The Old Dominion in the Seventeenth Century

*The Institute of Early American History and Culture
is sponsored jointly by The College of William and Mary in Virginia
and The Colonial Williamsburg Foundation.*

DOCUMENTARY PROBLEMS IN EARLY AMERICAN HISTORY

*The Old Dominion in the Seventeenth Century
A Documentary History of Virginia, 1606–1689*
Edited by Warren M. Billings (1975)

*The Great Awakening
Documents on the Revival of Religion, 1740–1745*
Edited by Richard L. Bushman (1970)

*The Glorious Revolution in America
Documents on the Colonial Crisis of 1689*
Edited by Michael G. Hall, Lawrence H. Leder,
and Michael G. Kammen (1964)

*Massachusetts, Colony to Commonwealth
Documents on the Formation of Its Constitution, 1775–1780*
Edited by Robert J. Taylor (1961)

*Prologue to Revolution
Sources and Documents on the Stamp Act Crisis, 1764–1766*
Edited by Edmund S. Morgan (1959)

The Old Dominion
in the Seventeenth Century

A Documentary History
of Virginia, 1606-1689

Edited by Warren M. Billings

Published for the
Institute of Early American History and Culture
at Williamsburg, Virginia
by The University of North Carolina Press
Chapel Hill

Copyright © 1975 by The University of North Carolina Press
All rights reserved
Manufactured in the United States of America

99   98   97   96   95   11   10   9   8   7

Library of Congress Catalog Card Number 74-8302

Library of Congress Cataloging in Publication Data

Billings, Warren M.   1940–   comp.
  The Old Dominion in the seventeenth century.

  (Documentary problems in early American history)
  Includes bibliographies.
    1. Virginia—History—Colonial period, ca. 1600–
1775—Sources.   I. Title.   II. Series.
F229.B615   975.5'02   74-8302
ISBN 0-8078-1234-x
ISBN 0-8078-1237-4 (pbk)

To Marcus B. Christian
Poet, scholar, and friend

Preface

Only by confronting a mass of primary sources from which he must reconstruct events, resolve conflicts in his evidence, and derive conclusions about the past does the student begin to appreciate the historian's craft. My purpose in editing this volume is to introduce students to some of the raw materials basic to an understanding of both seventeenth-century Virginia and the problem of creating a society in a new world.

What happened in Virginia's first century had profound meaning for the subsequent unfolding of the nation's history. Every student knows such episodes as the founding of Jamestown, the convening of the first General Assembly, and the arrival of the first Africans. These events are an integral part of the American past, but their significance is often ignored because they seem commonplace. England's successful planting of a colony in the New World broke ground for one of history's greatest population shifts; that first General Assembly established a valuable precedent for the emergence of representative political democracy in America; and the legacy of the Afro-American's experience in colonial Virginia has been a tragically bitter heritage whose effects are felt to this day.

Studying the Old Dominion in the seventeenth century is also valuable because it affords the opportunity to examine a time and a place so different from our own. Locked away in the extant documents is a fascinating story of how men and women struggled to adapt their values and traditions to new surroundings. Often ill-equipped for the struggle, but driven by a desire for a better life, these people endured painful failures and great tragedy. What they brought forth was better than what they had known, but by modern standards the quality of their new life was harsh and primitive. From our vantage point the costs of guaranteeing this improved life-style seem excessively high— among other things, the destruction of the Indians and the enslavement of the Negro.

Large portions of this story are obscured by a lack of evidence. Unlike the New England Puritans, few Virginia colonists left a record of their experiences, and fewer still are the number of these accounts that have survived. Over the past three hundred years, the ravages of time, carelessness, and war have exacted a frightful toll. Whole series of archives have been lost, destroyed, or damaged beyond repair. What remains is housed in widely located depositories, which makes access difficult at best and impossible at worst.

Thus this book is also an attempt to fulfill the long-felt need to make sources of Virginia history more accessible to students and scholars alike. Much of the seventeenth-century record still exists in unedited manuscript form. To be sure, some of the archives have appeared in print. Over the past one hundred and fifty years, for example, such scholars as William Waller Hening, R. A. Brock, Lyon G. Tyler, H. R. McIlwaine, and Susie M. Ames have edited and published significant segments of the colonial record. Generally, however, the published archives have long been out of print and often difficult to obtain, while the manuscripts require special skills for their utilization.

In compiling this collection, I have used previously published sources, but many of the documents that appear here have never been printed until now. All of the documents are arranged topically in chapters that are designed to illustrate Virginia's first century of development. The choice of topics depended upon several considerations: a few were obvious, some resulted from my own research interests, and others were dictated by the quality and quantity of surviving evidence. I used the chapter introductions to acquaint readers with the relation of a group of documents to its particular topic, rather than as commentaries upon the documents themselves. Each introduction concludes with a short list of suggested readings.

Documentary collections that are organized around a single problem are convenient devices for engaging and whetting novice historians' appetites for wider knowledge. They are no substitute for the thrill and frustration of actual archival research. It is my hope that, by the time students who read this book have digested the documents presented here, some will have developed a taste for research in the unpublished records of early Virginia history.

Any work of scholarship is a cooperative venture, and mine is no exception to this observation. I am deeply grateful to the Earl K. Long Library at the University of New Orleans for having acquired microfilm copies of Virginia's county court records. The following institutions, publishers, and individuals have graciously allowed me to reprint documents committed to their charge: the Public Record Office, the British Museum, the Mariner's Museum at Newport News, Va., the Alderman Library at the University of Virginia, the Library of Congress, the Earl Gregg Swem Library of the College of William and Mary, the Virginia State Library, the Massachusetts Historical Society, the Cambridge University Press, the University Press of Virginia, The University of North Carolina Press, the Marquis of Bath, and William M. E. Rachal.

I wish to thank my father, H. Warren Billings, for having made the drawings that appear in chapter 10. His interest in and knowledge of early American architecture helped shape my own curiosity about the past; so I now take this opportunity to discharge my debt to him.

I wish also to acknowledge the assistance and cooperation of those persons who helped this book to completion. For convincing me of the value of such an enterprise, I owe an especial debt to James H. Hutson. My own thinking about the document selection and the chapter introductions was sharpened by the trenchant criticisms of Carol Dunlap Billings, David R. Johnson, and Thad W. Tate, who read portions of the manuscript at various stages. An appreciation is due Frederick B. Alexius for having proofread the final version of the manuscript. Nita M. Walsh, Betty McKeon, and Carol Dunlap Billings contributed their skills as typists. Last, but by no means least, Norman S. Fiering and Joy Dickinson Barnes, editor and associate editor of publications at the Institute of Early American History and Culture, are due thanks for their shepherding of the book to publication.

WARREN M. BILLINGS

On Editing

Generally I have employed the expanded method of editing documents that is described in the *Harvard Guide to American History*. Abbreviations of military titles conform to modern usage, as does all typography, and proper names have been written out where abbreviated in the originals. Obvious typographical errors have been silently corrected, and I have occasionally added paragraphing (and an initial capital letter to open the paragraph) without mention. Words bracketed thus [?] were not clearly legible but represent the best guess of the editor. Any added punctuation is also enclosed in brackets, as are editorial clarifications of archaic terms or those that may be obscure in context. I have tried, however, to keep these intrusions to a minimum and have thus preferred to let the student confront some of the repeated eccentricities of seventeenth-century usage and spelling (such as "then" for "than") without explanation. Except for the above changes, the original orthography, capitalization, and punctuation have been retained.

The dates are Old Style throughout. As the English legal year used to begin on March 25, it was customary for contemporary writers to enter both years, i.e., January 1, 1660/61, in the interval between January 1 and March 25. That usage has been retained here.

Headings, divisions, and signatures to the documents generally follow their placement in the original, but in some cases the restrictions of typography and the need for clarity required changes in the arrangement of a document. In other words, no attempt has been made to render in type a facsimile of an original manuscript.

All citations to county records in the source lines are to the microfilm copies at the Virginia State Library, Richmond.

Contents

Preface *vii*

On Editing *x*

CHAPTER I. THE BEGINNINGS *3*

 Prelude to Settlement

1. *The Rationale for Colonization* *14*
2. *Supplies the Colonists Took to Virginia* *15*
3. *The First Settlers* *17*
4. *Instructions from the London Company
  to the First Settlers, November 1606* *19*
5. *George Percy's Account of the Voyage to Virginia
  and the Colony's First Days* *22*
6. *Some Contemporary Explanations for
  Virginia's Early Failures* *26*

 The Struggle for Survival

7. *A Share of Stock in the London Company, 1610* *27*
8. *The "Starving Time," 1609–1610* *28*
9. *Excerpts from the
  *Lawes Divine, Morall and Martiall, *1611* *29*
10. *Sir Thomas Dale's Plan
  for Revitalizing the Colony, 1611* *33*
11. *John Rolfe Experiments with Tobacco Growing, 1612* *36*

Virginia Transformed

12.   *The Beginning of Representative Government:*
      The London Company Creates a General Assembly   37

CHAPTER II. THE EVOLUTION OF SELF-GOVERNMENT
IN VIRGINIA: THE GOVERNOR, COUNCIL, AND
HOUSE OF BURGESSES   39

The Governor and Council

 1.   *Instructions to Sir William Berkeley, August 1641*   51
 2.   *The Burgesses Appoint the Council, 1652*   58
 3.   *The Governor and Council as Court, 1674*   58

The House of Burgesses

 4.   *Election of Burgesses, 1636*   62
 5.   *Freeholders Ordered to Meet with Their Burgesses, 1671* 62
 6.   *The Evolution of Burgess Representation*   62
      A. *An Act Authorizing Collection of Taxes*
          for Burgesses' Salaries, March 1642/43   62
      B. *An Act Limiting the Number of Burgesses a County*
          Could Elect and Defining Other Election
          Procedures, November 1645   63
      C. *An Act Authorizing the Assessment of Charges*
          for Parochial Burgesses, March 1658/59   63
      D. *An Act Limiting Counties to Elect*
          Only Two Burgesses, March 1660/61   63
      E. *An Act Requiring Counties to Elect*
          Two Burgesses, October 1669   63
      F. *An Act Fining Counties for Failing to Elect*
          Burgesses, October 1670   64
 7.   *Control over Legislative Procedures*   64
      A. *Members Freed from Arrest during*
          Assembly Sessions, 1623/24   64
      B. *Control over Members' Qualifications, 1663*   64
      C. *Selection of the Speaker, 1653*   64
      D. *Rules of Procedure, 1658/59*   65
 8.   *Initiation of Legislation*   66
      A. *Edmund Scarburgh's Petition to*
          the House of Burgesses, 1663   66
      B. *Scarburgh's Petition Becomes Law, 1663*   66

9. *Control over Taxation*   67
    A. *A Right Established, 1623/24*   67
    B. *A Right Reasserted, 1666*   67
10. *Control over Local Affairs: The General Assembly
    Creates the County Court System, 1634*   68

CHAPTER III. THE EVOLUTION OF SELF-GOVERN-
MENT IN VIRGINIA: LOCAL GOVERNMENT   69

    The Organization of County Government

1. *The Creation of Rappahannock County, 1656*   82
2. *The Appointment of County Officers*   83
    A. *Commission of the Peace, May 1652*   83
    B. *Sheriff's Commission, 1674*   84
    C. *Nominations for Sheriff, 1636*   84
    D. *The Justices' Control over Appointments
        to Their Courts, 1672*   85

    *The Growth of the County Courts'
    Statutory Control of Local Affairs*

3. *Acts of the Assembly, 1642/43–1661/62*   86
    A. *An Act Requiring Counties to Maintain
        Ferries and Bridges, March 1642/43*   86
    B. *An Act Empowering County Courts
        to Probate Wills, November 1645*   86
    C. *An Act Authorizing County Courts to Try All Cases
        at Common Law and in Equity, November 1645*   87
    D. *An Act Establishing County Courts and Their
        Justices, March 1661/62*   87
    E. *An Act Authorizing County Courts to Enact
        Local Bylaws, March 1661/62*   88

    The County Court as a Place of Record

4. *A Land Deed Recorded, 1638*   88
5. *A Deed of Sale, 1664*   89
6. *A Will Recorded and Probated, 1680*   89
7. *Mary Allen's Power of Attorney, 1665*   90
8. *Cattle Registry, 1665*   90
9. *A Coroner's Inquest, 1647*   90

    The County Courts' Administrative Duties

10. *County Court Procedure, 1675*   91

11.   *Justices Fined for Failing to Attend Their Court, 1663/64*   91
12.   *The Regulation of a Public House, 1667*   92
13.   *The Care of the Indigent and the Infirm*   92
      A. *Poor Relief, 1659*   92
      B. *The Care of an Idiot, 1661*   92
      C. *Tax Relief for an Aged Citizen, 1660*   93
14.   *County Defense, 1674*   93
15.   *Tax Collection, 1672*   94

      The Problems of Law and Order

16.   *Civil Justice*   95
      A. *A Debt Suit, 1655/56*   95
      B. *A Character Defamation, 1634*   95
      C. *Fighting in the Courthouse Yard, 1684*   96
      D. *A Justice Slandered, 1637*   96
      E. *A Chancery Suit, 1685*   96
      F. *A Violation of the Navigation Acts, 1685*   97
17.   *Criminal Justice*   99
      A. *Lower Norfolk Justices Assist
           in Capturing a Robber, 1685*   99
      B. *A Suspected Felon Is Bound Over
           to the General Court, 1658*   100
      C. *Grand Jury Presentments, 1684*   100
      D. *Petty Theft, 1650*   101
      E. *Petty Fraud, 1656*   101
      F. *An Assault, 1639*   101
      G. *Punishment of Fornication, 1641*   102
      H. *The Penalty for Adultery, 1642*   102
      I. *The Northumberland Court Stops
           an Illicit Affair, 1665*   103

CHAPTER IV. THE STRUCTURE OF SOCIETY   104

      The Character of Virginia's Population

1.   *An Excerpt from the Census of 1624/25*   116
2.   *Virginia's Population in 1634*   117
3.   *Sir William Berkeley's Estimate
      of Virginia's Population, 1670*   118
4.   *A Tithing List*   118
5.   *A Land Patent*   120

The Willoughby Family, 1610–1699

6. *The Original English Residence
   of Thomas Willoughby I*   120
7. *Thomas Willoughby I Arrives in Virginia*   120
8. *An Early Land Patent of Thomas Willoughby I*   120
9. *Offices Held by Thomas Willoughby I*   121
   A. *Commander of Forces Sent
      to Attack the Indians, 1627*   121
   B. *Monthly Court Judge, 1628/29*   121
   C. *Burgess, 1629/30, 1631/1632*   121
   D. *Justice of the Peace*   122
   E. *Member of the Council of State*   122
10. *Some Debts Owed to Thomas Willoughby I*   122
11. *The Lower Norfolk Justices Appoint
    Thomas Willoughby I to Recruit a Minister, 1655*   123
12. *Death of Thomas Willoughby I, 1658*   123
13. *Thomas Willoughby I's Children*   123
14. *Thomas Willoughby II Apprenticed
    as a Merchant Taylor, 1644*   123
15. *Thomas Willoughby II Refuses the Office
    of Justice of the Peace, 1656*   124
16. *Thomas Willoughby II Refuses Jury Service, 1656*   124
17. *Offices Held by Thomas Willoughby II*   124
    A. *His Appointment to the Bench of
       Lower Norfolk County, 1661*   124
    B. *Sheriff, 1666*   124
    C. *Fort Commissioner, 1667*   124
18. *The Wife of Thomas Willoughby II*   125
19. *Thomas Willoughby II's Children*   125
20. *Death of Thomas Willoughby II, 1672*   125
21. *Thomas Willoughby III's Appointment to
    the Bench of Lower Norfolk County, 1698*   125

Wider Kin Connections of the Willoughby Family

22. *The Husbands of Elizabeth, Daughter of
    Thomas Willoughby I*   126
    A. *Simon Overzee: Dutch Merchant*   126
    B. *George Colclough: London Merchant, Justice of the
       Peace, and Burgess for Northumberland
       County, Virginia*   126

C. *Isaac Allerton: New England Merchant, Justice of
the Peace, Burgess for Northumberland County,
Virginia, and Member of the Council of State*   *126*

CHAPTER V. BOUND LABOR: THE INDENTURED SERVANT   *127*

Procurement of Indentured Servants

1. *Richard Garford's Contract to Provide a Servant for
Thomas Workman, 1654*   *134*
2. *Servants Imported by Headright, 1652*   *135*
3. *Roger Jones's Indenture, 1688*   *135*
4. *Richard Willis Agrees to Teach
John Talbert a Trade, 1680*   *135*
5. *The Custom of the Country, 1656*   *135*
6. *The Sale of a Servant without an Indenture, 1665*   *136*

The Hazards of Servitude

7. *An Assault on Charity Dallen, 1649*   *136*
8. *James Revel Describes the Servant's Plight, ca. 1680*   *137*
9. *Edward Whittell Commits Suicide, 1664*   *143*

Problems Created by the Use of Servant Labor

10. *A Runaway, 1680*   *143*
11. *A Bastard Child, 1656*   *144*
12. *A Frivolous Lawsuit, 1681*   *144*
13. *Theft of Master's Goods, 1684*   *144*
14. *A Servant Assaults His Mistress, 1679*   *146*
15. *A Servant's Plot to Revolt, 1687*   *147*

CHAPTER VI. BOUND LABOR: SLAVERY   *148*

The Arrival of the Negro in Virginia, 1619

1. *A Relation from Master John Rolfe*   *155*

The Free Negro

2. *Anthony Johnson's Servant, 1655*   *155*
3. *Francis Paine's Will, 1673*   *156*
4. *Philip Mongom Is Accused of Stealing Hogs, 1659/60*   *157*
5. *John Francisco Maintains a Bastard Child, 1668*   *157*
6. *An Example of Intermarriage, 1671*   *157*

7. *John Francisco's Suit in Chancery, 1673/74* 158
8. *Susannah's Case, 1677* 158
9. *The Suit against Mary Williams, 1688* 158

Problems Created by the Use of Slave Labor

10. *Runaways* 158
    A. *Theoderick Bland Tries to Recapture Two
        Runaways, 1662* 158
    B. *Punishment of a Runaway Slave, 1689* 159
11. *Slave Insurrections* 159
    A. *A Rising on William Pierce's Plantation, 1640* 159
    B. *A Rising on the Northern Neck, 1680* 160
12. *The Difficulty in Maintaining Racial Separation* 160
    A. *Hugh Davis's Case, 1630* 160
    B. *William Watts's and Mary's Case, 1649* 161
    C. *William's Case, 1681* 161
    D. *Katherine Watkins's Case, 1681* 161
    E. *Rebecca Corney's Bastard, 1689* 163

The Paths to Freedom

13. *Mihill Gowen Is Set Free by His Master's Will, 1657/58* 164
14. *Antonio to Gain Freedom after Ten Years' Service, 1678* 164
15. *John and Isabell Daule Purchase Their Freedom, 1670* 164
16. *The Courts as an Avenue to Freedom* 165
    A. *The Case of Elizabeth Key, 1655/56* 165
    B. *Fernando Appeals His Suit to the General Court, 1667* 169
    C. *Jack Petitions Governor Berkeley and the General
        Court for His Freedom, 1665* 169
    D. *The General Court Sets Andrew Moore Free, 1673* 171
    E. *John Towe's Case, 1686* 171

The Evolution of Slavery's Definition in the Law

17. *Acts of the General Assembly, 1640–1680* 172
    A. *An Act Preventing Negroes from Bearing Arms, 1640* 172
    B. *An Act Taxing Negro Women, March 1642/43* 172
    C. *An Act Defining the Status of
        Mulatto Bastards, December 1662* 172
    D. *An Act Declaring That Baptism
        Does Not Bring Freedom, September 1667* 172
    E. *An Act Declaring How Negroes Belonging to
        Intestates Shall Be Disposed of, September 1671* 173

F. *An Act for Preventing Insurrections*
   among Slaves, June 1680   173

CHAPTER VII. TOBACCO AND TRADE   175

The Production of Tobacco

1. *How to Plant Tobacco, 1615*   182

The Tobacco Trade

2. *The Sale of Tobacco, 1651*   184
3. *A Bill of Exchange, 1668*   185
4. *Captain Yardley Buys Five Negroes, 1648*   186
5. *Correspondence between Merchants and Planters*   186
   A. *William Scopes to Thomas Willoughby,*
       Lemuel Mason, and John Holmes, 1653   186
   B. *James Gilbert to William Carver, 1667*   187
   C. *Abraham Wheelock to John Bowery, 1676*   188
6. *A Power of Attorney, 1657*   189
7. *A Bill of Lading and an Invoice of Goods*
   Bound for Virginia, 1661   190
8. *Correspondence between James Barton and*
   Thomas Wilke, 1680   191
9. *A Virginia Merchant's Stock*   192
10. *Jonathan Newell's Accounts, 1677*   198

CHAPTER VIII. INDIANS AND WHITES:
THE CONFLICT OF CULTURES   205

The Virginia Indians on the Eve of Colonization

1. *John Smith's Description of the Indian Way, 1612*   214

The Conflict of Cultures

2. *John Rolfe Requests Permission*
   to Marry Pocahontas, 1614   216
3. *The Massacre of 1622*   220
4. *The Governor and Council Threaten Reprisals*
   against the Indians, 1629   225
5. *Lower Norfolk County Sends Its Militia*
   against the Nanticokes, 1639   225
6. *The Peace Treaty That Ended*
   the Indian War of 1644–1646   226

7. *The English Formulate an Indian Policy*   228
   A. *An Act Outlawing the Killing of Indians,*
      October 1649   228
   B. *An Act Preventing the Kidnapping of*
      Indian Children, October 1649   228
   C. *An Act Granting Land to the Indians, October 1649*   229
8. *Sources of Potential Trouble between the Indians*
   and the English, 1661–1675   230
   A. *Indians Fined for Hog Stealing, 1660/61*   230
   B. *Indians Accused of Beating an Englishman, 1663/64*   230
   C. *Stafford Court Forbids Indians to Hunt in*
      Settled Areas, 1664   230
   D. *Indians Lose Suit to Recover Land, 1665/66*   230
   E. *Governor Berkeley's Formula for Quieting*
      the Northern Indians, 1666   231
   F. *Indians Suspected of Kidnapping a Servant Girl, 1668*   231
   G. *Indians Break into Robert Jones's House, 1669*   231
   H. *Accomack Court Orders Indians Whipped, 1671*   232
   I. *Whites Convicted of Stealing from the Indians, 1675*   232
9. *The Indian War of 1675–1677*   232
   A. *The Incident That Led to War, 1675*   232
   B. *The Governor and Council Act to Prevent War, 1675*   233
   C. *An Account of the Attack on the*
      Susquehannock Stronghold, 1675   234

   The Virginia Indians a Century after Colonization

10 *Robert Beverley's Estimate of the*
   Indian Population, ca. 1705   235

CHAPTER IX: UPHEAVAL AND REBELLION   236

   The Thrusting Out of Sir John Harvey, 1635

1. *The Mutineers' Complaints against Harvey:*
   Samuel Mathews to Sir John Wolstenholme   251
2. *Harvey's Account of His Troubles*   254

   The Lawne's Creek Rising, December 1673

3. *The Causes of Discontent*   258
   A. *The Dutch Burn the Tobacco Fleet, July 1673:*
      The Problem of Defending Virginia against Attack   258
   B. *Dissatisfaction with Sir William Berkeley's Leadership:*

The Council of State Defends the Governor against
Complaints of Mismanagement, October 1673   262

4. *The Prosecution of the Lawne's Creek Dissidents,*
   January 1673/74   263
   A. *The Warrants for the Arrest of the Dissidents,*
      January 3, 1673/74   263
   B. *Francis Taylor's Evidence, January 1673/74*   264
   C. *The Surry County Court's Verdict,*
      January 6, 1673/74   265
   D. *The General Court Confirms the Surry Court's*
      Verdict, April 1674   266
   E. *Governor Berkeley Cancels the Dissidents' Fines,*
      September 1674   266

Bacon's Rebellion, 1676

5. *The Causes of Discontent*   267
   A. *Frontier Planters Petition Governor Berkeley*
      to Commission Volunteers against the Indians,
      ca. Spring 1676   267
   B. *Nathaniel Bacon's Victory over the Indians,*
      April 1676   267
6. *Berkeley Attempts to Regain His Popularity*   269
   A. *Berkeley's Election Proclamation, May 10, 1676*   269
   B. *Berkeley's "Declaration and Remonstrance,"*
      May 29, 1676   270
7. *Berkeley Asks to Be Replaced*   272
8. *Bacon Is Elected Burgess for Henrico*   273
9. *Bacon's Submission*   273
10. *The June Assembly*   274
    A. *A Précis of the June Laws*   274
    B. *William Sherwood's Account of the*
       Assembly's Proceedings   276
11. *Bacon's "Manifesto"*   277
12. *Postrebellion Grievances*   280

The Plant-Cutter Riots, 1681–1683

13. *Two Accounts of the Riots*   282
    A. *Sir Henry Chicheley to Secretary Leoline Jenkins,*
       May 1682   282
    B. *Nicholas Spencer to Secretary Leoline Jenkins,*
       May 1682   283

14. *Governor Culpeper's Handling of the Plant Cutters,*
    January 1681/82   285

CHAPTER X. LIFE IN SEVENTEENTH-CENTURY
VIRGINIA   288

The Voyage to Virginia

1. *Henry Norwood's Passage to Virginia, 1649*   299

This New Land, Virginia

2. *Samuel Purchas's Description of Virginia, 1613*   303
3. *Two Views of Virginia's Promise*   304
   A. *John Pory Describes the Possibilities*
      for Advancement, 1619   304
   B. *Richard Frethorne's Account of*
      His Plight in Virginia, 1623   305

Houses and Household Property

4. *Types of Houses*   306
   A. *A Contract for a Frame House*   306
   B. *A Frenchman's Description of Housing*
      in Virginia, 1687   306
5. *Household Property*   307
   A. *William Harris's Estate, 1679*   307
   B. *John Waroe's Estate, 1650*   307
   C. *Jane Hartey's Estate, 1667*   308

Religious Life

6. *The Church*   317
   A. *The Creation of Christ Church Parish, 1666*   317
   B. *Petsworth Parish Builds a Church, 1677*   318
   C. *Recruiting a Minister, 1656*   319
   D. *The Vestryman's Oath, 1664*   319

Leisure Pursuits

7. *Amusements, Games, and Sports*   319
   A. *Horse Racing, 1674*   319
   B. *Ninepins, 1681*   320
   C. *Dicing, 1685*   320
   D. *Putt, 1685*   320
   E. *Hunting, 1680*   321

F. *Middlesex Court Acts to Conserve the*
   County's Fish Population, 1678   321
G. *Accomack Court Forbids a Company of Players from*
   Performing "The Bear and the Cub," 1663   ·   322

Epilogue   323

Illustrations

MAPS

Augustin Herrman's Map of Virginia and Maryland, 1670   2
(Courtesy of the Library of Congress)

Virginia from 1607 to 1624   8
Showing the English settlements along the James River, the Indian
villages within the ambit of Powhatan's authority, and the boundaries
of the four boroughs established in 1618. Locations are based on the
maps in Charles E. Hatch, *The First Seventeen Years: Virginia, 1607–
1624*, Jamestown 350th Anniversary Historical Booklet 6 (Williamsburg, Va., 1957), and Philip L. Barbour, ed., *The Jamestown Voyages
under the First Charter, 1606–1609*, Haklyut Society Publications, 2d
Ser., CXXXVI–CXXXVII (Cambridge, 1969), I. (Compiled by Warren M. Billings; drawn by Richard J. Stinely, Williamsburg, Va.)

Virginia in 1634   71
Showing the approximate boundaries of the eight original counties,
settlements along the York River, and churches. Locations of churches
here and in the following map are based on information in the articles
by George Carrington Mason in the *William and Mary Quarterly*, 2d
Ser., XVIII (1938)–XXIII (1943), and the *Virginia Magazine of
History and Biography*, LIII (1945)–LVII (1949). (Compiled by
Warren M. Billings; drawn by Richard J. Stinely, Williamsburg, Va.)

Virginia in 1668   72
Showing the formation of counties, and the locations of houses mentioned in the text and of churches established between 1634 and 1668.

(Compiled by Warren M. Billings; drawn by Richard J. Stinely, Williamsburg, Va.)

FIGURES

Figure 1. Wattle-and-Daub Cabins at Jamestown   291
(Conjectural drawing, courtesy of H. Warren Billings, Richmond, Va.)

Figure 2. The Framing of an Early Seventeenth-Century House   292
(Conjectural drawing, courtesy of H. Warren Billings, Richmond, Va.)

The Old Dominion in the Seventeenth Century

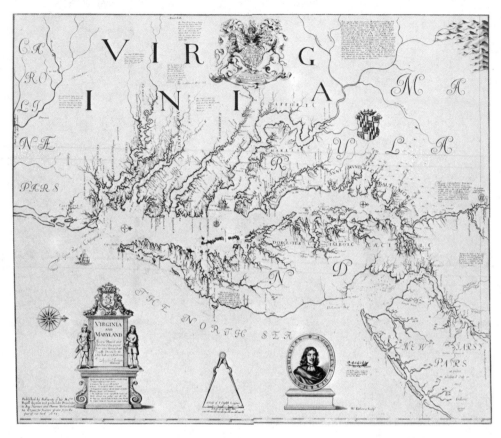

Augustin Herrman's Map of Virginia and Maryland, 1670
(Courtesy of the Library of Congress)

Chapter One

The Beginnings

After the failure of Sir Walter Ralegh's third attempt to plant a colony in the New World, Ralegh's contemporaries had kept alive the hope of establishing an English foothold in America. But the outbreak of the Anglo-Spanish War in 1588 had diverted attentions and energies towards warring upon Catholic Spain. The war dragged on until 1604, and while it lasted, the idea of erecting English colonies in Sir Walter's Virginia languished. Spurred by the return of peace, a group of well-connected merchants and public men from London and Plymouth solicited James I for a charter authorizing them to colonize in America. Over a year elapsed before these solicitations bore fruit; finally on April 10, 1606, the king granted the petitioners their charter.

James's patent authorized the creation of two companies to settle Virginia—one based in London, the other in Plymouth. It defined Virginia as the territory between the thirty-fourth and forty-fifth degrees of north latitude, or all the land between Passamaquoddy Bay in Maine and the Cape Fear River in North Carolina. This vast territory would be divided between the two companies, with the Plymouth Company exploiting the northern part and the London Company planting the southern region. In addition to describing the territorial limits, the charter provided a detailed explanation of how settlement should be undertaken, placed the responsibility for governing each colony in the hands of resident councils, and made these officers answerable to a royally appointed council that remained in England.

Some of the reasons for the colonizing venture may be drawn from the charter, and other explicit statements of purpose are to be found

[3]

in the promotional literature that preceded and followed the charter's promulgation. From the late sixteenth century onward colonial promoters like the two Richard Hakluyts publicized the advantages accruing to the nation from the establishment of colonies. An expansion of trade, a duplication of Spanish successes in the Indies, the need to acquire colonies as sources of supply, the furtherance of Protestantism—all of these and other reasons were put forward as the rationale for planting English settlements in America. Not least of all, of course, the Virginia adventurers hoped to make a profit from the risk of their capital or their lives (Document 1).

Attaining these ends depended upon the proper organization, financing, and management of a colonial venture, things that earlier undertakings had always lacked. To avoid the failures of the past, the patentees of 1606, especially the London group, drew from their own commercial experiences the chartered trading company as the model for managing their enterprise. The trading company minimized the financial risk to large and small investors alike. It also allowed for the investment of service as well as capital. Thus men who had no money, but who were willing to trade their labor for a share of the profits, could perform a vital role in the operation. Finally, the trading company could bring together the talents and expertise of specialists, providing thereby a fund of information and skills that could further enhance the chances of a successful adventure.

Armed with the charter, high purpose, and means, the backers of the London Company began preparations for an attempt to settle their part of Virginia. Over the summer and fall of 1606 the Londoners marshaled money, supplies, colonists, and ships. The amount and types of supplies the company raised are unknown, because no record of what was sent with the first settlers has survived. Some idea of the sorts of things that were necessary to sustain life during the initial phases of colonization may be deduced, however, from an inventory that Samuel Purchas compiled in the early 1620s (Document 2). If one is to judge from the list of recruits (Document 3), in choosing their first complement of colonists, company officials intended to send to America an exploratory expedition similar to the one Ralegh had employed in 1585. One of the expedition's apparent purposes was the establishment of a permanent settlement, but perhaps its first concern was erecting an outpost as a means of determining how the further exploitation of Virginia should proceed. The exploratory nature of the undertaking seems to be confirmed in the additional instructions (Document 4) that were issued to the colony's leaders shortly before they left England.

At length all was in readiness, and on December 20, 1606, three ships carrying a hundred men and four boys commanded by Christopher Newport, an old hand in the exploration of the North American coast, stood down the Thames for the New World. For six weeks contrary winds kept the little convoy in sight of England; when the winds shifted, the ships sailed to the Canary Islands, where the adventurers took on fresh water. Then, following a westerly course, the fleet made for the West Indies, arriving off Martinique late in March. After three weeks of rest in the islands, the colonists sailed north until they raised the Virginia Capes. On April 26 they put ashore a landing party and then spent the next seventeen days searching out a place to settle. By May 13 they had worked their ships up a river that they called James to a small peninsula on the river's north shore. They named the place Jamestown and set about building a fort and housing.

From the beginning troubles befell the Virginia venture. The first colonists were ill-equipped to cope with a hostile wilderness that admitted no mistakes. Neither the leaders, whom the company had drawn from the gentle ranks of English society, nor the artisans and craftsmen, upon whom the company depended to exploit the new land's bounty, had much prior preparation for the desperate struggle for survival that soon was visited upon them. As a result the men died at an appalling rate, carried off, in George Percy's words, by "diseases as Swellings, Flixes, Burning Fevers, and by warres, and some departed suddenly, but for the most part they died of meere famine" (Document 5). Within six months of their arrival in Virginia, all but thirty-eight of the settlers had perished.

Further difficulties arose from a confusion in the colony's management and the inability of the settlers to realize the colony's intended purpose. John Smith became the center of controversy when his colleagues banned him from his seat on the resident council. This and quarrels over what to explore, what to plant, and where to trade soon demonstrated the company's error in dividing political authority between England and Virginia. In addition, the reality of the situation failed to conform to the colonists' expectations of what they would find in Virginia. The Indians proved unfriendly; moreover, to the English they lacked the cultural attainments and the wealth of the indigenous peoples in the Spanish New World. There were neither gold mines nor the passage to the Orient. These impedimenta seemed to frustrate the dream of eventually turning Virginia into a profitably prosperous colony founded upon trade (Document 6).

Only the emergence of John Smith as the colony's leader and a redoubled effort by the company to infuse more men and supplies into the venture spared the colony from collapse. Until burns from a gunpowder explosion forced him to return to England in the summer of 1609, Smith kept the colony together. After his assumption of the council presidency in September 1608, he restored friendly relations with the Indians. At the same time he made progress in bettering living conditions at Jamestown. As a consequence of his forceful leadership, the colony passed the winter of 1608–1609 in comparative ease. Despite the improvements he had wrought, Smith had not solved the colony's basic problem—the need to discover some means by which the undertaking could be made profitable for its investors.

In an effort to resuscitate its flagging fortunes, the London Company secured from the crown a new charter that completely reorganized the Virginia operation. Along with creating a more centralized and efficient government for the colony, the Charter of 1609 turned the company into a joint-stock venture. The sale of corporate stock would give the company a new source of revenue (Document 7).

The reorganization of the London Company aroused new interest and hope in the future of Virginia, but, ironically, the colony almost failed as a result of the company's efforts. By the late spring of 1609 company officials raised a "supply" of five hundred colonists and nine ships and sent them to Virginia. At sea, plague and bad weather beset the convoy. A hurricane cut off the ship of the deputy-governor, Sir Thomas Gates, and it wrecked on the Bermuda coast. When four hundred leaderless survivors arrived at Jamestown in late summer, they were too sick to be of much use, but they quickly consumed the limited stores of food. That gone, the entire colony fell victim to disease and famine as winter set in. Between October 1609 and March 1610, the colony's population was reduced from five hundred to about sixty people (Document 8). So severe had the "starving time" been that when spring came, the survivors decided to give up and go home. Only the timely arrival of the governor, Thomas, Lord Delaware, and new colonists saved the colony from collapse.

Although the winter of 1609–1610 proved to be the nadir of the colony's struggle for existence, Virginia barely survived in the ensuing years. The thread that held the ailing colony together was a fortunate choice of governors and, beyond this, the company's dogged determination to surmount every obstacle to success. In the half-dozen years after 1610 Virginia's survival was the direct result of the stern government of Sir Thomas Gates and Sir Thomas Dale. Gates replaced the sickly Lord Delaware as governor in 1611. Even before replacing Delaware, however, he had instituted, at the company's behest, a series of regulations that subjected the colonists to martial law and discipline. To these regulations Sir Thomas Dale, whom the company had appointed marshal, added additional laws and ordinances. These severe laws, which became known as the *Lawes Divine, Morall and Martiall,* following their codification and publication by William Strachey in 1612, were strictly enforced by Dale (Document 9). For all of its severity and strictness, the introduction of the martial model of organization imposed upon the colony a regularity and order that it had never known before Gates's administration.

Besides restoring order to the struggling colony, Gates and Dale expanded the area of settlement, encouraged experimentation with staple crops, and subtly changed the nature of the colonial operation by introducing a degree of private land tenure. While Jamestown was an easy site to defend, its marshy terrain made it an unhealthful place in which to live. This was apparent from the start, but until Dale's arrival few steps had been taken to locate settlements elsewhere. In a letter to a friend (Document 10), Dale outlined a plan for expansion both as a means of better defense and a chance for utilizing the country's natural advantages. Shortly after he wrote the letter, Dale won Gates's approval to erect a new settlement at a place upriver from Jamestown, which he called "Henrico." As a result of Dale's endeavors, by the time he returned to England in 1616, the English had seated plantations on both sides of the James from its mouth to its falls (see the map on page 8).

With an advantage over the English both in numbers and knowledge of the countryside, the Indians continually posed a threat to the settlers. Relations between the Powhatan Confederacy and the English had always been tense, but they worsened after Smith's departure. So it was a matter of some urgency that Gates and Dale should seek to ease the tensions between the two peoples. An opportunity presented itself when Samuel Argall captured Powhatan's daughter Pocahontas in 1613. Her subsequent marriage to John Rolfe (see chapter 8) brought the long-sought peace.

Apart from his contribution to peaceable Indian relations, Rolfe played a prominent, if indirect, role in shaping the direction of Virginia's future development. It had been a goal of the London Com-

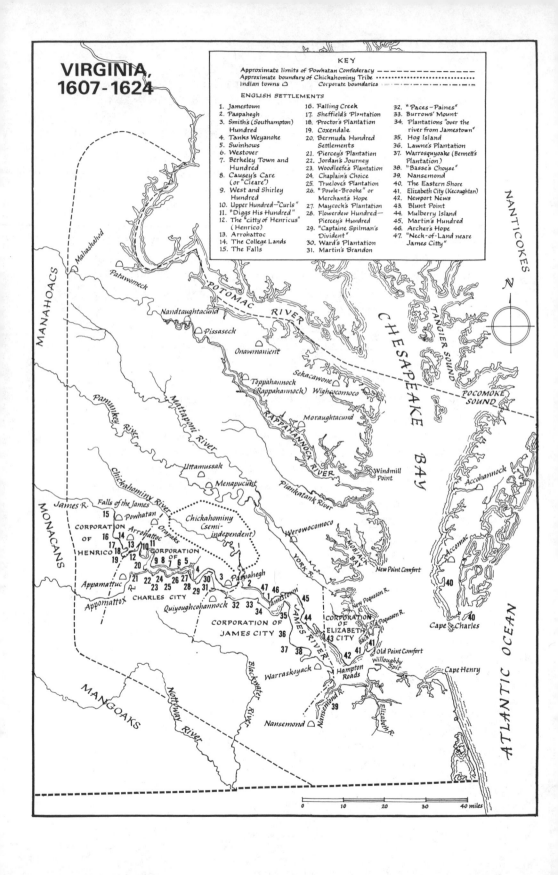

VIRGINIA, 1607-1624

KEY

Approximate limits of Powhatan Confederacy — — — — — —
Approximate boundary of Chickahominy Tribe ············
Indian towns ⌂   Corporate boundaries

ENGLISH SETTLEMENTS

1. Jamestown
2. Paspahegh
3. Smith's (Southampton) Hundred
4. Tanks Weyanoke
5. Swinhows
6. Westover
7. Berkeley Town and Hundred
8. Causey's Care (or "Cleare")
9. West and Shirley Hundred
10. Upper Hundred—"Curls"
11. "Diggs His Hundred"
12. The "city of Henricus" (Henrico)
13. Arrohattoc
14. The College Lands
15. The Falls

16. Falling Creek
17. Sheffield's Plantation
18. Proctor's Plantation
19. Coxendale
20. Bermuda Hundred Settlements
21. Piercey's Plantation
22. Jordan's Journey
23. Woodleefe's Plantation
24. Chaplain's Choice
25. Truelove's Plantation
26. "Powle-Brooke" or Merchant's Hope
27. Maycock's Plantation
28. Flowerdew Hundred— Piercey's Hundred
29. "Captaine Spilman's Divident"
30. Ward's Plantation
31. Martin's Brandon

32. "Paces—Paines"
33. Burrows' Mount
34. Plantations "over the river from Jamestown"
35. Hog Island
36. Lawne's Plantation
37. Warrosquyoake (Bennett's Plantation)
38. "Basse's Choyse"
39. Nansemond
40. The Eastern Shore
41. Elizabeth City (Kecoughtan)
42. Newport News
43. Blunt Point
44. Mulberry Island
45. Martin's Hundred
46. Archer's Hope
47. "Neck-of-Land neare James City"

pany to produce staple commodities both to further the national interest and to turn the colony into a profitable venture for its investors. From 1607 onwards, with the encouragement of the company and men such as Gates and Dale, the colonists had tried to produce, without measurable success, pitch, tar, soap ash, and silk. In the course of these endeavors Rolfe began to experiment with tobacco culture. Tobacco was in great demand in England, having been introduced there by Sir Francis Drake in 1586, and a species of the "joviall weed" grew in Virginia. But the Virginia variety, *nicotiana rustica,* bit the tongue, which made it unpalatable to English tastes accustomed to the milder West Indian varieties. Rolfe recognized the inferior quality of the local leaf, and in 1612 he tried raising a West Indian strain, *nicotiana tabacum.* Two years later he shipped four hogsheads of tobacco to London, thereby commencing the English-colonial tobacco trade and laying the basis for Virginia's subsequent economic viability. The speed with which the trade grew after 1614 justified Ralph Hamor's remark that no man had done more than Rolfe to secure the colony's future (Document 11).

However, it remained for the colonists and company officials to convince themselves that the key to success lay in transforming Virginia from a quasi-military outpost into a colony that possessed the attributes of a traditional social order. The colonists took to tobacco culture rather quickly, and their emulation of Rolfe's successes contributed to the introduction of limited private land tenure in Virginia. That change was the first of several steps that ultimately turned the colonial outpost into an agricultural community.

Until 1614 settlers who went to Virginia did so as servants. They were obligated to the company for seven years, during which they worked on company projects and drew their sustenance from a common storehouse. As events proved, this arrangement was conducive to neither hard work nor initiative, and it probably nurtured low morale among the colonists as well. By 1614, however, the indentures of the original colonists began to expire. Those who chose to remained in the colony as free laborers, and as more settlers completed their service, the number of free laborers grew. Soon the company allowed Dale to rent out to these colonists three acres of land in return for a month's service and a donation of corn to the common store. As a sop to those settlers still in company service, Dale gave every servant one month in each year to grow his own food. And to induce families to migrate to Virginia, Sir Thomas offered twelve acres of improved land rent free for one year. Dale's objective was an increase in food production, but instead of growing corn, those settlers who obtained private use of the land raised tobacco. This infusion of private tenure paved the way for individual land ownership a few years later.

Throughout the first ten years of Virginia's existence, company officials struggled to keep their colony vital. Undaunted by past failures, these men continued to search for ways to make Virginia self-sustaining and profitable. But fabulous expectations, a paucity of capital, a shortage of skilled colonists, and the lack of marketable commodities were constant plagues. Within three years of the 1609 reorganization, the company had become hard pressed for cash. In 1612 when the company secured a new charter, the most important new provision authorized the creation of a lottery. Armed with new hopes and additional funds raised from the sale of lottery tickets, company officials launched another attempt to revivify Virginia. But despite this latest transfusion of capital and men, Virginia, like a wounded albatross, limped along without showing a profit or even a hint of one.

Virginia's growing reputation as a deathtrap deterred people from going there, but the chief difficulty with the colony's population was its inability to exploit the country's most abundant resource—the land. Moreover, given the rigors of military discipline and the lack of a familiar social environment, there was little incentive to try. Artisans, craftsmen, gentlemen, and transported felons initially lacked the requisite skills for turning the Old Dominion into a prosperous agricultural community. Only after 1616, when the company declared a promised dividend in land rather than money, did company officials begin to realize that a possible salvation from their difficulties lay in transforming their colony from an outpost into a place that possessed many of the trappings of English society.

The slowness with which company officials came to this realization almost caused them to miss the significance of Rolfe's experiments with tobacco. Indeed, they were somewhat alarmed at the colonists' willingness to grow the weed to the exclusion of anything else. Consequently they sought to limit its growth until after 1618, when circumstances altered their aversion to it.

At the start of the colony's second decade, therefore, Virginia and the London Company remained in serious trouble. As a result of land policy, after 1614 settlements were widely scattered, and there was much confusion over land titles. The colony's economic foundations were as shaky as ever, and the colonists grew more restive when in 1616 Samuel Argall returned the colony to the strict discipline of Sir Thomas Dale's *Lawes*. In London the situation was little better, for the company verged on bankruptcy.

Against this background the company launched a new plan to invigorate its Virginia venture. Led by Sir Edwin Sandys, the newly chosen treasurer, the company embarked upon an ambitious course of action aimed at comprehensively reorganizing the entire colonial operation. The plan was embodied in a series of instructions and commissions, the so-called "Great Charter" of 1618, designed to reform land tenures, to improve local administration, and to supplant the *Lawes Divine, Morall and Martiall* with English common law and a more representative resident government. In short, the clear intent of the new program was to transplant as much of traditional English social order as the Virginia wilderness and the colonists' particular circumstances would allow.

In keeping with these instructions, Sandys authorized the newly appointed governor, Sir George Yeardley, to call together an assembly consisting of himself, a company-appointed council of state, and burgesses elected by the colony's freemen. (While the original instructions do not exist, Yeardley prepared a copy in 1621 for his successor, Sir Francis Wyatt [Document 12].) The assembly would meet annually except in cases of emergency, when it could be irregularly convened. It would serve as a court of justice, and the company gave it authority to enact such general laws and ordinances as should seem necessary. Such laws were subject to a gubernatorial veto and review by the company.

Upon his arrival in Virginia, Yeardley issued a call for the assembly, and on July 30, 1619, the first meeting of a representative legislative body convened in the little church at Jamestown. After electing a speaker and taking the oaths of allegiance and supremacy, the members proceeded to their business.

The assembly first considered its members' qualifications and ejected two, pending clarification of their patents from London. That done, it proceeded to its legislative business. The assembly's legislative work is divisible into four parts: examining the 1618 instructions to see what changes, if any, were desirable, enacting certain instructions into law, proposing new laws, and drafting petitions to the company. Six suggested revisions to the Great Charter were adopted, and the assembly enacted laws touching on such matters as Indian relations and the price of tobacco. After some criminal cases were resolved, "the intemperance of the weather and the falling sick of divers of the Burgesses" forced Yeardley on August 4 to prorogue the assembly to the following March.

In spite of the session's brevity, only five days, the General Assembly had achieved an important beginning. These twenty-seven men (the governor, six councillors, and twenty burgesses) ushered in a new era in colonial government. Although the assembly would undergo modifications in its functions, and its right to exist would be in doubt after the company lost its charter, that first meeting established a precedent for the evolution of representative political institutions and self-government in English North America.

Tragically, the high expectations of 1618 were soon dashed. Reorganization succeeded in streamlining land tenures and local administration and in introducing a more familiar form of government. An advertising campaign and the promise of cheap land swelled the colony's population to its highest level by the early 1620s. The settling of some women, children, and family units; the introduction of customary legal usages; and the advancement of agriculture were hopeful signs. But these changes did little to bail the company out of its underlying distress, because all of Sandys's schemes for restoring the company's fiscal health failed.

Sandys's leadership was itself a source of contention, and as the company's financial situation continued to worsen, opposition to Sir Edwin mounted. The crown's withdrawal of the company lottery in 1621 and the Indian attack on Virginia in 1622 (see chapter 8) were two blows from which the company never recovered. Loss of the lottery deprived the company of its chief source of operating revenue; without it company officials were hard pressed to keep operations going. The Indian attack, which killed some 350 settlers, plunged Virginia into a full-scale war that lasted until the late 1620s. To compound the colonists' difficulties, shortages of food and ammunition developed, and the colony was struck by a debilitating epidemic. These failures destroyed whatever resilience remained in the company's membership. Factionalism increased: the arguments became so rancorous that the crown intervened to prevent the company from destroying itself. When that tactic failed, James was left with no choice but to seek the company's destruction. To that end, in November. 1623 the crown's attorney-general, Thomas Coventry, brought suit upon a writ of *quo warranto* to show cause why the charter should not be voided against the company in the Court of King's Bench. Six months later the court ruled against the company, its charter was seized, and Virginia became England's first royal colony.

Despite the London Company's failures as a colonizing agency, it had achieved an important beginning for England's subsequent colonial enterprise. The company had succeeded in establishing a permanent English foothold in North America, and in the process provided future colonizers with a wealth of firsthand practical information about the New World. It had laid the foundation for Virginia's future economic growth. And most important, perhaps, the company began transplanting English conceptions of social order, law, and government to a new environment. For this reason alone the company period of Virginia history was enormously significant.

SUGGESTED READINGS

Primary Sources

*Bemiss, Samuel M., ed. *The Three Charters of the Virginia Company of London, with Seven Related Documents; 1606–1621.* Jamestown 350th Anniversary Historical Booklet 4 (Williamsburg, Va., 1957).

Tyler, Lyon Gardiner, ed. *Narratives of Early Virginia, 1606–1625.* Original Narratives of Early American History (New York, 1907), 245–278.

Secondary Sources

*Andrews, Charles M. *Our Earliest Colonial Settlements: Their Diversities of Origin and Later Characteristics* (Ithaca, N.Y., 1959 [orig. publ. New York, 1932]), 1–59.

*Craven, Wesley Frank. *The Southern Colonies in the Seventeenth Century, 1607–1689* (Baton Rouge, La., 1949), 60–138.

————. *Dissolution of the Virginia Company: The Failure of a Colonial Experiment* (Gloucester, Mass., 1964 [orig. publ. New York, 1932]).

Diamond, Sigmund. "From Organization to Society: Virginia in the

* Available in paperback.

Seventeenth Century." *American Journal of Sociology,* LXIII (1957–1958), 457–475.
Morton, Richard L. *Colonial Virginia.* 2 vols. (Chapel Hill, N.C., 1960), I, 1–122.

Prelude to Settlement

1. The Rationale for Colonization

[Thomas], Lord De la Ware, Sir Thomas Smith, Sir Walter Cope, Master Waterson, *A True and Sincere declaration of the purpose and ends of the Plantation begun in Virginia* . . . (London, 1610), in Alexander Brown, *The Genesis of the United States* (Boston, 1890), I, 339–340.

It is Reserved and onely proper to *Divine Wisdome* to forsee and ordaine, both the *endes* and *wayes* of every action. In *humaine prudence* it is all [that] can be required, to propose *Religious* and *Noble* and *Feasable* ends; and it can have no absolute assurance, and infalliblenesse in the *waies* and *meanes,* which are contingent and various, perhaps equally reasonable, subject to un-present circumstances and doubtfull events, which ever dignifie or betray the *Councell's* from whence they were derived. And the higher the quality, and nature, and more removed from ordinary action (such as those of which we discourse) the more perplexed and misty are the pathes there-unto.

Upon which grounds, We purpose to deliver roundly and clearly, our *endes* and *wayes* to the hopeful Plantations begun in *Virginia.* . . . The Principal and *Maine Endes* (out of which are easily derived to any meane understanding infinitlesse, and yet great ones) were *first* to preach and baptize into *Christian Religion,* and by propagation of the *Gospell,* to recover out of the Armes of the Divell, a number of poore and miserable soules, wrapt up unto death, in almost *invincible ignorance,* and to endeavour the fulfilling, and accomplishment of the number of the elect, which shall be gathered from out all corners of the earth; and to add our myte to the Treasury of Heaven, that as we pray for the coming of the Kingdome of Glory, so to expresse in our actions, the same desire, if God, have pleased, to use so weak instruments, to the ripening and consummation thereof.

Secondly, to provide and build up for the publike *Honour* and *Safety* of our *Gratious King* and his *Estates* (by the favor of our Superiors even in that care) some small Rampier of our owne, in this opportune and general summer of peace, by transplanting the rancknesse and multitude of increase in our people; of which there is left no vent, but age; and evident danger that the number and infinitnesse of them, will out-grow the matter, whereon to worke for their life and sustentation, and shall one infest and become a burthen to another. But by this provision they may be seated as a Bulwarke of defence, in a place of advantage, *against a stranger enemy,* who shall in great proportion grow rich in treasure, which was exhausted to a lowe estate; and may well indure an increase of his people long wasted with a continual war, and dispersed uses and losses of them: Both which cannot cho[o]se but threaten us, if we consider, and compare the ends, ambitions and practices of our neighbour countries, with our owne.

Lastly, the appearance and assurance of *Private commodity* to the *particular undertakers,* by recovering and possessing to themselves a fruitfull land, whence they may furnish and provide this Kingdome, with all such necessities and defects [Copper, Iron, Steel, Timber for ships, yards, masts, cordage, sope ashes (marginal note in original)] under which we labour, and are now enforced to buy, and receive at the curtesie of other Princes, under the burthen of great Customs, and heavy impositions, and at so high rates in trafique, by reason of the great waste of them from whence they are now derived, which threatens almost an impossibility long to recover them, or at least such losse in exchange, as both the Kingdome and Merchant, will be weary of the deerenesse and peril. These being the true, and essential ends of this *Plantation.* . . .

2. *Supplies the Colonists Took to Virginia*

Samuel Purchas, *Hakluytus Posthumus, Or Purchas His Pilgrimes; Contayning a History of the World in Sea Voyages and Lande Travells by Englishmen and Others* (Glasgow, 1905–1907), XIX, 164–167.

The Inconveniences that have happened to some persons which have transported themselves from England to Virginia, without provisions necessary to sustaine themselves, hath greatly hindered the Progresse of that Noble Plantation: For prevention of the like disorders hereafter, that no man suffer either through ignorance or misinformation; it is thought requisite to publish this short Declaration: wherein is contayned a particular of such necessaries, as either private Families or single persons shall have cause to furnish themselves with, for their better support at their first landing in Virginia; whereby also greater numbers may receive in part directions how to provide themselves.

Apparell for one man and so after the rate for more.

One Monmouth Cap	I.s.	10.d.
Three falling bands	I.s.	3.d.
Three shirts	7.s.	6.d.
One Waste-coate	2.s.	2.d.
One sute of Canvase	7.s.	6.d.
One sute of Frize [i.e., frieze, a heavy woolen having a shaggy uncut nap on one side]	10.s.	
One sute of Cloth	15.s.	
Three paire of Irish stockins	4.s.	
Foure paire of shooes	8.s.	8.
One paire of garters		10.
One doozen of points [i.e., cords used to lace up items of clothing]		3.d.

One paire of Canvase sheets	8.s.
Seven Ells [i.e., an archaic unit of measure equal to 45 inches] of Canvase, to make a bed and boulster, to be filled in Virginia	8.s.
One Rug for a bed 8.s. which with the bed serving for two men, halfe is	8.s.
Five Ells coorse Canvase, to make a bed at Sea for two men, to be filled with straw 4.s.	5.s.
One coorse Rug at Sea for two men, will cost 6.s. is for one	

[total]   4.li.

Victuall for a whole yeere for one man and so for more after the rate.

Eight bushels of Meale	2.li.	
Two bushels of Pease at 3.s.	6.s.	
Two bushels of Oatmeale 4.s. 6.d.	9.s.	
One gallon of Aquavitæ	2.s.	6.
One gallon of Oyle	3.s.	6.d.
Two gallons of Vinegar 1.s.	2.s.	

[total]   3.li.   3.s.

Armes for one man, but if halfe of your men have Armour it is sufficient, so that all have Peeces and Swords.

One Armour compleat, light		17.s.	
One long Piece, five foot or five and a halfe, neere Musket bore	1.li.	2.s.	
One Sword		5.s.	
One Belt		1.s.	
One Bandaleere		1.s.	6.d.
Twentie pound of Powder		18.s.	
Sixtie pound of shot or lead, Pistoll and Goose shot		5.s.	

[total]   3.li.   9.s.   6.d.

Tooles for a Family of sixe persons, and so after the rate for more.

Five broad howes [i.e., hoes] at 2.s. a piece	10.s.	
Five narrow howes at 16.d. a piece	6.s.	8.d.
Two broad Axes at 3.s. 8.d. a piece	7.s.	4.d.
Five felling Axes at 18.d. a piece	7.s.	6.d.
Two Steele Hand-sawes at 16.d. a piece	2.s.	8.d.
Two two-hand-sawes at 5.s. a piece	10.s.	
One whip-saw, set and filed with boxe, file and wrest	10.s.	
Two Hammers 12.d. a piece	2.s.	
Three shovels 18.d. a piece	4.s.	6.d.
Two Spades at 18.d. a piece	3.s.	
Two Augers 6.d. a piece	1.s.	
Six Chissels 6.d. a piece	3.s.	
Two percers [i.e., piercer, a tool for starting holes in wood or metal] stocked 4.d. a piece		8.d.

Three gimblets [i.e., gimlet, a small boring tool] 2.d. a piece				6.d.
Two hatchets 21.d. a piece			3.s.	6.d.
Two froves [i.e., froe, a wedge-shaped cleaving tool] to cleave pale [i.e., pallisades] 18.d.			3.s.	
Two hand-bils [i.e., a hook-bladed tool used for clearing brush] 20. a piece			3.s.	4.d.
One Grindlestone 4.s.			4.s.	
Nailes of all sorts to the value of		2.li.		
Two Pickaxes			3.s.	
[total]	6.li.	2.s.	8.d.	

Household Implements for a Family of six persons,
and so for more or lesse after the rate.

One Iron Pot		7.s.	
One Kettle		6.s.	
One large frying-pan		2.s.	6.d.
One Griddiron		1.s.	6.d.
Two Skillets		5.s.	
One Spit		2.s.	
Platters, dishes, Spoones of wood		4.s.	
[total]	1.li.	8.s.	

For Sugar, Spice, and fruit and at Sea for six men	12.s.	6.d.

So the full charge of apparell victuall, armes, tooles and houshold-stuffe, and after this rate for each person, will amount unto about the sum of	12.li.	10.s.
The passage of each man is	6.li.	
The fraight of these provisions for a man, will be about halfe a Tun, which is	1.li.	10.s.
So the whole charge wil amount to about	20.li.	

Nets, Hookes, Lines, and a Tent must be added if the number of people be greater, as also some Kine [i.e., livestock].

And this is the usuall proportion that the Virginia Company doe bestow upon their Tenants which they send.

3. *The First Settlers*

Edward Arber and A. G. Bradley, eds., *The Travels and Works of Captain John Smith, President of Virginia, and Admiral of New England, 1580–1631* (Edinburgh, 1910), I, 93–94.

Maister Edward Maria Wingfield. ⎫
Captaine Bartholomew Gosnoll. ⎪
Captaine John Smyth. ⎪
Captaine John Rat[c]liffe. ⎬ Councell.
Captaine John Martin. ⎪
Captaine George Kendall. ⎭

Maister Robert Hunt Preacher. }
Maister George Percie.
Anthony Gosnoll.   Gent.
Captaine Gabriell Archer.

Robert Ford.
William Bruster.
Dru[e] Pickhouse.
John Brookes.
Thomas Sands.
John Robinson.
Ustis Clovill.   Gent.
Kellam Throgmorton.
Nathaniell Powell.
Robert Behethland.
Jeremy Alicock.
Thomas Studley.
Richard Crofts.

Nicholas Houlgrave.
Thomas Webbe:
John Waler.
William Tankard.
Francis Snarsbrough.
Edward Brookes.
Richard Dixon.   Gent.
John Martin.
George Martin.
Anthony Gosnold.
Thomas Wotton, Sierg. [Surgeon]
Thomas Gore.
Francis Midwinter.

William Laxon.
Edward Pising.   Carpenters
Thomas Emry.
Robert Small.

Anas Todkill.
John Capper.

James Read, Blacksmith.
Jonas Profit, Sailer.
Thomas Couper, Barber.

John Herd, Bricklayer.
William Garret, Bricklayer.
Edward Brinto, Mason.
William Love, Taylor.
Nicholas Skot, Drum[mer].

John Laydon.
William Cassen.
George Cassen.
Thomas Cassen.
William Rods.
William White.
Ould Edward.   } Labourers.
Henry Tavin.
George Golding.
John Dods.
William Johnson.
William Unger.

William Wilkinson, Surgeon

Samuell Collier.
Nathaniel Pecock.
James Brumfield.   } Boyes.
Richard Mutton.

4. Instructions from the London Company to the First Settlers, November 1606

Philip L. Barbour, ed., *The Jamestown Voyages under the First Charter, 1606–1609,* Haklyut Society Publications, 2d Ser., CXXXVI–CXXXVII (Cambridge, 1969), I, 49–54.

As We Doubt not but you will have especial Care to Observe the Ordinances [i.e., the charter] set Down by the Kings Majestie and Delivered unto you under the privy Seal So for your better Directions upon your first Landing we have thought Good to recommend unto your Care these Instructions and articles following. When it Shall please God to Send you on the Coast of Virginia you shall Do your best Endeavour to find out a Safe port in the Entrance of Some navigable River making Choise of Such a one as runneth furthest into the Land. and if you happen to Discover Divers portable Rivers and amongst them any one that hath two main branches if the Difference be not Great make Choise of that which bendeth most towards the Northwest for that way shall You soonest find the Other Sea[.] When You have made Choise of the River on which you mean to Settle be not hasty in Landing Your Victual and munitions but first Let Captain Newport Discover how far that River may be found navigable that you may make Election of the Strongest most Fertile and wholesome place for if you make many Removes besides the Loss of time You Shall greatly Spoil your Victuals and Your cask[s] and with Great pain transport it in Small boats But if you Choose your place so far up as A Bark of fifty tuns will fleet then you may Lay all Your provisions a Shore with Ease and the better Receive the trade of all the Countries about you in the Land and Such A place you may perchance find a hundred miles from the Rivers mouth and the farther up the better for if you sit Down near the Entrance Except it be in Some Island that is Strong by nature An Enemy that may approach you on Even Ground may Easily pull You Out and if he be Driven to Seek You a hundred miles within the Land in boats you shall from both sides of your River where it is Narrowest So beat them with Your muskets as they shall never be Able to prevail Against You. And to the end That You be not Surprised as the French were in Florida by Melindus and the Spaniard in the same place by the french you shall Do Well to make this Double provision first Erect a Little Sconce at the Mouth of the River that may Lodge Some ten men With Whom you Shall Leave a Light boat that when any fleet shall be in Sight they may Come with Speed to Give You Warning. Secondly you must in no Case Suffer any of the natural people of the Country to inhabit between You and the Sea Coast for you Cannot Carry Your Selves so towards them but they will Grow Discontented with Your habitation and be ready to Guide and assist any Nation that Shall Come to invade You and if You neglect this You neglect Your Safety. When You have Discovered as far up the River as you mean to plant Your Selves and Landed your victuals and munitions to the End that Every man may know his Charge you Shall Do well to Divide your Six Score men into three parts whereof one forty of them you may appoint to fortifie and build of which your first work must be your Storehouse for Victual 30 Others you may imploy in preparing your Ground and Sowing your Corn and Roots the Other ten of these forty you must Leave as Centinel at the havens mouth The Other forty you may imploy for two Months in Discovery of the River above you and on the Contrary [country?] about you which Charge Captain Newport and Captain Gosnold may under-take[.] of these forty Discoverers when they Do Espie any high Lands or hills Captain Gosnold may take 20 of the Company to Cross Over the Lands and Carrying half a Dozen pickaxes to try if they Can find any mineral. The Other twenty may go on by River and pitch up boughs upon the Banks Side by which the Other boats Shall follow them by the Same turnings You may also take with them a Wherry Such as is used here in the Thames by Which you may Send back to the President for supply of munition or any Other want that you may [be?] not Driven to Return for Every Small Defect.

You must Observe if you Can Whether the River on which you Plant Doth Spring out of Mountains or out of Lakes if it be out of any Lake the passage to the Other Sea will be the more Easy and it is Like Enough that Out of the same Lake you shall find Some Spring which run the Contrary way toward the East India Sea for the Great and famous River of Volga Tan[a]is and Dwina have three heads near joynd and Yet the One falleth into the Caspian Sea the Other into the Euxine Sea and the third into the Polonian Sea. In all Your Passages you must have Great Care not to Offend the naturals if You Can Eschew it and imploy Some few of your Company to trade with them for Corn and all Other lasting Victuals if you [they?] have any and this you must Do before that they perceive you mean to plant among them for not being Sure how your own Seed Corn will prosper the first Year to avoid the Danger of famine use and Endeavour to Store yourselves of the Country Corn. Your Discoverers that passes Over Land with hired Guides must Look well to them that they Slip not from them and for more Assurance let them take a Compass with them and Write Down how far they Go upon Every point of the Compass for that Country having no way nor path if that Your Guides Run from You in the Great Woods or Deserts you Shall hardly Ever find a Passage back. And how Weary Soever your Soldiers be Let them never trust the Country people with the Carriage of their Weapons for if they Run from You with Your Shott which they only fear they will Easily kill them all with their arrows And whensoever any of Yours Shoots before them be sure that they be Chosen out of your best Markesmen for if they See Your Learners miss what they aim at they will think the Weapon not so terrible and thereby will be bould . . . d [?—bould] to Assaillt You. Above all things Do not advertize the killing of any of your men that the Country people may know it if they Perceive they are but Common men and that with the Loss of many of theirs they may Deminish any part of Yours they will make many Adventures upon You if the Country be popalous[.] you Shall Do well also not to Let them See or know of Your Sick men if you have any which may also Encourage them to many Enterprizes. You must take Especial Care that you Choose a Seat for habitation that Shall not be over burthened with Woods near your town for all the men You have Shall not be able to Cleanse twenty acres in a Year besides that it may Serve for a Covert for Your Enimies round about You neither must You plant in a low and moist place because it will prove unhealthful[.] You shall Judge of the Good Air by the People for Some part of that Coast where the Lands are Low have their people blear Eyed and with Swollen bellies and Legs but if the naturals be Strong and Clean made it is a true sign of a wholesome Soil. You must take Order to Draw up the Pinnace that is Left with You under your fort and take her Sails and Anchors A Shore all but a Small Kedge [i.e., a small anchor] to ride by Least Some ill Disposed Persons Slip away with her. You must take Care that your Marriners that Go for wages Do not marr your trade for those that mind not to inhabite for a Little Gain will Debase the Estimation of Exchange and hinder the trade for Ever after and there fore you Shall not admit or Suffer any person whatsoever other then Such as Shall be appointed by the president and Councel there to buy any Merchandizes or Other things whatsoever. It Were Necessary that all Your Carpenters and Other such like Workmen about building Do first build Your Storehouse and those Other Rooms of Publick and necessary Use before any house be Set up for any private person and though the Workman may belong to any private persons yet Let them all Work together first for the Company and then for private men And Seeing order is at the same price with Confusion it shall be adviceably done to Set your houses Even and by a line that You[r] Streets may have a Good breadth and be carried Square about your market place and Every Streets End opening into it that from thence with a few feild peices you may Command Every street throughout which marketplace you may also fortify if you shall think it needful. You Shall do well to Send a perfect relation by Captain Newport of all that is Done of what height you are Seated how far into the Land what Comodities you find what Soil Woods and their Several Kinds and so of all Other things Else to advertise particularly and to Suffer no man to return but by pasport from the president and Councel nor to write any Letter of any thing that may Discourage others. Lastly and Cheifly the way to prosper and to Obtain Good Success is to make yourselves all of one mind for the Good of your Country and your own and to Serve and fear God the Giver of all Goodness for every Plantation which our heavenly father hath not planted shall be rooted out.

5. *George Percy's Account of the Voyage to Virginia and the Colony's First Days*

Barbour, ed., *Jamestown Voyages*, I, 129–146.

On Saturday, the twentieth of December in the yeere 1606 the fleet fell from London, and the fift of January we anchored in the Downes: but the winds continued contrarie so long, that we were forced to stay there some time, where wee suffered great stormes, but by the skilfulnesse of the Captaine wee suffered no great losse or danger.

The twelfth day of February at night we saw a blazing Starre, and presently a storme. The three and twentieth day we fell with the Iland of Mattanenio [Martinique] in the West Indies. The foure and twentieth day we anchored at Dominico, within fourteene degrees of the Line, a very faire Iland, the Trees full of sweet and good smels inhabited by many Savage Indians, they were at first very scrupulous to come aboord us. . . . [Percy describes explorations and also encounters with Indians on various Caribbean islands touched on by the colonists prior to their arrival in Virginia.]

The tenth day [of April] we set saile, and disimboged out of the West Indies, and bare our course Northerly. The fourteenth day we passed the Tropicke of Cancer. The one and twentieth day, about five a clocke at night there began a vehement tempest, which lasted all the night, with winds, raine, and thunders in a terrible manner. Wee were forced to lie at Hull that night, because we thought wee had beene nearer land than wee were. The next morning, being the two and twentieth day wee sounded; and the three and twentieth and foure and twenteth day, but we could find no ground. The five and twentieth day we sounded, and had no ground at an hundred fathom. The six and twentieth day of Aprill, about foure a clocke in the morning, wee descried the Land of Virginia: the same day wee entred into the Bay of Chesupioc [Chesapeake] directly, without any let or hindrance; there wee landed and discovered a little way, but wee could find nothing worth the speaking of, but faire meddowes and goodly tall Trees, with such Fresh-waters running through the woods, as I was almost ravished at the first sight thereof.

At night, when wee were going aboard, there came the Savages creeping upon all foure, from the Hills like Beares, with their Bowes in their mouthes, charged us very desperately in the faces, hurt Captaine Gabrill Archer in both his hands, and a sayler in two places of the body very dangerous. After they had spent their Arrowes, and felt the sharpnesse of our shot, they retired into the Woods with a great noise, and so left us.

The seven and twentieth day we began to build up our Shallop: the Gentlemen and Souldiers marched eight miles up into the Land, we could not see a Savage in all that march, we came to a place where they had made a great fire, and had beene newly a rosting Oysters: when they perceived our comming, they fled away to the Mountaines, and left many of the Oysters in the fire: we eat some of the Oysters, which were very large and delicate in taste.

The eighteenth day we lanched our Shallop, the Captaine and some Gentlemen went in her, and discovered up the Bay, we found a River on the Southside running into the Maine; we entered it and found it very shoald [i.e., shallow] water, not for any Boats to swim: Wee went further into the Bay, and saw a plaine plot of ground where we went on Land, and found the place five mile in compasse, without either Bush or Tree, we saw nothing there but a Cannow, which was made out of the whole tree, which was five and fortie foot long by the Rule. Upon this plot of ground we got good store of Mussels and Oysters, which lay on the ground as thicke as stones: wee opened some, and found in many of them Pearles. Wee marched some three or foure miles further into the Woods, where we saw great smoakes of fire. Wee marched to those smoakes and found that the Savages had beene there burning downe the grasse, as wee thought either to make their plantation there, or else to give signes to bring their forces together, and so to give us battell. We past through excellent ground full of Flowers of divers kinds and colours, and as goodly trees as I have seene, as Cedar, Cipresse, and other kindes: going a little further we came into a little plat of ground full of fine and beautifull Strawberries, foure times bigger and better than ours in England. All this march we could neither see Savage nor Towne. When it grew to be towards night we stood backe to our Ships, we sounded and found it shallow water for a great way, which put us out of all hopes for getting any higher with our Ships, which road at the mouth of the River. Wee rowed over to a point of Land, where wee found a channell, and sounded six, eight, ten, or twelve fathom: which put us in good comfort. Therefore wee named that point of Land, Cape Comfort.

The nine and twentieth day we set up a Crosse at Chesupioc Bay, and named that place Cape Henry. Thirtieth day, we came with our ships to Cape Comfort; where we saw five Savages running on the shoare; presently the Captaine caused the shallop to be manned, so rowing to the shoare, the Captaine called to them in signe of friendship, but they were at first very timersome, until they saw the Captain lay his hand on his heart: upon that they laid down their Bowes and Arrowes, and came very boldly to us, making signes to come a shoare to their Towne, which is called by the Savages Kecoughtan. Wee coasted to their Towne, rowing over a River running into the Maine, where these Savages swam over with their Bowes and Arrowes in their mouthes. . . .

The twelfth day [of May] we went backe to our ships, and discovered a point of Land, called Archers Hope, which was sufficient with a little labour to defend our selves against any Enemy. The soile was good and fruitfull, with excellent good Timber. There are also great store of Vines in bignesse of a mans thigh, running up to the tops of the Trees in great abundance. We also did see many Squirels, Conies, Black Birds with crimson wings, and divers other Fowles and Birds of divers and sundrie collours of crimson, Watchet, Yellow, Greene, Murry, and of divers other hewes naturally without any art using.

We found store of Turkie nests and many Egges, if it had not beene disliked, because the ship could not ride neere the shoare, we had setled there to all the Collonies contentment.

The thirteenth day, we came to our seating place in Paspihas Countrey, some eight miles from the point of Land, which I made mention before: where our shippes doe lie so neere the shoare that they are moored to the Trees in six fathom water.

The fourteenth day we landed all our men which were set to worke about the fortification, and others some to watch and ward as it was convenient. The first night of our landing, about midnight, there came some Savages sayling close to our quarter: presently there was an alarum given; upon that the savages ran away, and we not troubled any more by them that night. Not long after there came two Savages that seemed to be Commanders, bravely drest, with Crownes of coloured haire upon their heads, which came as Messengers from the Werowance of Paspihae; telling us that their Werowance was comming and would be merry with us with a fat Deare. . . .

The nineteenth day, my selfe and three or foure more walking into the Woods by chance wee espied a path-way like to an Irish pace: we were desirous to knowe whither it would bring us; wee traced along some foure miles, all the way as wee went, having the pleasantest Suckles, the ground all flowing over with faire flowers of sundry colours and kindes, as though it had beene in any Garden or Orchard in England. There be many Strawberries, and other fruits unknowne: wee saw the Woodes full of Cedar and Cypresse trees, with other trees, which issues out sweet Gummes like to Balsam. . . .

At Port Cotage in our Voyage up the River, we saw a Savage Boy about the age of ten yeeres, which had a head of haire of a perfect yellow and a reasonable white skinne, which is a Miracle amongst all Savages.

This River which wee have discovered is one of the famousest Rivers that ever was found by any Christian, it ebbes and flowes a hundred and threescore miles where ships of great burthen may harbour in safetie. Wheresoever we landed upon this River, wee saw the goodliest Woods as Beech, Oke, Cedar, Cypresse, Wal-nuts, Sassafras and Vines in great abundance, which hang in great clusters on many Trees, and other Trees unknowne, and all the grounds bespred with many sweet and delicate flowres of divers colours and kindes. There are also many fruites as Strawberries, Mulberries, Rasberries and Fruits unknowne, there are many branches of this River, which runne flowing through the Woods with great plentie of fish of all kindes, as for Sturgeon all the World cannot be compared to it. In this Countrey I have seene many great and large Medowes having excellent good pasture for any Cattle. There is also great store of Deere both Red and Fallow. There are Beares, Foxes, Otters, Bevers, Muskats, and wild beasts unknowne.

The foure and twentieth day wee set up a Crosse at the head of this River, naming it Kings River, where we proclaimed James King of England to have the most right unto it. When wee had finished and set up our Crosse, we shipt our men and made for James Fort. By the way wee came to Pohatans Towre where the Captaine went on shore suffering none to goe with him, hee presented the Commander of this place with a Hatchet which hee tooke joyfully, and was well pleased.

But yet the Savages murmured at our planting in the Countrie, whereupon this Werowance made answere againe very wisely of a Savage, Why should you bee offended with them as long as they hurt you not, nor take any thing away by force, they take but a little waste ground, which doth you nor any of us any good. . . .

The fifteenth day of June, we had built and finished our Fort which was triangle wise, having three Bulwarkes at every corner like a halfe Moone, and foure or five pieces of Artillerie mounted in them, we had made our selves sufficiently strong for these Savages, we had also sowne most of our Corne on two Mountaines, it sprang a mans height from the ground, this Countrey is a fruitfull soile, bearing many goodly and fruitfull Trees, as Mulberries, Cherries, Walnuts, Ceders, Cypresse, Sassafras, and Vines in great abundance.

Munday the two and twentieth of June, in the morning Captaine Newport in the Admirall departed from James Port for England.

Captaine Newport being gone for England, leaving us (one hundred and foure persons) verie bare and scantie of victualls, furthermore in warres and in danger of the Savages. We hoped after a supply which Captaine Newport promised within twentie weekes. But if the beginners of this action doe carefully further us, the Country being so fruitfull, it would be as great a profit to the Realme of England, as the Indies to the King of Spaine, if this River which wee have found had beene discovered in the time of warre with Spaine, it would have beene a commoditie to our Realme, and a great annoyance to our enemies. . . .

The sixt of August there died John Asbie of the bloudie Flixe. The ninth day died George Flowre of the swelling. The tenth day died William Bruster Gentlemen, of a wound given by the Savages, and was buried the eleventh day.

The fourteenth day, Jerome Alikock Ancient, died of a wound, the same day Francis Midwinter, Edward Moris Corporall died suddenly.

The fifteenth day, their died Edward Browne and Stephen Galthrope. The sixteenth day, their died Thomas Gower Gentleman. The seventeenth day, their died Thomas Mounslic. The eighteenth day, there died Robert Pennington, and John Martine Gentleman, The nineteenth day, died Drue Piggase Gentleman. The two and twentieth day of August, there died Captaine Bartholomew Gosnold one of our Councell, he was honourably buried, having all the Ordnance in the Fort shot off with many vollies of small shot. . . .

The foure and twentieth day, died Edward Harington and George Walker, and were buried the same day. The sixe and twentieth day, died Kenelme Throgmortine. The seven and twentieth day died William Roods. The eight and twentieth day died Thomas Stoodie, Cape Merchant.

The fourth day of September died Thomas Jacob Sergeant. The fift day, there died Benjamin Beast. Our men were destroyed with cruell diseases as Swellings, Flixes, Burning Fevers, and by warres, and some departed suddenly, but for the most part they died of meere famine. There were never Englishmen left in a forreigne Countrey in such miserie as wee were in this new discovered Virginia. Wee watched every three nights lying on the bare cold ground what weather soever came warded all the next day, which brought our men to bee most feeble wretches, our food was but a small Can of Barlie sod [i.e., soaked] in water to five men a day, our drinke cold water taken out of the River, which was at a floud verie salt, at a low tide full of slime and filth, which was the destruction of many of our men. Thus we lived for the space of five moneths in this miserable distresse, not having five able men to man our Bulwarkes upon any occasion. If it had not pleased God to have put a terrour in the Savages hearts, we had all perished by those vild [i.e., vile] and cruell Pagans, being in that weake estate as we were; our men night and day groaning in every corner of the Fort most pittifull to heare, if there were any conscience in men, it would make their harts to bleed to heare the pittiful murmurings and out-cries of our sick men without reliefe every night and day for the space of sixe weekes, some departing out of the World, many times three or foure in a night, in the morning their bodies trailed out of their Cabines like Dogges to be buried: in this sort did I see the mortalitie of divers of our people.

It pleased God, after a while, to send those people which were our mortall enemies to releeve us with victuals, as Bread, Corne, Fish, and Flesh in great plentie, which was the setting up of our feeble men, otherwise wee had all perished. Also we were frequented by divers Kings in the Countrie, bringing us store of provision to our great comfort.

The eleventh day, there was certaine Articles laid against Master Wingfield which was then President, thereupon he was not only displaced out of his President ship, but also from being of the Councell. Afterwards Captaine John Ratcliffe was chosen President.

The eighteenth day, died one Ellis Kinistone which was starved to death with cold. The same day at night, died one Richard Simmons. The nineteenth day, there died one Thomas Mouton.

William White (having lived with the Natives) reported to us of their customes in the morning by breake of day, before they eate or drinke both men, women and children, that be above tenne yeeres of age runnes into the water, there washes themselves a good while till the Sunne riseth, then offer Sacrifice to it, strewing Tobacco on the water or Land, honouring the Sunne as their God, likewise they doe at the setting of the Sunne.

6. *Some Contemporary Explanations for Virginia's Early Failures*

> William Simmonds, *The Proceedings of the English Colonie in Virginia Since their first beginning from England in the Yeare of our Lord, 1606 till this present 1612, with all their accidents that befell them in the Journies and Discoveries* (Oxford, 1612), 76–78.

Those temporall proceedings, to some maie seeme too charitable, to such a dailie daring trecherous people [i.e., the Indians]; to others unpleasant that we washed not the ground with their blouds, nor shewed such strange inventions in mangling, murdering, ransaking, and destroying (as did the Spaniards) the simple bodies of those ignorant soules; nor delightful, because not stuffed with relations of heaps and mines of gold and silver, nor such rare commodities as the Portugals and Spaniards found in the East and West Indies. The want whereof hath begot us, that were the first undertakers, no lesse scorne and contempt, than their noble conquests and valiant adventures (beautified with it), praise and honor. Too much, I confesse, the world cannot attribute to their ever memorable merit. And to cleare us from the worlds blind ignorant censure, these fewe words may suffise to any reasonably understanding.

It was the spaniards good hap to happen in those parts where were infinite numbers of people, whoe had manured the ground with that providence that it afforded victuall at all times; and time had brought them to that perfection [that] they had the use of gold and silver, and [of] the most of such commodities as their countries affoorded: so that what the Spaniard got was only the spoile and pillage of those countrie people, and not the labours of their owne hands.

But had those fruitfull Countries beene as Salvage [i.e., savage], as barbarous, as ill-peopled, as little planted laboured and manured, as *Virginia*; their proper labours, it is likely would have produced as small profit as ours. But had *Virginia* bin peopled, planted, manured, and adorned with such store of pretious Jewels and rich commodities as was the Indies: then, had we not gotten and done as much as by their examples might bee expected from us, the world might then have traduced us and our merits, and have made shame and infamy our recompence and reward.

But we chanced in a lande, even as God made it. Where we found only an idle, improvident, scattered people, ignorant of the knowledge of gold, or silver, or any commodities; and carelesse of anything but from hand to mouth, but for ba[u]bles of no worth; nothing to encourage us but what accidentally wee found nature afforded. Which ere we could bring to recompence our paines, defray our charges, and satisfie our adventurers; we were to discover the country, subdue the people, bring them to be tractable civil and industrious, and teach them trades that the fruits of their labours might make us recompence, or plant such colonies of our owne that must first make provision how to live of themselves ere they can bring to perfection the commodities of the countrie: which doubtless will be as commodious for England as the west Indies for Spaine, if it be rightly managed. . . .

The Struggle for Survival

7. *A Share of Stock in the London Company, 1610*

Egerton Manuscripts, 2087, British Museum.

Whereas the Mayor Juratts and Cominaltye of the Towne and Porte of Dover have payde in readye monye to Sir Thomas Smyth Knight Treasurer of Virginia, the some of Twentye fyve pounds for three adventures towards the sayd voyadge. It is agreed that for the same, they the sayd Mayor, Juratts and Cominaltye, and there successors, shall have notablye accordinge to there adventures, these full part of all suche landes—Tenementes, and heredita-mentes, as shall from tyme to tyme be there recovered, planted and inhabited, And of suche Mynes, and Minnerales of Golde, silver, and other Metall or Treasure Pearles, precious stones, or anye kinde of was or marchandizes, co-modeties, or profitts whatsoever which shalbe obteyned, or gotten in the sayd voyage, accordinge to the portion of monye by them ymployed to that use, in an ample manner as anye other adventurer therein shall reteyne for the like sume. Written this 23th of Maye Domini *1610*[.]

8. *The "Starving Time,"* 1609–1610

Arber and Bradley, eds., *Travels and Works of John Smith*, II, 498–499.

Now we all found the losse of Captaine *Smith,* yea his greatest maligners could now curse his losse: as for corne provision and contribution from the Salvages, we had nothing but mortall wounds, with clubs and arrowes; as for our Hogs, Hens, Goats, Sheepe, Horse, or what lived, our commanders, officers and Salvages daily consumed them, some small proportions sometimes we tasted, till all was devoured; then swords, armes, pieces, or any thing, wee traded with the Salvages, whose cruell fingers were so oft imbrewed in our blouds, that what by their crueltie, our Governours indiscretion, and the losse of our ships, of five hundred within six moneths after Captaine *Smiths* depar-ture [October 1609–March 1610], there remained not past sixtie men, women and children, most miserable and poore creatures; and those were preserved for the most part, by roots, herbes, acornes, walnuts, berries, now and then a little fish: they that had startch in these extremities, made no small use of it; yea even the very skinnes of our horses.

Nay, so great was our famine, that a Salvage we slew and buried, the poorer sort tooke him up againe and eat him; and so did divers one another boyled and stewed with roots and herbs: And one amongst the rest did kill his wife, powdered [i.e., salted] her, and had eaten part of her before it was knowne; for which hee was executed, as hee well deserved: now whether shee was better roasted, boyled or carbonado'd [i.e., grilled], I know not; but of such a dish as powdered wife I never heard of.

This was that time, which still to this day [1624] we called the starving time; it were too vile to say, and scarce to be beleeved, what we endured: but the occasion was our owne, for want of providence industrie and govern-ment, and not the barrennesse and defect of the Countrie, as is generally sup-posed; for till then in three yeeres, for the numbers were landed us, we had never from *England* provision sufficient for six moneths, though it seemed by the bils of loading sufficient was sent us, such a glutton is the Sea, and such good fellowes the Mariners; we as little tasted of the great proportion sent us, as they of our want and miseries, yet notwithstanding they ever over-swayed and ruled the businesse, though we endured all that is said, and chiefly lived on what this good Countrie naturally afforded. Yet had wee beene even in Paradice it selfe with these Governours, it would not have beene much better withe us; yet there was amongst us, who had they had the government as Captaine *Smith* appointed, but that they could not maintaine it, would surely have kept us from those extremities of miseries. This in ten daies more, would have supplanted us all with death.

But God that would not this Countrie should be unplanted, sent Sir *Thomas Gates*, and Sir *George Sommers* with one hundred and fiftie people most happily preserved by the *Bermudas* to preserve us [May 21, 1610]. . . .

9. *Excerpts from the* Lawes Divine, Morall and Martiall, *1611*

William Strachey, comp., *Lawes Divine, Morall and Martiall,* ed. David H. Flaherty (Charlottesville, Va., 1969), 10–17, 19, 21, 24–27.

1   First since we owe our highest and supreme duty, our greatest, and all our allegeance to him, from whom all power and authoritie is derived, and flowes as from the first, and onely fountaine, and being especiall souldiers emprest in this sacred cause, we must alone expect our successe from him, who is onely the blesser of all good attempts, the King of kings, the commaunder of commaunders, and Lord of Hostes, I do strictly commaund and charge all Captaines and Officers, of what qualitie or nature soever, whether commanders in the field, or in towne, or townes, forts or fortresses, to have a care that the Almightie God bee duly and daily served, and that they call upon their people to heare Sermons, as that also they diligently frequent Morning and Evening praier themselves by their owne exemplar and daily life, and dutie herein, encouraging others thereunto, and that such, who shall often and wilfully absent themselves, be duly punished according to the martiall law in that case provided. . . .

6   Everie man and woman duly twice a day upon the first towling of the Bell shall upon the working daies repaire unto the Church, to hear divine Service upon pain of losing his or her dayes allowance for the first omission, for the second to be whipt, and for the third to be condemned to the Gallies for six Moneths. Likewise no man or woman shall dare to violate or breake the Sabboth by any gaming, publique, or private abroad, or at home, but duly sanctifie and observe the same, both himselfe and his familie, by preparing themselves at home with private prayer, that they may be the better fitted for the publique, according to the commandements of God, and the orders of our Church, as also every man and woman shall repaire in the morning to the divine service, and Sermons preached upon the Saboth day, and in the afternoon to divine service, and Catechising, upon paine for the first fault to lose their provision, and allowance for the whole weeke following, for the second to lose the said allowance, and also to be whipt, and for the third to suffer death. . . .

9   No man shal commit the horrible, and detestable sins of Sodomie upon pain of death; and he or she that can be lawfully convict of Adultery shall be punished with death. No man shall ravish or force any woman, maid or Indian, or other, upon pain of death, and know the[e] that he or shee, that shall commit fornication, and evident proofe made thereof, for their first fault shall be whipt, for their second they shall be whipt, and for their third they shall

be whipt three times a weeke for one month, and aske publique forgivenesse in the Assembly of the Congregation.

10   No man shall be found guilty of Sacriledge, which is a Trespasse as well committed in violating and abusing any sacred ministry, duty or office of the Church, irreverently, or prophanely, as by beeing a Church robber, to filch, steale or carry away any thing out of the Church appertaining thereunto, or unto any holy, and consecrated place, to the divine Service of God, which no man should doe upon paine of death: likewise he that shall rob the store of any commodities therein, of what quality soever, whether provisions of victuals, or of Arms, Trucking stuffe [i.e., trading cloth], Apparrell, Linnen, or Wollen, Hose or Shooes, Hats or Caps, Instruments or Tooles of Steele, Iron, etc. or shall rob from his fellow souldier, or neighbour, any thing that is his, victuals, apparell, household stuffe, toole, or what necessary else soever, by water or land, out of boate, house, or knapsack, shall bee punished with death. . . .

13   No manner of Person whatsoever, contrarie to the word of God (which tyes every particular and private man, for conscience sake to obedience, and duty of the Magistrate, and such as shall be placed in authoritie over them[ )], shall detract, slander, calumniate, murmur, mutenie, resist, disobey, or neg-lect the commaundments, either of the Lord Governour, and Captaine Gen-erall, the Lieutenant Generall, the Martiall, the Councell, or any authorised Captaine, Commaunder or publike Officer, upon paine for the first time so offending to be whipt three severall times, and upon his knees to acknowl-edge his offence, with asking forgivenesse upon the Saboth day in the assem-bly of the congregation, and for the second time so offending to be con-demned to the Gally for three yeares: and for the third time so offending to be punished with death. . . .

15   No man of what condition soever shall barter, trucke, or trade with the Indians, except he be thereunto appointed by lawful authority, upon paine of death.

16   No man shall rifle or dispoile, by force or violence, take away any thing from any Indian comming to trade, or otherwise, upon paine of death.

17   No Cape Marchant, or Provant [i.e., provision] Master, or Munition Master, or Truck Master, or keeper of any store, shall at any time imbezell, sell, or give away any thing under his Charge to any Favorite, of his, more than unto any other, whome necessity shall require in that case to have extra-ordinary allowance of Provisions, nor shall they give a false accompt unto the Lord Governour, and Captaine Generall, unto the Lieutenant Generall, unto the Marshall, or any deputed Governor, at any time having the com-maund of the Colony, with intent to defraud the said Colony, upon paine of death. . . .

19   There shall be no Capttain, Master, Marriner, saylor, or any else of what quality or condition soever, belonging to any Ship or Ships, at this time remaining, or which shall hereafter arrive within this our River, bargaine, buy, truck, or trade with any one member in this Colony, man, woman, or child, for any toole or instrument of iron, steel or what else, whether apper-taining to Smith Carpenter, Joyner, Shipwright, or any manuall occupation, or handicraft man whatsoever, resident within our Colonie, nor shall they buy

or bargaine, for any apparell, linnen, or wollen, householdstuffe, bedde, bedding, sheete towels, napkins, brasse, pewter, or such like, eyther for ready money, or provisions, nor shall they exchange their provisions, of what quality soever, whether Butter, Cheese, Bisket, meal, Oatmele, Aquavite, oyle, Bacon, any kind of Spice, or such like, for any such aforesaid instruments, or tooles, Apparell, or householdstuffe, at any time, or so long as they shall here remain, from the date of these presents upon paine of losse of their wages in *England*, confiscation and forfeiture of such their monies and provisions, and upon peril beside of such corporall punishment as shall be inflicted upon them by verdict and censure of a martiall Court: Nor shall any officer, souldier, or Trades man, or any else of what sort soever, members of this Colony, dare to sell any such Toole, or instruments, necessary and usefull, for the businesse of the Colonie, or trucke, sell, exchange, or give away his apparell, or household stuffe of what sort soever, unto any such Seaman, either for mony, or any such foresaid provisions, upon paine of 3 times severall whipping, for the one offender, and the other upon perill of incurring censure, whether of disgrace, or addition of such punishment, as shall bee thought fit by a Court Martiall.

20 Whereas sometimes heeretofore the covetous and wide affections of some greedy and ill disposed Seamen, Saylers, and Marriners, laying hold upon the advantage of the present necessity, under which the Colony sometimes suffered, have sold unto our people, provisions of Meale, Oatmeale, Bisket, Butter, Cheese etc., at unreasonable rates, and prises unconscionable: for avoiding the like to bee now put in practise, there shall no Captain, Master, Marriner, or Saylor, or what Officer else belonging to any ship, or shippes, now within our river, or heereafter which shall arrive, shall dare to bargaine, exchange, barter, truck, trade, or sell, upon paine of death, unto any one Landman member of this present Colony, any provisions of what kind soever, above the determined valuations, and prises, set downe and proclaimed, and sent therefore unto each of your severall ships, to bee fixed uppon your Maine mast, to the intent that want of due notice, and ignorance in this case, be no excuse, or plea, for any one offender herein. . . .

23 No man shall imbezell, lose, or willingly breake, or fraudulently make away, either Spade, Shovell, Hatchet, Axe, Mattocke, or other toole or instrument uppon paine of whipping.

24 Any man that hath any edge toole, either of his owne, or which hath heeretofore beene belonging to the store, see that he bring it instantly to the storehouse, where he shall receive it againe by a particular note, both of the toole, and of his name taken, that such a toole unto him appertaineth, at whose hands, upon any necessary occasion, the said toole may be required, and this shall he do, upon paine of severe punishment.

25 Every man shall have an especiall and due care, to keepe his house sweete and cleane, as also so much of the streete, as lieth before his door, and especially he shall so provide, and set his bedstead whereon he lieth, that it may stand three foote at least from the ground, as he will answere the contrarie at a martiall Court. . . .

31 What man or woman soever, shall rob any garden, publike or private, being set to weed the same, or wilfully pluck up therein any roote, herbe, or

flower, to spoile and wast or steale the same, or robbe any vineyard, or gather up the grapes, or steale any eares of the corne growing, whether in the ground belonging to the same fort or towne where he dwelleth, or in any other, shall be punished with death. . . .

All such Bakers as are appointed to bake bread, or what else, either for the store to be given out in generall, or for any one in particular, shall not steale nor imbezell, loose, or defraud any man of his due and proper weight and measure, nor use any dishonest and deceiptfull tricke to make the bread weigh heavier, or make it courser upon purpose to keepe backe any part or measure of the flower or meale committed unto him, nor aske, take, or detaine any one loafe more or lesse for his hire or paines for so baking, since whilest he who delivered unto him such meale or flower, being to attend the businesse of the Colonie, such baker or bakers are imposed upon no other service or duties, but onely so to bake for such as do worke, and this shall hee take notice of, upon paine for the first time offending herein of losing his eares, and for the second time to be condemned a yeare to the Gallies, and for the third time offending, to be condemned to the Gallies for three yeares.

All such cookes as are appointed to seeth [i.e., boil], bake or dresse any manner of way, flesh, fish, or what else, of what kind soever, either for the generall company, or for any private man, shall not make lesse, or cut away any part or parcel of such flesh, fish, etc. Nor detaine or demaund any part or parcell, as allowance or hire for his so dressing the same, since as aforesaid of the baker, hee or they such Cooke or Cookes, exempted from other publike works abroad, are to attend such seething and dressing of such publike flesh, fish, or other provisions of what kinde soever, as their service and duties expected from them by the Colony, and this shall they take notice of, upon paine for the first time offending herein, of losing his eares, and for the second time to be condemned a yeare to the Gallies: and for the third time offending to be condemned to the Gallies for three yeares.

All fishermen, dressers of Sturgeon or such like appointed to fish, or to cure the said Sturgeon for the use of the Colonie, shall give a just and true account of all such fish as they shall take by day or night, of what kinde soever, the same to bring unto the Governour: As also of all such kegges of Sturgeon or Caviare as they shall prepare and cure upon perill for the first time offending herein, of loosing his eares, and for the second time to be condemned a yeare to the Gallies, and for the third time offending, to be condemned to the Gallies for three yeares. . . .

The Summarie of the Marshall Lawes

Thee are now further to understand, that all these prohibited, and forefended [i.e., forbidden] trespasses and misdemenors, with the injoyned observance of all these thus repeated, Civill and Politique Lawes, provided, and declared against what Crimes soever, whether against the divine Majesty of God, or our soveraigne, and Liege Lord, King *James,* the detestable crime of Sodomie, Incest, Blasphemie, Treason against the person of the principall Generals, and Commaunders of this Colonie, and their designs, against detracting, murmuring, calumniating, or slaundering of the Right Honourable the Councell resident in England, and the Committies there, the general Councell, and chiefe Commaunders heere, as also against intemperate raylings, and base unmanly speeches, uttered in the disgrace one of another by the worser sort, by the most impudent, ignorant, and prophane, such as have neither touch of humanitie, nor of conscience amongst ourselves against Adultery, Fornication, Rape, Murther, Theft, false witnessing in any cause, and other the rest of the Civill, and Politique Lawes and Orders, necessarily appertaining, and properly belonging to the Government of the State and Condition of the present Colony, as it now subsisteth: I say thee are to know, that all these thus joyned, with their due punishments, and perils heere declared, and published, are no lesse subject to the Martiall law, then unto the Civill Magistrate and where the Alarum, Tumult, and practise of arms, are not exercised, and where these now following Lawes, appertaining only to Martiall discipline, are diligently to be observed, and shall be severely executed.

1. No man shall willingly absent himself, when hee is summoned to take the oath of Supremacy, upon paine of death.

2. Every Souldier comming into this Colonie, shall willingly take his oath to serve the King and the Colonie, and to bee faithfull, and obedient to such Officers, and Commaunders, as shall be appointed over him, during the time of his aboad therein, according to the Tenor of the oath in that case provided, upon paine of being committed to the Gallies.

3. If any Souldier, or what maner of man else soever, of what quality or condition soever he be, shal tacitely compact, with any Sea-man, Captain, Master, or Marriner, to convay himselfe a Board any shippe, with intent to depart from, and abandon the Colony, without a lawful Passe from the Generall, or chiefe commander of the Colonie, at that time, and shall happen to bee prevented, and taken therwith, before the shippe shall depart out of our Bay, that Captaine, Maister or mariner, that shall so receive him, shall lose his wages, and be condemned to the Gallies for three yeeres, and he the sworne servant of the Colony, Souldier, or what else, shall bee put to death with the Armes which he carrieth.

4. When any select, and appointed Forces, for the execution and performance of any intended service, shall bee drawne into the field, and shall dislodge from one place unto another, that Souldier that shall quit or forsake his Colors, shall be punished with death.

10. *Sir Thomas Dale's Plan for Revitalizing the Colony, 1611*

Thomas Dale to Lord Salisbury, August 1611, C.O. 1/1, 94–95, Public Record Office.

. . . Yet now at length let me boldly affirme it unto your Lordship (and laying for the same, my life to [paine?] if I performe it not) that with the expence of so mutch Monie as now at once disbursed, to furnish hither 2000 men, to be here by the beginning of next Aprill, I wold in the space of two yeares (my number still made good) render this whole Countrie unto his Majestie, settle a Colonie here secure for themselves, and readie to favore all hir [ends?] and expectations, for by the severall Plantations and Seates which I would make, I shold so over master the subtile-mischeivous Great Powhatan, that I should leave him either no roome in his Countrie to harbour in, or drawe him to a firme association with our selves, and he being brought to this shift of fortune to seeke a straunger Countrie, or to accept of a well liked condition of life with us [how?] would it strike upon the neighbour Salvadges confining him, (who in all probabilitie of reason[)] may be wun then unto our owne conditions.

And that it may be thus wrought, I humbly beseetch your Lordship to pardone my weaknes, if unto your habler [i.e., abler] Judgment I presume to present the meanes thus unto your Honnor. All the Tract of Land which lieth betweene our River, which we call the Kings River [i.e., the James], and that whereupon Powhatan dwelleth (which may be in some places twentie miles over, and from Point Comfort [at the mouth of the James River] up to the Falls extendeth in length some 150 miles) is all in the commaund, and containeth the principallest Seates of Powhatan, which I would thus secure unto us, (and by haveing them, of necessitie be commaunders of the oposite South Shoare).

Att Point Comfort I would first fortefie to secure as above, and hold open the mouth of our River, to lett shipping into us: And where the two Princes Forts there are, at Keoughtan, fashion and lay out a spatious and commodious Towne, for a chiefe Commander, where is allreadie 2 or 3000 acors of cliered ground to sett Corne, and plant Vine; and Vines growe naturallie there, in great abundance; withall, this place is apt for fishing, as likewise there growes our best silk grass.

Some 15 miles from hence at a place called Kiskaick somewhat short of Powhatans cheif Towne (called Worowocomaco upon the North side of the River) should my second Plantation bee, for that would make good the inland, and assure us likewise of Pamunkie River.

My third should hould as it doth at James Towne.

My fourth should be at Arsahattacks 80 miles up our River from James Towne, where I have surveied a convenient, strong, healthie, and [sweete?] seate to plant a new Towne in, (according as I had in my instructions upon my departure) there to build, from whence might be no more [remove?] of the principall Seate; and in that forme to build, as might accomodate the inhabitants, and become the Title and Name, which it hath pleased the Lords allreadie to appoint for it.

A fift I could advise to be tenn miles above this, to commaund the head of the River, and the many fruitefull Islands in the same: Those divisions (like Nurseries) sending out smaller Settlements, (upon some places yet of Moment) would marck my former promise, concerning the full possession of Powhatans Countrie, and this Countrie of it self, would affoard many excellent Seates for many A thowsand Householder.

And believe it right noble Lord without these Forces to make good these severall Seates (the haveing whereof not onely secures our lives from the subtile Indian, but brings us in plentie of wherewith[al] to feed our lives, to cloath our Bodies, and to explore the hidden and unknowne commodities of the whole Countrie). It shalbe in vaine to strive any longer to settle a handfull of wretched and untoward people here, and great expectations to be placed over their labours, with waking and jeleous eyes, expecting the returne of sutch retributions, and benefites, secrett commodities, and ritches, which is as impossible for them to get, either into their possession, or knowledg, as it is to prise and weigh the mountaines.

I have sene (right excellent Lord) a spatious and fruitfull [Circuit?] of ground even from Point Comfort up to the Falls, upon many seates both upon the one and the other Shoare, and in all places within the lower Countrie finde that plentie of Corne, which our Companie Adventurers in England hardly believe can be here at all, and at the Falls I cannot onely testifie of Corne but of all probabilities of Mines, when our tyme shall [serve?] (which may not be yet) and where I gathered many scattered peeces of Cristall.

I am not ignorant (noble Lord) how cold the devotions of men take this great worcke, and some former slaunders yet upon itt (not removed) deterr many a meane man from his personall adventure hither, howbeit I am right well assured if we once had here the number of 2000 men as aforesaid I should in little tyme even satisfie the worst and widest assertion of him who most malignes it, or flies from it: for the two Plantations the one at Arsahatacks, the other at the head of the Falls upon the mainc of Tanx Powhatans [i.e., "Little Powhatan," one of the great chief's sons] land do so neerely neighbour all the chiefe and onely varietie and [chaunge?] of Townes and howses belonging to the Great Powhatan as either he would [desire?] friendship with us, or will leave them to our possession his countrie and thereby leave us in Securitie. Upon them we might norish our owne Breeders, and hunt, and fowle upon the land, and fish in the Rivers, and plant our Corne and Vines, boldly and with saftie, by which meanes we should no more lament us of want or scarcitie of any provision, and onely the not haveing of sufficient of provision (and in that good kindes likewise) hath bin and is yet the greatest enemie unto the speedie peopling of this Colonie: And upon the Arrival of those 2000 men (may they be here before the next Aprill though sent at two severall tymes) if but sent hither furnished with six moneths provision of corne, I wold never after chardg the Companie for any Commoditie or supplie in that kinde againe for them, so long as they staid in the Countrie.

And sithence [i.e., seeing that] (noble Lord) I know well (the Colonie standing in sutch condition and state as it doth) how hard it is to procure so many men in so short tyme, I have (under your Lordships pardone) conceived that if it will please his Majestie to banish hither all Offenders condemned betwixt this and then to die out of common Gaoles [i.e., jails], and likewise to continew that graunt for 3 yeres unto the Colonie (and thus doth the Spaniard [i.e., the king of Spain] people his Indies) it would be a readie way to furnish us with men, and not allways with the worst kinde of men either for birth, spiritts, or Bodie, and sutch who wold be right glad so to escape a just sentence to make this their new Countrie, and plant and inhabite herein with all diligence, cheerfullnes and Comfort: whereas now sutch is the universall disposition throughout our whole little Colonie (as by reason of some present want of our english provisions) as everie man all-most laments himself of being here, and murmurs at his present State, though haply he could not better it in England, not taking unto them so mutch patience untill some few yeres have accomplisht the fullnes of our better store by the growth and increase of our Cattle, planting and tilling of our corne and Vines, and indeede (right noble Lord) our discontented Companie makes good that old saying Jejunus exercitus non habet aures [i.e., "a hungry army is not ready to listen"].

Nor can I conceive how sutch people as we are inforced to bring over hither by peradventure, and gathering them up in sutch riotous lasie [i.e., lazy] and infected places can intertaine themselves with other thoughts, or put on other behaviour then what accompanies sutch disordered Persons, so prophane, so riotous, so full of mutenie and treasonable Intendments, as I am well to witness in a parcell of 300 which I brought with me, of which well may I say not many give testimonie besides their names that they are Christians, besides of sutch diseased and crased bodies as the Sea hither and this Clime here but a little scortching them, render them unhable fainte, and desperate of recoverie as of 300 not threescore may be called forth or imploied upon any labour or service.

Thus (my right noble Lord) I have presumed to apeale to you from your grave and serious affaires to peruse a tedious Storie of the Condition wherein your Colonie hath ever heretofore and now for the present remaineth: some meanes likewise I have presumed as I conceive it to offer unto your Lordship how it may be truly recovered and prosper with greater comfort both to the Adventurers at home and to us here. . . .

11. *John Rolfe Experiments with Tobacco Growing, 1612*

Ra[l]phe Hamor, *A True Discourse of the Present Estate of Virginia, and the successe of the affaires there till the 18 of June. 1614* . . . (London, 1614), 24.

. . . The valuable commoditie of Tobacco of such esteeme in England (if there were nothing else) which every man may plant, and with the least part of his labour, tend and cure will returne him both cloathes and other necessaries. For the goodnesse whereof, answerable to *west-Indie Trinidado* or *Cracus* [i.e., Caraccas] (admit there hath no such bin returned) let no man doubt. Into the discourse wherof, since I am obviously entred, I may not forget the gentleman, worthie of much commendations, which first tooke the pains to make triall thereof, his name Mr. John *Rolfe, Anno Domini* 1612. partly for the love he hath a long time borne unto it, and partly to raise commodity to the adventurers, in whose behalfe I witnesse and vouchsafe to holde my testimony in beleefe, that during the time of his aboade there, which draweth neere upon six yeeres, no man hath laboured to his power, by good example there and worthy incouragement into England by his letters, then he hath done. . . .

Virginia Transformed

12. The Beginning of Representative Government:
The London Company Creates a General Assembly

Susan Myra Kingsbury, ed., *The Records of the Virginia Company of London* (Washington, D.C., 1906–1935), III, 482–484.

To all people to whom these presents shall come bee seen or heard, the Treasuror, Council and Company of Adventurers and planters of the Citty of London for the first Collony in Virginia send greetings Knowe yee That wee the said Treasuror Counsell and Company takeing into our Carefull Consideration the present state of the said Colony in Virginia: And intending by the devine assistance to settle such a forme of government ther as may bee to the greatest benefitt and comfort of the people and whereby all Injustice grevance and oppression may bee prevented and kept of as much as is possible from the said Colony have thought fitt to make our Entrance by ordayning and establishing such supreame Counsells as may not only bee assisting to the Governor for the time being in administration of Justice, and the executing of other duties to his office belonging, but also by ther vigilent Care and prudence may provide as well for remedy of all inconvenyencies groweing from tymc to tymc, As also for the advancing of Encrease strength stabillitie and prosperytie of the said Colony[.]

Wee therefore the said Treasuror Counsell and Company, by authoritie directed to us from his Majestie under his great scale upon mature deliberation doe hereby order and declare, That from hence forward ther bee towe Supreame Counsells in Virginia for the better government of the said Colony as aforesaid. The one of which Counsells to bee called the Counsell of State and whose office shall Cheiflie bee assisting with ther Care advise and circomspection to the said Governor shall be Chosen nominated placed and displaced from tyme to tyme by us the said Treasurer Counsell and Company and our successors, which Counsell of State shall Consiste for the present onlie of those persons whose names are here inserted vizt. [names omitted] Which said Counsellors and Counsell wee Earnestlie Pray and desier, and in his Majesties name strictlie charge and Comand, That all factious parcialties and sinester respects laid aside they bend ther care and Endeavors to assist the said Governor first and principallie in advancement of the honor and service of almightie god, and the Enlargement of his kingdom amongste those heathen people, And next in the erecting of the said Colonie in one obedience to his Majestie and all lawfull Authoritie from his Majestie dirived, And lastlie in maytayning the said people in Justice and Christian Conversation among themselves and in strength and habillytie to with stand ther Ennimies, And this Counsell is to bee alwaies or for the most part residing about or neere the said Governor, The other Counsell more generall to bee called by the Governor and yeerly of Course and no oftener but for very extreordynarie and Important occasions shall consist for present of the said Counsell of State and of Tow Burgesses out of every towne hunder [i.e., hundred] and other particuler plantation to bee respetially [i.e., especially] Chosen by the inhabitants. Which Counsell shalbee called the generall Assemblie, wherin as also in the said Counsell of State, all matters shall be decyded determined and ordred by the greater part of the voyces then present, Reserveing alwaies to the Governor a negative voyce, And this generall assembly shall have free power, to treat Consult and conclude as well of all emergent occasions concerning the pupliqe [i.e., public] weale of the said colony and everie part thereof, as also to make ordeine and enact such generall lawes and orders for the behoof of the said colony and the good government thereof as shall time to tyme appeare necessarie or requisite. Wherin as in all other things wee requier the said gennerall Assembly, as also the said Counsell of State to imitate and followe the policy of the forme of government, Lawes Custome manners of loyall and other administration of Justice used in the Realme of England as neere as may bee even as ourselves by his Majesties Letters patente are required. Provided that noe lawes or ordinance made in the said generall Assembly shalbe and continew in force and validytie, unlese the same shalbe sollemlie ratified and Confirmed in a generall greater Court of the said Court here in England and so ratified and returned to them under our seale. It being our intent to affoord the like measure also unto the said Colony that after the government of the [*said Colony, shall once have been well framed and settled accordingly, which is to be done by us as by authoritie derived from*] his Majestie and the sa[*me shall*] have bene soe by us declared, No orders of our Court afterwarde shall binde [*the said*] colony unlese they bee ratified in like manner in ther generall Assembly.

In wittnes wherof wee have hereunto sett our Comon seale the 24th day of [*July*] 1621, and in the yeare of the raigne of our governoure Lord James by the [Grace] of God of England Scotland France and Ireland King defendor of the [faith] vizt. of England France and Scotland the Nyneteenth and of Scotland the fower and Fiftieth.

Chapter Two

The Evolution
of Self-Government
in Virginia

The Governor, Council, and
House of Burgesses

By 1689 Virginians had acquired a remarkable measure of self-government. Self-government did not come at once; nor was it the by-product of a conscious design on the colonists' part. Instead it was due to a lengthy adaptation of the rich English political heritage to new circumstances. Often the need to raise taxes, to settle land titles, or to defend the colony provided the motive force for molding that heritage to new situations, although accident and the crown's inattention also contributed to the evolution of political institutions in the Old Dominion. The solutions of the moment became precedents for the future, and throughout the seventeenth century the gradual unfolding of custom and precedent laid the foundations for Virginia's self-governing tradition. This evolutionary process operated at two distinct, somewhat independent, levels of development. One involved the governor, the Council of State, and the House of Burgesses; the other embraced local government.

On several occasions between 1606 and 1624 the London Company had modified its methods of governing Virginia. The charter of 1606 had created a resident council and a president to manage local affairs. When that arrangement proved unworkable, the company replaced it with a governor and a council. Then an assembly and a degree of home rule were added. By the time the crown seized the London Company's charter, the basic outlines of Virginia's provincial government had emerged.

The dissolution of the London Company cast into limbo the General Assembly and all the other provisions for limited self-government that had been granted in the Great Charter of 1618. It also thrust the responsibility for ruling the infant colony upon the crown. Arranging a permanent government for Virginia was therefore a major concern for James I and the Privy Council. Within a month of the order dissolving the company, James turned the task of governing Virginia over to a commission headed by council president Henry Mandeville. The Mandeville Commission came to an abrupt end at the king's sudden death in March 1625. So the matter of what to do with Virginia passed to James's son Charles I. Shortly after ascending the throne, the new monarch proclaimed Virginia a royal colony.

Although the transition to the status of royal colony occurred at a time of crisis, the changeover was marked by continuity. While the crown moved slowly towards a solution to the Virginia problem, it governed Virginia in accordance with procedures established by the London Company. Initially the Mandeville Commission had taken immediate steps to remove any doubts about the source of public authority in the colony by securing a royal commission and instructions for the company's last governor, Sir Francis Wyatt. From that time forward Virginia's governors would be royal appointees who served at the king's pleasure or until they retired or died.

A royal governor's powers derived from his commission and instructions. For a guide in drafting these documents, crown officials followed the usage that had been adopted in company days. By the time Charles appointed Sir William Berkeley governor in 1641, the commission and instructions had become somewhat standardized.

Sir William's instructions (Document 1) are important for what they reveal about the governor's role vis-à-vis the crown and the colonists. The governor was the king's surrogate; as such, the office was in theory the most prestigious and powerful political position in Virginia. To the governor belonged the power of appointment to all the colony's lesser offices; he enforced royal policy and dispensed patronage, justice, and land. The governor ordered the coming and going of the General Assembly, and his assent was necessary for a bill to become law: his veto automatically killed a measure. In brief, the governor exercised an extraordinarily broad degree of control over the direction of the colonists' lives. To be sure, the accretions of custom and gubernatorial acquiescence eroded a governor's ability to use these wide powers, but the crown's conception of the office remained unaltered after 1624. Down to 1689, save for the hiatus of the Interregnum, when the House of Burgesses chose the chief executive, successive monarchs viewed Virginia's governor as the linch-pin between themselves and their colonial subjects.

Assessing the performances of Virginia's governors between 1624 and 1689 is a difficult task. The absence of records all but obscures the abilities of most governors and their influence upon the colony's development. Perhaps only four governors stand out as more than mere signatures on long-forgotten documents: Sir John Harvey (1630–1635), Sir William Berkeley (1641–1652, 1660–1676), Thomas, Lord Culpeper (1680–1683), and Francis, Lord Howard of Effingham (1684–1688). Harvey is noteworthy only because his unpopularity with the council caused his expulsion from Virginia in 1635 (see chapter 9). Berkeley's association with Bacon's Rebellion in 1676 has made him a central character in Virginia history. Culpeper and Howard each played a part in the crown's attempt to break the House of Burgesses during the 1680s. Of the four, Sir William Berkeley left the most lasting impression on a maturing Virginia.

Berkeley's vigorous suppression of Bacon's Rebellion has earned him the enmity of many Virginia historians. That enmity has obscured the governor's rather considerable accomplishments. A younger son of Sir Maurice Berkeley, of Bruton, Somerset, Sir William's family connections and his own abilities had opened the door to opportunities usually denied to younger sons in England. The beginning of his career was consistent with that of other genteel Virginia immigrants in the middle decades of the seventeenth century: he quickly became a leading planter and the owner of a large plantation at Green Spring.

Unlike any of his predecessors and few of his successors, Sir William developed a deep and intimate knowledge of Virginia during the thirty-five years he lived there. He played a vital role in shaping the colony's rapid expansion throughout the 1640s, 1650s, and 1660s. During these crucial years the power and influence of local government increased at the expense of institutions at the provincial level. Berkeley did nothing to check this development; indeed, he encouraged it by sanctioning the division of power and responsibility between the two jurisdictions. He also maintained a tolerably successful Indian policy for nearly thirty years. In addition, he tried to ease Virginia into the emerging commercial system that the home government began to implement following the Stuart restoration in 1660.

Ultimately his knowledge and ability failed him. Toward the end of his career Berkeley seriously misjudged the mood of his people. That mistake contributed to the outbreak of Bacon's Rebellion, which caused a diminution of Berkeley's reputation as the century's most popular and effective governor.

In its effort to maintain a degree of tranquility in Virginia after the dissolution of the London Company, the crown had left the governor's council undisturbed. The king merely reconfirmed the existing councillors in their offices, and the council continued to function as the colony's principal administrative agency. Consequently, few changes in either the council's composition or its duties occurred in the years immediately after the company's demise. In time, however, the council matured into a potent and specialized political institution.

A procedure for appointing councillors became standardized rather quickly. In 1624 the Mandeville Commission had established a precedent by including the names of the councillors in Sir Francis Wyatt's commission. Thereafter the crown nominated the council at the beginning of a reign or a governor's administration. A change in reigns or governors did not involve wholesale changes in council membership, since the crown usually continued existing councillors in office. Vacancies created by retirement or death could be filled, subject to royal approval, by the governor. Generally a seat on the council carried life tenure, although councillors could be dismissed for incurring the displeasure of the king or governor.

Only once during the entire colonial period was this procedure disrupted. When Virginia surrendered to Oliver Cromwell in 1652, the General Assembly agreed to an arrangement whereby the House of Burgesses would elect councillors annually (Document 2). This arrangement ended with the Restoration in 1660.

Throughout most of the seventeenth century the council consisted of twelve to sixteen members. Beyond the stipulation that governors should avoid choosing "necessitous people, or people much in debt," since the councillors received no salaries, there were few formal qualifications for the office. For its councillors the London Company had selected men from the higher ranks of English society or men who were well versed in Virginia affairs. That tendency continued for some years after 1624, but increasingly the membership came to be drawn almost exclusively from an emerging Virginia society. After 1650 virtually all the appointees were long-term residents of Virginia who had given extensive service in local government or the House of Burgesses. The reason for their choice is obvious enough. Given the nature of the council's duties, a wide understanding of the workings of Virginia's political institutions was a necessary prerequisite to service on the council.

Less apparent, perhaps, is what a seat on the council represented in terms of a developing colonial social structure. Power and prestige attached to the office; therefore membership on the council marked an individual as a man of superior skill and wealth who had surpassed his competitors in the rough-and-tumble world of Virginia politics. Like other immigrants, those who succeeded to the council were usually driven by the passion for social advancement. Land and familial connections were the keys that opened the door to social and political preferment in a rapidly expanding society. The men who became councillors often arrived in Virginia with some competitive advantages. Frequently they had the backing of family or money with which they could insinuate themselves into a local office. Thereafter their luck, skill, and overweening ambition pushed them to the top of Virginia society. Having once reached the pinnacle, they sought to solidify their power. By 1689 the councillors had monopolized all of the collectorships and the other lucrative patronage positions that were at the governor's disposal. The office gave them access to large tracts of land, which they grabbed off at every opportunity. Intermarriage kept the dilution of power at a minimum. In brief, the great conciliar families successfully adapted traditional English social values to the Virginia environment. Their success mirrored the Virginia gentry's emergence and the consolidation of its control of the avenues to social, political, and economic power at all levels of colonial life.

As the composition of the council changed, its duties became more specialized. Owing to the destruction of most of the council records, this transformation cannot be examined closely, but its outlines may be sketched in broad strokes. From the beginning the council had been assigned three large areas of responsibility: to advise the governor on all matters of state, to legislate, and to dispense justice. Even before the dissolution of the London Company, some modification of these duties had occurred. The creation of the General Assembly in 1618 had cast the council in the role of the legislature's upper house.

Together with the governor, the council had also been charged with the colony's daily management. Much of its time was thus taken up in settling estates, land titles, and petty legal disputes. After 1624 the scope of these activities began to narrow. A major change came in 1634 when the General Assembly erected the county form of local government. Increasingly after that date the assembly assigned more of the mundane affairs of local administration to the county courts.

Released from the press of routine business, the council assumed more specialized tasks. In its capacity as the General Court, for example, the council evolved into a high court of appeals. Although it always retained original jurisdiction in criminal cases involving life or limb, most of the council's juridical activity involved hearing cases on appeal from the county courts (Document 3). In its role as advisor to the governor, the council aided the chief executive in developing colonial policy. When a governor was absent or there was a lapse between terms, its president served as interim governor.

Throughout the seventeenth century the council was the dominant component of the General Assembly. Individual members served as floor managers in the House of Burgesses and assisted in drafting legislation. Their assent was necessary for a bill to become law. When conflicts between the governor and the burgesses arose, the council frequently sided with the chief executive. This alignment was especially apparent during the 1680s when Governors Culpeper and Howard attempted to curb the powers of the house. But the flirtation with the crown was brief, for the councillors soon discovered that the home government's assaults on the house posed a threat to their own power. By the century's end they had joined forces with the burgesses to resist the crown's further incursions.

But for much of the century the General Assembly, and the House of Burgesses in particular, remained an amorphous institution whose authority lacked clear definition. Only when Governors Culpeper and Howard challenged it did the house grow conscious of its powers and become capable of resisting assaults on its prerogatives. These observations should not, however, diminish the importance of legislative developments in the years between 1624 and 1689. During this interval the assembly acquired some fundamental rights; in a few instances it even assumed powers that did not belong to Parliament. By trial and error the burgesses learned the legislator's craft, the mysteries of power, and the uses to which power could be put. Briefly stated, the experimentation with the forms and processes of representative government established the customs, usages, prec-

edents, and laws that became the foundation for Virginia's self-
governing tradition.

It should be reiterated that the rise of representative government
in the Old Dominion after 1624 was unanticipated. Indeed, at the
time of the crown's seizure of the London Company's charter, there
was some doubt as to the General Assembly's continued existence.
The crown's commission to Sir Francis Wyatt contained no provision
for the assembly's continuance. That oversight probably resulted from
an uncertainty over how best to govern the colony, rather than from
the crown's desire to stifle any tendency toward self-government, but
the failure to sanction the assembly created some problems in Virginia. The assembly was popular with the colonists, and it had proven
to be an effective instrument of government. Furthermore, the colonists saw its continuation as a bulwark against any efforts to return
the colony's management to the hands of a revived company. The
colonists therefore mounted a campaign to legitimize the assembly.
For fifteen years they persisted, and finally, in 1639, their persistence
bore fruit. Charles I authorized annual meetings of the General Assembly when he again commissioned Sir Francis Wyatt as the colony's governor.

Even as the colonists strove to preserve their assembly, the members set in train a cautious movement towards establishing procedures
for electing burgesses, fixing a basis for representation in the house,
and acquiring some legislative privileges and powers. For their mod-
els the burgesses had English history, Parliament, and their own experience. There is considerable evidence to suggest that all three
played decisive roles in shaping the assembly's growth.

The method used to elect burgesses before the General Assembly
created the county form of local government in 1634 is unclear. After
that date the following procedure seems to have emerged fairly quickly. Some time prior to the convening of the assembly the governor
issued an election proclamation to the county courts and an election
writ to the respective sheriffs. Then the sheriff ordered all qualified
voters to meet at an appointed day to choose their representatives
(Document 4). It also became customary for voters to meet with their
burgesses to air grievances at some point before the assembly sat
(Document 5).

Voter qualifications underwent several changes before 1689. At
first it appears that only those males who possessed a fifty-acre free-
hold were entitled to vote. In the 1640s, however, the assembly extended the privilege to all free males, but in 1670 the franchise was

again restricted to freeholders. Except for a temporary extension to freemen in May 1676, the concept of equating the right to vote with property ownership remained unchanged for the duration of the colonial period.

Gradually the counties became the units of representation in Virginia. Before the General Assembly established the county court system, burgesses tended to represent ecclesiastical parishes, and a parish could elect as many burgesses as it chose to pay. For some years after 1634 both parochial burgesses and county burgesses sat in the house. In time, however, the assembly began to eliminate the parish as a basis of representation. A first step in that direction occurred in March 1642/43, when the assembly required the county courts to raise burgess salaries through county taxes (Document 6A). Then in November 1645 the legislature reduced the number of burgesses from all local jurisdictions to four (Document 6B), and in March 1658/59 it empowered the parish vestries to raise funds to pay the salaries of their respective burgesses (Document 6C). An act of March 1660/61 eliminated parochial burgesses altogether by restricting the number of representatives to two, although it did not require the election of any burgesses (Document 6D). That requirement did not become law until 1669, and the following year the assembly enacted stiff penalties for any county that failed to elect two representatives (Documents 6E and 6F).

By 1670, then, the General Assembly had fashioned representation into a mirror that reflected local interests. That this possibility should have materialized was not inconsistent with the character of seventeenth-century Virginia politics. After 1634 the number of counties proliferated, and for the remainder of the century a principal occupation of the assembly was attending to the problems of rapidly expanding local communities. Because nearly all of the men who served in the House of Burgesses before 1689 were simultaneously members of the county courts, they used their legislative authority to consolidate the power of the men who had the greatest acquaintance with local affairs, themselves and the other members of the courts. To protect that power and to insure local interests a continued hearing at the provincial level of government, the counties had to be transformed into the units of representation. Burgesses thus became, in Bernard Bailyn's phrase, "attorneys of their constituencies."

Unwittingly the General Assembly had adopted a theory of representation akin to one that had flourished in medieval England. On that groundwork the Virginians, like colonists elsewhere in English

North America, continued to construct a novel system of direct representation. But as early as the fifteenth century the English had begun to abandon the medieval conception for one which held that members of Parliament represented the whole realm as well as the particular electors who had chosen them. By the time the Virginians settled the matter, therefore, the drift of political thought in England was already moving towards a theory of virtual representation. No one grasped the implications of what the General Assembly had done. Unconcerned with theory, the burgesses sought to resolve new problems, while the crown paid scant attention to what occurred in its remote colony. Only when the constitutional crises that led to revolution arose in the eighteenth century did the diverging views of representation become apparent.

The General Assembly's control of legislative apportionment is also indicative of the powers that the House of Burgesses began to accumulate during the seventeenth century. These powers may be divided into four categories: control over internal proceedings, the right to initiate legislation, control over taxation, and control of local affairs. The circumstances leading to the burgesses' assumption of control over their own proceedings are unclear. Of course, there was the example of Parliament to follow, but too much can be made of that model. The discrepancies of practice in the General Assembly indicate that the burgesses sometimes only vaguely understood how Parliament operated. Certainly the enlargement of its authority cannot be attributed solely to a desire to curb executive interference; examples of such interference in house deliberations are rare before Lord Culpeper's administration in the last quarter of the century. It seems more likely that as the burgesses came to represent local interests, they sought to consolidate their power further by gaining some measure of influence over apportionment, elections, members' qualifications, selection of the Speaker, and the rules of order in the house itself.

Two of the first privileges that the burgesses secured were freedom from arrest during assembly sessions and the right to judge members' credentials. Freedom from arrest was established by statute in March 1623/24 (Document 7A), and although there were subsequent revisions in the law, the basic principle remained untrammeled. At the very first session of the General Assembly in 1619, two burgesses had been ejected because of improper credentials (see chapter 1), thereby laying down a precedent for fixing the qualifications of burgesses in the future. Apparently the house continued to expand this right, for there are hints that it disciplined refractory members in the 1640s. Some time before the middle of the century the house created a standing committee on elections, and in the 1660s members were expelled for their religious nonconformity (Document 7B).

Another important element in controlling internal proceedings was the election of the chief officers of the house, the Speaker and the clerk. The Speaker presided over the house and spoke for the membership, while the clerk took minutes and kept records. It appears that at an early date the burgesses won the exclusive right of electing the Speaker. The concurrence of the governor and the council was sought at least until mid-century (Document 7C), but no evidence survives to indicate that any serious disputes occurred between the executive and the house over the Speaker's selection. Until the 1680s the burgesses regularly elected their own clerk without gubernatorial meddling—a fundamental departure from Parliament, where the crown made the appointment. An erosion of that right commenced when imperial authorities instructed Culpeper and his successors to wrest it from the burgesses. Ultimately the house gave way, and by the end of the century the governor chose the clerk.

A final ingredient for controlling internal proceedings was the authority to regulate the rules of order. Nothing indicates an unwillingness by the crown or the governors to concede such authority to the burgesses. In all likelihood, the house assumed this right at an early date, although no rules of order are known to exist before 1659 (Document 7D).

Among the preeminent powers belonging to elected legislative bodies are the right to initiate legislation and control of the purse. In 1619 the burgesses first laid claim to the initiation of legislation, but their success in making good that claim prospered slowly. For much of the century the governor provided the impetus for a considerable portion of the substantive law adopted by the General Assembly. But as the assembly's deliberations were increasingly taken up with local matters, the initiative began to shift to the burgesses. An insight into the shift is revealed in a petition to the house by Edmund Scarburgh, a burgess for Northampton County (Document 8A). During the General Assembly of 1663 Scarburgh petitioned the assembly to enact some legislation beneficial to his constituents. The subsequent adoption of Scarburgh's petition into law suggests that by the 1660s the burgesses had already won a ponderable degree of freedom in adopting legislation not proposed by the governor.

The importance of this right is evinced by the widening competence of Virginia legislators and by the growing complexity and variety of the legislation enacted as the century wore on. Early statutes were poorly drawn; often they lacked penalties for their violation, and their provisions were difficult to interpret. Late seventeenth-century statutes by comparison exhibit careful drafting and clearer intent. The scope of the early laws was limited to narrow areas such as price fixing or defense. Within a matter of a few years, however, the assembly broadened its field of legal activity to include virtually every conceivable human endeavor, from regulating intimate family situations and religion to disbursing public monies.

Control of the purse was the seventeenth-century House of Burgesses' most priceless legacy. English precedents for this right existed long before the settlement of Virginia; it came along with the rest of the colonists' intellectual baggage. The burgesses asserted their claim to the privilege in 1624, when the assembly denied the governor authority to impose taxes (Document 9A). In 1629 they established some control over expenditures. They began to draft budgets, to fix the salaries of public officials, the governor included, and to require the county courts to collect the taxes levied at each meeting of the assembly. The right became exclusive in 1666. That year Governor Berkeley suggested that several councillors assist the house in apportioning annual taxes. The burgesses rebuffed the suggestion, and the executive's interference with their prerogative never again constituted a serious issue (Document 9B).

Through its power to establish courts and to delineate their jurisdiction, the General Assembly gained some influence in local affairs. The precedent for the assumption of this particular prerogative dated to 1634, when the legislature divided Virginia into the eight original counties. From that point forward the assembly constantly broadened the right by continually adopting statutes that detailed the county courts' responsibilities. Exercising this authority gave the assembly a power that did not belong to Parliament.

By the end of the seventeenth century the House of Burgesses had achieved an impressive start in its quest for power. By accident, default, and necessity, it had garnered an important share in regulating colonial life, and to that end, the whole growth process had afforded valuable instruction in the practice of self-government. While the house had succumbed to some infringements on its authority, it had stoutly resisted others. The membership had learned the practical skills required of legislators and much about the nature of power. Yet much remained to be accomplished. In some areas the house had only nebulous powers; in other areas it had none at all. The house had only recently begun to sit apart from the council, and its internal procedures were deficient. The burgesses had not perfected techniques to bind the executive to their will, let alone muster a sustained effort to combat challenges by imperial authorities. Conscious of its burgeon-. ing power, yet still weak and uncertain, the adolescent house groped for maturity.

SUGGESTED READINGS

Bruce, Philip Alexander. *Institutional History of Virginia in the Sev-enteenth Century: An Inquiry into the Religious, Moral, Educa-tional, Legal, Military, and Political Condition of the People. . . .* 2 vols. (New York, 1910), II, 229–522.

*Craven, Wesley Frank. *The Southern Colonies in the Seventeenth Century, 1607–1689* (Baton Rouge, La., 1949).

————. ". . . And So the Form of Government Became Perfect." *Virginia Magazine of History and Biography,* LXXVII (1969), 131–145.

*Kammen, Michael. *Deputyes and Libertyes: The Origins of Repre-sentative Government in Colonial America* (New York, 1969).

*Pole, J. R. *The Seventeenth Century: The Sources of Legislative Power.* Jamestown Essays on Representation (Charlottesville, Va., 1969).

Rainbolt, John C. "The Alteration in the Relationship between Lead-ership and Constituents in Virginia, 1660 to 1720." *William and Mary Quarterly,* 3d Ser., XXVII (1970), 411–434.

————. "A New Look at Stuart 'Tyranny': The Crown's Attack on the Virginia Assembly, 1676–1689." *Virginia Magazine of History and Biography,* LXXV (1967), 387–406.

*Washburn, Wilcomb E. *Virginia under Charles I and Cromwell, 1625–1660.* Jamestown 350th Anniversary Historical Booklet 7 (Williamsburg, Va., 1957).

*Wertenbaker, Thomas J. *The Government of Virginia in the Sev-enteenth Century.* Jamestown 350th Anniversary Historical Book-let 16 (Williamsburg, Va., 1957).

————. *Virginia under the Stuarts, 1607–1688* (Princeton, N.J., 1914).

* Available in paperback.

The Governor and Council

1. Instructions to Sir William Berkeley, August 1641

Entry Book of Letters . . . , 1607–1662, C.O. 5/1354, 224–241, Public Record Office.

Charles Rex
Instructions to Sir William Berkeley Knight One of the Gentlemen
of Our Privy Chamber, Governor of Virginia,
and to the Council of State there.

Service of God and Provision for Ministers.
1.   That in the first place you be carefull Almighty God may be duly and daily served according to the forme of Religion Established in the Church of England both by Your selfe and the people under your charge, which may draw down a Blessing upon all your endeavours: And let every Congregation that hath an able Minister build for him a convenient Personage House, To which for his better maintenance over and above the usuall Pension you lay 200. Acres of Gleable lands for the clearing of that Ground, every of His Parishioners for three yeares shall give some days labours of themselves, and their Servants, and see that you have a speciall care that the Glebe lands be sett as neer his Parsonage House as may be, and that it be of the best conditioned land. Suffer no Invasion in matters of Religion and be carefull to appoint Sufficient and conformable Ministers to each Congregation, that may Chatechise and instruct them in the Grounds and Principles of Religion—

Oaths of Supremacy and Allegiance to be Administered,
The Refusers sent home.
2.   That you Administer the Oaths of Allegiance and Supremacy to all such as come thither, with intention to Plant themselves in the Country which if he shall refuse he is to be returned and shiped from thence home, and Certificate made to the Lords of the Councill; the same Oath is to be Administered, to all other persons when you shall see it fitt as Mariners, Merchants, etc. to prevent any danger by Spyes—

Justice to be administered according to the laws of England.
3.   That Justice be equally Administed to All His Majesties Subjects there residing, and as neere as may be after the forme of his Realm of England and vigilant care to be had to prevent Corruption in Officers tending to the delay or preverting of Justice—

Calling a Generall Assembly yearly, and the Governor
therein to have a Negative voice.
4.   That you and the Councellors as formerly once a year or oftner if urgent occasion shall require, Do Summon the Burgesses of all and Singular the Plantations there which together with the Governor and Councill makes the Grand Assembly, and shall have Power to make Acts and laws for the Government of

that Plantation, correspondant as near as may be to the laws of England in which Assembly the Governor to have a Negative Voice as formerly.

Quarterly Courts and access to all Suitors.

5.   That you and the Councill Assembled are to set down the fittest months of the Quarterly meeting of the Councill of State, whereat they are to give their attendance for one whole week, or more if need shall require to advise and consult upon matter[s] of Councill and State, and to decide and determine such causes as shall come before them, and that free access be admitted to all Suitors, to make known their particular Grievances, be it against what person soever wherein the Governor for the time being as formerly, is to have but a casting voyce, if the number of Councellors should be equally devided in Opinion, besides the Quarterly meeting of the Councill it shall be lawfull for you to Summons from time to time Extraordinary meetings of the Councill according to Emergent occasions.

Manner of proceeding against such as are of Councill where necessity requireth—

6.   In case there shall be necessary cause to proceed against any of the Councill for their own persons they are in such cases to be Summoned by you the Governor to appear at the next Quarter Sessions of the Councill holden[,] there to abide their sensure or otherwise if you shall think it may concerne either the safety or quiet of that State to proceed more speedily wih such an Offender It shall be lawfull to Summon a Councill Extraordinary Whereat Six of the Council at least are to be present with you, and by the Major part of their Voyces Commit any Councillors to safe Custody, or upon Bayle to abide the Order of the next Quarter Councill—

Courts of Justice for Suits of lower Value and Smaller Offences.

7.   For the ease of the Country and quicker dispatch of businesses you the Governor and Councill may appoint in places convenient Inferior Courts of Justice and Commanders for the same to determine of suits not exceeding the value of ten pounds, and for the punishment of such Offences as you and the Councill shall think fitt to give them power to hear and determine—

Governor appoint Officers to Execute Orders, the Councill and some principal Officers excepted.

8.   The Governor shall appoint Officers of Sealing of Writts and Subpenas, and such Officers as shall be thought necessary for the Execution of the Councill Orders. As Also the Acts and laws of the General Assembly, and for punishing any neglect or contempt of the said Orders, Acts, or laws, respectively, And shall nominate and appoint all other publique Officers under the degree of the Councill, the Capt. of the Fort, Muster Master, and Surveyor General excepted—

Councellors exempted from publique charges and 10 of his Servants.

9.   That since the Councill attend His Majesties Service, and the publique busi-

ness to the great hinderance of the private, that they and ten Servants for every Councellor be exempted from all publique charges and contributions Assessed, and levyed by the General Assembly (a Warr defensive, assistance towards the building of a Town, or Churches and the Ministers duties excepted)—

To make probate of Wills in every
Colony with a Caution.

10. To avoid all Questions concerning the Estates of persons dying in Virginia, it shall be lawfull as it hath been used heretofore, to make Probates of Wills, and [in] default of a Will to grant letters of Administration in the Colony, *Provided* alwayes that such to whom Administration is granted do put in sufficient Security to be accomptable to such persons in England, or els where unto whom of Right those Estates belong, And that such Probate of Wills, and letters of Adm:nistration shall be and abide in full force and vertue, to all intents and purposes—

A Muster Master Generall to be, And All
persons above 16. to beare Arms.

11. To the End the Country may be the better served against all Hostil Invasions, it is requisite that all persons from the Age of 16. to be Armed with Arms both Offensive and defensive, And if any person be defective in this kind, Wee strictly charge you to Command them to Provide themselves of sufficient Arms within one year or sooner if possible it may be done, and if any shall faile to be Armed at the end of the Term limitted Wee will that you punish them severely—

The Muster Master.

12. And for that Arms without the knowledge of the use of them are to no effect, Wee ordain that there be one Muster Master Generall appointed for the Colony, who shall 4. times in the year, and oftner (if Cause be) not only view the Arms, Ammunition and furniture of every person in the Colony, but also Train and exercise the people, touching the use and Order of Arms, and shall also certify the defects if any be either of appearance or otherwise to you the Governor and Councill. And being informed that the place is voyd by the death of George Dunn, Wee do nominate and appoint Our Trusty and Welbeloved John West Esq., being recommended unto us for his sufficiency and long experience in the Country to be Muster Master of the said Colony, and for his Competent maintenance Wee Will that the Governor and Councill so Order the business at a Generall Assembly that every Plantation be rated equally according to the number of persons, wherein you are to follow the Course practiced in the Realm of England—

Maintenance for the Captain of the Fort
and 10 Guarders.

13. That you Cause likewise 10. Guarders to bee maintained for the Port [i.e., fort] at Point Comfort and that you take Course that the Capt. of the said Fort have a Competent allowance for his Service there, Also that the said Fort be well kept in reparation and provided with Ammunition.

All but new Comers and the Councellors to be
Rated for maintenance of a Warr.

14.   That new Comers be exempted the 1st. yeare from going in person or con-tributing to the Wars, save only in defence of the place where they shall in-habit, and that only when the enemies shall assail them but all others in the Colony shall go or be rated to the maintaining of the Warr proportionably to their abilitys, neither shall any man be privileg'd for going to the War that is above 56. years old, and under 60. respect being had to the Quality of the person, that Officers be not forced to as private Soldiers or in places Inferior to their degrees, unless in case of extream necessity—

Trade with the Savages forbidden
without speciall Licence.

15.   That you may better avoid and prevent the treachery of the Salvages Wee strictly forbid all persons whatsoever to receive into their houses the person of any Indian, or to converse or trade with them, without the special licence and Warrant given to that purpose according to the Commission—inflicting se-vere punishment upon the Offenders.

Beacons to be Erected in places convenient and duly watched
or Alarum to be taken by shooting off 3. peices.

16.   For preventing of all Surprizes as well of the Treacherous Savages, as any Foraine Enemy, Wee require you to Erect Beacons in Severall parts of the Countries by firing whereof the Country may take notice of their attempts and draw to their designed Rendezvous, the Erecting of their Beacons, and their watching them to beare the Charge of the Country as shall be determined by a Generall Assembly, or otherwise by the shooting off 3. peices, whereby they may take the Alarum, as shall be found most convenient—

Everyone according to proportion of land to build a house. A house
also for publique meeting, and power given to remove from
James Town, to some other place more convenient.

17.   That for raising of Towns everyone that hath or shall have a Grant of 500. Acres of land, shall within a convenient time, build a convenient house of Brick of 24. foot long and 16. foot broad with a Cellar to it, and so propor-tionably for grants of larger or lesser quantity. And the Grounds and Plat-forms for the Towns to be laid out in such forms and Order as the Governor and Councill shall appoint. And that you cause at the publiq charge of the Country a convenient house to be built where you and the Councill may meet and sitt for the dispatching of the publick Affairs and hearing of Causes. And because the Buildings at James Town are for the most part decayed, and the place found to be unhealthy, and in convenient in many respects, It shall be in the power of you and the Councill with the advice of the Generall Assembly to choose such other Seate for the Chiefe Town and Residence of the Gover-nor, as by them shall be judged most convenient, retaining the Ancient name of James Town—

To Grant Patents of lands 50. Acres to every person
Transported thither since Middsummer 1625.

18.   That you shall have Power to Grant Patents, and assign such proportion of

land to all Adventurers and Planters as have been usefull heretofore in the like cases either for Adventurers of money, Transportation of people thither according to the Orders of the late Company, and since allowed by His Majesty. And likewise that there be the same proportion of fifty Acres of land Granted and Assigned for every person transported thither since Midsummer 1625. And that you continue the same Course to all persons Transported thither untill it shall be otherwise determined by His Majesty.

To Grant New Patents for confirming and settling Estates of
such as have by Order seated upon Estates.

19.   Whereas the greatest part of land upon James River hath been formerly granted either to particular persons or publick society, but being by them either not Planted att all, or for many years deserted, divers Planters have by Orders and leave of the Governor and Councill in Virginia set down upon those lands or some part of them which was absolutely necessary for the defense and security of the Colony against the Indians, That the Governor confirm those lands unto the present Planters, and Possessors thereof, And that the like Course be taken for Planting new Patents in any other places so implanted or deserted as aforesaid whereat it shall be found necessary, And in case the former Proprietors make their Clearing thereunto, that there be assigned to them the like quantities in any other part of the Colony not actually possessed where they shall make choice.

To examin whether the Passengers have had room
and provision during the Voyage—

20.   That you call for the Charter Parties that Masters of ships bring along with them, and streightly examin whether they have truly performed the Conditions of their Contracts. And farther diligently to Inquire and examin whether they have given sufficient and wholsome food and drink with convenient room to the Passengers during the Voyage. And that no Servants be discharged the Ships and turned a Shore as formerly untill their Masters have notice and sufficient time to send for them, And that upon complaint in any of these particulars you give such Redress as Justice shall require—

Not to go on board upon Arrival of Ships without leave

21.   That in regard you may daily expect the Coming of a Forain Enemy wee require you soon after the first landing that you publish by Proclamation throughout the Colony, That no person whatsoever upon the Arrivall of any Ship shall dare to go on Board without the express warrant from the Governor and Councill least by that means they be Surprized to the great prejudice if not the overthrow of the Plantation—

Master[s] not to break Bulke untill they come to James Towne.

22.   And to avoid that intollerable abuse of ingrossing Comodities and forestalling the Markit, That you require all Masters of Ships not to Break Bulk untill they arrive at James Citty or otherwise without special Order from you the Governor and Councill, and that care be taken that there be sufficient storehouses and Warehouses for the same, and convenient buying of their Goods, as they shall arrive[.]

Wine and Strong Waters not to be sold to persons likely to abuse
them, Unwholsom drink the vessels to be Staved.

23.   That you endeavour by severe punishment to suppress drunkness. And
that you be carefull that great Quantity of Wine and strong Waters be not sold
into the hands of those that be likliest to abuse it, but that so near as you can
it may be equally disposed for the releife of the whole Plantation. And if any
Merchant or other for private heire [i.e., hire] shall bring in any corrupt or
unwholesome Wines, Waters, or any other liquors, such as may endanger the
health of the ,people, and shall so be found upon the Oaths of sufficient persons appointed for the Tryall, That the Vessell be Staved—

Empaling and fencing in of Orchards etc.

24.   That speciall care be taken for the preservation of Neat Cattle, and that
the Females be not killed up as formerly, whereby the Colony will in short
time have such plenty of Victualls that much people may come thither for the
setting up of Iron Works and other Staple Commodities, That you cause the
people to plant such store of Corne, as there may be one whole years provision before hand in the Colony, least in relying upon one single Harvest, by
Draught Blasting or otherwise they fall into such want and famine as formerly
they have endured, And that the Plow may go, and the English be sowed in
all places convenient. And that no Corne or Cattle be sold out of the Plantation without leave from the Governor and Councill—

25.   That they apply themselves to the Impaling of orchards and gardens for
Roots and fruits, which that Country is so proper for and that every Planter
be compelled for every 200 Acres Granted unto him to inclose and sufficiently
Fence, either with Pales or Quick sett, and ditch, and so from time to time to
preserve inclosed and Fenced a Quarter of an Acre of Ground in the most Convenient place near his dwelling house for Orchards and Gardens—

Stinting [i.e., limiting the growth of] Tobacco.

26.   That Whereas your Tobacco falleth everyday more and more to a baser
price that it be Stinted to a farr less proportion then hath been made in the
last year 1637 not only to be accounted by the Plants, but by the Quantity
when 'tis cured. And because the Great Debts of the Planters in Tobacco occasioned by the excessive Rates of Commodities, have been the Stinting thereof
so hard to be put in Execution, that the Course Comanded by his Majesty in
his letter of the 22th of Aprill in the 13th year of his Raign for regulating the
Debts of the Colony be duly observed, And also not to suffer men to build slight
Cottages, as heretofore hath been there used, And to remove from place to place
only to Plant Tobacco, That Tradesmen and Handycrafts men be compelled to
follow their Severall Trades and occupations and that you draw them into
Towns—

To raise Staple Commodities Hemp Flax etc.
Plant Vines and Mulberry Trees.

27.   Wee require you to use the best endeavor to cause the people there to apply themselves to the raising of more Staple Comodities as Hemp and Flax,
Rope Seed and Madder [i.e., a red dye root] Pitch and Tarr for Tanning of

Hydes, and leather, likewise every Plantation to Plant a Proportion of Vines answerable to their Numbers, and to Plant White Mulbery Trees, and to attend Silk Worms—

Tobacco not to be raised at any certaine
Prizes but left free.

28.   That the Merchant be not constrained to take Tobacco at any Price in Exchange for his Wares, But that it be lawfull for him to make his own Bargain for his goods he so changeth, Notwithstanding any Proclamation there published to the Contrary—

Restraining the Merchants from bringing in
excessive quantities of strong liquors.

29.   That no Merchant shall be suffered to bring in Ten pounds worth of Wine, or Strong Waters, that brings not in one Hundred Pounds worth of necessary Commodities, and so rateably. And that every Merchant who desireth a Warrant for the recovery of his debts shall bring in a Bill of Parcells with the Rates of the severall Commodities—by the certainty of the Debts and the Comodities thereof may the better appeare—

Bond to be taken of all ships to bring their goods into His Majesties
Domminions, that his Majesty may have his Customes.

30.   That Whereas many ships laden with Tobacco and other Merchandize from thence carry the same imediately into Foreine Countries, Whereby His Majesties looseth the Custom and thereupon due nothing being Answered in Virginia, you be very carefull that no ship or other Vessell whatsoever depart from thence fraighted with Tobacco or other Comodities which that Country shall afford, before Bond with sufficient Securities be taken to His Majesties use to bring the same directly into His Majesties Domminions, and not els where, and to bring a Bill of lading from thence, that the staple of those Comodities may be made here, Whereby His Majestie after so great expense upon that Plantation and so many of His Subjects Transported thither may not be defrauded of what shall be justly due unto him, for Custom and other duties upon those Goods. Those Bonds to be Transmitted to the Councill here, and from thence to the Exchequer, That the delinquent may be proceeded with according to due course of law—

Not to Trade with any Foraine Ships but
upon great necessity.

31.   Next That you strictly and resolvedly forbid All Trade or Trucking for any Merchandize whatsoever with any ship other then His Majesties Subjects that shall either purposly or casually come to any of the Plantations. And that if upon some unexpected occasion and necessity the Governor and Councill shall think fitt to admitt such intercourse which wee admitt not but upon some extremity, That good Caution and Bond be taken both of the Master as also the Owner of the said Tobacco, or other Comodities so laden that they shall (danger of the Sea excepted) be brought to our Port of London, there to pay unto us such duties as are due upon the same—And to Conclude, That in all things

according to your best understanding you endeavour the extirpation of Vice, and the encouragement of Religion, Vertue, and Goodness[.]

Charles

2. *The Burgesses Appoint the Council, 1652*

William Waller Hening, ed., *The Statutes at Large; Being a Collection of All the Laws of Virginia, from the First Session of the Legislature, in the Year 1619* (Richmond, New York, and Philadelphia, 1809–1823), I, 371–372.

AFTER long and serious debate and advice taken for the settleing and governing of Virginia, It was unanimously voted and concluded, by the commissioners appointed here by authority of parliament and by all the Burgesses of the severall countys and plantations respectively, untill the further pleasures of the states be knowne: That Mr. Richard Bennett, Esq. be Governour for this ensuinge yeare, or untill the next meeting of the Assembly, with all the just powers and authorities that may belong to that place lawfully: And likewise that Col. William Clayborne be Secretarie of State, with all belonging to that office, and is to be next in place to the Governour, next that the Councill of State be as followeth, (vizt.) Capt. John West, Col. Samuel Mathewes, Col. Nathaniel Littleton, Col. Argoll Year[d]ly, Col. Thomas Pettus, Col. Humphrey Higgi[n]son, Col. George Ludlow; Col. William Barnett, Capt. Bridges Freeman, Capt. Thomas Harwood, Major William Taylor, Capt. Francis Epps and Lt. Col. John Cheesman, and they shall have power to execute and do right and equall justice to all the people and inhabitants of this collony according to such instructions as they have or shall receive from the Parliament of England and according to the knowne lawe of England: And the acts of Assembly here established; And the said Governour, Secretary and Council of State are to have such power and authorities and to act from time to time, as by the Grand Assembly shall be appointed and granted to their severall places respectively for the time abovesaid: of which all the people which inhabitt or be in this country are hereby required to take notice and accordingly conforme themselves thereunto. God save the Common-Wealth of England and this countrey of Virginia.

3. *The Governor and Council as Court, 1674*

H. R. McIlwaine, ed., *Minutes of the Council and General Court of Colonial Virginia, 1622–1632, 1670–1676, with Notes and Excerpts from Original Council and General Court Records, into 1683, Now Lost* (Richmond, Va., 1924), 371–374.

The Ninth *Aprill* 1674
present
GOVERNOR [Sir William Berkeley]   *Edward Diggs*   Col. [Nathaniel] *Bacon*
Col. [Thomas] *Swann   Henry Corbyn*   Col. [Thomas] *Beale*
Lt. Col. [Daniel] *Parke   Thomas Ballard*   Col.[Joseph] *Bridger* Esquires

Whereas it Appeares to this Court that *Marmaduke Newton* Did most wickedly and maliciously abuse Col. *Nathaniel Bacon* one of his majesties Councell of State in most abusive Language this Court have thought fitt that the Said *Newton* be fined Twenty pound *sterling* but uppon his Submission in Court *It is ordered* he pay two barrells of powder one to *James Citty* fort and the other to *Nanzemond* fort, And Ask the Said Col. *Bacon* forgiveness uppon his Knees (which he Accordingly Did) and pay all Costs Lt. Col. *William Cole* and Major [Miles] *Carey* are Impowered to receive the powder and to be Acountable to both forts.

It is ordered that all the Bussiness Betweene Mrs. *Randolph* Administratrix of Mr. *Henry Randolph* and the Creditors to the Said Mr. *Randolphs* Estate be Refferred to the next Assembly

It is ordered Mr. *Richard Laurence* be fined four hundred pound tobacco and Caske which is to Goe towards the fort at *James Citty*, for Entertaineing the Honorable Governors Servants.

Whereas It Appeares to this Court that *Peter Starke* hath A better right to The Land that *Anthony Vauson* Escheated [i.e., land that had reverted to the crown because there were no heirs] in *Yorke* County, *It is therefore ordered* that the Said *vauson* Assigne over all his rights of the Said Escheate to the Said *Starkey*, and that *Starkey* pay unto the Said *Vauson* fifteene hundred pound of tobacco and Caske in full [payment] of all charges Suspended by him in and about the Escheate.

It is ordered that Mr. *Thomas Bowler* Give an Account uppon oth [i.e., oath] of what bills bonds and morgages have Come to his hands belonging to the Estate of Mr. *John Sauners* Deceased [to] the next General Court.

Mrs. *Anna Bland* Administratrix of *Theodorick Bland* Esquire presents An Account Debtor and Creditor of the Said *Holmwoods* Estate To this Court, where it Appeares she hath paid beyond Assetts. *It is therefore ordered* She have a *Quietas Est* [i.e., "he is quit," a writ indicating that an executor has satisfied all claims against an estate], from the Said *Holmwoods* Estate.

In the Differrence Betweene *Thomas Warwell* and Mr. *William Thompson* uppon An Appeale from a virdict of A Jury Confirmed in *Surrey* County Court, *It is ordered* the business be Refferred back to that Jury or Some other who are to further Enquire into the Differrence, and to make report to that County Court

Mr. *James Minge* and Mr. *Joseph Chipp* being Appointed to Audite the Accounts of Mr. *George Reeves* Administrator of *Thomas and Francis Reeves* Against their Estates who have Returned their Report under their hands to this Court that they find the Said *George Reeves* hath paid Beyond Assetts, *It is therefore ordered* the Said Mr. *George Reeves* have A *Quietas Est*

Lt. Col. *John West* presents An Inventory uppon oth of the Estate of Mrs. *Mary Marsh* Deceased, *which is ordered to be Recorded.*

Whereas Mr. *Samuel Arnall* Did in his life time Convey to Lt. Col. [John] *West* a Certaine Plantation with the Appurtenances in *New Kent* County for Tenn Thousand pound of Tobacco and Caske and one *John Wilson* who marryed the Relict [i.e., widow] of the Said *Arnall* being in possession of the Same and pretending that the Said Land was made over only in Trust to the

Said Lt. Col. *John West* and the matter being fully heard by this Court *It is the Opinion of this Court* that the Conveyance is Good, *It is therefore ordered* that the Sherriffe of *New Kent* Doe forthwith putt the Said Lt. Col. *John West* in possession of the Said Land but that uppon payment to Lt. Col. *John* [*West*] of the Said Tenn Thousand pound of tobacco and Caske the Same Shall returne and be Rendred by the Said Lt. Col. *West* to Such persons of whome of right it belongs, And the Said Lt. Col. *John West* hath Judgment Against the personall Estate of the Said *Arnall* In the hands of the [said] *Wilson* for payment of Two Thousand one hundred Sixty Six pound of tobacco and Caske Nine hundred pound of *Muscavado* Sugar and one able man Negro with Costs

Upon the Petition of Captain *John West* on behalfe of himselfe and the rest of the Administrators of Col. *Edmund Scarburgh* Deceased Concerning A negro woman called *black mary* purchased by the Said Administrators from Col. *John Vassall, It is ordered* that the Said negroe woman returne to her Service, And that the Administrators Aforesaid with the first opportunity take Care to write to Col. *Vassall* to know whether the Said negroe woman was A Slave or free, and if Appear she was noe slave when bought, then they to pay her for her Service what this Court shall Adjudge.

Col. *Nathaniel Bacon Thomas Ballard* Esquires and Mr. *John Page* or any two of them are Desired at Such time as they Appoint to Audite all Accounts Concerning the Estate of *John Grove* Deceased to the End it may Appeare to this Court what the Executors have received of the Said Estate and paid out of the Same, and that they make report thereof to next Generall Court.

Mr. *Francis Sawyer* hath order Granted to take upp and pattent what wast land is Adjoyning to his lands in *Elizabeth* river (being Two Devidents [i.e., parcels of land]) provided he prejudice noe former Grant, Entring rights According to Custome

Captain *Southey Littleton* hath order Granted to pattent Two hundred and Fifty Acres of Land in *Maggety* bay in *Northampton* County formerly granted to *Daniell Neck* and for want of Seateing by him Deserted Entring rights According to Custome.

Captain *Edward Boeman* hath order Granted to pattent Six hundred Acres of Land at *Mosongo* Creeke formerly Granted to *Richard Johnson* and for want of Seateing by him Deserted Entring rights According to Custome

Afternoone
[present]

GOVERNOR   *Thomas Ludwell* Secretary   *Edward Diggs*   Col. *Bacon*
Major Gen. *Bennett*   Col. *Swann*   Henry *Corbyn*   Col. *Beale*
Lt. Col. *Parke*   Col. *Bridger*   Esquires

Col. *John Custis* and Col. *Stringer* is Added to An Order that past this Court for to Enquire into the bounds of Mr. *Savages* Land and Mr. *Harmonsells*

Mr. *John Winn* minister of *Abbington* Parish in *Gloster* County complayning to this Court, that *Henry Whiteing* of *Ware* Parish did breake open his tobacco house, and take away part of a hoggshead of tobacco, as in his Petition is Sett Downe and made Divers other Complaints therein, *This Court Doth therefore referre* Complaint of the Said *Gwinn* [Winn] to be Enquired into and Examined by *Gloster* Court both parties have Due notice to be present, and after Examination the Court are to report how they find the whole matter to this next Generall Court.

The Differrence Betweene *Argall Yardly* Plaintiff and *Edward Dolby* Defendant about Land is Refferred to Capt. *Robert Beverly* Surveyor to Survey and Lay out the Said Land According to *Yardlys* pattent (and if the said Capt. *Beverly* thinke fitt that A Jury be Impannell[ed] and if they find that *Dolby* is within *Yardlys* bounds then he to pay all Costs) and if they Doe not Agree report is to be made to next Court for Judgment

Refferrence Betweene *John Stith* and Mr. *Rowland Place* to the 2d Day of next Generall Court

It is ordered that *Ambrose White* Appeare at the next Generall Court to Answer the Complaint of *Edward Smale.*

The Differrence Betweene Mrs. *Tabitha Browne* the relict and Administratrix of Mr. *Devereaux Browne* and *Edward Greenely* about the Said *Greenelys* freedome and severall Goods and other things Claymed by the Said Mrs. *Browne* Being heard *It is the Opinion of this Court* that the Said *Greenely* is noe Servant, and the Accounts Betweene them are Refferred to Lt. Col. *Phillip Ludwell* and Col. Custis to Audite [and?] Examine them, and Report thereof to the Sixth Day of next Generall Court.

Nonsuite [i.e., a judgment against a plaintiff who has failed to produce adequate evidence to support his case] is Granted *Edward Greenely* Against Capt. *John Culpeper* noe petition being Entred, *It is therefore ordered* he pay Damages According to Act with Costs

There being formerly A Differrence Betweene Mr. *Humphrey Gwinn* and Mr. *Richard Young* Concerning A wager of One Thousand pound of tobacco which Depended Severall Courts in *Gloster* County and in this Court untill which [the?] said *Young* [has?] paid Three Thousand and Three hundred Seventy one [pounds of?] tobacco and Caske *It is the Opinion of this Court and Accordingly ordered* that the Said *Young* be Allowed by the said *Gwynn* four hundred pound Tobacco and Caske out of the Same Charged to him and that Mr. *Gwyn* pay Costs of this Suite.

Refferrence Betweene Col. *Cut{h}bert* Potter and Mrs. *Elizabeth Newell* Administratrix of Mr. *Jonathan Newell* Deceased till Col. *Potter* Come in.

Refferrence Betweene Mrs. *Elizabeth Newell* Administratrix of Mr. *Jonathan Newell* and *David Newell* till next Court.

Refferrence Betweene *Thomas Lambert* and *David Jones* till the third Day of next Generall Court.

The Court Adjorned till the meeting of the Next Assembly.

Test{e}

Henry Hartwell
Clerk of Council

The House of Burgesses

4. Election of Burgesses, 1636

Northampton County Order Book, 1632–1640, 84.

According to an order of Court from the Governor and councell for the election of Burgesses out of this county the comander with the consent of the Comissioners appoynted the Inhabitants of this County to meete togaether at the Sheriffes house, Wher [the] 15th day of February were come togaether and made Choyce of Mr. John How and Mr. William Roper for Burgesses and for their Charges it was then agreed on that they should have 1500 lbs. of Tobacco

Teste Henry Bagwell Clerke

5. Freeholders Ordered to Meet with Their Burgesses, 1671

Accomack County Order Book, 1671–1673, 16.

Ordered that a Note be sett up at the Court door by the Clarke to give the Freeholders of the upper parts of this County notice to meet their respective burgesses upon Satterday come seven[n]ight being the 26th of instant August at the house of Mr. Thomas [Fowler?] there to present their Agrievances according to the Law of this Country.

6. The Evolution of Burgess Representation

A. AN ACT AUTHORIZING COLLECTION OF TAXES FOR BURGESSES' SALARIES, MARCH 1642/43

Hening, ed., *Statutes at Large,* I, 267.

Be it further enacted and confirmed by the authoritie of this present Grand Assembly that the inhabitants of the several counties and precincts shall be assessed in the defraying of the Burgesses charges expended in their imployment to be levied by the sheriff of each county respectively, And upon refusall in case of nonpayment to make seizure by vertue of this authoritie, Allways provided that the Burgesses produce their charge to the countie courts, who are hereby required to rayse proportionably upon the estates of tithable persons, And be it further enacted and confirmed that if any assembly be sumoned and disolved before the First of March the charge of the Burgesses to be levied that present yeare, *Provided,* that if it happen in or after March to be satisfied the following yeare, And it is further enacted and confirmed by the authoritie aforesaid, that if any Burgesses shall employ their owne servants in their publique service as by attendance upon any Burgesses, The inhabitants of the severall precincts respectively are to allow worke for so many days as they are soe employed.

B. AN ACT LIMITING THE NUMBER OF BURGESSES A COUNTY
COULD ELECT AND DEFINING OTHER ELECTION PROCEDURES,
NOVEMBER 1645

Hening, ed., *Statutes at Large*, I, 299.

BE it enacted by the authority of the Governour, Council and Burgesses of this present Grand Assembly, That whereas the certain number of Burgesses for the several countyes of this collony have been divers times augmented and lessened without any certain rule for the same: that hereafter for all ensueing Assemblies no county shall exceed the number of 4 Burgesses, (except the county of James Cittie onely, which shall elect 5 Burgesses for the said county and one for James Citty) And that the election of all Burgesses be performed in those places where the county courts be held, (those places excepted which are published by act of Assembly;) also the sherriffs shall give notice of such elections to the severall inhabitants 6 days at least before the time of meeting to that place.

C. AN ACT AUTHORIZING THE ASSESSMENT OF CHARGES FOR
PAROCHIAL BURGESSES, MARCH 1658/59

Hening, ed., *Statutes at Large*, I, 520–521.

WHEREAS many disputes and controversies have arose about the defraying of the charge of the paroachiall Burgesses, by reason the vestrys of the said parishes have not been sufficiently qualified for laying the same uppon the people, *It is hereby enacted and ordained*, That the vestrie of any parish which shall elect any Burgess shall be impowered to order payment for his charges, And in case any persons within the parish electing shall refuse to make payment according to their order, then the collectors shall by vertue of that order make distresse [i.e., seize property as security] for the same, which shall be accounted authentique in any court of judicature within this collonie.

D. AN ACT LIMITING COUNTIES TO ELECT ONLY TWO BURGESSES,
MARCH 1660/61

Hening, ed., *Statutes at Large*, II, 20.

WHEREAS the charge of assemblies is much increased by the great number of Burgesses, *Bee itt enacted* that hereafter no county shall send above two Burgesses who shall be elected at those places in each county where the county courts are usually kept, provied allwaies that James Citty being the metropolis of the country shall have the priviledge to elect a Burgesse for themselves and every county that will lay out one hundred acres of land and people itt with one hundred tithables persons, that place shall enjoy the like liberty and priviledge.

E. AN ACT REQUIRING COUNTIES TO ELECT TWO BURGESSES,
OCTOBER 1669

Hening, ed., *Statutes at Large*, II, 272–273.

WHEREAS severall inconveniencies have arisen by the act giveing liberty to the counties to chuse one or two burgesses at discretion as the retarding the busines at the house when those single burgesses are upon committees, or of any suite of their owne, or difference between diverse parishes of the counties, or have their appearance hindred by sicknes or otherwise, in all which occasions the county that sends, or parte of it are deprived of the priviledge of their representative, *It is enacted* that each county after this present session shalbe enjoyned to returne two burgesses for the better service of the publique.

F. AN ACT FINING COUNTIES FOR FAILING TO ELECT BURGESSES, OCTOBER 1670

Hening, ed., *Statutes at Large*, II, 282–283.

WHEREAS the act for electing two burgesses for each county for want of a Fine hath not had that due observance it ought, *It is enacted* that every county not sending to every session of assembly two burgesses shall be fined ten thousand pounds of tobacco to the use of the publique.

7. *Control over Legislative Procedures*

A. MEMBERS FREED FROM ARREST DURING ASSEMBLY SESSIONS, 1623/24

Hening, ed., *Statutes at Large*, I, 125.

That no burgesses of the General Assembly shall be arrested during the time of the Assembly, a week before and a week after upon pain of the creditors forfeiture of his debt and such punishment upon the officer as the court shall award.

B. CONTROL OVER MEMBERS' QUALIFICATIONS, 1663

Hening, ed., *Statutes at Large*, II, 198.

September 12th, 1663.

WHEREAS Mr. John Hill high sheriff of Lower Norfolk hath represented to the house that Mr. John Porter, one of the burgesses of that county was loving to the Quakers and stood well affected towards them, and had been at their meetings, and was so far an anabaptist as to be against the baptising of children, upon which representation the said Porter confessed himself to have and be well affected to the Quakers, but conceived his being at their meetings could not be proved, upon which the oaths of allegiance and supremacy were tendred to him which he refused to take; whereupon it is ordered that the said Porter be dismissed this house.

C. SELECTION OF THE SPEAKER, 1653

Hening, ed., *Statutes at Large*, I, 378, 377.

IT is ordered, that Lt. Col. Edward Major, Lt. Col. George Fletcher, Mr. William Hockaday and Mr. William Whittby, attend the Governor and Councill, to request of them their reasons, wherefore they cannot joyne with us the

Burgesses in the business of this Assembly, about the election of Lt. Col. Walter Chiles for Speaker of this Assembly.

Lt. Col. Walter Chiles haveing by plurality of votes been chosen Speaker of this Assembly: And this day representing to the house his extraordinarie occasions in regard of the dispatch of some shipping now in the country in which he is much interested and concerned, The house upon his desire have given him leave to follow his private affairs notwithstanding the election aforesaid.

July the 5th, 1653

GENTLEMEN,

NOT to intrench [i.e., encroach] upon the right of Assemblies in the free choice of a speaker, nor to undervalue Lt. Col. Chiles, but onely by way of advice, It is my opinion, the Council likewise concerning [i.e., concurring] therein, That it is not so proper nor so convenient att this time to make choice of him for that there is something to be agitated in this Assembly concerning a shipp lately arrived, in which Lt. Col. Chiles hath some interest, for which and some other reasons we conceive it better at present to make choice of some other person amongst you whom you shall agree upon.

Your reall servant,
RICHARD BENNETT

July the 5th, 1653.
Vera copia,
JOHN CORKER, Clerk to the Burgesses.

D. RULES OF PROCEDURE, 1658/59

Hening, ed., *Statutes at Large*, I, 507–508.

ORDERS IN THE HOUSE.

1. That no Burgesse shall absent himselfe from attendance on the House without leave first obteined (unlesse prevented by sicknesse) when any matter shall be debated of; But that every member shall keepe good order, and give due attention to the reading or debateing of whatsoever shall be proposed or presented to the consideration of the House: And that every Burgesse shall, with due respect, address himselfe to Mr. Speaker in a decent manner, And not entertaine any private discourse, while the publique affairs are treated off.

2. That any member of this house for everie time of his absence upon call of the clerke shall forfeit twenty pounds of tabacco to be disposed of by the major part of the house upon every Saturday in the afternoon, lawfull impediments excepted.

3. That the first time any member of this house shall by the major part of the house adjudged to be disguised with overmuch drinke he shall forfeit one hundred pounds of tobacco, and for the second time he shall be soe disguised, he shall forfeit 300 of tobacco and for the 3d offence 1000 lb. tobacco.

4. That upon debate of any thing proposed by the Speaker, The party that speaketh shall rise from his seate and be uncovered [i.e., bareheaded] dureing the time he speaketh, wherein no interruption shall be made untill he have finished his discourse, upon the penalty of one hundred pounds of tobacco.

5. That no irreverent or indigne forme of speech be uttered in the House by any person against another member of this House, upon the penalty of Five hundred pounds of tobacco, The House to be judge therein and the severall Fines to be disposed of by the House as abovesaid.

8. *Initiation of Legislation*

A. EDMUND SCARBURGH'S PETITION TO THE HOUSE OF BURGESSES, 1663

Hening, ed., *Statutes at Large*, II, 202–203.

It is humbly proposed that the acts concerning hides may be enlarged to calves and deer skins so well as hides, and that a commission throughout the country may be qualyfied by injunction in the act to receive all proofs that shall be presented them for detecting those persons that convey hides or skins out of the country contrary to the act and to give warrants for sumoning witnesses and order to make search for hides and skins.

Calves skins and deer skins included; any perticular justice to send a warrant for search; 3 or more one being of the quorum to take evidences.

———

WHEREAS there is thefts committed dayly on the south side of James river by the Indians, as stealing of hogs, robbing of hedges in the night, stealing tobacco and corn out of the fields, and our neighbouring Indians being taxed therewith, say that it is by the Tuscarodoe Indians which lie skulking about our English plantation and there covertly have underhand dealings with the English and can never be taken by reason [that] the law prohibiting the Indians to come within the English bounds without badges doth only inflict a punishment upon the Indians so coming but no mulct [i.e., penalty] upon the English for not taking such Indians as come in without badges, so by reason of their sinister ends the law is seldom put into execution for prevention of which mischeif or peradventure a greater if not timely prevention put a stop to it, it is humbly proposed that if any Indian or Indians shall be found at the house of any English within the English bounds not having a badge with him or them according to law, that then the Englishman so entertaining such Indian or Indians pay the like value as is amerced for the Indians to pay, and the one half of both to the informer.

And I will thank, praise, and go on with them in the work.

Your honours most humble servant,
EDMUND SCARBURGH.

October 15th, 1663.

B. SCARBURGH'S PETITION BECOMES LAW, 1663

Hening, ed., *Statutes at Large*, II, 185.

Act III
An act prohibiting the exportation of Deere skins or Calve skins, etc.

WHEREAS it appeares that the skins of Deer and Calves are according to their quantity as usefull and benefitiall to the country as hides, for promoteing the manufacture of shooes, *It is therefore enacted* that all such skins shall be included in the act against exportation of hides or leather, with five hundred pounds of tobacco to be forfeited by the buyer or seller of the same, *And be it further enacted* that any perticuler justice be impowered to send his warrant aboard any ship, sloope or vessell for search or detection of such offences, and that three or more (one being of the quorum) may examine and take evidence for the proofe thereof, and that a court may be called if requested by the party concerned according to a former act for dispatch of maritime affaires to passe judgment thereupon, and for what shall be found aboard any ship, sloope or vessell as aforesaid to give sentence for confiscation thereof.

Act IV
An act prohibiting the entertainment of Indians without badges.

SINCE it is manifest that diverse thefts are comitted by Indians on the southside of James river, for which the neighbouring Indians being taxed say, and affirme it to be done by the Tuscarores and other remote nations who lying skulking about the English plantations for private sinister comerce cannot be soe safely discovered and taken by the reason that the penalty, by law for Indians comeing in without a badge is laid on the Indians only, and not on the English entertayning them, *Be it therefore enacted* that what Englishman soever shall privately entertaine any Indian or Indians of any nation not haveing a badge according to law shalbe lyable to the same censure and penalty as the law imposes upon an Indian, for such their illegall comeing in, and that the informer or discoverer thereof shall have halfe the said penalty.

9. *Control over Taxation*

A. A RIGHT ESTABLISHED, 1623/24

Hening, ed., *Statutes at Large,* I, 124.

That the Governor shall not lay any taxes or ymposies upon the colony their lands or comodities other way than by the authority of the General Assembly, to be levyed and ymployed as the said Assembly shall appoynt.

B. A RIGHT REASSERTED, 1666

H. R. McIlwaine, ed., *Journals of the House of Burgesses of Virginia, 1659/60–1693* (Richmond, Va., 1914), 43.

The Honourable Governor sent Knowledge of his pleasure to the House that two or more of the Council might Joyn whith the House in Granting and Confirming the Sum of the Levy.

The Humble Answer of the House is that they conceive it their priviledge to lay the Levy in the House and that the House will admit nothing without reference from the Honourable Governor and Council unless it be before adjudged or Confirmed by Act or Order and after passing in the house shall be presented to their Honours for their approbation or Dissent.

Mr. [Thomas] *Ballard* Major [John] *Weir* and Capt. [Joseph] *Bridger* are appointed to present this answer to the Governor and Council.

This is willingly assented to and desired to remain on Record for a Rule to walk by for the future which will be Satisfactory to all.

William Berkeley

10. *Control over Local Affairs: The General Assembly Creates the County Court System, 1634*

Hening, ed., *Statutes at Large*, I, 224.

In 1634. The country divided into 8 shires, which are to be governed as the shires in England.

The names of the shires are,

James City	*Warwick River*
Henrico	*Warrosquyoake*
Charles City	*Charles River*
Elizabeth Citty	*Accawmack*

And Lieutenants to be appointed the same as in England, and in a more especial manner to take care of the warr against Indians. And as in England *sheriffs* shall be elected to have the same power as there; and *sergeants*, and *bailiffs* where need requires.

Commissioners, instead of £5 causes, may determine £10 causes and one of the council to have notice to attend and assist in each court of shire.

Chapter Three

The Evolution
of Self-Government
in Virginia

Local Government

Throughout the seventeenth century it was the vitality of local government that gave strength to the Old Dominion's growing tradition of self-government. Like the emergence of the General Assembly, the rise of the county form of local government was unplanned. Because the form of Virginia's local government so closely resembled its English counterpart, it is easy to ignore the significance of localism in the development of the colony's political institutions. Following the establishment of the county court system in 1634, a profound alteration in the character of these institutions occurred. The courts' creation induced a fundamental decentralization and dispersal of power within the colony's institutional structure by splitting the powers and duties of government among the courts, the governor, and the General Assembly.

Within thirty years' time, law, custom, and local conditions enlarged that division until the county courts became the branch of government with which the colonist had the most frequent contact and intimate knowledge, while the General Assembly assumed more of a purely legislative role. As local government became a focal point of the settlers' daily existence, some planters employed what family ties, influence, and wealth they possessed to fashion it into an institutional device for founding a ruling elite akin to the traditional English ruling classes. In turn, this elite provided the manpower from which justices of the peace, burgesses, and councillors were drawn.

When the General Assembly erected the county form of local government, it responded to the twin pressures of a swiftly growing colony and the necessity for a more effective system of local administration. Between 1607 and 1634 the colony's settled area had extended outward from the original settlement at Jamestown. Colonists had inhabited both sides of the James River from its falls to its mouth, the York-James Peninsula, and the Eastern Shore, and by 1634 they were just beginning to push into the region north of the York River (see the maps on pages 71 and 72). As long as the settlements remained close to Jamestown and the population was small, the governor and his council could adequately discharge the tasks of local government. By the late 1620s, however, not a few of these chores had been assumed by an irregular patchwork of monthly courts and particular plantations. The result was an overlapping of jurisdictions and an ineffectual dispensation of justice. The decision to create the county courts not only eliminated delays and inefficiencies but also provided the means for extending a uniform system of justice and government throughout Virginia in the future.

Initially the General Assembly divided Virginia into eight large, three-sided counties, but the colony experienced its own "great migration" after 1634, and by 1668 a total of twenty counties had been erected. As population increased, county-building followed a common pattern. Because the courthouse was a center of attention, the distance a colonist had to travel in order to file a lawsuit or a land deed, or to have a will probated, was a matter of concern. Given the difficulty of land travel in the seventeenth century, journeys of more than a day posed extreme hardships for the colonist whose business required legal remedies. Therefore, as soon as a sufficient number of colonists had seated a remote area in a county, they petitioned the assembly to divide the existing county into two smaller ones. If the assembly concurred with the petitioners' demands, it ordered the division, and the governor, with the council's advice, appointed officers for the new county (Document 1).

Governing each county was a court consisting of justices of the peace, a sheriff, a clerk, their deputies, and minor officials such as constables, tithe-takers, and surveyors of the highways. Like their counterparts in England, the individual justices took depositions, issued warrants, and disposed of minor disputes; collectively, at monthly

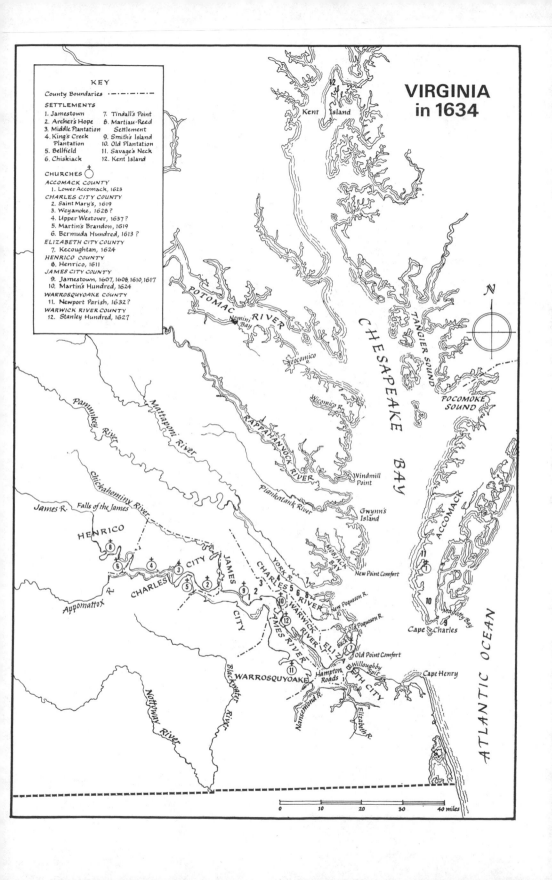

VIRGINIA in 1634

KEY

County Boundaries — · — · —

SETTLEMENTS
1. Jamestown
2. Archer's Hope
3. Middle Plantation
4. King's Creek Plantation
5. Bellfield
6. Chiskiack
7. Tindall's Point
8. Martiau-Reed Settlement
9. Smith's Island
10. Old Plantation
11. Savage's Neck
12. Kent Island

CHURCHES ⚲

ACCOMACK COUNTY
1. Lower Accomack, 1623

CHARLES CITY COUNTY
2. Saint Mary's, 1619
3. Weyanoke, 1628?
4. Upper Westover, 1637?
5. Martin's Brandon, 1619
6. Bermuda Hundred, 1613?

ELIZABETH CITY COUNTY
7. Kecoughtan, 1624

HENRICO COUNTY
8. Henrico, 1611

JAMES CITY COUNTY
9. Jamestown, 1607, 1608, 1610, 1617
10. Martin's Hundred, 1624

WARROSQUYOAKE COUNTY
11. Newport Parish, 1632?

WARWICK RIVER COUNTY
12. Stanley Hundred, 1627

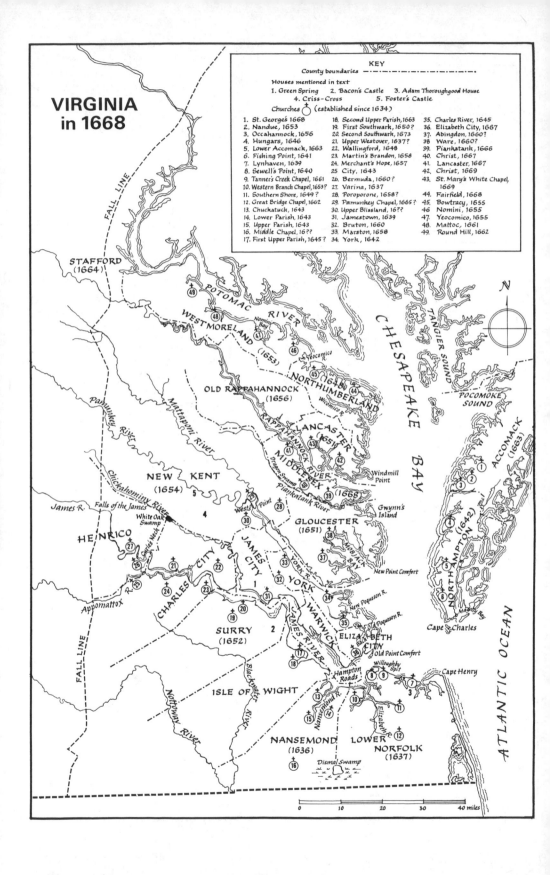

VIRGINIA
in 1668

KEY

County boundaries

Houses mentioned in text
1. Green Spring   2. Bacon's Castle   3. Adam Thoroughgood House
4. Criss-Cross   5. Foster's Castle

Churches (established since 1634)

1. St. George's 1668
2. Nandue, 1653
3. Occahannock, 1656
4. Hungars, 1646
5. Lower Accomack, 1663
6. Fishing Point, 1641
7. Lynhaven, 1639
8. Sewell's Point, 1640
9. Tanner's Creek Chapel, 1661
10. Western Branch Chapel, 1653?
11. Southern Shore, 1649?
12. Great Bridge Chapel, 1662
13. Chuckatuck, 1643
14. Lower Parish, 1643
15. Upper Parish, 1643
16. Middle Chapel, 16??
17. First Upper Parish, 1645?

18. Second Upper Parish, 1663
19. First Southwark, 1650?
20. Second Southwark, 1673
21. Upper Westover, 1637?
22. Wallingford, 1648
23. Martin's Brandon, 1658
24. Merchant's Hope, 1657
25. City, 1643
26. Bermuda, 1660?
27. Varina, 1637
28. Poroporone, 1658?
29. Pamunkey Chapel, 1665?
30. Upper Blissland, 16??
31. Jamestown, 1639
32. Bruton, 1660
33. Marston, 1658
34. York, 1642

35. Charles River, 1645
36. Elizabeth City, 1667
37. Abingdon, 1660?
38. Ware, 1660?
39. Piankatank, 1666
40. Christ, 1667
41. Lancaster, 1667
42. Christ, 1669
43. St. Mary's White Chapel, 1669
44. Fairfield, 1668
45. Bowtracy, 1655
46. Nomini, 1655
47. Yeocomico, 1655
48. Mattoc, 1661
49. Round Hill, 1662

STAFFORD (1664)

WESTMORELAND (1653)

OLD RAPPAHANNOCK (1656)

NORTHUMBERLAND (1656)

LANCASTER (1651)

MIDDLESEX (1668)

NEW KENT (1654)

GLOUCESTER (1651)

HEINRICO

JAMES CITY

CHARLES CITY

YORK

WARWICK

SURRY (1652)

ELIZABETH CITY

ISLE OF WIGHT

NANSEMOND (1636)

LOWER NORFOLK (1637)

ACCOMACK (1663)

NORTHAMPTON (1642)

CHESAPEAKE BAY

TANGIER SOUND

POCOMOKE SOUND

ATLANTIC OCEAN

POTOMAC RIVER

RAPPAHANNOCK RIVER

Pamunkey River

Mattaponi River

Chickahominy River

James R.

Falls of the James

White Oak Swamp

Appomattox

Blackwater River

Nottoway River

Dismal Swamp

Cape Charles

Cape Henry

Old Point Comfort

Hampton Roads

New Point Comfort

Windmill Point

Gwynn's Island

Dragon Swamp

Piankatank River

York River

Elizabeth R.

Nansemond R.

Cape Henry

Willoughby Spit

FALL LINE

0   10   20   30   40 miles

meetings of court, they settled petty criminal offenses and civil suits. As the term *justice of the peace* implies, their general responsibility was the maintenance of what the seventeenth-century English jurist Michael Dalton called "the Amity, Confidence and Quiet that is between men."

The sheriff performed a variety of tasks that ranged from policing his county to gathering taxes and overseeing the election of burgesses. At first appointments to the shrievalty were independent of the courts, but by the middle of the century the justices had adopted the English practice of nominating one of their number for the post, and the governor customarily complied with their wishes. The governor's control over appointments was further neutralized when the custom of rotating the shrievalty among the justices became law by an act of assembly in March 1661/62.

Clerks usually held their office for life. Their chief duty was to record the business of court and colonist. Maintaining accurate records required much of their time, for in addition to enrolling depositions, indictments, and orders, the clerks registered land deeds and wills in the county archives—a departure from English practice. Because Virginia clerks were essentially scriveners rather than conservators of the peace, the prototype for their office seems to have been a blending of the record-keeping functions of the English *custos rotulorum* and his subordinate, the clerk of the peace.

As the governor received his commission from the king, so justices, sheriffs, and clerks derived their authority from commissions issued by the governor. The justices' commission (Document 2A) contained the names of the men appointed to office. Listed in order of seniority of service, the first four judges constituted the quorum, which meant that at least one of these men had to attend every meeting of court. Together the justices-in-quorum could sit in place of the full commission. The document also delineated the bounds of the justices' authority; it enjoined the magistrates to keep the peace and to enforce the statutes committed to their charge. A commission remained in force until the monarch died or until a governor chose to issue a new one or was replaced. If during the interval between the issuance of the commissions, justices died, the governor merely appointed replacements.

Sheriffs' and clerks' commissions were less elaborate. Actually, after it became customary to draw candidates for the shrievalty from the county benches, the provisions of the commission of the peace applied to them as well as the other justices. Once the custom had become established, a letter of appointment from the governor sufficed (Document 2B). Similarly, since clerks were not peace officers, simple letters of appointment served as their commissions.

Until 1662 Virginia law specified neither the size of the county courts nor the qualifications of their members, but at its March 1661/62 sitting the General Assembly adopted a law fixing the number of justices at eight and requiring that only the "most able, honest and judicious" men be named to the courts. Long before the assembly attempted this definition of qualifications, however, an informal procedure for screening prospective justices had come into use. An adaptation of traditional political and social values to a colonial context, it had a profound impact upon the structure of Virginia society.

The power to appoint justices and other court officers belonged, of course, to the governor, but by the 1660s usage, necessity, and the law had reduced that power to a formality. For appointment to the benches of the original eight counties, the governors had selected councillors, militia officers, or judges from the defunct monthly courts. This arrangement had been satisfactory for as long as the number of counties remained constant, but in the two decades after 1648 the number of counties doubled. For the courts of these new counties the governor had to choose men with little or no legal training. To cope with an increasingly complex office, the appointees could depend only upon acquired experience and common sense. As the General Assembly reduced the governor's control over local affairs and as the distances between court and capital made it impractical for the justices to seek his advice, the chief executive's acquaintance with local government declined. Consequently these developments helped the justices to consolidate their control over appointments to all local offices. With increasing frequency after 1648, the justices recommended sheriffs, clerks, and new members of the bench to the governor, and he followed their advice. The practice is recorded as early as 1636 (Document 2C), in the 1650s it was customary, and by Berkeley's second administration it had become inviolable (Document 2D).

Virginia's rapid expansion after 1634 produced a need for men to fill newly created county offices. Once the demand for officeholders had outdistanced the supply of qualified colonists already living in Virginia, the way to upward political and social mobility opened to a number of immigrants. A reservoir of talented and grasping new settlers was available, for the erection of the county courts coincided with the migration to Virginia of some fairly prosperous and socially well-connected Englishmen. For these ambitious colonists county office-holding presented certain advantages. A seat on the bench was useful for developing business contacts with other planters and gaining a measure of influence over a county's economy. It also proved advantageous in acquiring land, and it could lead to marriage into prominent colonial families, thereby assuring a further step upward. A system of courts whose authority enlarged with each passing year offered the opportunity to shape and to direct the colony's political life and opened the door to membership in the House of Burgesses and the Council of State. Such reasons for pursuing county offices were compelling motives for colonists who had moved to Virginia in the hope of finding improved social status.

Having gained the power and prestige of public office, successful immigrants tried to bequeath their advantage to their descendants. Although these immigrants usually did not spring from the English ruling classes, they were close enough to have observed the workings of the traditional social order. They were cognizant of an inextricable relationship between social status and political power, for they had learned that in England high social standing belonged to the squire, who held office and enforced the law. Armed with that knowledge, they sought to reproduce the familiar relationship by transmuting the office of justice of the peace into a bridge between the Old Dominion's political and social strata.

For half a century the General Assembly continually augmented the powers of government of the county courts. Throughout the first eighteen years of the courts' existence, the foundations of their authority were laid. Initially the courts were assigned jurisdiction over petty criminal offenses and civil cases, but the assembly soon gave them responsibility for housekeeping tasks like maintaining bridges and ferries (Document 3A). A significant addition to their competence occurred in 1645 when the assembly empowered the courts to probate wills and to try all cases in common law and equity (Documents 3B and 3C). In England the right to probate wills belonged to ecclesiastical courts, but since the Anglican establishment had not been transferred to Virginia, many of its powers devolved on the governor and council. Assigning the probation of wills to the county courts relieved the governor of a burdensome chore and also spared the remotely situated colonist a difficult journey to Jamestown. Similarly, by giving local courts original jurisdiction in most civil cases, the assembly eased the strain on the governor and council. Before 1645 it had been customary for the governor and council, sitting in quarterly sessions, to try all civil suits involving amounts above £10. But as the statute noted, "the great distance of many parts of this collony from James Citty" and an increase in the number of suits had made that arrangement impractical. The courts' powers increased in other areas as well: by 1652 they were beginning to combine various criminal, civil, ecclesiastical, and administrative jurisdictions that fell within the purview of separate English courts or political subdivisions.

An opportunity to diminish the courts' widening authority presented itself in 1652. The capitulation of Virginia to the dominion of the English Commonwealth in March raised the prospect of alterations in the structure of the colony's local government. But such a prospect never became a reality, because the parliament men were more concerned about reducing Virginia to their authority than they were about tinkering with politics. Parliament's apparent willingness to leave things unchanged is evidenced by the fact that when the General Assembly met in April to bring Virginia's legal code into conformity with the situation in England, the assemblymen did not impair the county courts' jurisdiction.

Indeed, throughout the decade between 1652 and 1662 the assembly continued its augmentation of the courts' competence. When the General Assembly of March 1661/62 revised Virginia's entire legal code, its chief concern was the enhancement of local government. To that end it expanded still further the county courts' wide jurisdiction. Two laws (Documents 3D and 3E) exemplify that intention. One granted local magistrates the same authority enjoyed by English justices of the peace; the other empowered them to enact bylaws. In effect, these laws both recognized the pivotal importance of the county courts and gave additional sanction to the division of power between county and province that had been occurring since 1645. Save for an additional refinement, that division was now complete, although the assembly continued to give the courts more authority until the end of the century.

The statutory authority that the General Assembly assigned to the county courts may be divided into three broad areas: record keeping, administration, and the maintenance of public order. In an age when few men were literate and communications with the outside world were hazardous and slow, the county court as a place of record provided a valuable service by preserving in relative safety the intimate details of a colonist's life. Such information could protect an estate, free a servant who had served his time, or show that a planter had cleared his debts with a London merchant, for a county's records were recognized as evidence in any law court.

Of all the records kept in a county's archives, none were of greater importance than land deeds and wills. Land was a principal basis of wealth in Virginia, so it was necessary to devise a means for effecting clear title to it. Apparently one of the reasons for creating the court system had been the desire to formulate a method of registering land patented by headright, for the earliest court records contain numerous certificates for land thus claimed. Putting these certificates in the record attested to their validity and provided grounds for prosecuting fraudulent claimants. Once a headright had been proven, the certificate was forwarded to Jamestown, a deed was issued, and the colonist recorded a copy of the deed at the courthouse (Document 4). In the event that a tract of land was subsequently sold, a deed of sale testified to the transaction (Document 5).

Wills are the instruments by which property of all sorts is disposed according to the wishes of the deceased. Many colonists did not own enough property to warrant drafting a will. At the opposite extreme, some planters owned so much that they required a lengthy and complex document to distribute their acquisitions. The property of those settlers who fell between these extremities could be passed on in a short, written will (Document 6) or in an oral statement taken at the deathbed in the presence of witnesses. However it was made, the value and necessity of having a copy of the will in the county archives is obvious enough. Recording a written will prevented tampering; in the case of a nuncupative will, recordation proved its existence. Besides land titles and wills, the court records contained business accounts, contracts, inventories of estates, powers of attorney (Document 7), livestock brands (Document 8), and even letters to family and friends in England. In addition to chronicling these facts about the personal lives of local inhabitants, the clerks maintained a record of the courts' official proceedings. They enrolled every trial, order, or decision in the record books, as well as the reports of constables, appraisers, or coroner's juries (Document 9). To read these records, in short, is to become familiar with the seventeenth-century Virginian's world. Often the details of that world are trivial or boring. Sometimes they are tantalizingly sketchy. But taken in toto they reveal much about how the colonist coped with a novel environment by adapting what he knew to his new surroundings.

Just as the settlers depended upon the courts to preserve a record of their lives, the General Assembly depended upon the courts to administer the affairs of local communities. The courts' administrative powers were wide-ranging. Courts fixed their own rules of procedure (Document 10), fined justices who failed to attend sessions (Document 11), regulated public houses (Document 12), and cared for the indigent and the infirm (Documents 13A, 13B, 13C). In addition, they probated wills, set prices and wages, drew parochial boundaries, and recruited ministers. The burden of defending the colony also fell upon the county courts. By law each county was required to maintain a militia force commanded by several justices, to instruct the militias in the art of warfare, and to equip them with adequate arms and provisions. To defend against an invasion or Indian attack, the General Assembly often ordered the building of forts in coastal or frontier counties, and the affected colonists were expected to provide labor or funds (Document 14).

Perhaps the most significant administrative responsibility that the courts exercised involved laying and collecting taxes. Although the House of Burgesses assumed the power to tax at an early point in its development, it never possessed the machinery for collecting public revenues. After 1634 raising the taxes that the house had voted became the courts' duty. They also acquired the authority to levy local taxes in order to defray the costs of county government.

A county levy consisted of two parts—the local contribution to general provincial revenue needs and the taxes set aside for the county's own operating expenses. Local taxes served a variety of purposes. The largest regular expense was the salaries of the county burgesses. Other regular expenses might include payment of shrieval and clerical fees; reimbursements to local citizens for services to the county; the maintenance of bridges, roads, or ferries; the payment of bounties on predators; and care of the indigent. There might also be extraordinary expenses such as building forts, warring on Indians, or purchasing law books for the justices.

Once each year, usually in October or November, each court met in fiscal session and received an assessment from the General Assembly, to which the justices added that year's estimated local expenses. By dividing the number of tithable persons in the county (all males above the age of sixteen and women field hands) into the total sum of the levy, the justices arrived at the proportion of tax owed by individual taxpayers. Because of the scarcity of coin in Virginia, these computations were always based upon tobacco as the medium of exchange, and once they were completed, the justices instructed the sheriff to collect the requisite poundage of tobacco from each family head. If a family head failed to pay his taxes, the court was empowered to take legal action against the offender.

There were few limitations on the county courts' power to tax. The tax laws did no more than fix the fees that sheriffs, clerks, and burgesses could collect for discharging their duties; prohibit justices from receiving a salary; and require the counties to keep accurate lists of tithable persons. None of these prohibitions or requirements infringed on the judges' powers. Nor did custom or law allow any active citizen participation in raising local taxes. Indeed, there was no sanction, legal or otherwise, to prevent courts from sitting in executive session when preparing levies. The General Assembly rarely interfered with the courts' taxing powers, and then only when flagrant statutory violations occurred. Their authority to tax almost without restriction is an example of the county courts' high degree of independence from the provincial government. By 1676 this virtually untrammeled power would be a source of popular irritation.

The record-keeping and administrative functions of the county courts are probably less familiar to modern students than is their more obvious responsibility for maintaining law and order. As court of the first instance in "all causes of what value or nature whatsoever not touching life or member," the county courts tried a wide variety of civil and criminal cases. Most civil suits involved the recovery of debt (Document 16A), but the justices also settled numerous personal disputes such as character defamation (Document 16B) and fights (Document 16C), in addition to enforcing community respect for themselves (Document 16D). After 1645, when the General Assembly authorized them to try all cases in common law and equity, the justices frequently sat as a court of chancery to determine suits for which there was no relief by statute or at the common law (Document 16E). Following the adoption of the navigation system by the home government in 1660, the courts occasionally tried violations of the acts of trade and navigation (Document 16F).

Except for capital crimes, the county courts tried all criminal offenses. Even though they lacked felony jurisdiction, the local magistrates played a role in bringing suspected felons to justice (Document 17A). In instances where a felony had been committed, the justices ordered the suspect's arrest. A common arrest procedure was for a judge to issue a warrant of hue and cry, which commanded all people in a community to assist the sheriff in capturing the suspected criminal. Once an arrest had occurred, the courts found witnesses, gathered evidence, and conducted a preliminary hearing. If the court decided that a crime had been committed, and the evidence was sufficient, it bound the suspect over to the General Court for trial (Document 17B).

Instances of capital crimes were fairly rare, so the courts' attention was taken up with prosecuting misdemeanors. To assist in suppressing crime, every county court convened a grand jury, which sat for an entire year, to investigate possible breaches of the law. Twice during their term, usually in April and December, the grand jurors presented their indictments to the justices for action (Document 17C). Indictments might concern petty theft (Document 17D), fraud (Document 17E), or assault (Document 17F), but the most numerous violations of law were moral offenses, the commonest of which were begetting a bastard (see chapter 5), fornication (Document 17G), and adultery (Document 17H). Traditionally the prosecution of such lapses in moral behavior had belonged to ecclesiastical courts, but since there was no church establishment, local courts were empowered to handle them. Once again new circumstances had forced a fundamental alteration of accepted practices.

The punishment of crimes falling within the county courts' jurisdiction depended upon the degree of their severity. Except in rare instances jails performed no other role in penalizing the offender than holding him for trial, but the judges had a variety of other punitive devices. The most frequent forms of punishment were penance, fines, and corporal punishment, none of which was necessarily required for particular crimes. A thief, for example, might be whipped, fined, and required to make restitution for his offense, while a slanderer might get off with no more than a public apology. Common scolds could be ducked, put in the stocks, or whipped. To be sure, some offenses carried a specific penalty: fornication required penance, and bastardy was invariably punished by fining the reputed father and whipping the mother.

No one who lived in Virginia questioned the right of the county courts to regulate personal conduct or to interfere in matters of private morals. Indeed, had the justices not sought to enforce church attendance, curb public drunkenness, and prevent illicit affairs between married men and women (Document 17I), their neighbors would have considered them derelict. Both judge and ordinary citizen alike thought that it was the magistrate's solemn duty to hold every person accountable to a socially acceptable code of personal and moral behavior. Furthermore, they believed that every citizen was obliged to bring any violation of that code to the authorities' attention.

By now the importance of the county court system as the kingpin of the Old Dominion's political and legal structure ought to be apparent. The General Assembly's creation of the system had interposed a governing authority between governor and colonist, thereby decentralizing Virginia's political institutions. After 1634 political power was no longer centered in one place; now it was dispersed. In the seventeenth century most of the government's concerns were private or local in nature. Because of this the justices of the peace were the agents of government with whom the colonist dealt most frequently. As their responsibilities increased, it was the courts, rather than the governor and council, that provided a place of record and a mechanism for solving personal and community problems requiring legal remedy. For much of the century, therefore, the courts were focal points of life and power in Virginia. Only towards the century's end, when the hazards of living in a new world began to recede and the challenges to the General Assembly materialized, did the courts dwindle in importance.

SUGGESTED READINGS

Ames, Susie M. *Studies of the Virginia Eastern Shore in the Seventeenth Century* (Richmond, Va., 1940).

Billings, Warren M. "The Growth of Political Institutions in Virginia, 1634 to 1676." *William and Mary Quarterly,* 3d Ser., XXXI (1974), 225–242.

Bruce, Philip Alexander. *Institutional History of Virginia in the Seventeenth Century: An Inquiry into the Religious, Moral, Educational, Legal, Military, and Political Condition of the People. . . .* 2 vols. (New York, 1910), I, 463–696.

*Craven, Wesley Frank. *The Southern Colonies in the Seventeenth Century, 1607–1689* (Baton Rouge, La., 1949), 262–309.

*Hiden, Martha Woodroof. *How Justice Grew. Virginia Counties: An Abstract of Their Formation.* Jamestown 350th Anniversary Historical Booklet 19 (Williamsburg, Va., 1957).

———. "Seventeenth Century Virginia Parochial and County Court Records." *Virginia Magazine of History and Biography*, LVI (1948), 125–141.

———. "Virginia County Court Records: Their Background and Scope." *Virginia Magazine of History and Biography*, LIV (1946), 3–16.

Robinson, Morgan Poitaux. *Virginia Counties: Those Resulting from Virginia Legislation.* Virginia State Library, *Bulletin*, IX (Richmond, Va., 1916).

*Robinson, W. Stitt, Jr. *Mother Earth: Land Grants in Virginia, 1607–1699.* Jamestown 350th Anniversary Historical Booklet 12 (Williamsburg, Va., 1957).

The Organization of County Government

1. The Creation of Rappahannock County, 1656

Lancaster County Order Book, 1657–1666, 319.

At a grand Assembly helde at James Cittie 11th December 1656

Whereas a petition of the inhabitants of the Lower parts of Lancaster county sheweinge their vast distance from the County Court was presented to the honorable Assembly by Capt. Moore Fanteleroy and their desire of haveinge the County devided, It is ordered that according to an order of Court deviding the saide County at present into parishes bee for the future the bounds of the Two Countyes (vizt.) the lower part of Mr. Bennetts lande knowen by the name of Naemhocke on the southside the Easter[n]most branch of Moratticock [i.e., Morattico] Creeke on the Northside the River bee the lower most bounds of the upper Countie[;] the lower Countie to retaine the name of Lancaster, and the upper Countie to bee named Rappahannocke Countye, and notwithstandinge this Devision both Countyes to be lyable to the Burgesses Chardge of this present Assembly.

The Commissioners for the Countie of Rappahannocke are as followeth (vizt.)

Col. Moore Fantelroy		The militia
Lt. Col. Toby Smith		Col. Moore Fanteleroy
Mr. James Bagnole	of the Quorum	Lt. Col. Toby Smith
Capt. William Underwood		Major Thomas Goodrich
Mr. Thomas Lucas, Sr.		Capt. William Underwood
Mr. Andrew Gilson		Capt. Francis Slaughter
Mr. Francis Slaughter		Capt. Richard Lees
Mr. Richard Lees		
Mr. William Johnson		
Mr. humphrey Booth		

Vera Copia
Teste   Henry Randolph   Clerk of the Assembly

* Available in paperback.

At a Court helde at James Citty the 13th of December 1656
present the Governor and Councell
Mr. William Johnson by the Court elected Sheriffe for Rappahannock County this ensueing year to be sworne the next Court there.

Teste Nicholas Meriweather, Clerk of Council

The Commission of Lancaster Countie

Col. John Carter			Mr. Rowland Lawson
Lt. Col. Henry Fleete	} of the Quorum		Mr. Edmond Kempe
Major Thomas Bries			Mr. Richard Parrott
Mr. David Fox			Mr. Cuthbert Potter
Mr. George Marsh			the first [three] of the militia
Mr. John Montayne			
Mr. Raleigh Traverse			

Vera Copia Teste Henry Randolph
Clerk of the Assembly

According to the aforesaide act the oath of a Commissioner was administered to mr. James Bagnoll Major Thomas Goodrich Capt. William Underwood Mr. Andrew gilson Capt. Francis Slaughter and mr. humphrey Booth[.] According to an order mr. William Johnson was sworne high sheriffe of the County of Rappahannocke[.] Clement herbert was like wise sworne undersheriffe of the said County. According to Col. William Claybourne his letter of Recommendation Anthony Stephens is admitted and Sworne Clerke of the said Countie of Rappahannocke, and the said Anthony Stephens is likewise sworne a surveyour.

2. *The Appointment of County Officers*

A. COMMISSION OF THE PEACE, MAY 1652

Northumberland County Order Book, 1650–1652, fol. 76.

To all men whome these presents shall come I Richard Bennett Esq. Governor and Captaine Generall of Virginia send Greetings in our Lord God everlasting. Whereas for the ease of the Countrey and greater dispatch of business, The Governor and Councell of State have [therefore?] appointed, in places convenient inferiour Courts of Justice and Commissioners for the same to determine of suites and for the punishment of offences as the Governor and Councell shall thinke fitt to give them power to heare and determine. And Whereas by Act of Assembly beareing Date at James Citty the 12th of May 1652 it was thought fitt that Commissioners should be appointed in every County for the Keeping of County Courts six times in the year [according?] to the 69th Act of Assembly 1642 and oftner upon extraordinary Causes required and agreed upon by the Major part of the [Court?]. Now, know yee That I the said Richard Bennett, Esq. in the name of the Keeper of the Liberty of England by Act of Parliament accordingly have assigned and for the time being [have] appointed you and every [one] of you whose names are here [inscribed?] to be the present Commissioners for the County of Northumberland Col. John Mattrom Lt. Col. George Fletcher Mr. Thomas Speke Mr. John Trussell Mr. William Presly Mr. Nicholas Pope Major [Thomas] Baldridge Mr. John Hollowes Mr. Walter Broadhurst Mr. Samuel Smith and Mr. Nicholas Morris Giveing and granting [to all or any four of?] them whereof Col. John Mattrom Lt. Col. George Fletcher Mr. Thomas Speke and Mr. John Trussell to be alwayes one [all such power?] to heare and determine all suites and Controversies between [party and party?] it being lawfull for any persons to appeale to the Quarter Court att James Citty in any matter depending before them according to the 5th Act of Assembly 1647 with power to them and every [one] of them to take depositions and examinations for the learneing of the truth. And that you be carefull for the Conservation of the peace and the quiet government and safety of the people there resideing or living and that you keepe or cause to be kept and observed all Orders of Court and proclamations directed to your hands from the Governor and Councell and according to the same and as neere as may be according to the lawes of England to afflict punishment upon offenders and deliquents and to doe and execute whatsoever a Justice of a peace or two or more Justices of the peace may doe or execute such offences only excepted as concerne the taking of life or member, And further you are hereby required from time to time to keepe or cause to be kept by the [Clerk?] of your Court Recordes of all matters and Controversies decided and agreed upon by you or any fower of you as aforesaid provided further and it is hereby intended that those of the Councell of state in this Colony are to sett and be of this Commission and to take their places and have their voices in Judicature according to their degrees in Councell upon emergent occasions with the advice of one or more Commissioners to call and keepe a Court in the absence of those of the Quorum herein named and authorized untill I by Commission under my hand signify to the Contrary. Given under my hand this 28th of May 1652. By Command of the Governor Councell and Burgesses

Robert Huberd Clerk of Council   Vera Copia.

B. SHERIFF'S COMMISSION, 1674

> Westmoreland County Deeds and Wills, 1665–1677, fol. 181.

I doe hereby appoynt mr. John Frodesham to be sherriffe of Westmoreland for this ensuing yeare 1674 and doe Order that and accordingly at the usuall time he be sworne Given under my hand this 7th November 1673

William Berkeley

C. NOMINATIONS FOR SHERIFF, 1636

> Northampton County Order Book, 1632–1640, 77.

At this Court these names underwritten were chosen for choyse of a sheriffe to be presented to the governor and counsel at the next quarter court

Mr. nathaniell Littleton	Mr. Alexander Mountney
Mr. John Neale	Mr. William Roper
Mr. Edward Drewe	Mr. Henry Wilson

D. THE JUSTICES' CONTROL OVER APPOINTMENTS TO THEIR COURTS, 1672

Lower Norfolk County Deeds and Wills, E, fol. 132.

To the Right Honorable Sir William Berkeley
knight Governor and Captain Generall of Virginia
Lemuel Mason
Humbly prayes that Mr. William Daynes, Esq. may bee aded to the Comission for the County Court of Lower Norfolk and bee of the quoram next unto Mr. John Porter, Esq. hee having beene formerly a Justice of the said County and in Regard of the Remotenesse of the Inhabitants one from the other who Cannott without great trouble goe to a Justice for the determination of differences that lyeth in theire power to decide hee [i.e., Mason] humbly Prayeth that Mr. Anthony Lawson may also bee added to the said Comission, and that the said Comission may bee Renewed and That each Justice may know his degree and take place accordingly, and further that Your Honor will bee pleased to Cause the Comission for the militia for the said County to bee sent downe being boath for the Court and malitia as followeth If your Honor think fitt

Justices		Commission for the malitia wanting
Lemuel Mason		My [i.e., Mason's] Captain Lieutenant and Ensigne
Lt. Col. Thorowgood		
Mr John Porter, Squire		Lt. Col. Adam Thorowgood
Mr. William Daynes, Esq.	of the	his Lieutenant and Ensigne
Mr. Thomas fulcher	quoram	Major Francis Sayer
Mr. William Robinson		his Lieutenant and Ensigne
Mr. Francis Sayer		Capt. John Hatton
Mr. George Fouler		his Lieutenant and Ensigne
Mr. William Andrews		Capt. Robert Bray
Mr. Robert Bray		his Lieutenant and Ensigne
Mr. Adam Keeling		Capt. William Robinson
Mr. John Hatton		the horse his Lieutenant and Ensigne
Mr. Malachi Thruston		
Mr. Anthony Lawson		

Lemuell Mason

This petition is granted Except Mr. William Daynes and Comission to issue accordingly unlesse the said Mr. daynes desires to bee in the place he was formerly

October 2 *1672*   William Berkeley

The Growth of the County Courts' Statutory Control of Local Affairs

3. Acts of the Assembly, 1642/43–1661/62

A. AN ACT REQUIRING COUNTIES TO MAINTAIN FERRIES AND BRIDGES, MARCH 1642/43

> William Waller Hening, ed., *The Statutes at Large; Being a Collection of All the Laws of Virginia, from the First Session of the Legislature, in the Year 1619* (Richmond, New York, and Philadelphia, 1809–1823), I, 269.

WHEREAS for the more ease of travellers, It was enacted by the Assembly in January 1641, that all this countrey respectively provide and maintain Ferrys and bridges and the leavy for payment to the Ferrymen to be made by the comissioners where the Ferry is kept, And where one creeke parts two counties, there each of them to contribute towards the maintenance of the said Ferries, and bridges should be built and provided by the first of September following, And that all passengers whether strangers or others should be freed from payment otherwise then by the leavie, And that the Ferrymen should give their due attendance from sunne rising to sunne setting, *This present Grand Assembly to all intents and purposes doth hereby confirme the same.*

B. AN ACT EMPOWERING COUNTY COURTS TO PROBATE WILLS, NOVEMBER 1645

> Hening, ed., *Statutes at Large,* I, 302–303.

WHEREAS the estates of the deceased persons in this collony have been much wronged by the great charge and expences which have been brought in by the administrators thereof by pretence of their attendance at James Cittye and the distance of their habitations from thence, *For remedy whereof*, and because the abuses may be better knowne and prevented in the place where the decedent dwelt and the estates belonging to orphans and absent men may be better conserved, *Be it enacted*, That all administrations shall be granted at the county courts where such person or persons did reside or inhabitt, And all probats of wills there made and the wills recorded together with the appraisments, inventories and accounts belonging to the same there examined and allowed, And accordinglie as the comissioners of the said county courts shall see cause, to give certificate to the secretaries-office at James Citty for a quietus est [i.e., "he is quit," a writ indicating that an executor has satisfied all claims against an estate] to be given to the administrators of course, and likewise that all such administrations being granted and made there, be sent up to the said office to be exemplified under the seale of the collony.

C. AN ACT AUTHORIZING COUNTY COURTS TO TRY ALL CASES AT
COMMON LAW AND IN EQUITY, NOVEMBER 1645

Hening, ed., *Statutes at Large,* I, 303–304.

WHEREAS the great distance of many parts of this collony from James Citty
hath occasioned much trouble and charge to the inhabitants by their frequent
repair thither for the dispatch of their busines in suits of law, *it is thought fit
and accordinglie enacted,* that all causes of what value soever between party
and party shall be tryed in the countie courts by verdict of a jurie if either
party shall desire it, which jurors shall be chosen of the most able men of the
county who shall of course be empannelled by the sherriff for that purpose: but
if the defendant before the hearing of the cause shall desire releife in equity,
and to be heard in way of chancery, then the proceedings by the way of jury
at common law shall be stayed until the other party have answered the particulars of his petition upon oath and the cause heard accordingly: Upon
which hearing, The comissioners shall either proceed to make a final end, or
decree in the said cause, or else finding noe such cause of releife in equitie
as was pretended, then to remit the cause back againe to be tryed by a jury as
aforesaid: And the jurors to be kept from food and releife till they have
agreed upon their verdict according to the custome practised in England, Also
it shall be lawfull for any person or persons haveing cause of equity to take
out sumons under the hand of one of the comissioners of the quorum in way of
subpoena to be entred in the Clerkes booke, commanding the appearance of
any person or persons to answer the complaint of the plaintiff who shall ex-
hibitt his petition, to which the defendant shall be bound to answer upon oath
as aforesaid, And the court is hereby authorized to appoint such times and
orders as they shall think fitt For the hearing of all the aforesaid chancery
causes, Be it alsoe enacted, That the clerkes of the courts shall from time to
time keep records of the proceedings of all actions and causes aforesaid, and
noe depositions shall be taken but in court, or before two of the comissioners
the plaintiff and defendant being present or some appointed by the said plaintiff and defendant.

D. AN ACT ESTABLISHING COUNTY COURTS AND THEIR JUSTICES,
MARCH 1661/62

Hening, ed., *Statutes at Large,* II, 69–71.

BEE *it also enacted* that for the more due administration of justice in the
several counties, and the greater ease of the people in obtaining the same the
courts be continued in each county as of long time hath been accustomed,
and that the said courts doe consist of eight of the most able, honest and judicious persons of the county, which eight or any foure of them; whereof one to be
always of the *quorum* are to bee impowred by commission from the governor
for the time being to act according to the laws of England, and of this country
and to impower them severally and out of court to act, and doe all such things
as by the laws of England are to be done by justices of the peace there, *And be
it enacted* that those persons soe comissionated take the oaths of allegiance

and supremacy, and the oath of a justice of peace, that they be called justices of the peace that the courts be stiled county courts, and further, that the said justices doe keep the said courts precisely upon the dayes appointed, by this, and former acts of assembly (vizt.)

Henrico, the 1st. day	Northampton, the 28th. day
Charles Citty, the 3d. day	New-Kent, the 28th day
James Citty, the 6th. day	Gloucester, the 16th day
Isle of Wight, the 9th. day	Lancaster
Nansemum, the 12th. day	Rappahannock
Lower Norfolk, the 15th day	Surry
Elizabeth Citty, the 18th. day	Northumberland
Warwick County, the 21st. day	Westmerland
Yorke County the 24th day	

And all adjournments, by all meanes possibly be avoyded and that all the justices of the said courts respectively shall duly attend the same, and shall not depart or absent themseves from thence without the licence and consent of the rest of the justices there present, and if any of them shall happen to have a lawful cause of absence, it is thought fitt that in such cases they shall upon the first day of the court signify the same to the court by writing and that they make good proof of the truth thereof at the next ensuing court or else being delinquent in the premisses every justice soe offending shall forfeit for every time of his absence three hundred pounds tobacco, to be imposed by the court and disposed off to the good of the county.

E. AN ACT AUTHORIZING COUNTY COURTS TO ENACT LOCAL BYLAWS, MARCH 1661/62

Hening, ed., *Statutes at Large*, II, 171–172.

WHEREAS oftentimes some small inconveniencies happen in the respective counties and parishes which cannot well be concluded in a general law, *Bee it therefore enacted,* that the respective counties and the severall parishes in those counties shall have liberty to make lawes for themselves, and those that are soe constituted by the major part of the said counties or parishes to be binding upon them as fully as any other act.

The County Court as a Place of Record

4. A Land Deed Recorded, 1638

Isle of Wight County Deeds and Wills, Book A, 1636–1767, 66.

TO ALL TO WHOM these presents shall come I Sir John Harvey Knight Governor and Captain General of Virginia *etc.* NOW KNOW YEE that I the said

Sir John Harvey Knight do with the consent of the Council of State according-
ingly give and grant unto Peter Knight Merchant TWO hundred acres of
Land scituate lying and being in the County of the Isle of Wight bounding
upon the main Creek S.E. easterly and South West or Westerly into the Woods
butting upon the Land of Lt. John Upton Southerly and upon the Plantation
called by the name of the Batchelors Plantation Northerly the said Two Hundred acres of Land being due unto him the said Peter Knight by assignment
and Exchange by and with the said Lt. Upton to and with Mr. Thomas Hill
for Two Hundred acres in any other place ungranted And by the said Thomas
Hill. Conveyed Bargained and Sold to Mr. Peter Knight Merchant for a valuable Consideration TO HAVE AND TO HOLD the said two hundred acres of
Land etc. ut in allis [i.e., as in other cases]: GIVEN at James City under my
Hand and Sealed with the Seal of the Colony this 13th of March 1638
Richard Kemp   Secretary   John Harvey

5. A Deed of Sale, 1664

Old Rappahannock County Deeds and Wills, 1665–1677, 1.

I WILLIAM WEST do by these presents assigne over unto William Gibson
for a valluable consideration received in hand all my right Interest and title
of a third part of Land which I West bought of Francis Triplet and do by
these presents sell and set over from me and my heires unto William Gibson
his heirs or assignes for ever as witness my hand December the 3rd 1664
Signed and Sealed in presence of us   William West seal
Enoch Doughty
James T. Gullock
his mark

6. A Will Recorded and Probated, 1680

Lancaster County Wills and Inventories, 1674–1689, fols.
73–74.

In the name of God Amen I Jonathan Bates being very Sicke and infirme in
body but of sound and perfecte memory doe make this my last will and testament as followeth
1st. I will and bequeath my body to the earth to be decently buried and soule
to God that gave it mee trusting in his mercy through Jesus Christ for eternall
salvation
2nd. I will and desire that my mare and Colte which are [word illegible] and
made over to mr. Benjamin Dogget for performance of Covenant betweene
him and mee bee apprized by John England and Thomas Heydon and mr.
Benjamin Dogget to have the refusall of them being soe apprized and if
hee thinke fitt they should bee soulde to any other person then that, hee should
bee first, provide[d] what [i.e., that] my Cropp of Corne and tobacco fall
short of payeing him the Covenant I made with him and alsoe foure hundred
pounds of tobacco for finishing the Crop and alsoe my Severall Charges and

if there bee any tobacco left to pay it to my Creditors proportionably to their debts

3rdly. I doe hereby constitute and appointe mr. Benjamin Dogget my sole Executor of this my last will and testament and Witness my hand and Seale this fifteene day of October in the year of Lord God Sixteene hundred and eighty

Jonathan Bate   the seale

[probated in Lancaster County Court, December 8, 1680]

Teste John Stretchly   Clerk of Court

Signed Sealed and delivered in the presence of
Robert Webb
Henry Bell

7. *Mary Allen's Power of Attorney, 1665*

Old Rappahannock County Deeds and Wills, 1665–1677, 58.

KNOW ALL MEN by these presents that I Mary Allen do by virtue hereof Constitute make and ordaine John Speed my Lawfull Attorney to acknowledge my dower of one hundred and ten acres of Land unto James Coghill from me my heirs unto him and his heirs for ever In witness I have hereunto set my hand and seal February 5th 1665

Mary Allen seal

Peter Cornewell
Richard Manford

8. *Cattle Registry, 1665*

Northampton County Deed Book, 1651–1654, fol. 227.

Lt. Col. [William] Kendalls marke of Cattle, Cropt on both Eares, slitt on the Left Eares and some of them branded on the horne and Buttock with WK.

9. *A Coroner's Inquest, 1647*

Lower Norfolk County Order Book, 1646–1651, fol. 41.

June 12th 1647

Wee whose names are hereunder written being impanelled and sworne as a Coroners Inquest to viewe the body of perrigrine Bland whoe departed this lyfe the eleaventh of this Instant June, have according to our Charge duely viewed the Corps and the place where it was found dead, and made diligent inquiry concerning all Circumstances and passages, which passed immediately before his death as well upon oath as otherwyse doe declare and testify to the best of our knowledg and Judgments, That neyther any act of his owne nor anything done to him the said Mr. Peregrine Bland by any other, hath beene the cause or occasion of his soe strange and sodayne [i.e., sudden] death; but rather doe conceive that he dyed a Naturall death, having finished the Course which God had appoynted him in this lyfe, And that he was not sensible of death when it came upon him, but determined his lyfe in his Sleepe, And wee are the rather induced to this opinion because that as he was seene Sleepinge soe he was found dead with his eyes and mouth closed, and his armes and other partes of his body lying after the same manner as they were when he was Sleeping. And in testimony that wee have herein delivered our verdict fully and freely to the best of our abilityes, we have hereunto sett our hands the day and yeare first above written. [names of jurors omitted]

The County Courts' Administrative Duties

10. *County Court Procedure, 1675*

Lancaster County Order Book, 1666–1680, 208.

Ordered by this Court that the rules and orders hereafter herein mentioned and prescribed Bee duely observed of all manner of persons whose occasions shall now, or att any tyme hereafter require their attendance at this Court upon penaltie herein mentioned and the further displeasure of this Court.
1. That noe person presume to move the Court for any thing, but by petition.
2. That noe person presume to smoake tobacco or to bee topered [i.e., drunk] in the Face of this Court upon the penaltie of lyeing in the Stocks one houre or payeing 100 lbs. of tobacco to bee disposed off by the further order of this Court.
3. That no person presume to speake to any business in Court, wherein hee is not onely called, and concerned, or permitted by the Court.
4. That noe petition bee presented to this Court but in a faire legible hand, otherwise the petition to be evicted. Ordered that these rules and orders be published and affixed in a conspicuous place for the view of all persons that now pretend ignorance.

11. *Justices Fined for Failing to Attend Their Court, 1663/64*

Northumberland County Order Book, 1652–1665, fol. 189.

Whereas mr Peter Knight Capt. John Rogers Capt. William Nutt and mr. Francis Clay Justices of the peace for this County have failed in giveing their attendance at this Court It is therefore ordered that they the said Justices shall pay each of them three hundred pounds of Tobacco fine according to act of assembly and by the Sherriffe forthwith to be levyed and disposed of according to the said act.

12. *The Regulation of a Public House, 1667*

York County Order Book, 1665–1672 (transcript), 201.

Robert Weekes is Suspended from keeping ordinary and retailing any Liquors untill hee hath given bond and security to sell according to the rates prescribed by Act of Assembly.

13. *The Care of the Indigent and the Infirm*

A. POOR RELIEF, 1659

Lower Norfolk County Order Book, 1656–1666, 236.

Whereas the Court are informed of the sad Condition of frances Porter Widow of Henry porter late deceased being very poore and Left with two smal young Children, and having nothing to releeve herselfe nor them, neither for the back nor belly, the Court have requested Mr. John Martin to furnish the said distressed Widdow With Corne and necessaries to the value of Three hundred and fifty pounds of tobacco and Caske Which the Court doe oblige themselves shalbee Satisfied out of the next yeares Levies.

B. THE CARE OF AN IDIOT, 1661

Surry County Deeds and Wills, 1652–1672, fol. 45.

30 die January 1661.

The Commissioners of Surry County the last Court held at Southwork for the County the 15th Day of this instant January having referred to placing ordering and disposing of John Deane an Iddiott formerly servant unto Mr. William Simmons unto Lt. Col. George Jordan and Mr. Thomas Warren who have accordingly have this day Examined the said Iddiott touching his consent and desire with whom hee is minded and willing to live for this ensuing yeare as also with whom hee might have the best termes in consideration of his labor, Hee hath voluntarily made choyce to live with Robert House and it is likewise found that the said house is willing to give him the best consideration, whereupon hee is placed with the said House for this insuing yeare upon these termes following (vizt.) That the said Robert house shall during the said time carefully looke after and provide for him both in sicknesse and in health meat drinke washing and lodgeing and all other measures needfull and sufficient above the degree of an ordinary or Common Servant to pay his levyes and all other charges and to pay unto whom the said court shall shall [*sic*] appoint and order, at the next crop three hundred and fifty pounds of Tobacco and caske to bee imployed according to their direction for the said John his best use and benefitt, that the said John shall bee free the first day of January next; and that the said house shall then present him to the next Court as well and justly cloathed as hee receives him, that hee shall not assign or sell him to any person during the said time, that hee shall use him well during the said time and take care and charge of his cattle for the time hee shall live with him as for his owne and returne them and their increase when hee shall bee free at the time aforesaid

Dated the day and yeare above written

Recorded the 4th March

1664 Teste Robert Stanton

C. TAX RELIEF FOR AN AGED CITIZEN, 1660

York County Order Book, 1657–1662 (transcript), 204.

John Bates of Middletown parish in this County an auncient Inhabitant of this Collony being Sixty two yeares of Age and thereby disabled to worke as formerly is discharged from the Countrey and County Leavyes by this Court for the future

14. *County Defense, 1674*

Lower Norfolk County Deeds and Wills, E (Orders), fol. 104.

Whereas by act of assembly made at James Citty the 20th day of october Last It was Enacted that there should bee a fort Erected in Elizabeth River att the Charge of the County provided that the Inhabitants did Condescend thereunto, and this day They being all sumoned togeather to that purpose and haveing unanimously voted for the Same and Referred the Choice of place, modell, and meanes to Erect the Same to the Justices of This County, It is therefore by them ordered that It bee built upon foure fording point, being a point of Land belonging to the orphants of Nicholas Wise deceased, that the modell bee in [the] forme of a halfe moone, and for the avoiding of the great Charge that may accrew yearely If tobacco were to bee levied for defraying the Charge of the whole work: It is ordered that Each tythable in this County shall work two days upon the same or hier persons in their Roome to performe the said two days work, and that Each man doe find himself dyett and such tools as hee shall bee appointed to bring; by the severall officers that Shall Sumons them to the said work, and also further order that Mr. George fouler and Mr. Malachy thruston [two of the J.P.'s] bee Requested to agree with patrick Twige for the overseeing the Workmen att as Reasonable Tearmes as may bee, [he] to bee paid in tobacco the next Croop, which agreement by them soe made, tobacco shall bee Raysed for the Same in the next County Levy, and that Col. Lemuel Mason [the senior J.P.] Issue forth his warrants from time to time to the Constables of James Creek for the warning [of] soe many men for Each day as Col. Mason shall think fitt, untill the whole precincts of James Creek have accomplished the 2 days work, and then Major francis Sayer [another J.P.] to doe the like for the Southerne Branch precincts; then Capt. John Hatton [another J.P.] for the Westerne Branch precincts; then Mr. John Porter, Sr. [another J.P.] for the Eastern branch precincts; then Mr. George fouler for the little Creek precincts; then Capt. Robert Bray [another J.P.] for the Eastern

Shore precincts and then Mr. Adam Keeling [another J.P.] for the westerne
Shore precincts; and It is also further ordered that what person soever haveing
notice given him as aforesaid of the time hee Ought to performe the said
Work, that Shall peremtorily Refuse or neglect to Come and perform the same
by himselfe or another in his Roome Shall forfeit and pay the sume of twenty
five pounds of tobacco Each day for the use of the said fort, which said sume
of 25 lbs. of tobacco Shall bee levied by the sherif by distrainte as in Case
of other publique dues or Levyes.

15. Tax Collection, 1672

Lancaster County Order Book, 1666–1680, 243–244.

The County of Lancaster being indebted in the [amount and?] quantity of
23287 lbs. of tobacco have ordered that a Levye of 50 lbs. of tobacco per poll
be raised upon the severall persons hereafter mentioned by the Sheriffe of
this County and by hym paid to the severall persons hereafter mentioned according to orders hereafter exprest (vizt.)

To the order of Assembly		11284
To Samuell Jewell	200	
To Capt. [David] Fox	100	
To Henery Clarke	500	
To Joseph Ball	500	
To William Pritchard	500	
To Samuell Jewell	500	
To Sir Henry Chicheley	7500	
To Mr. [Henry] Randolph	318	
To Sallory	1025	
	11284	

To the County Ordered   12003
(vizt.)

To Col. William Ball for Burgesses Charges for	
24 dayes	3600
To Cask	360
To Mr. [Thomas] Haynes for ditto	3600
To Cask	360
To Col. Ball for Ferry	1200
To Cask	120
To Dominic Theriott for Candles	100
To Cask	010
To Col. Ball for attending the General Court	800
To Cask	080
To Mr. Randolph for Acts and Orders	320
To Cask	032
	10582

To Joseph Whittaker for wolves head		200
To Cask		020
To the Courts Comission		100
To Cask		010

	330
	10582
	10912
To Salary	1091
	12003

Tithables	466	To publiq	11284
Levye	50	In toto	23287

	000
	2330
	23300
rests	13
	23287

The Problems of Law and Order

16. Civil Justice

A. A DEBT SUIT, 1655/56

Charles City County Order Book, 1655–1665, fol. 1.

Whereas Henry Hawkins is indebted by bill to John Burton 600 lb tobbacco and cask payable att Powells Creeke: Itt is therefore ordered that the said Hawkins shall make payment thereof with costs, als[o] execution.

B. A CHARACTER DEFAMATION, 1634

Northampton County Order Book, 1632–1640, fol. 34.

At this Court Edward Drew preferred a petition against Joane Butler for calinge of his wife common Cunted hoare and upon due examination, and the Deposition of John Halloway and William Basely who affirmeath the same one oath to be true that the syd Joane Butler used those words. Upon due examination it is thought fit by this board that the syd Joane Butler shalbe drawn over the Kings Creeke at the starne of a boate or kanew from on[e] kow pen to the other, or else the next Sabath day in the tyme of devyne servis betwext the first and secound lesson present her selfe befor the minister and say after him as followeth, I Joane Butler doe acknowledge to have called Marie Drew hoare, and thereby I confesse I have done her manefest wronge, wherefor

I desire befor this congregation, that the syd Marie Drew, will forgive me, and alsoe that this congregation, will joyne, and praye with me, that God may for give me.

C. FIGHTING IN THE COURTHOUSE YARD, 1684

Lower Norfolk County Order Book, 1675–1686, 230.

Whereas Capt. John Gibbs and Henry Gibbs his brother some time before the setting of this Court and afterwards the Court being sett did in the Court house yard draw their Swords in a quarrell between them and others whereby much mischiefe might have Insued had It nott been prevented by the standers by, and then Capt. John Gibbs being thereupon seazed by the Sheriff drew a pistoll out of his pockett, It is thereupon ordered that the Sheriff take the said Capt. John Gibbs and henry his brother and them disarme and In safe prison to deteyne until they Enter Into bond with good security for their future good behaviour.

D. A JUSTICE SLANDERED, 1637

Lower Norfolk County Order Book, 1637–1646 (transcript), 1–2.

The deposition of Gilbert Guy, age 28 years or thereabouts Sworn and Examined, Sayeth That being at the house of William Fowler, discoursing with him concerning certain cask found by the Servant of Capt. Adam Thorougood [one of the justices of the peace] by the Seaside, but afterwards being seized and fetched away by the aforesaid William Fowler, the aforesaid deponent told him it would vex him to have the said casks taken away from him, Thereupon the wife of the said William Fowler asked who would take them from him? The said deponent answered Capt. Thorougood, upon which she the said Anne Fowler answered "Let Capt. Thorougood Kiss my arse."

William Tanner, age 36 years or thereabouts, Sworn and examined sayeth; That being in company with Gilbert Guy at the house of William Fowler, he the said deponent heard Gilbert Guy tell William Fowler that it would vex him to have the casks which he had fetch'd home taken from him Whereupon the wife of the said Fowler asked who would take them from him? The said Gilbert answered, Capt. Thorougood, upon which she, the said Anne Fowler[,] answered "Let Capt. Thorougood Kiss my arse."

Whereas it doth appear to this court by the oaths of several witnesses that Anne Fowler the wife of William Fowler of Linhaven, planter, did, in a shameful uncomely and irreverent manner, bid Capt. Adam Thorougood Kiss her arse, with the assignation of many unusual terms, It is therefore ordered that the said Anne Fowler shall, for hir offense, receive twenty Stripes upon the bare shoulders and ask forgiveness of the said Capt. Thorougood here now in Court and also the ensuing Sunday at Linhaven.

E. A CHANCERY SUIT, 1685

Middlesex County Order Book, 1680–1694, 216–217.

Mr. Thomas Stapleton haveing Brought an Action of the Case to this Courte against Sarah Williamson and declareing *etc.*, And the Fact being referred to

Mr. Richard Willis, Mr. John Nicholls, David Barwick, Augustine Scarboro, Thomas Radley, Alexander Murray Who say upon their oathes that they find for the Plaintiff and Damages One hundred pounds of Tobaccoe It is therefor Ordered That the Said Sarah Williamson doe forthwith deliver to the Said Thomas Stapleton the horse Demanded by his said Declaration, and pay him the Said Sume of One hundred pounds of Tobaccoe and Costs Upon the Petition of Sarah Williamson an Injunction in Chancery is Granted her to Stopp the Proceedings of the foregoeing Judgement to the end She may be heard in Equity upon all the matter in the Said Judgement Conteyned at the next Courte held for this County And Mr. Augustine Cant and Mr. Phillip May became Security that the above named Sarah Williamson shall pay and Satisfie to the Said Thomas Stapleton as Such Damages as Shalbe awarded against her by reason of the Said Injunction and Stopping the Said Proceedings.

F. A VIOLATION OF THE NAVIGATION ACTS, 1685

Westmoreland County Order Book, 1675–1689, 374–377.

Whereas the Ship Endeavour of Weymouth in England Richard White Master was seized by Capt. Thomas Allen Commander of his majesties Ketch The Quaker For that the said Master and his merchant Mr. Phillip Lynes or one of them having contrary to the severall Acts of parliament loaden and shipped Tobacco of the groweth of the province of Maryland in and upon the said Shipp (vizt.) Thirteen hogsheads without Cocquett [i.e., cocket, a document certifying that customs duties have been paid on a ship's cargo] and in defraud of his Majesties Customes and the said phillip Lynes by notice given him from the said Nicholas Spencer Esq. his majesties Collector for potomack district in Virginia appearing to Justifye his good, The said Nicholas Spencer Esq. in behalfe of his majestie prefers to this Court Declaration against the said phillip Lynes thereby setting forth. That the said phillip Lynes in the moneth of July last past secretly conveyed on board the said shipp Endeavour and now riding att Anchor in the port of Yeocomoco whereof the said Richard White then was and still remayneth Master Thirteene Hoggsheads of Leafe Tobacco contayning by estimation Five Thousand Two hundred pounds of Tobacco and the same secretly and privately exported out and from the province of Maryland and transported the same partly beyond the seas without paying the Customes thereon due and payable unto the Kings Majestie in despight of and contrary to an Act of parliament in that case made and provided wherefore on the behalfe of his majestie the said Nicholas Spencer Esq. demanded Judgment of the Court against the said phillip Lynes for the sume of Fower hundred Thirty and seaven pounds, six shillings and Eight pence sterling money being the Forfeiture imposed for the breach of the said Act of parliament. To which Declaration the said phillip Lynes appeared and prayed respite and time to put in his plea in writing which being granted for some hours, Hee the said Lynes came and delivered theis pleas following, desiring they might be recorded (vizt.) First hee pleads That the Fact layd forth in the Declaration to be committed in Maryland, hee humbly conceived this Court had noe Jurisdiction of for that there is a particular officer of his majestie to examine and inquire into all offenses of such nature there committed as he is ready to make appeare. also that he cannot legally here bee presented for any offense committed in Maryland Itt being a distinct Jurisdiction and Government of ittselfe and seeing the Fact according to the Declaration is sett forth and layd to bee done and committed in Maryland hee ought there to have his Tryall and prosecution. Secondly If the Courts in Virginia without a speciall Command from his Majestie according to the Charter and my Lord [Francis] Howards [the baron of Effingham, the governor of Virginia] Commission and the several Commissions from him distributed to the several County Courts have not power by vertue of theire said Commissions Itt being a speciall cause and consequently requireth a special Commission and belongs properly and perticuliarlye to the Court of Admiraltye and ought there to bee determined or att least to his Majesties Court of Exchequer (in which it ought to have its determination). Therefore hee humbly conceives That without speciall Command from my Lord Howard This Court hath noe Jurisdiction of his Cause both which hee prays his Counsell may Argue. Thirdly admitting that the Court had Jurisdiction and that it had a legall constitution and Authoritie yett hee humbly conceives hee is not legally summoned and brought to his Tryall For by the Law of England All persons whatsoever that are prosecuted either Criminally Cappitally or Civilly have had due processe first proceeded against them as all that are arrested criminally or capitally are first committed being first sett forth in the Warrant or other order for the committment, and in all Civill Causes by a lawfull writt duely taken out and legally executed neither of which course was observèd to this defendant. Wherefore hee craves the benefitt of Magna Charta, Cha. 29th wherein are theis expresse words nullus liber homo capitur aut imprisone tuo aut alignio modo distraitur et nisi per legem Terra [no man may be imprisoned or his property distrained without due process of law] and now contrary to this law we are destroyed without either Committment or lawfull process and consequently contrary to the Law of the Land. Fourthly admitting there was a lawfull process yett the Declaration is soe generall and uncertaine that the defendant knows not how to Answeare to the same and by the Law of England for want of certainty in the Declaration the suite ought to abate Coke 9 fol. 48 [i.e., a reference to the *Reports* of Sir Edward Coke] where for the uncertaintye of a Declaration the Suite by Judgment of the Court was abated, now in this breach of an Act of parliament is sett forth, but noe particular Act mentioned or specified whereby he may be enabled to plead to the same and by my Lord Cooke [i.e., Coke] 3 fol. 37 where there is a generall mention of the breach of an Act of parliament and not the particular Statute mentioned for that uncertainty the suite abated. To the first of which pleas being to the Jurisdiction of the Court The Counsell for the King replyed That the Action is transitory and not locall nor tyed by the Law to any one particular place or Jurisdiction, but that all his majesties Courts have an originall Jurisdiction in themselves to heare and adjudge pleas of this nature upon the breach of penall statutes for defrauding of his majesties Customes. Upon which the Court overruled the plea as to theire Jurisdiction. To the second the Kings Councell argued in the further Vindication of the Jurisdiction of the Court that this way of proceeding secundum Legem Terra [i.e., "according to the law"], the fact being layd down to have been committed infra Corpus Comitatus et non super altum Mare [i.e., "within the bounds of a county and not on the high seas"] and consequently not properly to be Tryed by the Court of Admiraltye but by Twelve men according to the Laws of the Land which aforesaid plea The Court over-ruled And adjudged theire owne Jurisdiction to bee good against all the Assertions of the defendant. To the Third the Kings Councell Argued That the defendants exception against the processe was not good, for that the defendant had such notice as was possible to be given him hee being in Maryland and likewise argued That the way of proceedinge upon penall Statutes is by Bill plaint or information. The last which is fully exhibited against the defendant, who appeared and had lyberty given him by the Court to consider of the same To which he made the aforesaid plea. And therefore the Kings Councell demanded the Judgment of the Court as to the validity of the proceedings which the Court adjudged legal and regular. To the Fourth The Kings Councell argues that [the Declaration?] was soe certaine and full as the Law required in Cases of this nature and that there needed noe other or further certaintye to make good in Law the said Declaration then what was there conteyned and demanded the Judgment of the Court concerning the same. And the Court did adjudge the said Declaration good sufficient and overruled the defendant. Whereupon the Kings Counsell demanded Judgment for the King against the defendant unless he pleaded over, And the defendant pleaded not guilty. Upon which Issue being Joyned An able Jury was Empanelled and sworne whose names are as followeth [names omitted] Who find specially (vizt.) That itt appears to us by the Bill of Lading Invoice and other papers delivered to us That there was Thirteen hoggsheads of Tobacco more exported by the defendant than what was indicted or expressed in the said Cocquett and doe humbly crave the Judgment of the Court whether the aforesaid writings are sufficient Evidence in Law. And upon theire oathes say That if the Court shall adjudge the said papers and writings to be sufficient Evidence in Law: They find for the King But if the Court shall adjudge the said papers and writings noe sufficient Evidence in Law they find for the defendant. Whereupon the Court nemine contradicent [i.e., "without dissent"] did Adjudge the said papers and writings to be good and sufficient Evidence in Law. And the Jury withdrawing by order of the Court to find the neate Quantity of the said Thirteene Hoggsheads of Tobacco, Returne and upon theire oathes say that the said Thirteene Hoggsheads of Tobacco conteyned Three Thousand Eight Hundred and Nynteen pounds which comes to Six Hundred Thirty and Six pounds eight pence sterling money according to the Acts of Parliament in that case made and provided. But in regard that the Collector had declared for noe more than Fower hundred Thirty seaven pounds six shillings and eight pence sterling money The Court order Adjudge and Condemne the defendant phillip Lynes in the said sume of Fower hundred Thirty and seaven pounds six shillings and eight pence with costs and charges of suite als[o] Execution.

17. Criminal Justice

A. LOWER NORFOLK JUSTICES ASSIST IN CAPTURING A ROBBER, 1685

Lower Norfolk County Order Book, 1675–1686, 281.

Whereas by vertu of a hue and Cry from one of the Chiefe magistrates of North Carolina In persuite of one Smith, that was formerly aprehended with

Roger Michell and his Complices that Robed the house of Nicholas Smith in Pagan Creek, one John Smith was this day aprehended and brought before this Court upon suspition of being the same person, and It apearing to this Court In all Likelyhood that the said Smith Is the same man mentioned in that hue and Cry, It is ordered that the Sheriff take the said Smith into his Custody, and him forthwith to convey Into the Isle of Wight County where the fact was Comitted, and after also all papers now taken Convey him beefore the Honorable Col. Joseph Bridger Esq. [a member of the Council] to be further dealt with as his honor shall think fitt.

B. A SUSPECTED FELON IS BOUND OVER TO THE GENERAL COURT, 1658

Charles City County Order Book, 1655–1665, 157.

The Court hath ordered that Thomas Hux Barbara Huxe Nicholas Marcellis Bridgett Willyard Ann Townshend and Jane Bayley shall personally appeare at James Citty the 2 day of this present Quarter [General] Court before the Governor and Councell then and there to give evidence, viva voce, on the behalfe of his Highnesse the Lord Protector against Thomas Till a person then and there to be tryed for the suspison of fellony and in case of any of their failing to forfeit and pay to his Highnesse the Lord protector each of them 2000 lbs. of good merchantable tobacco and caske als[o] execution.

The Court finding by the evidences against Thomas Till that the suspison and occasion against him are high and criminall doth therefore order and require the sheriff of this County to convey and deliver the said Till, a person, according to act, to receive his tryall before the Honorable Governor and Council this present Quarter Court.

C. GRAND JURY PRESENTMENTS, 1684

Henrico County Deed Book, 1677–1692, 336.

To the Right Worshipful Justices for the Court of Henrico Abraham Womeck humbly presents the misdemeanors of these men underwritten

Thomas Wells and his wife the 5th and 6th day of June to Swearing and Cursing in a horible nature and at severall other times that I can't remember the days of the monethe.

Major Thomas Chamberlain on the same time to Swearing and Cursing.

Mr. James Brain by his own confession Drunk.

Mr. Peter Roland at the same time dr[u]nk.

and Edward Stratton Jr. at the same time.

Thomas Wells having an English wench brought to bed with a Bastard.

Recordat per Henry Randolph Clark Curia

To the Right Worshipful Court of Henrico County

Edward Stratton Jr. humbly sheweth as being on[e] of the Grand-jury of inquest.

Thomas Wells for swearing severall wicked Oaths.

Mihill Turpin for being drunk by his own Confession.

Thomas Lockett for being drunk by his own confession.

Will Puckett for being drunk by his own confession.
Abraham Womeck for being drunk by his own confession.
Nicholas Dison for being drunk by his own confession.
Mihill Turpin for fighting.
Henry Hatcher for being drunk.
Richard Ligon for Fighting.
Thomas Bagly informs against Richard Ligon for Striking him severall blowes

Recordat per Henry Randolph Clark Curia

D. PETTY THEFT, 1650

Northumberland County Order Book, 1650–1652, fol. 43.

Whereas it appeareth to this court that Phillipe Bagley did unlawfully carry away certaine goodes belonginge to William Hardich vizt. six yards of tradinge Cloath one gunn twenty five arm lengths and five [*sic*] of Rohannocke [i.e., roanoke, an inferior kind of wampum made from oyster shells] pretendinge that he [purchased?] the said goods of Thomas Waggatt as also it appeareth that the said Bagley hath no place of Residence but liveth an unlawfull Course of life about the Cuntry It is therefore ordered that the said William Hardich shall receave his gunn and tradinge cloath of the Sheriffe in whose hands they remaine and that the said Bagley shall remaine in the Sheriffes hands till he hath paid the twenty five Armes Lengthes of Rohannocke with Court Charges And for the said Bagley his abuse herein he is ordered by this Court to receave fifteen Strips upon the bare shoulders And so depart the County.

E. PETTY FRAUD, 1656

Charles City County Order Book, 1655–1665, 45.

Itt is ordered by the Court that execution be issued out against the estate of Michaell Fletcher for the value of 1818 lb. of tobacco and cask and all charges at the suite of Capt. Henry Perry esq. And Whereas it appeareth to the Court that the said Fletcher hath deceitfully and fraudulently taken tobacco out of severall caskes received and in the roome thereof putt in bad tobacco, tobacco stalkes and dirt, Itt is ordered that the said Fletcher shall forthwith be Comitted to the sherrifs custody and there remaine till such time that he stand at the Court doore for one hour with a paper in his hatt written in Capitall letters these words Be hold and beware by my example how yee cheate and abuse tobacco already received and that he stand one whole yeare bound to his good behaviour, and give security for the performance.

F. AN ASSAULT, 1639

Lower Norfolk County Order Book, 1637–1646 (transcript), 30–31.

Whereas Cole Garison, Mariner, hath without any occasion or cause, wounded Robert Clayton, Mariner, after a Most desperate and dangerous manner, as by sufficient proof appeareth, It is therefore ordered that the aforesaid Garrison shall forthwith put in Sufficient security to pay, within ten days after the ship Pelicans arrival in England, ten pounds sterling unto Johnathan Longworth, chirugeon [i.e., surgeon], for the care of the said wound and sixteen pounds sterling unto the said Clayton for his wrongs and damages by him received.

G. PUNISHMENT OF FORNICATION, 1641

> Lower Norfolk County Order Book, 1637–1646 (transcript), 100–101, 120.

Whereas Christopher Burrough and Mary Somes are presented to this Court by the Church wardens of Linhaven Parish for committing of fornication, with absolute testimony of the same, It is therefore ordered that the said Christopher and Mary shall, according to the statute of England, do penance in their parish church the next sabbath the minister preacheth at the said church, standing in the middle alley of the said church upon a stool in a white sheet, and a white wand in their hands, all the time of Divine Service and shall say after the Minister such words as he shall deliver unto them before the Congregation there present and also pay the charges of Court.

Thomas Tooker and Elizabeth Hauntine are to undergo the like penance at their Parish church according to the tenor of this order and so is Savill Gaskine and his wife and to pay the Court charges. . . .

Whereas Elizabeth Tooker [Elizabeth Hauntine] was ordered by a court holden the 12th of April 1641, for the foul crime of fornication committed by her, to do penance in their chapel of ease, situated in Elizabeth River according to the full intent and meaning of the said order, and she, the said Elizabeth, being brought to the said Chapel of Ease to perform the said penance, in which time of performance and exhortation delivered unto her by the minister admonishing hir to be sorry for hir foul crime committed, but she the said Elizabeth not regarding the good admonition of the said minister, nor obeying the tenor of the said order did, like a most obstinate and graceless person, cut and mangle the sheet wherein she did penance, It is Therefore ordered that the said Elizabeth shall receive at present, 20 lashes on the bare back and, on the Sunday come fort night, do penance in the aforesaid Chapel of Ease according to the tenor of the said spiritual laws and forms of the Church of England in that case provided.

H. THE PENALTY FOR ADULTERY, 1642

> Lower Norfolk County Order Book, 1637–1647 (transcript), 180.

Whereas Frances Dyer, the wife of John Dyer, hath committed adultery with Hugh Wood at several times, as appears by divers testimonies and her own confession, It is therefore ordered that the Said Francis Dyer and Hugh Wood shall ask Almighty God forgiveness upon their bare knees in the presence of this court for their said heinous offense against His Divine Majesty committed and that they shall each of them severally receive fifteen lashes upon their bare backs.

I. THE NORTHUMBERLAND COURT STOPS AN ILLICIT AFFAIR, 1665

Northumberland County Order Book, 1652–1665, fol. 420.

Whereas It appeares to this Court that there hath been unlawfull familiarity and meetings between Mr. Charles Ashton and Mrs. Susanna Lyndsay, It is Ordered that Mr. David Lyndsay in behalfe of his wife, and that the said Charles Ashton doe severally give bond with security for their good behaviour, and they have noe further unlawfull conferences, otherwise the sheriff to take them into safe Custody.

Chapter Four

The Structure
of Society

At the end of the seventeenth century a clearly defined social order prevailed in Virginia. But like so much else in the history of the Old Dominion's first century, the shape that order took conformed to no prearranged scheme. Instead the structure merely happened as circumstances forced the colonists to alter their expectations of what a proper society should be.

Because of the manner in which it matured, historians have long argued about the nature of Virginia society, how it developed, and the character of its population. Owing to the frequent uncertainty or paucity of the surviving record, controversy about such questions will always exist. In recent times, however, some scholars have begun a fresh examination of the evidence in an effort to minimize the conflicts and to seek areas of general agreement. The reassessment is still in its infancy, but the results achieved thus far make it possible to limn a sketch of what Virginia's people and society were like by 1700.

Except for a few thousand Africans and an even smaller contingent of continental Europeans, Virginia was colonized by Englishmen. So obvious is that fact that its significance is easily ignored. It meant that Virginia's law, language, and customs would be English in origin, and all non-English immigrants would forever be compelled to cast off their own ways and take on those of transplanted Englishmen.

Unlike some of the other English colonies planted in America before 1700, Virginia experienced slow population growth during its first decades of existence. Upwards of six thousand Englishmen moved to Virginia between 1607 and 1625, but most of these colonists either failed to survive the rigors of the wilderness or returned home. A census taken in 1624/25 shortly after the crown voided the London Company's charter listed slightly more than twelve hundred inhabitants. Most of the colonists who migrated in the company period, therefore, had relatively less impact upon the development of Virginia than did later arrivals.

Turning Virginia into a royal colony did little at first towards diminishing its deadly reputation. A decade after the dissolution of the London Company, the number of settlers had risen to about five thousand, but the 1630s marked a dramatic turning point in the colony's population growth. Throughout the period that falls roughly between the years 1634 and 1674, there was a great surge of colonists moving to Virginia. By the mid–1670s more than forty thousand immigrants had settled there. Thereafter, for reasons that are not yet altogether clear, the rate of migration slowed down as the century drew to a close.

The population explosion and the attendant growth in the number of counties after 1634 are two of the more striking developments in Virginia's history (see the maps in chapter 3). This rapid growth directly influenced the shape of the colony's political and social institutions. It provided some of the new immigrants with the chance to carve out political and economic domains for themselves and their progeny. And it contributed to the decentralization of authority, the lack of political cohesiveness, and the relative impermanence in social arrangements that were quite characteristic of Virginia throughout most of the seventeenth century.

The majority of the post–1634 immigrants can be described only in general terms. Traditionally Virginians have regarded themselves as descendants of Charles I's gentlemen cavaliers. This interpretation of the origins of Virginia's population enjoyed a long history, even though it has been challenged by the more prosaic explanation that common laborers, undesirables, and felons populated Virginia. To be sure, an assortment of armigerous royalists and rogues could be found huddled in the tween decks of Virginia-bound ships. But the bulk of the immigrants were rather ordinary, middling sorts of Englishmen. Driven by the vexations and troubles of a society in the throes of dynamic change, these restless immigrants left England in search of the promise of a richer life that Virginia seemed to offer.

These new arrivals both created the need for changes in Virginia's institutions and aided in their reshaping. Merely by arriving in the numbers that they did, the immigrants forced a fundamental reordering of the colony's basic political organization. The General Assembly's differentiation of a provincial and local government for Virginia was a direct consequence of the increase in population. Moreover, unlike the first colonists, those who came after 1634 intended to stay and reap whatever bounty the land offered—something that the backers of the London Company had tried and failed to bring about after 1618. The post–1634 immigrants eventually transformed Virginia from a tenuous outpost into a colonial society that bore a resemblance to what they had left behind.

In order to understand what these colonists created, it is necessary to delineate the structure of the society that began to emerge after 1634. To that end one must appreciate the conceptions of social order that the immigrants brought with them from England and the conditions that forced them to modify those notions.

A man's status in seventeenth-century English society rested upon his possessing certain skills that placed him within a recognizable hierarchy of vocations. The basic dichotomy was between those individuals who worked with their hands and those who did not. High status was accorded to those who lived off unearned incomes or who engaged in gentle rather than menial callings. Professions such as business, the law, the church, and the military provided the channels for upward mobility for the skilled, regardless of their origins. Englishmen also acknowledged an inseparable link between social structure and political authority, since the state was scarcely distinguishable from a more general social authority. Because their position as England's natural leaders entailed upon them the responsibility of governing others, the "better sort" of Englishmen demanded and received deference from their social inferiors.

The English immigrant brought these ideas with him to Virginia. But the traditional forms of social cohesion and control functioned badly for lack of a material basis of support. Settlers who were unwilling to work with their hands stood little chance of surviving in the wilderness, where survival depended upon one's ability to wrest a living from the land. That had been evident from the earliest days of the colony, when John Smith complained of the abundance of gentlemen who came with the first boatloads of colonists.

Land, the immemorial badge of social distinction in England, was everywhere in abundance. Primogeniture, the legal device that kept

English lands in the control of relatively few families by requiring the settlement of a father's real property upon his eldest son, never performed its intended role in Virginia. Released from the restraints imposed by law and the constraints of an island kingdom, any Englishman on coming to Virginia conceivably could become a landowner. Thus, while it would be a factor in determining one's status, the mere acquisition of land did not automatically guarantee an immigrant a high position in an emerging Virginia society.

Few Englishmen who engaged in gentle callings ever migrated to the Old Dominion. For the most part, those who did went before 1624, only to die or return to England during the period of the company's rule. After 1634 there were scarcely any gentry or landed aristocrats; nor were there many lawyers, clergymen, doctors, or other professional men. Those colonists who settled in Virginia during the "great migration" were mostly indentured servants or the younger sons of substantial English families with mercantile connections. The latter group of immigrants, motivated partly by ambition and partly by necessity, began to assume a variety of roles that in England would have been undertaken by men belonging to different social groups. Often such a colonist was at once a farmer, a merchant, an attorney, a militia officer, and sometimes a magistrate.

As the century progressed, a hierarchy of vocations developed in Virginia, but a blurring of traditional categories occurred. The fundamental dichotomy in colonial society was between servants and planters. Providing he survived the vagaries of servitude, some movement up the hierarchy was possible for the immigrant servant. Freemen may be ranked in a series of status levels ranging from the small planters to the members of local ruling elites, who wielded an enormous presence in their respective communities. Family connections, luck, influence, and an ability to survive in the Virginia wilds were the keys to advancement. Possession of a major public office was a mark of great achievement.

The servants and slaves who comprised the lower of Virginia's two major social groups lacked any significance in the social order, aside from the fact that they worked as bound laborers. In addition to representing a prodigious economic investment for their employers, servants constituted a sizable portion of the colony's population—perhaps as much as 50 percent at any given point before 1700. Until the last third of the century, slavery's importance as a labor system was trifling, since the number of black slaves was quite small. It seems clear that planters preferred the indentured laborers until the sources of white labor began to dry up.

Indentured servants probably fared no better or worse than the slaves, but their bondage was temporary. Servants came to Virginia, served their time, and earned their freedom. Upon becoming freemen they passed into the planters' ranks.

The planter group is too large and diverse to be dealt with as a single unit. Some planters owned land, voted, paid taxes, and held political office; others did not possess these attributes. This large group is divisible, however, into three subgroups based upon varying degrees of wealth and vocational status: the small planter, the middling planter, and the great planter, or member of the colony's ruling elite.

Arriving at sound generalizations about the small planters is difficult, because they left scant evidence of their existence. Some were immigrants who had just enough money to get to Virginia and sue out a headright in hopes of improving their lot. Others may have been tradesmen and craftsmen seeking to perform their callings in a new environment. Many others—just how many remains to be determined—were former servants. Whether or not servitude conferred land ownership upon them is uncertain. Some indentures provided land as a reward for service, but it is also evident that by the 1670s a sizable class of landless ex-servants was living in the colony. Where it is possible to fix the ownership of real property for them, the small planters' holdings, ranging between perhaps fifty and two hundred acres, are indicative of their social standing. Except for occasional service in minor county posts, few small planters ever held public office. The conclusion to be drawn, then, is that the colonists who may be placed in the small planter subgroup were the least successful of the post–1634 immigrants. How much coming to Virginia bettered their condition is an open question.

Planters in the middle rank, however, seem to have experienced an improvement in their condition. They had come to Virginia at their own expense and were able to pay the passage of a few servants, on whom they patented headrights. Taking up tobacco planting, they acquired as much land as their means allowed. In addition to farming, the middling planters engaged in a variety of commercial activities, ranging from factoring for English, Dutch, or New England merchants to tavern keeping. From their ranks the county courts recruited local officials such as constables, undersheriffs, deputy clerks, churchwardens, grand jurymen, and surveyors of the highways. They also formed the pool from which arose the great planters who governed the colony.

The great planters shared several traits in common. All were large landholders. For example, among the 375 men who may be classified as great planters in the years between 1660 and 1676, the average holding was forty-two hundred acres. In their respective communities they were the chief sources of credit and the men in closest touch with England's financial centers. Their families were closely related by kinship and personal ties. Great planters took their turns as justices of the peace, sheriffs, burgesses, and members of the governor's council. It was they who sought to duplicate the familiar relationship between social position and political authority and thereby to claim the deference due society's natural leaders.

Such claims to dominance did not go unchallenged. In terms of their social origins, the great planters were similar to other settlers who emigrated to Virginia from the 1630s onward. But as the younger sons of well-to-do English families, their connections at home and in the Old Dominion gave them a competitive edge over the others, and they used this advantage to push their way to the top rung of Virginia society. Their claim to leadership did not have the sanction of ancient usage or custom: it was founded upon nothing else than their having outstripped their rivals. Only their ability to remain on top ultimately convinced their beaten competitors that the great planters were there to stay. The length of time required for that acceptance contributed to the social instability that typified Virginia for most of the seventeenth century.

It is not yet possible to measure precisely the distances between these three planter subgroups. An accurate, detailed investigation of landholdings and other wealth remains to be undertaken, and until such studies are forthcoming, the matter is largely conjectural. One may assume that in Virginia the distances between these subgroups were shorter than between their English analogues. It may also be surmised that in the 1630s and 1640s, when the colony's society was relatively undifferentiated, the gap between great planter and small was narrow. But as time passed, and more immigrants settled in Virginia, the uneven rates of success widened the margin considerably.

How much movement through the ranks of Virginia society was possible after 1634 is a question that also awaits additional study. All servants experienced upward mobility upon acquiring their freedom, but how much further they could expect to rise is guesswork. There are examples of men like Abraham Wood, Thomas Ludwell, and the first Adam Thoroughgood rising from servants to the ranks of the governing elite, but these are exceptional cases indeed. Elevation to the middling planter subgroup was about the most a servant might expect to attain. Similarly, the degree of vertical mobility experienced by those colonists who became middling planters is difficult to assess. Some of them went no higher than the level they attained upon their arrival in Virginia, while others clawed their way into the ranks of the great planters. Of course, it was the great planters who enjoyed the most spectacular successes after moving to America.

In brief, then, this rough sketch of colonial society provides an explanation of how after 1634 a social order gradually evolved in Virginia. A more discerning portrait of that evolution must await the conclusion of the studies of the Old Dominion's social structure that are now in progress.

The current examination of Virginia's social history is proceeding along two lines of inquiry. One approach lies in investigating the colony's population with the intention of describing such characteristics as its age and composition, the ratio of males to females, the number and size of households, the amounts of labor employed by individual householders, migration trends, and how these characteristics changed over time. The other approach involves examining the origins and the development of the colony's governing elite. Here the concern is with discovering who the great planters were, what their kin connections were, what their original English residences and vocations had been, when they emigrated to America, what offices they held, when they took office, and what amounts of property they acquired. Both modes of inquiry are based upon similar forms of historical evidence, but each rests upon different methodological foundations. Taken together, they hold the promise of clearing up and removing much of the mystery and error that up to now have surrounded the study of Virginia's social order.

Methodologically, the analysis of Virginia's population must follow the techniques developed by demographers and other social historians that have been so profitably used in the recent New England town studies. Instead of relying upon literary evidence, this type of analysis depends upon court records, tax lists, church registers, censuses, inventories, and wills. To be sure, making such documents yield up their wealth requires considerable ingenuity on the historian's part, but the first obstacle to be faced—and this is especially true of the extant record for seventeenth-century Virginia—is the frequent absence of such data.

Only one comprehensive census of the inhabitants of Virginia was taken in the seventeenth century, the muster of 1624/25 (Document 1). The muster reveals a relatively small population that was predominantly male and lacked the stabilizing influence of the family. It also records what supplies and weapons the colonists possessed. As Irene Hecht has shown, the existence of the muster allows some demographic comparisons with other English colonies (see the Suggested Readings for Hecht's article). But since the document is unique, its value for establishing long-term population trends in Virginia is limited. None of the other known contemporary estimates of population is particularly helpful in that endeavor because they lack the muster's attention to detail (Documents 2 and 3).

Given the absence of censuses of the quality of the muster of 1624/25, another type of demographic data, the tithing list, becomes important. Throughout the court records of Accomack, Lancaster, Northampton, and Surry counties, scattered lists survive for the last half of the century. These lists name the householder and record the number of taxable males, all who were above the age of sixteen, in each household. The Surry and Northampton lists also include the names of all the servants (Document 4).

The information thus provided can be developed into patterns that reflect trends in the evolution of Virginia's social structure. For example, using the names provided in the Surry and Northampton lists, the mobility of servants might be plotted. Also, comparisons of the number of households can be used as a measure of the varying degrees of prosperity in the respective counties. The number of laborers in individual households could serve as an index of wealth. And merely by charting the size of households over time, it becomes possible to offer some observations about their changing character.

As revealing as these and other possibilities may be, the results of such endeavors are limited by the relative scarcity of the tithing lists. When the limitations of the tithing lists have been reached, other sources must be sought. Among the most valuable of these are the land records that were kept by the secretary of the colony.

For most of the seventeenth century, the fifty-acre headright was the basic device for distributing land in Virginia. Introduced by the

London Company in 1617 as an inducement to settlement, its use continued after the company's fall. Any immigrant who paid his passage to America, or that of another, was entitled to claim a headright. After 1634 all he had to do was file a certificate in the county court attesting that he had transported himself. Then the governor issued a patent for the land. One copy was recorded in the secretary of the colony's office for safety and for keeping track of what land had been distributed.

Each patent records the same information: the name of the patentee, the date of the patent, its location, its size, and most often the names of the individuals upon whom the patent was sued (Document 5). What makes these patent records unique among the sources of seventeenth-century Virginia history is their continuity. Despite the fraudulent abuse of the system, which was ultimately abandoned in 1714, the land patents are the only unbroken record of land use in the period. Therein lies their great value to the social historian.

Wesley Frank Craven's recent study, *White, Red, and Black: The Seventeenth-Century Virginian*, is a model example of the kinds of results that may be obtained by a careful analysis of the land patents. Besides providing valuable information about the character and the flow of English and African immigration to Virginia, these records have much to tell about other facets of the colony's social order. For example, they can be used to develop a comprehensive study of landholdings among all the patentees. Or, by focusing upon those patentees who sued out headrights upon Africans, insights into the evolution and use of black labor could be developed. And the patents are quite useful for determining the approximate arrival date of an individual planter, as well as how much land he acquired over a lifetime. It is at this juncture that the patent records become necessary for examining the rise of the great planters.

Tracing the activities of the great planters has, until recently, been the province of genealogists. Indeed, they can be credited with perfecting the methodological tool that the demographer calls "family reconstitution." How a family can be reconstituted may be illustrated by the rise to prominence of the family of Thomas Willoughby.

In 1610, as a young man of seventeen, Thomas Willoughby the immigrant left Rochester in Kent for Virginia (Documents 6 and 7). His age at the time of his migration suggests that he might have been a younger son in search of the advancement that the accident of birth had denied him. But whether or not he was entitled to be called a gentleman, as he was styling himself by the 1620s, is uncertain.

Willoughby's early years in the New World are clouded by a dearth of evidence. He may have done some soldiering prior to his coming, or soon thereafter, for he was listed in the muster of 1624/25 as "Ensigne Thomas Willoby." By the 1620s, though, Willoughby clearly had begun to acquire land and political offices. Although his name does not appear in the land patent records until 1628 (Document 8), he had already sued out patents to three hundred acres of land as early as 1626. And by the time he died, Willoughby had amassed over thirty-six hundred acres of land by patent.

His military experiences probably account for his gradual insinuation into the colony's political life. In 1627 Governor George Yeardley and the Council of State appointed him to the command of a militia force sent to attack hostile Indians (Document 9A). Thereafter Willoughby served as a judge on one of the monthly courts that preceded the county court system and sat in the House of Burgesses (Documents 9B and 9C). After the General Assembly erected the county courts, he became one of the first justices of the peace in Lower Norfolk County following its formation in 1637 (Document 9D). By the 1640s he had been elevated to a seat on the Council of State, a post he apparently occupied until the Interregnum (Document 9E).

In addition to these public duties, Willoughby performed other community services. For his neighbors he was one of the chief creditors in the county. As such, his name regularly appears in court records as a suitor in debt actions (Document 10). Since he also engaged in a wide range of commercial activities and even made frequent trips to London, it may be surmised that he was also a contact for city merchants as well. And on more than one occasion Willoughby was asked by county officials to do such tasks as buy law books for the court or recruit a minister from England (Document 11).

Thomas Willoughby died in England sometime before August 1658 (Document 12). He left two daughters and a son (Document 13), but since he died intestate, there is no record of how his property was distributed among his heirs.

The son, also named Thomas, was born in Virginia in 1632. His father intended that he should be trained in a mercantile calling, for the elder Willoughby sent the boy to the Merchant Taylors' School in London when he was twelve (Document 14). The earliest evidence of Thomas II in the records of Lower Norfolk County occurs in April 1656, when he turned down an appointment to the bench, and a month later when he was fined for refusing jury duty (Documents 15 and 16). His refusal of both responsibilities may have resulted from his royalist sympathies, a supposition that is borne out by his acceptance of a commission as a justice of the peace a year after Sir William Berkeley's restoration as governor in 1660 (Document 17A).

Like his father, Willoughby held several other county posts during his tenure on the Lower Norfolk Court. A colonel in the county's militia, he also served one term as sheriff in 1666 (Document 17B). At the time of the Second Anglo-Dutch War he was one of the commissioners appointed to oversee the construction of a fort on the lower James River (Document 17C). But unlike the elder Willoughby, the son never served in the House of Burgesses or on the Council of State.

Sometime prior to 1659 young Willoughby married Sarah Thompson, daughter of a planter in Northumberland County (Document 18). The union produced a son and a daughter who grew to adulthood (Document 19). By August 1672 Thomas Willoughby II was dead at the age of forty (Document 20).

Not until 1686 is there any notice of Willoughby's son, Thomas III, in the Lower Norfolk County records. In that year he sold part of his patrimony to John Gascott. His name appears again three years later when he disposed of more of his inheritance. Then in 1698 Thomas Willoughby III was named to the county court, where he remained until his death (Document 21).

The influence of the Willoughby family extended beyond the boundaries of Lower Norfolk County. Over the length of the seventeenth century the family established ties with those of other great planters. When Thomas Willoughby II's wife's sister married Peter Presly, Willoughby became related to one of the rising Northern Neck families. It was through Thomas's sister Elizabeth, however, that the Willoughbys became allied with some of the post–1634 immigrants who like Thomas the immigrant also aspired to gentility.

During her lifetime Elizabeth Willoughby wedded three husbands. The first was Simon Overzee, a Dutch merchant who traded widely in the lower James River basin, the counties along the Chesapeake Bay, and Maryland (Document 22A). Overzee died in 1660, and within the year Elizabeth took her second husband, George Colclough (Document 22B). The younger brother of a wealthy, well-placed London grocer, and himself a merchant, Colclough had settled in Northumberland County around 1651. By 1656 he was a magistrate and a burgess for the county. The marriage lasted until Colclough's death in 1662. Thereupon, the widow Colclough married

Isaac Allerton, the son of a Plymouth, Massachusetts, merchant, who also resided in Northumberland (Document 22C). Either just before or soon after they were wed, Allerton was commissioned a justice of the peace. Subsequently he became a member of the House of Burgesses and eventually won a seat on the governor's council.

Three men with high social aspirations were therefore able to help translate their ambitions into reality by strategic marriages into one of the colony's old, established, and politically prominent families. In this respect they contributed to the weaving of the complicated web of kinship that evolved between the great planter families throughout the seventeenth century.

Of course, not all of the progenitors of the great planter families established themselves as early or as quickly as the Willoughbys. What happened to the Willoughby family is fairly typical of only about a third of the familial clans who dominated Virginia society by 1700. The remaining two-thirds could date their progress to gentility only from the 1640s and 1650s. What gave them their start, in part, was the availability of widows, daughters, and sisters in respectable families like that of Thomas Willoughby I.

Because they have left more of a record of their accomplishments, reconstituting great planter families like the Willoughbys is easier than developing demographic trends for the whole of Virginia's population. Both endeavors are necessary, though, since they complement each other by filling in the blank spaces in the story of how Englishmen molded their conceptions of social order to suit new conditions. The work now underway is gradually enabling scholars to understand more about the structure of seventeenth-century Virginia society than ever before.

SUGGESTED READINGS

*Bailyn, Bernard. "Politics and Social Structure in Virginia." In *Seventeenth-Century America: Essays in Colonial History,* ed. James Morton Smith (Chapel Hill, N.C., 1959), 90–115.

Bridenbaugh, Carl. *Vexed and Troubled Englishmen, 1590–1642* (New York, 1968).

*Campbell, Mildred. "Social Origins of Some Early Americans." In *Seventeenth-Century America,* ed. James Morton Smith (Chapel Hill, N.C., 1959), 63–89.

Craven, Wesley Frank. *White, Red, and Black: The Seventeenth-Century Virginian* (Charlottesville, Va., 1971), 1–39.

Hecht, Irene W. D. "The Virginia Muster of 1624/5 as a Source for Demographic History." *William and Mary Quarterly*, 3d Ser., XXX (1973), 65–92.

Jester, Annie Lash, comp. and ed., in collaboration with Martha Woodroof Hiden. *Adventurers of Purse and Person, Virginia, 1607–1625* ([Princeton, N.J.], 1956).

Morgan, Edmund S. "Headrights and Head Counts: A Review Article." *Virginia Magazine of History and Biography*, LXXX (1972), 361–371.

Stone, Lawrence. "Social Mobility in England, 1500–1700." *Past and Present*, XXXIII (1966), 16–55.

Wertenbaker, Thomas J. *The Planters of Colonial Virginia* (Princeton, N.J., 1922).

*Wright, Louis B. *The First Gentlemen of Virginia: Intellectual Qualities of the Early Colonial Ruling Class* (San Marino, Calif., 1940).

Wrigley, E. A., ed. *An Introduction to English Historical Demography, from the Sixteenth to the Nineteenth Century* (London, 1966).

The Character of Virginia's Population

1. An Excerpt from the Census of 1624/25

C.O. 1/3, 169, Public Record Office.

A Muster of the Inhabitance of the Easterne Shore over the Baye

Capt. William Epes his Muster (in the William and Thomas)
Margrett Epes in the George 1621

Servants

Nicholas Raynberd age 22 in the Swan 1624
William Burditt age 25 in the Susan 1615

* Available in paperback.

Thomas Cornish age 25 in the Dutie 1620
Peeter Porter age 19 in the Tiger 1621
John Baker age 20 in the Ann 1623
Edwards Rogers age 26 in the Ann 1623
Thomas Worden age 24 in the Ann 1623
Benjamin Knight age 28 in the Bona Nova 1620
Nicholas Granger age 15 in the George 1618
William Munnes age 25 in the Sampson 1619
Henrie Wilson age 24 in the Sampson 1619
James Blackborn age 20 in the Sampson 1619
Nicholas Summerfield age 15 in the Sampson 1619

Provision

Corne	65 barrells
hoges	2

Armes

powder	120 lbs.
lead	200 lbs.
peeces	5
Armores	6
Coates of steele	6
Coates of Male [*i.e.*, mail]	4
howses	2
forte	1
Stores	1
shallop [*i.e.*, a small open boat]	1

2. *Virginia's Population in 1634*

C.O. 1/8, 155, Public Record Office.

A List of the Nomber of men women and children Inhabitinge in the severall Counties within the Colony of Virginia. Anno Domini *1634*.

Imprimis from Arrowhattocks to Sherley hundred one [i.e., on] both sides the river beinge within the Countie of Henrico } 419

Item from Sherley hundred Iland to Weyanoke one both sides the river beinge within the Countie of Charles Citty } 511

Item from Upper Chippoaks Creeke to Lawnes Creek on the Southward side and from Checkohominey river to Kethes Creeke one the Northward side of the river beinge within the Countie of James Citty } 886

Item from Kethes Creeke and Mulberry Iland to Maries mount one the Northward side of the river, beinge within the Countie of War-rike river   } 811

Item from Lawnes Creeke to Warrosquyoake Creeke on the south-ward side of the river beinge within the County of Warrosquyoake   } 522

Item from Maries mount to Fox hill within the plantations of the Back river and the old pocolson [*i.e.*, Poquoson] river one the Northward side, and from Elizabeth river to Chesepiake river on the southward side of the river beinge within the Countie of Eliza-beth Citty   } 856

Item in the plantations of Kiskyake Yorke and the New Pocolson beinge within the Countie of Charles River   } 510

Item in the plantations on the Easterside of Chesepiake Bay beinge within the Countie of Accawmacke   } 396

The whole nomber is   4914

After this List was brought in there arrived a Ship of Holand with 145. from the Bermudas. And since that, 60. more in an English Shipp which likewise came from the Bermudas.

3. *Sir William Berkeley's Estimate of Virginia's Population, 1670*

> "Enquiries to the Governor of Virginia," 1670, in William Waller Hening, ed., *The Statutes at Large; Being a Collection of all the Laws of Virginia, from the First Session of the Legislature, in the Year 1619* (Richmond, New York, and Philadelphia), II, 515.

15. What number of planters, servants and slaves; and how many parishes are there in your plantation?
Answer. We suppose, and I am very sure we do not much miscount, that there is in Virginia above forty thousand persons, men, women and children, and of which there are two thousand *black slaves*, six thousand *christian servants*, for a short time, the rest are born in the country or have come into settle and seat, in bettering their condition in a growing country.

4. *A Tithing List*

> Northampton County Order Book 9, 1666–1674, fol. 40.

A List of Tythables in Northampton County Anno Domini 1667 delivered in att a Court held in the said County the 9th September *1667*

Sampson Rogers ⎫
George Roman ⎬ —2
Amos Harris—1
Henry Reade ⎫
Morgan Poulden ⎬ —3
William Starns ⎭
John Haggaman—1
Mason Patrick ⎫
Richard Watkins ⎬ —3
Teage Harman ⎭
Robert Miller—1
John Abraham ⎫
Thomas Wilson ⎪
Nicholas [Harwood?] ⎬ —6
Richard Jeffreys ⎪
William Bider ⎪
Arthur Upshott ⎭
Robert Blades ⎫ —2
Isaac Jacobs ⎭
John Doson ⎫
Francis [Bradley?] ⎬ —4
Stephen Avis ⎪
Arthur [Armitige?] ⎭
Philip Jacob ⎫ —2
Thomas Bullock ⎭
John Dalby ⎫ —2
James Sanders ⎭
John Senior—1
Thomas Bagley—1
Brian Kehorne ⎫ —2
John [Wrager?] ⎭
John Dolby, Jr. ⎫
John Shamell ⎪
John Reede ⎬ —5
Derek Johnson ⎪
John Dolby, Sr. ⎭
Stephen Long ⎫ —2
Peter Long ⎭
Robert Gaskins ⎫
Robert Butler ⎪
Nathaniel Stalley ⎬ —5
A Negro woman ⎪
William Gaskins ⎭
Abraham Wisterhouse ⎫
Lawrence Cline ⎪
WilliamWisterhull ⎬ —5
John Greene ⎪
William Wisterhouse ⎭
Josias [Combes?] ⎫
William [Combes?] ⎪ —4
[name illegible] ⎬
Henry Combes ⎭
John [Epanes?]—1
Francis Darling—1

—————
54

Richard Nottingham ⎫ —2
William Swift ⎭
William Satehall—1
Martin Only ⎫ —2
Robert Foster ⎭
John Ferry ⎫ —2
Ralph Warrell ⎭
William Stockley ⎫
John Begna ⎬ —3
John Stockely ⎭
Pearce Davis ⎫ —2
Thomas Davis ⎭
James Davis, Jr. ⎫
Edward Ashley ⎪
John Hoswell ⎬ —6
John Robins ⎪
Abraham Bonage ⎭
James Davis, Sr. ⎫
John Field ⎪
Mathew Hauslett ⎬ —5
John Denny ⎪
A Servant Boy ⎭
John Andrews
Paule Wimborough ⎫ —2
John Wimborough ⎭
John Wimborough Jr.—1
Samuell [Fiskell?] ⎫
Jacob Hill ⎬ —3
Simon [Fiskell?] ⎭
Owen Howell ⎫
John Howell ⎪
Isaack Russell ⎬ —5
Henry Newton ⎪
John Kendall ⎭
Thomas Evans ⎫ —2
[Irmstrong?] Foster ⎭
Richard Gilbert ⎫ —2
John Evens ⎭
John Whitehead—1
[Irmstrong?] Foster ⎫
John [Samess?] ⎬ —3
William Foster ⎭
Thomas Fox ⎫ —2
Henry Hill ⎭
Jeremy Waller—1
Richard Shikes ⎫
Richard Wildsgage ⎬ —3
Robert Wilson ⎭
Thomas Asell—1
Francis Roberts—1
George Boice—1
Henry Force ⎫
Peter [name illegible] ⎪
David Price ⎪
John [Halssa?] ⎬ —8
[Jenny?] ⎪
Henry [name illegible] ⎪
[name illegible] ⎪
Capt. Isaack Foxcroft ⎭

—————
59

Thomas Nealey—1
Edmund Flyn—1
Harman Johnson ⎫
Ervin Loyd ⎪
Francis Owings ⎬ —4
Capt. William Jones ⎭
Walter Mills—1
George Smith ⎫
William Scardon ⎪
William Palmer ⎪
Henry ⎪
Richard Beard ⎬ —10
John Collins ⎪
Two Negroes ⎪
Thomas Fascue ⎪
Capt. William Spencer ⎭
Thomas Dimmer ⎫
Jonathan Newton ⎬ —4
Lambert Genton ⎪
William [Armour?] ⎭
Christopher Young—1
Christopher Stanley—1
Nicholas Granger ⎫ —2
John Lucas ⎭
Richard [Jutock?] ⎫ —2
John Darby ⎭
Abraham Heath—1
Edward Stevens ⎫
William Tipshott ⎬ —3
John Wilson ⎭
John Colt ⎫ —2
Andrew Whittington ⎭
John Abbott ⎫ —2
Francis Church, Jr. ⎭
John Basy—1
William Kennett—1
John Mapp ⎫
Thomas Collins ⎬ —3
Peter Watson ⎭
Thomas Kendall ⎫ —2
John Lyon ⎭
William Hickman ⎫
Joseph Hickman ⎬ —3
Thomas Risse ⎭
Dunkin Macknabb—1
John Plumb ⎫ —2
Michaell Graney ⎭
Phillip Mongom ⎫ —2
Mary Mongom ⎭
John Clarke—1
Richard Aust ⎫ —2
Anthony Blase ⎭
John Tatum ⎫ —2
Cornelius Brice ⎭
William Huston—1
John Floyd ⎫ —2
[Abraham?] Sheppard ⎭
Samuel [Chase?]—1

—————
59

5. A Land Patent

Virginia Land Patent Book 3, 1652–1655, 28.

To all etc.   Whereas etc.   Now Know Yee that I the said Richard Bennet Esquire give and grant unto Rawleigh Travers Three hundred Acres of land situate on the southsid of Rappahannock River . . . The said land being due unto the said Rawleigh Traverse by and for the transportation of six persons into this Colony . . . Proved and Dated the 9th of March 1653

Mary Marloe, John Heath, Anthony Negroe, Mary Negro: and one hundred acres by assignment from Mr. Spry . . .

The Willoughby Family, 1610–1699

6. The Original English Residence of Thomas Willoughby I

C.O. 1/4, 38.

[1626]   Thomas Willowby of Rochester in the County of Kent gentleman aged 27 yeares or thereabouts sworne and examined as aforesaid; Saieth and deposeth uppon his oath; That this Examinate is now bound a passenger for Virginia in the said shippe the Peter and John of London . . .

7. Thomas Willoughby I Arrives in Virginia

C.O. 1/3, 158.

Ensigne Thomas Willoby His Muster

Thomas Willoby aged 25 in the Prosperous 1610

Servants
John Chaundler aged 24 in the Hercules 1609
Thomas aged 20 in the greate hopewell 1623
Robert Bennett aged 24 In the Jacob 1624
Niccolas Davis Aged 13 in the Mariegould 1618

8. An Early Land Patent of Thomas Willoughby I

Virginia Colonial Land Patent Book I, Pt. 1, 1623–1643, 63, Virginia State Library, Richmond.

By the Governor and Capt. Generall of Virginia
To all to whome these presents shall come I Francis West Esq Governor and Capt. Generall of Virginia send greeting . . . Whereas by Orders and Consti-

tutions formerly made and established for the affaires of this Colony It hath been ordeyned and appointed that all devidents of Lands any way due or belonging to any assignee to them according to the severall Conditions in the same mentioned Now Know Yee that I the said Francis West doe with the consent of the Councell of State give and graunt unto Ensigne Thomas Willoughby of Elizabeth Citty gentleman . . . fifty acres of Land . . . In witness whereof I the said Francis West have hereunto sett my hand and the seale of the Colony the Seventeenth day of November [1628]. . . .

9. *Offices Held by Thomas Willoughby I*

A. COMMANDER OF FORCES SENT TO ATTACK THE INDIANS, 1627

> H. R. McIlwaine, ed., *Minutes of the Council and General Court of Colonial Virginia, 1622–1632, 1670–1676, with Notes and Excerpts from Original Council and General Court Records, into 1683, Now Lost* (Richmond, Va., 1924), 151.

A COURT at *James Citty* the 4th day of *July* 1627. . . .

At this Court was thought fitt that we should draw out partyes from all our plantations and goe uppon the Indians and cutt downe their corne, and further that we should sett uppon them all in one day, *vizt.* the first of August next: . . . For the Chesapieacks [*i.e.*, Chesapeake], Ensigne [Thomas] *Willoby*.

B. MONTHLY COURT JUDGE, 1628/29

> McIlwaine, ed., *Minutes of the Council and General Court*, 193.

A COURT at James Citty the 7th of *March* 1628 . . .

For the ease of the people and according to the order established in the generall assembly[,] *It is ordered* that a . . . Commission for a monethly Court at *Elizabeth Citty* [be drawn,] the Commissioners whereof to be *vizt.* . . . Lt. *Willoughby*. . . .

C. BURGESS, 1629/30, 1631–1632

> William G. Stanard, *The Colonial Virginia Register* (Albany, N.Y., 1902), 56; Hening, ed., *Statutes at Large*, I, 154.

BURGESSES FOR THE ASSEMBLY
OF 1629/30 . . .

The Upper Part of Elizabeth City: Thomas Willoughby
William Kemp
Thomas Hayrick

A GRAND ASSEMBLY
Holden at James Citty the 21st of February, 1631/32 . . .

The names of the Burgesses were viz[t.]: . . .

Waters Creeke and the upper } Capt. Thomas Willoughbye
parrish of Elizabeth Citty

D. JUSTICE OF THE PEACE

> Lower Norfolk County Order Book, 1637–1646 (transcript), 39.

At a Court
holden the 2nd day of March at Capt John Sibseys 1639

Lower Norfolk County   Present
Capt. Thomas Willoughby
Capt. John Sibsey   Lt Francis Mason
Mr. Henry Seawell   Mr. William Julian

E. MEMBER OF THE COUNCIL OF STATE

> Lower Norfolk County Order Book, 1637–1646 (transcript), 78.

At a court holden at James City the 4th of February 1640
present—Sir Francis Wyatt, Knight, Governor etc

Capt. John West   Mr. Argoll Yerdly
Capt. Samuel Mathews   Mr. George Minifee
Capt. William Perce   Capt. William Brocas
Capt. Thomas Willoughby   Mr. Ambrose Harmer
Mr. Roger Wingate

10. *Some Debts Owed to Thomas Willoughby I*

> Lower Norfolk County Order Book, 1637–1646 (transcript), 74.

Whereas it appears to this Court that Ralph Clarke deceased was indebted unto Capt. Thomas Willoughby in his life time the sum of 3£. 10.s. sterling and 96 lbs. of tobacco—It is therefore ordered that Thomas Causon, the executor of the said Ralph's estate shall put in sufficient security for the shipping of such a quantity of tobacco as two sufficient men shall think fit, for to satisfy the said debt, the said tobacco being to be shipped a board any ship or ships which the said Capt. Willoughby shall appoint and likewise for the sum of 9£. 10s. . . .

11. *The Lower Norfolk Justices Appoint Thomas Willoughby I to Recruit a Minister, 1655*

> Lower Norfolk County Order Book, 1651–1656, fol. 158.

Honored Sir

You are hereby intreated, and both by the Countie and the Court fully impowered[,] to provide A Minister of Gods word for us, whereby our necessities [are] to you very well knowne maye be supplyed, for which if you please to undertake for us, wee shall with A generall Consent be very thanckfull to you. . . .

From Linhaven Court this
24th of Maye 1655 subscribed

To Captaine Thomas Willoughbye, esq.
Theis present

Your assured friends
John Sidney
Thomas Lambert
Francis Emperor
Thomas Bridge
Lemuell Mason
John Porter, Sr.
John Porter, Jr.

12. *Death of Thomas Willoughby I, 1658*

> Lower Norfolk County Deeds, Wills, and Orders, Book D, 1656–1666, 162.

[August 16, 1658.] Upon the petition of Mr. Thomas Willoughby, A Commission of Administration is granted unto him, upon his fathers estate Capt. Thomas Willoughby who deceased in England, hee putting in security according to Law.

13. *Thomas Willoughby I's Children*

> Virginia Colonial Land Patent Book 3, 1652–1655, 321.

To all etc.   Whereas etc.   Now Knowe yee that I the said Richard Bennett Esq. etc. give and grant unto Capt. Thomas Willoughby two thousand nine hundred Acres of Land . . . for the transportation of twenty Eight persons into this Collony . . .
Alice Willoughby
Thomas Willoughby
Elizabeth Willoughby

14. *Thomas Willoughby II Apprenticed as a Merchant Taylor, 1644*

> Mrs. E. P. Hart, ed., *Merchant Taylors' School Register, 1561–1934* (London, 1936), II, n.p.

Willoughby, Thomas 1644–47 [this interval represents the period of apprenticeship]; b. 25. 12. 1632 at Virginia, America; s[on] of Capt. Thomas (merchant) of Red Lyon Alley, St. Botolph, Aldgate [London]. . . .

15. Thomas Willoughby II Refuses the Office of Justice of the Peace, 1656

Lower Norfolk County Order Book, 1651–1656, fol. 210.

[April 15, 1656.] Mr. Thomas Willoughby hath refused to be sworne a Commissioner for the County.

16. Thomas Willoughby II Refuses Jury Service, 1656

Lower Norfolk County Order Book, 1651–1656, fol. 219.

[May 15, 1656.] Thomas Willoughby is fined by the Court One hundred and Fifty pounds of tobacco for his offence and contempt to the Court In saying hee would not obey their [said?] order to bee of a jury. . . .

17. Offices Held by Thomas Willoughby II

A. HIS APPOINTMENT TO THE BENCH OF LOWER NORFOLK COUNTY, 1661

Lower Norfolk County Deeds, Wills, and Orders, Book D, 1656–1666, 303.

Lower Norfolk Att a Court held the 15th August 1661 at Thomas Hardings Present Francis Morrison esq. Governor and Capt. Generall of Virginia

Col. John Sidney
Maj. Lemuell Mason
Mr. Thomas Browne
Mr. Thomas Willoughby   } Commissioners
Capt. Richard Foster
Mr. John Martin

B. SHERIFF, 1666

Lower Norfolk County Deeds and Wills, Book E (Orders), 1666–1675, fol. 12.

[February 28, 1666.] Whereas It was ordered that Col. Miles Cary should bee paid out of the Levy of Lower Norfolk County Tenn Thousand pounds of Tobacco and Mr. Thomas Willoughbie Sheriffe and Collector of the said County haveinge made it appeare . . . that he hath satisfied the same . . . it is ordered that the said Mr. Willoughby be discharged from the said Debt accordinge to Act.

C. FORT COMMISSIONER, 1667

Lower Norfolk County Deeds and Wills, Book E (Orders), 1666–1675, fol. 19.

[October 15, 1667.] Ordered that Lt. Col. Willoughby and Mr. Fulcher be authorized and appointed to meete the Commissioners of the association for Nansemond Fort the 29th of October and to Act according to the Act of Assembly for building the Fort there.

18. *The Wife of Thomas Willoughby II*

Land Patent Book 5 (copy), 1661–1666, 502.

. . . The said Land being formerly granted unto Richard Tompson by two several Patents the one for Five hundred and Sixty Acres dated the fourth of april one thousand six hundred and fifty nine; the other for Forty eight Acres dated the fifteenth of December one thousand six hundred and fifty one, and after the [said] Richard Tompsons decease became due unto Sarah and Elizabeth Tompson Heirs of the aforesaid Richard and by Mr Thomas Willoughby and Mr Peter Presly who married the said Sarah and Elizabeth Tompson . . .

19. *Thomas Willoughby II's Children*

Lower Norfolk County Deeds and Wills, Book E, 1666–1675, fol. 19.

September 15 *1673*

In the name of god amen I Sarah Willoughby of the County of Lower Norfolk widow being sick, butt of perfect memory doe make this my last will and testament. first I bequeath my soul to almighty god my saviour and my body to bee buried in a most Christian manner, and for my goods and Chattells I give to my two Children, Thomas and Elizabeth Willoughby and the two to bee sole Executors. . . .

20. *Death of Thomas Willoughby II, 1672*

Lower Norfolk County Deeds and Wills, Book E, 1666–1675, fol. 125.

15th August *1672*

An Inventory and apraisement of the Estate of Lt. Col. Thomas Willoughby deceased taken and appraised by us underwritten this 15th day of May *1672*.
. . .

21. *Thomas Willoughby III's Appointment to the Bench of Lower Norfolk County, 1698*

Lower Norfolk County Deeds, Wills, and Orders, 1695–1703, fol. 126.

A[t a Court the 19th of] July 1698

present Capt. John [Hatton   Mr. Ja]mes Wilson   Mr. Mathew Godfrey Mr. Thomas [Hodgis   Mr. Thomas] Willoughby

Wider Kin Connections of the Willoughby Family

22. The Husbands of Elizabeth, Daughter of Thomas Willoughby I

A. SIMON OVERZEE: DUTCH MERCHANT

> Lower Norfolk County Deeds, Wills, and Orders, Book D, 1656–1666, 261.

[August 15, 1660.] Upon the petition of Thomas Willoughby in the behalf of Mrs. Elizabeth Oversee Widdow order for a Commission of Administration is granted unto her upon her husbands estate Mr. Symon Overzee, shee giving Caution according to Course.

B. GEORGE COLCLOUGH: LONDON MERCHANT, JUSTICE OF THE PEACE, AND BURGESS FOR NORTHUMBERLAND COUNTY, VIRGINIA

> Lower Norfolk County Deeds, Wills, and Orders, Book D, 1656–1666, 292.

[March 1, 1660.] At Adam Hayes his request A Reference is granted unto him until the next Court against Mr. Willoughby Attorney of Mr. [George] Colclough who married the relict [i.e., widow] and administratrix of Symon Overzee then to bee heard and determined.

C. ISAAC ALLERTON: NEW ENGLAND MERCHANT, JUSTICE OF THE PEACE, BURGESS FOR NORTHUMBERLAND COUNTY, VIRGINIA, AND MEMBER OF THE COUNCIL OF STATE

> Lower Norfolk County Deeds, Wills, and Orders, Book E, 1656–1666, fol. 375.

[August 17, 1663.] WHEREAS Mr. Thomas Willoughby Attorney of Mr. George Colclough obteyned an Order in June Court 1662 against Thomas Harvy for the some [i.e., sum] of 3284 lbs of tobacco and caske, being due by bill. Uppon the petition of the said Mr. Willoughby the said order is revived on the behalfe of Isaacke Allerton who married the relict and Administratrix [i.e., Elizabeth Willoughby-Overzee] of the said Colclough.

Chapter Five

Bound Labor

The Indentured Servant

A colonial society is imperfect because it lacks some of the essential attributes of a matured social organism. An example of this observation is the characteristically chronic demand for labor in Virginia throughout the seventeenth century. The organizers of the original Virginia venture had recognized the need for workers to aid in the clearing and planting of a settlement; to that end they had recruited laborers in the first complement of immigrants for the new colony. For the duration of the London Company's control of the colony, supplying Virginia with a competent work force had remained a continuing concern of the company's backers. The successful cultivation of tobacco increased the demand for labor as it became apparent that tobacco culture was a way to economic survival in a hostile wilderness. The difficult task of recruiting and maintaining an adequate labor force still remained, however. During the seventeenth century Englishmen devised two solutions to the problem: indentured servitude and chattel slavery.

Although both servitude and slavery had Old World antecedents, the forms that they took in Virginia were unique, and both represent institution building in response to specific New World situations for which there were few known precedents. Servitude and slavery in Virginia were more than sets of arrangements governing the relationship between employer and employee; they were also instruments of social control designed to regulate, as strictly as law and community attitudes allowed, the lives of unruly and potentially quite dangerous immigrants. Both institutions may have emerged at approximately

the same point in time, but for most of the seventeenth century indentured servitude predominated. At century's end it had begun to be
replaced by chattel slavery. Slavery's growth as a labor system and a
means of manipulating race relations cannot be understood in isola-
tion from indentured servitude, for the latter provided the institutional model for the former.

The concept of bound labor was not unknown to seventeenth-
century Englishmen. Serfdom had been the lot of agricultural workers
in medieval times, some crimes carried service as punishment for
their commission, and many well-to-do households employed servants.
By far, however, the most commonly recognized form of bound labor
was apprenticeship, that period of time when a young person bound
himself out to a craftsman for the purpose of learning a trade. Apprenticeship had been confined to craft guilds until 1562, when Parliament adopted the Statute of Artificers, which imposed a national
system of apprenticeship upon all who would enter industrial callings.
A modified form of apprenticeship appeared in Virginia at an early
date, after officials of the London Company promised settlers land in
return for their service. By 1619 the customs of indentured servitude
were becoming fixed; the first General Assembly provided for the
recording and enforcing of contracts between masters and servants.
Although the precise origins of servitude in Virginia have remained
obscure, it seems clear enough that the institution was patterned after
a mixture of well-tried English usages.

While the purpose of indentured servitude as a labor system is
evident, two other functions are perhaps less obvious. The trade in
servants for Virginia became a lucrative occupation for those persons
who engaged in it. Indeed, this trade was an important source of investment for English merchants of all sorts, from the innholder with
a relative or a friend in the colony and a few pounds sterling to invest
(Document 1) to the great London and Bristol goldsmiths, cloth
merchants, and grocers who had numerous contacts and large sums
to venture. In addition to benefiting from the labor it supplied, some
Virginia planters also used the trade for speculative purposes. For
them there was a return to be made both in selling servant indentures
and the land acquired by patenting servant headrights (Document 2)
and in acting as brokers between Virginia and England.

Indentured servitude also enabled people to get to Virginia—not
the poor, but the restless, skilled men and women for whom America
promised a new and possibly better life. Judging from the evidence, it
appears as though servitude was tailor-made for the young, since most

servants were under the age of twenty-five. Of course, young people were easier to uproot and to ship across the seas, but because so many servants had completed apprenticeships or were the children of yeoman farmers, they were possibly driven by the belief that an unsettled England dimmed their prospects for pursuing a trade or a traditional calling at home. Servitude seemed to satisfy the needs of middling sorts of Englishmen, who saw in the institution a marvelous opportunity to try one's luck in America at someone else's expense in return for a few years of service. And come they did. Most of Virginia's population increase between 1634 and 1674 was the direct result of an influx of men and women who had willingly sold themselves into bondage.

These immigrants bound themselves to service with a document known as an "indenture." As the word implies, indentured servitude was a contractual arrangement between two consenting parties. The simplest form of indenture merely stated that a servant agreed to serve the master for a specified number of years at whatever work the master required, in return for which the master promised to furnish passage to Virginia and to supply the servant's food, clothing, and shelter during his term (Document 3). Sometimes the indenture included the master's promise to teach the servant a trade or to give him an additional reward for the faithful performance of his duties (Document 4).

The length of service varied but generally ranged between four and seven years. A youngster might be bound until he attained his majority, while the servant who learned a trade might have an additional year or two tacked on to the normal period of bondage. In any case, when the term expired, servants were entitled to freedom dues. By law every freed servant could claim as his due "the custom of the country," a bushel of corn and a new suit of clothes (Document 5). Other dues might include a tract of land, money, livestock, or tools. Whether or not a servant received these additional items depended upon his skill in negotiating their inclusion in his indenture.

Relatively few planters went to England to recruit their work forces, so prospective servants bargained for their indentures with a resident merchant, a planter's agent, or a ship's captain, and when they arrived in Virginia, their indentures were sold at dockside. Those bondsmen who landed in the colony without an indenture were likewise sold, but their terms were longer than that of an indentured servant (Document 6).

Although bound to another man's bidding, the servant did not lose his freedom completely. He could sue and be sued by others in court, and the law allowed him to give evidence to any matter of fact that he had witnessed. Married servants were not separated from their spouses and children, nor were single bondsmen prevented from marriage. Like free men, male servants were required to join the militia. Few servants passed from rags to riches, but no stigma attached itself to the men and women who got their start in Virginia as bondsmen. A temporary condition, indentured servitude neither stripped the servant of his humanity nor systematically degraded him. Unlike slavery the institution was not intended to reduce the servant to a nonthinking, childlike dependant.

On the face of it, then, servitude would appear to have been well-suited to the needs of servant and master alike. A closer inspection of the institution reveals otherwise, because its operation proved less than ideal. In practice, servitude visited hardship, danger, and even death upon the servants. Like other immigrants, every man or woman who contemplated servitude immediately faced being torn from familiar surroundings and enduring the rigors of the passage to Virginia. The mental strain upon the farm lad or girl who at a young age left family and friends forever, as well as the terrifying experience of being at sea for months below decks in tiny cramped ships, can only be imagined. If one survived the shock of being uprooted and the terrors of the voyage, he next confronted the necessity of adjusting to life in a primitive agricultural community. Tobacco farming was an unfamiliar occupation for the thousands of servants who emigrated from England, and under any circumstances, there was nothing particularly edifying about spending a minimum of four years working for someone else's profit. The work was arduous and unending: there were fields to be cleared and crops to be planted and harvested—all had to be accomplished speedily, with a minimum of tools or labor-saving devices. The workday was long, and there was little amusement or recreation to relieve the tedium of routine agricultural procedures. Moreover, failure to plant, to sucker, or to top the tobacco at the appropriate time in the growing season could mean the loss of a crop, just as failure to have the tobacco harvested and cured could cause the planter to miss the fall sailing of the tobacco fleet. Without meeting these deadlines, planters could not have sustained life in Virginia.

These were but a few of the hardships that indentured servants faced. In theory, the law protected servants from privation and physical harm, but mistreatment at their masters' hands was not an uncommon occurrence. The surviving records of every seventeenth-century Virginia county contain vivid testimony of the harsh usage that many servants endured. Administering corporal punishment to a refractory servant was the master's legal prerogative, but beatings were often the penalty for minor infractions. Sometimes beatings were so severe that the servants were mauled or maimed (Document 7). Maidservants were inviting targets for abuse. Not infrequently they were subjected to sexual assaults or made pregnant by their masters or other free men. Pregnancy during service meant time added on to the original term, and if a father could not be discovered, the child was bound out to the local parish until his thirty-first birthday. In addition to the beatings and assaults, the county archives disclose a dreary litany of overwork, poor housing, and inadequate diet and clothing.

Only in rare instances have a servant's recorded feelings about his lot survived (Document 8). Much may be inferred, however, from servants' actions as revealed by numerous entries in court record books. That servitude was an unpleasant condition is demonstrated by the repeated incidence of drunkenness, runaways, and suicides (Document 9) among the servile population.

To their credit, local magistrates tried to ameliorate the bondsmen's lot whenever a dispute between master and servant came to their attention. Their willingness to hear servants' complaints is remarkable, but it was difficult for the judges to scrutinize closely masters who lived on plantations scattered widely about a county. Also, the justices did not make a habit of scouring their jurisdictions for breaches of the laws relating to a master's treatment of his servants. The servant had to initiate legal action, and it was he who reaped the consequences if he failed to convince the court that a wrong had been done him. For this reason, the number of recorded suits against masters is not a very accurate index of how servants were treated.

The hazards connected with servitude were by no means solely the lot of the servants. As a group they posed a considerable amount of difficulty for the planters and the community at large. By its very nature the institution created a constant turnover in the planters' work force. A continuing concern of every planter who employed servants, therefore, was how to replenish his laborers as their indentures expired. Recruiting a complement of bondsmen was always risky business. Acquiring servants required contacts, capital, and time—commodities that were at a premium for a great many planters. The supply of prospective servants coming into the colony could easily be disrupted. Shippers regularly lost cargoes of bondsmen to storms and pirates; wars and changed economic conditions threatened to impede the flow; many servants could not stand the effects of the passage; and there was always the chance that the crown's policy of encouraging migration to America might change. Indeed, the risks seemed endless.

His troubles did not end once a planter had recruited his labor force. Young and resentful of authority, many servants turned out to be quite unmanageable and even dangerous. If there was one problem that surpassed all others, it was the runaway servant (Document 10). Bondsmen frequently ran off because of ill-treatment, but others absconded for different reasons. Some were not temperamentally suited to agricultural labor, others had no intention of ever fulfilling their indentures, and a few were perhaps lured by the call of the wild. Not as prevalent as runaways, but a trial nevertheless, were the maidservants who bore bastard children (Document 11). Judging from the available evidence, the colony's rate of illegitimacy was highest among servants. Whatever moral implications this may have, its existence placed a burden upon the planters since they had to care for the women during their pregnancies. Then too, servants exercised their right to sue in court against their masters. Sometimes there was substance to these suits, but court records suggest that many of the actions were dilatory (Document 12). Also, the master's storehouse, household possessions, and livestock were inviting targets for the mischievous bondsman (Document 13). Finally, the danger of physical harm for the master's family or of insurrection always existed (Documents 14 and 15).

Because colonial society lacked adequate methods for calling its citizenry to account, difficulties with servants deterred the planter from his principal occupation. Every servant who ran away, bore an illegitimate child, filed a frivolous court action, or stole property cost the planter dearly in lost labor and time. There were few effective means of restraining the indentured servant's vicious tendencies. The responsibility for maintaining discipline and order among his laborers belonged to the master. To an extent his success in realizing that responsibility depended upon the servant's willingness to abide by the conditions of his bondage. Many bondsmen proved refractory. It was the recalcitrant servant who most often availed himself of the opportunities for mischief provided by a settlement pattern of widely scattered and remotely situated plantations.

When breaches of the law occurred, local authorities stepped in, but the amount of restraint that they could apply was frequently minimal. The task of chasing down or breaking up roving gangs of runaways in thinly settled areas was beyond the abilities of the sheriff and his deputies. The courts could not prevent the clogging of their dockets with cases involving servants. They might punish the bastard bearer, the petty thief, or the incendiary, but punishment did not put an end to illegitimacy, pilferage, and rebelliousness among the servants.

Out of the desire to assist in controlling an unruly population and the need to protect the rights of masters and servants, Virginia lawmakers wrote an extensive corpus of legislation governing indentured servitude. This legislation may be grouped into several categories: some laws distinguished between free men and servants, others defined the rights of masters and servants, and another group supported the masters by throwing the weight of government behind their efforts to maintain an orderly work force.

Beginning as early as 1619, the drafting of servant law became an integral task of virtually every General Assembly that sat during the remainder of the century. This preoccupation with bondsmen reflects the evolution of an institution and the legislators' growing skill at drafting law, but it also indicates the assembly's continued concern for the colony's peace and safety. A society where more than half of the population was always in bondage verged on trouble. For this reason, the laws tended to be harshly punitive and weighted in the master's favor.

Despite all of the impedimenta that inhered in it, indentured servitude endured as the mainstay of Virginia's labor system. But throughout the seventeenth century, some planters turned to an alternative form of labor—chattel slavery.

SUGGESTED READINGS

Primary Sources

Hening, William Waller, ed. *The Statutes at Large; Being a Collection of All the Laws of Virginia from the First Session of the Legislature, in the Year 1619.* 13 vols. (Richmond, New York, and Philadelphia, 1809–1823), I, II, III.

Secondary Sources

Bruce, Philip Alexander. *Economic History of Virginia in the Seventeenth Century: An Inquiry into the Material Condition of the*

People, Based upon Original and Contemporaneous Records. 2 vols. (New York, 1895), I, 572–634, II, 1–57.

Morgan, Edmund S. "The First American Boom: Virginia 1618 to 1630." *William and Mary Quarterly,* 3d Ser., XXVIII (1971), 169–198.

*Morris, Richard B. *Government and Labor in Early America* (New York, 1946).

*Smith, Abbot Emerson. *Colonists in Bondage: White Servitude and Convict Labor in America, 1607–1776* (Chapel Hill, N.C., 1947).

Procurement of Indentured Servants

1. Richard Garford's Contract to Provide a Servant for Thomas Workman, 1654

Lower Norfolk County Order Book, 1651–1656, fol. 86.

Recorded this 20th Day of June 1654

Be it known unto all men by these presents that I Richard Garford of London Inhoulder doe Confess and acknowledge my selfe to owe and stand indebted unto Thomas Workman of the Little Creeke in the County of Lower Norffolk in Virginia, planter, his Executors Administrators or assignes the full and Just some of Tenn pounds of good and lawfull money of England to be paid uppon demand of the abovesaid Thomas Workman or his true and lawfull Atterny or Attornyes at the now dwelling house of Mr. Willyam Garford Innkeeper at the Red Lyon in fleet streete without either Equevocation fraud or delay, and to the true performance of the same well and truly to bee made and done I bind my selfe my Executors Administrators and Assignes, firmly by these presents in witnesse heereof I have hereunto sett my hand and seale this 4th day of Aprill 1653

Richard Garfford

The Condition of this obligation is such that the within bounden Richard Garford or his Assignes shall well and truly deliver or cause to be delivered unto the above mentioned Thomas Workman, his Executors Administrators or assignes here in Virginia a sound and able man servant betweene Eighteene and 25 yeres of age that shall have fower yeres to serve at the least, and that in the first second or third shipp that shall arrive in the Port of James River

* Available in paperback.

in Virginia from London, that then the bond above to be voyd and of noe effect or else to stand in full force and vertue

Richard Garfford

Sealed and delivered in the presence of
Thomas Ward

2. Servants Imported by Headright, 1652

Northumberland County Order Book, 1652–1665, fol. 389.

According to sufficient proofe made to this Court there is due to Robert Wyard 150 Acres of land for the transportation of these persons following into this Colony vizt.

Richard Phillips
Richard Howes
Edward Dunkly

3. Roger Jones's Indenture, 1688

Middlesex County Order Book, 1680–1694, 343.

Roger Jones Servant to Mr. William Churchill Comes and acknowledges that hee is freely Willing to Serve his Master Seaven yeares from his Arival, The said Churchill promising that hee will imploy his said Servant in the Stoar and other his occasions and not imploy him in Common workeing in the Ground.

4. Richard Willis Agrees to Teach John Talbert a Trade, 1680

Middlesex County Order Book, 1680–1694, 380.

John Talbert Servant to mr. Richard Willis Comes in Court and Acknowledges to Serve the Said Willis one Compleate Yeare more then by his Indenture Expressed, In Consideration the Said Willis doth promis to keep the Said Talbert Constantly at the Shoomakers Trade and not to worke in the ground and also to give the Said Talbert a New Searge Suite Shooes Stock and hatt more then the Law Enjoynes att the time of his Freedome.

5. The Custom of the Country, 1656

Charles City County Order Book, 1655–1665, 36.

Itt is ordered that Corn and cloathing According to Custome be forthwith paid to Thomas Chappell late Servant to John Richards deceased out of the said Decedants estate by the executors or administrators thereof, also execution with Costs.

6. *The Sale of a Servant without an Indenture, 1665*

Surry County Deed Book, 1652–1672, 252.

Know all men by these presents that I lott Richards of the Citty of Bristoll Merchant haveing transported in the ship Called the ranee bow of the above Citty att my personal Cost and Charge one Sarvant boy by name William freeman being about eleven yeares old and haveing noe indenture for him I doe by these presents assigne over the said Sarvant unto John Barnes of Lower Chipoaks or to his assigns for the full tearme of eight yeares from the arrival of the ship he came in which was in November 64 and att the Expiration of the abovesaid Right is to be absolutly free from the said Barnes and alsoe my self as witness my hand the 18 February Anno 1664 the said Barnes to pay his full due According to the Custom of this Country

Teste William Cokerham   Lott Richards
                                                    Recorded 14th March 1664

The Hazards of Servitude

7. *An Assault on Charity Dallen, 1649*

Lower Norfolk County Order Book, 1646–1651, fol. 120.

The deposition of Joseph Mulders Aged 23 yeares or thereabouts Sworne and examined Sayeth

That Deborah Fernehaugh, the Mistress of this deponent, did beate her mayd Sarvant in the quartering house before the dresser more Liken a dogge then a Christian, and that at a Certaine time, I felt her head, which was beaten as soft as a sponge, in one place, and that as there shee was a weeding, shee complayned and sayd, her backe bone as shee thought was broken with beating, and that I did see the mayds arme naked which was full of blacke and blew bruises and pinches, and her necke Likewise and that afterwards, I tould my Mistress of it and said, that two or three blowes, could not make her in such a Case, and after this my speeches shee Chidge [i.e., chided] the said mayd, for shewing her body to the men, and very often afterwards she the said mayd would have showen mee, how shee had beene beaten, but I refused to have seene it, saying it concernes me not, I will doe my worke and if my Mistress abuse you; you may complaine, and about 8 dayes since, being about the time shee last went to Complaine, I knew of her goeing, but would not tell my mistress of it, although shee asked mee, and sayd I could not chuse but know of it, and further hee sayeth not

sworne the 31th July 1649   The Marke of
Thomas Bridge Clerk of Court   Joseph X Mulders

Michaell Mikaye aged 22 yeares of there abouts, sworne and examined, sayeth verbatim as the above mentioned deponent sayeth and deposeth and further sayeth not

sworne the 31th July *1649*   The Marke of
Thomas Bridge Clerk of Court   Michael X Mikay

Upon the depositions of Joseph Mulders and Michaell Mikaye of the misusage of Charetie dallen, by her Mistress Deborah Fernehaugh, and by many other often Complaints, by other sufficient testimonies, and although the said Deborah hath had advertisement thereof from the Court yet persisteth in the very Ill usadge of her said sarvant, as appeareth to the board, It is therefore ordered that the said Charetie Dallen shall no longer remaine in the house or service with her said Mistress, but is to bee and Continue at the house of Mr. Thomas Lambard [Lambert], untill such time as the said Deborah Fernehaugh shall sell or otherwise dispose of her said servant, for her best advantage of her the said Deborah.

8. *James Revel Describes the Servant's Plight, ca. 1680*

> James Revel, "The Poor Unhappy Transported Felon's Sorrowful Account of His Fourteen Years Transportation at Virginia in America," ed. John Melville Jennings, *Virginia Magazine of History and Biography*, LVI (1948), 189–194.

PART I

My loving Countrymen pray lend an Ear,
  To this Relation which I bring you here,
My sufferings at large I will unfold,
  Which tho' 'tis strange, 'tis true as e'er was told,
Of honest parents I did come (tho' poor,)
Who besides me had never Children more;
Near Temple Bar was born their darling son,
And for some years in virtue's path did run.

  My parents in me took great delight,
And brought me up-at School to read and write,
And cast accompts likewise, as it appears,
Until that I was aged thirteen years.

  Then to a Tin-man I was Prentice bound,
My master and mistress good I found,
They lik'd me well, my business I did mind,
From me my parents comfort hop'd to find.

  My master near unto Moorfields did dwell,
Where into wicked company I fell;
To wickedness I quickly was inclin'd
Thus soon is tainted any youthful mind.

  I from my master then did run away,
And rov'd about the streets both night and day:

Did with a gang of rogues a thieving go,
Which filled my parents heart with grief and woe.
   At length my master got me home again,
And used me well, in hopes I might reclaim, . . .
I promis'd fair, but yet could not refrain,
   But to my vile companions went again: . . .
One night was taken up one of our gang,
Who five impeach'd and three of these were hang'd.
   I was one of the five was try'd and cast,
Yet transportation I did get at last; . . .
   In vain I griev'd, in vain my parents weep,
For I was quickly sent on board the Ship:
With melting kisses and a heavy heart,
I from my dearest parents then did part.

PART II

In a few Days we left the river quite,
   And in short time of land we lost the sight,
The Captain and the sailors us'd us well,
But kept us under lest we should rebel.
   We were in number much about threescore,
A wicked lowsey crew as e'er went o'er;
Oaths and Tobacco with us plenty were,
For most did smoak, and all did curse and swear.
   Five of our number in our passage died,
Which were thrown into the Ocean wide:
And after sailing seven Weeks and more,
We at Virginia all were put on shore.
   Where, to refresh us, we were wash'd and cleaned
That to our buyers we might the better seem;
Our things were gave to each they did belong,
And they that had clean linnen put it on.
   Our faces shav'd, comb'd out our wigs and hair,
That we in decent order might appear,
Against the planters did come down to view,
How well they lik'd this fresh transported crew.
The Women s[e]parated from us stand,
As well as we, by them for to be view'd;
And in short time some men up to us came,
Some ask'd our trades, and others ask'd our names.
   Some view'd our limbs, and other's turn'd us round
Examening like Horses, if we're sound,
What trade are you, my Lad, says one to me,
A Tin-man, Sir, that will not do, says he[.]
   Some felt our hands and view'd our legs and feet,
And made us walk, to see we were compleat;
Some view'd our teeth, to see if they were good,

Or fit to chew our hard and homely Food.
   If any like our look, our limbs, our trade,
The Captain then a good advantage made:
For they a difference made it did appear.
'Twixt those for seven and for fourteen year.
   Another difference there is alow'd,
They who have money have most favour show'd;
For if no cloaths nor money they have got,
Hard is their fate, and hard will be their lot.
   At length a grim old Man unto me came,
He ask'd my trade, and likewise ask'd my Name:
I told him I a Tin-man was by trade,
And not quite eighteen years of age I said.
   Likewise the cause I told that brought me there,
That I for fourteen years transported were,
And when he this from me did understand,
He bought me of the Captain out of hand,

PART III

Down to the harbour I was took again,
   On board of a sloop, and loaded with a chain;
Which I was forc'd to wear both night and day,
For fear I from the Sloop should get away.
   My master was a man but of ill fame,
Who first of all a Transport thither came,
In Reppahannock county we did dwell,
Up Reppahannock river known full well,
   And when the Sloop with loading home was sent
An hundred mile we up the river went
The weather cold and very hard my fare,
My lodging on the deck both hard and bare,
   At last to my new master's house I came,
At the town of Wicocc[o]moco call'd by name,
Where my Europian clothes were took from me,
Which never after I again could see.
   A canvas shirt and trowsers then they gave,
With a hop-sack frock in which I was to slave:
No shoes nor stockings had I for to wear,
Nor hat, nor cap, both head and feet were bare.
   Thus dress'd into the Field I nex[t] must go,
Amongst tobacco plants all day to hoe,
At day break in the morn our work began,
And so held to the setting of the Sun.
   My fellow slaves were just five Transports more,
With eighteen Negroes, which is twenty four:
Besides four transport women in the house,
To wait upon his daughter and his Spouse,

We and the Negroes both alike did fare,
Of work and food we had an equal share;
But in a piece of ground we call our own,
The food we eat first by ourselves were sown,
    No other time to us they would allow,
But on a Sunday we the same must do:
Six days we slave for our master's good,
The seventh day is to produce our food.

    Sometimes when that a hard days work we've done,
Away unto the mill we must be gone;
Till twelve or one o'clock a grinding corn,
And must be up by daylight in the morn.

    And if you run in debt with any one,
It must be paid before from thence you come;
For in publick places they'll put up your name,
That every one their just demands may claim,
    And if we offer for to run away,
For every hour we must serve a day;
For every day a Week, They're so severe,
For every week a month, for every month a year
But if they murder, rob or steal when there,
Then straightway hang'd, the Laws are so severe;
For by the Rigour of that very law
They're much kept under and to stand in awe.

PART IV

At length, it pleased God I sick did fall
But I no favour could receive at all,
For I was Forced to work while I could stand,
Or hold the hoe within my feeble hands.

    Much hardships then in deed I did endure,
No dog was ever nursed so I'm sure,
More pity the poor Negroe slaves bestowed
Than my inhuman brutal master showed.

    Oft on my knees the Lord I did implore,
To let me see my native land once more;
For through God's grace my life I would amend
And be a comfort to my dearest friends.

    Helpless and sick and being left alone,
I by myself did use to make my moan;
And think upon my former wicked ways,
How they had brought me to this wretched case.

    The Lord above who saw my Grief and smart,
Heard my complaint and knew my contrite heart,
His gracious Mercy did to me afford,
My health again was unto me restor'd.

    It pleas'd the Lord to grant me so much Grace,

That tho' I was in such a barbarous place,
I serv'd the Lord with fervency and zeal,
By which I did much inward comfort feel.

    Thus twelve long tedious years did pass away,
And but two more by law I had to stay:
When Death did for my cruel Master call,
But that was no relief to us at all.

    The Widow would not the Plantation hold,
So we and that were both for to be sold,
A lawyer rich who at James-Town did dwell,
Came down to view it and lik'd it very well.

    He bought the Negroes who for life were slaves,
But no transported Fellons would he have,
So we were put like Sheep into a fold,
There unto the best bidder to be sold,

PART V

A Gentleman who seemed something grave,
Unto me said, how long are you to slave;
Not two years quite, I unto him reply'd,
That is but very short indeed he cry'd.

    He ask'd my Name, my trade, and whence I came
And what vile Fate had brought me to that shame?
I told him all at which he shook his head,
I hope you have seen your folly now, he said,

    I told him yes and truly did repent,
But that which made me most of all relent
That I should to my parents prove so vile,
I being their darling and their only child.

    He said no more but from me short did turn,
While from my Eyes the tears did trinkling run,
To see him to my overseer go,
But what he said to him I do not know.

    He straightway came to me again,
And said no longer here you must remain,
For I have bought you of that Man said he,
Therefore prepare yourself to come with me.

    I with him went with heart oppressed with woe,
Not knowing him, or where I was to go;
But was surprised very much to find
He used me so tenderly and kind.

    He said he would not use me as a slave,
But as a servant if I well behav'd;
And if I pleased him when my time expir'd,
He'd send me home again if I required.

    My kind new master did at James Town dwell;
By trade a Cooper, and liv'd very well:

I was his servant on him to attend.
Thus God, unlook'd for raised me up a friend.

PART VI

Thus did I live in plenty and at ease,
   Having none but my master for to please,
And if at any time he did ride out,
I with him rode the country round about.
   And in my heart I often cry'd to see,
So many transport fellons there to be;
Some who in England had lived fine and brave,
Were like old Horses forced to drudge and slave.
   At length my fourteen years expired quite,
Which fill'd my very soul with fine delight;
To think I shoud no longer there remain,
But to old England once return again.
   My master for me did express much love,
And as good as his promise to me prov'd:
He got me ship'd and I came home again
With joy and comfort tho' I went asham'd,
   My Father and my Mother wel I found,
Who to see me, with Joy did much abound:
My Mother over me did weep for Joy,
My Father cry'd once more to see my Boy;
   Whom I thought dead, but does alive remain,
And is returned to me once again;
I hope God has so wrought upon your mind,
No more wickedness you'll be inclined,
   I told them all the dangers I went thro'
Likewise my sickness and my hardships too;
   Which fill'd their tender hearts with sad surprise,
While tears ran trinkling from their aged eyes.
   I begg'd them from all grief to refrain,
Since God had brought me to them home again,
The Lord unto me so much grace will give,
For to work for you both While I live,
   My country men take warning e'er too late,
Lest you should share my hard unhappy fate;
Altho' but little crimes you here have done,
Consider seven or fourteen years to come,
   Forc'd from your friends and country for to go,
Among the Negroes to work at the hoe;
In distant countries void of all relief,
Sold for a slave because you prov'd a thief.
   Now young men with speed your lives amend,
Take my advice as one that is your friend:
For tho' so slight you make of it while here,
Hard is your lot when once the[y] get you there.

9. *Edward Whittell Commits Suicide, 1664*

Accomack County Order Book, 1663–1666, fol. 67.

Jurymen Summoned to view the Corps of Edward Whittell Servant to John Reney of the County of Accomack, who was found hanged in a tobacco house on the plantation [where] the said Reney now lives upon the 8th of Aprill 1664 The Jury whose names are hereunto Subscribed haveing viewed the Corpes and place where the said Whittell had hanged himself, and examined two Evidences doe finde that the said Whittell for want of Grace was guilty of his owne death

[jurors' names omitted]

John Crook aged 25 yeares Sworne and examined Saith that your deponent comeing to the house of John Reney the said Reney missing one of his Servants makeing enquirey after him the said Servant was found hanged on a barr in a tobacco house, the deponent supposing that there was life Remaining in him cut the said Servant downe, Supposing therby to preserve him and further your deponent Saith not.
Sworne before me the 8th April 1664.   John Crooke
Hugh Yeo

Thomas Middleton aged 21 years or their about Sworne and examined saith your deponent goeing forth to worke the 8th of this instant Aprill in the morninge with the rest of your deponent's fellow servants one Edward Whittell being one of them the said Whittell complayning that hee was not very well, went as your deponent thought into the house, your deponents master coming and mising the said Whittell asked your deponent where hee was, whereupon your deponent makeing search where the said Whittell was gon found him hanged in the tobacco house and further saith not.
Sworne before me the 8th Aprill 1664   the marke of
Hugh Yeo   Thomas X Middleton

Problems Created by the Use of Servant Labor

10. *A Runaway, 1680*

Middlesex County Order Book, 1680–1694, 362.

Adam Ballentine Servant to mr. Robert Price Comes in Court and vollentaryly Acknowledges to Serve his said Master two yeares and a halfe In Recompense of his often runing away after his first time by Indenture is over.

11. *A Bastard Child, 1656*

Charles City County Order Book, 1655–1665, 53.

Whereas Ann Parke servant to Elizabeth Hatcher widdow is Complained of and proved to have Comitted Fornication and borne a Child in the time of her service: It is therefore ordered that the said Ann shall double the time of service due to be performed by her to her mistress or her assigns, from the time of her departure, according to act in that Case made and provided.

12. *A Frivolous Lawsuit, 1681*

Accomack County Order Book, 1678–1682/83, 260.

Whereas William Wallworth and Benedict Talbot Servants to Capt. Hilary Stringer brought an information to this Court on behalf of his Majesty against theire Master Capt. Hilary Stringer wherein they accused their Said Master for occasioning the death of a Servant woman named Ellinor Tanner late Servant to Capt. Hillary Stringer and alledging the Neighborhood to be well knowing of the truth thereof the Court takeing the same into due examination and haveing maturely weighed and considered all things alleadged by the said Servants against theire said Master and allsoe a former examination of the Court of Northampton taken thereupon as allso all other evidences presented and likewise all the Neighborhoods testimonys that know anything relating thereto It appeares to the Court a most false and most malitious accusation by the said servants combination contrived thereby hopeing to acquitt themselves of the notorious wrong they had done their said Master the Court doe adjudge the said information so brought by the said Servants on behalf of his Majesty against their said Master to be notoriously false and Scandallous and order that the Said Servants make Satisfaction by Service after theire time by Indenture or Custome be expired for all charges whatsoever accrewed by reason of their Said Causless information and complaint against their Said Master and that the Said Capt. Stringer to pay the present charge thereof:

13. *Theft of Master's Goods, 1684*

Accomack County Deeds, Wills, and Inventories, 1676–1690, fols. 389–390.

A Declaration or Confession of [Roger] Court Crotosse one of Col. John Wests Servants of some misdemeanors Comitted or done by him or other Servants belonging to the said Col. West.
1st. Saith that about a year since he went from mary branch to his masters mill [with] John Fisher a Servant to his master alsoe (being miller) to fetch some meale the miller not being within[,] this declarant Saith he went into the mill and there lookinge for meale found in a Caske amongst Some woole and yarne a turkey warme and the feathers pluckt of[f] and the neck twisted about which Turkey this declarant drest and with a negro of his masters Eat it, And about two nights after this declarant goeing from mary branch to Chequon-

essex with one Sandy Coloured Turkey and one black turkey under his armes John Fisher then had this declarant to say nothing but come to the mill at night and he should eate parte of them which this declarant did and eate parte of one of them but did not See the other

2nd. That at the last Springe the aforesaid John Fisher perswaded this declarant and Thomas Hartly (another of Col. Wests Servants) to kill a Lamb and lent us his knife to kill it which accordingly we did and carried into the Swamp and [word illegible] drest it some of it wee then Eat and next morning he went with us and he Eat what he would and Said it was well done

3rd. That about August last the said John Fisher perswaded this declarant and a negro Tony to carry a Sheep from Chequonessex to mary branch and there kill it but if it were not fatt then lett it loose amongst the Sheep there att mary branch And there take one of the best of those Sheep and kill it accordingly wee carry away a Sheep upon the horse Tyger from Chequonessex and killed it att mary branch house but did not Exchange it as he ordered: The next day John Fisher came and Eat Some of it and Carryed some of it with him.

4th. That about the last of August last this declarant and the aforesaid John Fisher and the aforesaid Thomas Hartley (by Fishers perswasions) killed a Sow att Chequonessex house and by the said John Fishers order fleade [i.e., flayed] her and tyed up her gutts in the skin and Stones with them and threw them into the pond afterwards wee tooke a Pott and the Sowe and carryed them into the Swamp and there drest halfe of it and the rest wee Eat at the Indian towne.

5th. That about the seaventh day of october last this declarant beinge att breakfast att Chequonessex house heard mr Francis Chambers bid the aforesaid John Fisher Catch two piggs and bring them in afterwards this declarant beinge at plow the said Fisher bad[e] him goe along with him to help him and take his gun with him which he accordingly did And shott one pigg and would have carried that into the house but the said John Fisher would not but had him goe kill another for one would not doe but this declarant could not[.] there upon the said Fisher said he would roast that and gott a Spitt for the purpose and asked this declarant if he Could gett fire who answered he could not thereupon the said Fisher Stopt the touchhole of the Gunn and gott fire and there roasted it and Eat it[.] In the time the pigg was roasting old mr Johnson Came to the fire but the said Fisher seeing him come ran away with the spitt and kept out of sight untill the old man went away

6th. That abought a fortnight or three weeks since this declarant and the aforesaid John Fisher Thomas Hartley and Jack A negro at two severall times killed four piggs one of them being marked with my masters marke carryed them away and Eate them.

[7th.] That on Tuesday last was a fortnight att night to this declarant and the said Thomas Hartley sitting by the fire in the middle roome the said John Fisher came to us and bad[e] us goe along with him (which we did) then he went out with us to the henhouse and said Jonny Negro had hid a bag of potatoes there and that he would steale them whereupon he put downe a board by the doore and then unlockt the doore And tooke the Potatoes presently after the same night this declarant and Thomas Hartley went to the henhouse againe and tooke a Turkey and a hen and carryed them into the shoomakers shop loft and there pluckt them and boyled them in the shop

8th. That about a week since my master Calling this declarant the said Fisher and Hartley to question for our misdemeanors Afterwards the said Fisher said to us that if he was brought to any damage he would begone and if he could gett there he would send his master a very Loveing Letter that his sheep his hoggs and turkeys were very fat *etc.*

9[th.] That what is above written and declared is very true And that this Declarant can depose to the same when Called Dated this 6th day of November anno Domini *1684*

10[th.] allso this declarant farther saith that there was another sheep killed by him and John Fisher which he did not remember when he was examined before Col. [Daniel] Jenifer.

The marke of
Roger X Court Crotosse

14. *A Servant Assaults His Mistress, 1679*

Accomack County Order Book, 1678–1682/83, 88–89.

The Examination of Elizabeth Bowen Widdow—
saith—That on Sunday evening being the eighteenth day of May *1679* Thomas Jones her servant did come into her Roome and with a naked Rapier in his hand did tell her he would kill her and said shee had sent Will Waight to her Mothers and that shee had got a master for them, but hee would bee her Master and allso said that he would not kill her if shee would let him lye with her all night and bade her goe to bed and she answered she would not and Runn in with his Rapier and bent it, then he said he woald cutt her throat but she getting [to] the dore did run out of dores and he after her and ketched [her] in the yard and as she was standing did endeavour to cutt her throat with a knife but could not and then he threw her down and did there allso indeavour to cutt her throat but she prevented it by defending her throat with her hands and bending the knife hee took her [petti]coats and threw [them] over her head and gave her two or three blows in the face with his fist and bade her get her gun and did in this act with the Knife scurrify her throat and brest and cut her right hand with six or seven cutts very much and that she with bending the Rapier and knife cut her hands and fingers very much

Elizabeth Bowen

Whereas Elizabeth Bowin Widdow did by her examination upon oath in open Court declare that Thomas Jones her servant in a most barbarous and villanous nature sett upon and most desparately attempted to murder the said Bowin with a naked Rapier and Knife to cut her throat which had been perpatrated and committed had it not bee[n] Providentially and strongly prevented by the said Bowins resistance recieving severall wounds in her endeavours to prevent the sam[e] which was allso confessed by the said Jones: The Court takeing the same into their serious Considerations do order as a just reward for his said horrid offense and crime that the sherriff Forthwith take him into Custody and that he forthwith receive thirty nine lashes on the bare back well laid on: and to have his haire cutt off and an Iron Coller forthwith put about his neck dureing the Courts pleasure and after the time for which he was to serve his said mistriss is expired to serve his said mistriss or assignes one whole yeare according to Act for laying violent hands on his said mistriss and allso two yeares for his wounding her as aforesaid and after due punishment inflicted accordingly The Court do further order that the sherriff deliver the said Jones to the said Elizabeth Bowin or order (it being by her request) and the said Bownig [*sic*] to Pay Court Charges the said Jones makeing satisfaction for the same after his time of service is expired—

15. *A Servant's Plot to Revolt, 1687*

Middlesex County Order Book, 1680–1694, 309–310.

Upon Examination of John Nickson a man Servant belonging to Ralph Wormeley Esq. who was Comitted to this Common Goall for having with diverse other ill disposed Servants and others entered into a Disigne and Conspiracy to procure Gunnes powder and Shott and other Armes and to Assemble themselves together with Designe to Runnaway and with Force and Armes as aforesaid to withstand and Oppose all persons that should endeavour to Suppress them; And the same tending to the greate disturbance of his Majesties Peace and the Terrour of his Leige People It is therefore ordered that the said John Nickson bee returned into the said Goall there to bee kept in safe Custody until the next Court held for this County And that in the meane time Strict inquiry bee made after all the Rest of the said Conspirators in order to their Apprehention And being procceded against with the said Nickson According to Law, and that all person that Can give any Evidence against the said Nickson And his said Accomplishes [i.e., accomplices] bee Supened or bound over to appeare to give their Evidence on behalfe of our Sovereign Lord the King.

Chapter Six

Bound Labor

Slavery

One of the most intriguing, albeit abhorrent, phenomena in Virginia's early colonial history was the appearance of chattel slavery. Slavery's emergence presents historians with the complex puzzle of determining why the English, whose own traditions did not include it, should have seen in slavery the ultimate remedy for the planters' labor difficulties, as well as the ideal instrument for controlling relations between themselves and the Old Dominion's African colonists. Shrouded by a dearth of evidence, the riddle of the Negro's enslavement remains mysterious and controversial. No one can say with assurance that the "twenty negars" whom John Rolfe mentioned in his oft-quoted remark were the first Africans to settle in Virginia. Neither can one conclude that slavery began in August 1619 when that now-famous skipper of a Dutch man-of-war sold his cargo of blacks to the English, for no clue to the fate or status of those unwilling immigrants now exists (Document 1). But the year 1619 and the Dutchman's cargo may be used as convenient points of departure for discussing the evolution of slavery.

The arrival of twenty Africans in 1619 did not signal the start of a massive black migration to Virginia or the rapid transition from indentured to slave labor. Precise figures on the number of blacks who settled in the colony are impossible to obtain, but the data that survive argue that throughout the century Virginia's Negro population was small in relation to that of the English. An estimate made in 1649, which has been confirmed by modern scholarship, fixed the number of the Old Dominion's black colonists at mid-century at three hundred. A recent study concludes that slightly more than six thousand settlers of African origins, most of whom had arrived since 1660, were living in Virginia as the seventeenth century drew to a close.

How the African colonists got to Virginia is conjectural. Traditionally historians have held that until the passage of the navigation acts Dutch traders were the chief sources of supply, but this view is questionable. Although the Dutch had enjoyed fairly wide trading privileges in the colony prior to 1660, the population statistics just cited suggest that Africans were not a major item in the Dutch-Virginia trade. Even Englishmen who dealt in African labor seem not to have rated Virginia as having a high market potential. Following the chartering of the Royal African Company in 1672, for example, trade between the company and the colony was slow to develop. The likeliest explanation is that the blacks living in Virginia by 1700 had been recruited mostly from other New World colonies through contacts that the Virginia colonists had themselves developed. Some Virginians had regular dealings with New Netherland, New England, and the West Indies, and there is evidence showing that from an early date one of the items of this commerce was Negro labor (see chapter 7).

However they got there, not all Africans who went to Virginia met the same fate. Indeed, before the 1660s, when the colony's lawmakers began to give slavery statutory definition, the English seem to have been rather ambivalent in their relationships with the blacks. Scant evidence of the Negro's presence exists for the interval between 1619 and the creation of the county court system of local government in 1634, and what remains is difficult to interpret. From the 1630s, though, the record is fuller. By then, surviving wills, inventories, and deeds of sale indicate that it was a customary practice to hold some Negroes in a form of life service. But it is equally clear that other blacks were commonly treated as indentured servants, who, when they completed their terms, passed into the ranks of free men.

The factors that determined how certain Negroes became indentured servants are difficult to discern. Conceivably some blacks had lived in freedom in the colonies from which they had migrated, and for them servitude in Virginia promised a chance for an improvement in life-style. A Negro's religion may also have affected his status. All of the identifiable free blacks had Christian names, and until the General Assembly outlawed it, baptism could be grounds for a black bondsman to secure his release from life service. Also, some Englishmen, at least before the 1660s, probably treated a black man just as any other laborer who should be set free at the end of a specific period of service. While a satisfactory answer to the question may never be forthcoming, the important point to note is that a significant number of Negroes who settled in Virginia after 1619 never became slaves.

Free blacks enjoyed many of the same privileges and rights that belonged to Englishmen. They owned property, including in at least one instance servants and slaves, and a few even acquired enough material substance to warrant leaving wills (Documents 2 and 3). Records show various Negroes committing petty offenses, performing useful community services, and occasionally intermarrying with whites (Documents 4 through 6). Free men also had access to the courts: they could sue, be sued, and give evidence (Documents 7 through 9).

One can only speculate about whether or not a free black who met the franchise requirements was entitled to vote in elections for the House of Burgesses. Since voting was done orally, no record of seventeenth-century voting behavior exists. But there is nothing to suggest that during the seventeenth century qualified blacks were prevented from casting their ballots. There were no laws aimed at disfranchising them until 1725, and no challenge to black voters has come to light in local records, though such challenges do exist for Englishmen. In the absence of contrary evidence, it is perhaps safe to assume that if a black could qualify as a freeholder, he could vote.

Certain distinctions set free blacks apart from the English, however. One was the Englishmen's habit of identifying Negroes by race in court records. Some scholars have taken this practice as proof of an English antipathy towards black colonists, but too much can be made of it, since clerks customarily noted the nationality of everyone who was not English. Such notations are probably rather more indicative of a suspicion of foreigners in general rather than Africans in particular. More to the point are those disabilities that the English imposed upon free black men. As early as 1640, for example, the General Assembly debarred Negro men from keeping arms and serving in the militia. After 1643 black women, unlike their English counterparts, were liable to be taxed along with all males above the age of sixteen who lived in the colony. Later on, blacks were forbidden to own English servants, and their freedom of movement was otherwise restricted. By the end of the century the position of free blacks had deteriorated from what it had been fifty or sixty years earlier. Still, it was better than that of the enslaved blacks.

Those Negroes who were cast into slavery came to that condition gradually, but the process by which they became enslaved has remained obscure because the institution first evolved through practice and custom before it was sanctioned and defined in Virginia law. From the point of earliest known contact in 1619, the Englishmen's need for labor and their peculiarly hostile attitudes about blacks, as well as the Africans' heritage and color, made the Negroes especially susceptible to enslavement. And as time passed, the English, without apparent thought, slowly adapted themselves to the idea of keeping men in perpetual bondage. In the course of gaining some measure of acceptance as an alternate system of labor, slavery produced certain practical problems that ultimately required legal solutions. In concert with hardening English attitudes and an increased number of blacks settling in Virginia, these problems combined to accelerate slavery's statutory definition in the years after 1660.

In all respects save one, the working conditions of an emerging slavery probably differed little from those of indentured servitude. Lacking contrary evidence, there is little reason to believe that slaves were treated any differently than servants; so any planter who employed slave labor experienced some of the same problems of those who worked indentured servants. Like indentured bondsmen, slaves pilfered their masters' storehouses, broke tools, and otherwise made nuisances of themselves. They ran off with about the same frequency as servants, and although they were no easier to catch, their color made runaway slaves less difficult to identify (Documents 10A and 10B). Slaves also might rebel. Only two uprisings are known to have occurred before 1700, but neither of them reached the proportions of similar insurrections in the West Indies (Documents 11A and 11B).

Wherever blacks and whites lived and worked together, an especial problem soon became manifest: it was difficult to maintain racial separateness and to prevent interracial fornication. From the beginning the English evinced an abiding concern over miscegenation, but neither concern nor the stringent punishment of offenders prevented its occurrence throughout the seventeenth century (Documents 12A through 12E). The Englishmen's attitudes toward miscegenation were conditioned by their prejudices and suspicions of Africans, as well as by the rather practical matter of what should become of the offspring of casual unions between whites and blacks. Were these children to be treated as Englishmen or Africans, servants or slaves, Christians or heathens?

Although he was *"filius nullius, filius populi,"* a bastard born to English parents was nonetheless a Christian and an Englishman, who could not therefore be enslaved. Thus, in Virginia illegitimate children of white indentured servants were baptised and could not be held in servitude beyond the age of majority without indentures, unless their fathers were unknown, in which case they served until their thirty-first birthday. But a mulatto bastard was different because one of his parents was an African and possibly a heathen to boot. If one of his parents was a slave, would such a child be one too? If a slave, could the child escape slavery because he was part English or had been baptised? English law and custom could provide few answers to these questions, because neither had contemplated the existence of mulattoes or the circumstances that produced them. Here then was a legal no-man's-land, through which the English colonists had to plot a course without the aid of many known or useful precedents to guide them. As a result, it took years before a solution to the matter materialized, and until then, confusion over the mulatto's status persisted.

Because slavery had grown to adolescence without any statutory sustenance, a similar sort of confusion reigned in other areas of the relationship between master and slave. Many Englishmen understood a slave to be a man who had completely lost his freedom, "even against nature," but until the 1660s that conception of slavery was rather loosely applied to the Negro bondsman. Consequently there were means by which a slave sometimes escaped his bondage. As a reward for faithful service, a master might manumit his slave by last will and testament (Document 13), or he might free him after the slave had served a specified term of years (Document 14). A few slaves even managed to purchase their freedom (Document 15). These avenues to liberty were not unique to slavery in Virginia. Instead they probably represent adaptations of what was generally known about slavery from classical times or in the Spanish and West Indian colonies. But a rather more novel approach to freedom came through the colony's judicial institutions, for it appears that slaves, like black indentured servants, had the right to sue in colonial courts.

There are at least five known instances where slaves sued for their freedom in colonial courts. The grounds upon which each litigant based his claim varied. In one case a mulatto named Elizabeth Key argued that her paternity, her religion, and the violation of a contractual arrangement that her father had made entitled her to her freedom (Document 16A). Another slave, Fernando, tried to convince the courts that his conversion to Christianity altered his status from slave to servant (Document 16B). Each of the three remaining cases hinged upon the question of whether or not the petitioners were actually servants rather than slaves (Documents 16C, 16D, 16E). The outcome of each is immaterial; the important point is that for a time even slaves had a right to sue in court. As long as that right remained, the Virginia slave's loss of freedom was not complete, and a slave could subject his master to lengthy and costly litigation that might result in the winning of his release from bondage.

Despite the potential aggravation that such litigation posed, the English moved slowly to close off this legal route to freedom. Perhaps this slothfulness continued because until the 1660s the number of blacks living in the colony was so small. Awareness of their existence was comparatively slight, and they presented only occasional problems for those few Englishmen who owned them. Since there were no laws to prevent it, some Englishmen likely followed their kinder instincts and occasionally freed mulattoes who could prove English paternity or slaves who became Christians.

The year 1660, however, marks a turning point in English attitudes towards slavery. After that date white colonists began to perceive the meager rights that they had inadvertently conceded to blacks as threats to the commonweal and to their own self-interests. Building upon the few laws pertaining to blacks that had been enacted prior to 1660 (Documents 17A and 17B), the General Assembly wrote the peculiar institution into Virginia law, and from the 1660s the few opportunities for slaves to escape their bondage rapidly disappeared. This change in attitude is probably attributable to a rising black population, which increased the frequency of runaways, miscegenation, and court actions brought by slaves. It may also have been due to a realization of the need to bring statute law into conformity with custom. Such action would remove doubts and inconsistencies about who was and who was not a slave, while it would eliminate the bases for blacks' claims to freedom.

In the process of regularizing custom by statutory means, the General Assembly formally stripped the Negro of his humanity and reduced him to a chattel who had neither a legal personality nor freedom of movement. The laws that the assembly adopted fell into three general categories: defining who was a slave, establishing the master's property rights over his slaves, and using the power of the colony's governing authorities to assist the master in maintaining discipline among the slaves (Documents 17C through 17F). Ultimately these laws would be codified into Virginia's first slave code, which the assembly wrote in 1705.

At the end of the seventeenth century indentured servitude was still Virginia's dominant system of labor, but the English colonists had already made a fateful commitment to replace it with slavery. Contemporary English attitudes conspired with slowly evolving legal judgments to regard slavery as a viable alternative to indentured servitude and a solution to the problems of race relations. The tragic result of that "unthinking decision" was a bitter heritage that has yet to run its course.

SUGGESTED READINGS

Primary Sources

Hening, William Waller, ed. *The Statutes at Large; Being a Collection of All the Laws of Virginia, from the First Session of the Legislature, in the Year 1619.* 13 vols. (Richmond, New York, and Philadelphia, 1809–1823), I–III.

Secondary Sources

Billings, Warren M. "The Cases of Fernando and Elizabeth Key: A Note on the Status of Blacks in Seventeenth-Century Virginia." *William and Mary Quarterly*, 3d Ser., XXX (1973), 467–474.

Brewer, James H. "Negro Property Owners in Seventeenth-Century Virginia." *William and Mary Quarterly*, 3d Ser., XII (1955), 575–580.

Bruce, Philip Alexander. *Economic History of Virginia in the Seventeenth Century: An Inquiry into the Material Condition of the People, Based upon Original and Contemporaneous Records.* 2 vols. (New York, 1895), II, 57–131.

Craven, Wesley Frank. *White, Red, and Black: The Seventeenth-Century Virginian* (Charlottesville, Va., 1971), 73–111.

————. "Twenty Negroes to Jamestown in 1619?" *Virginia Quarterly Review*, XLVII (1971), 416–420.

*Curtin, Philip D. *The Atlantic Slave Trade: A Census* (Madison, Wis., 1969).

Degler, Carl N. "Slavery and the Genesis of American Race Prejudice." *Comparative Studies in Society and History*, II (1959–1960), 49–66.

Handlin, Mary F. and Oscar. "Origins of the Southern Labor System." *William and Mary Quarterly*, 3d Ser., VII (1950), 199–222.

*Jordan, Winthrop D. *White over Black: American Attitudes toward the Negro, 1550–1812* (Chapel Hill, N.C., 1968), 3–98.

————. "Modern Tensions and the Origins of American Slavery." *Journal of Southern History*, XXVIII (1962), 18–30.

Palmer, Paul C. "Servant into Slave: The Evolution of the Legal Status of the Negro Laborer in Colonial Virginia." *South Atlantic Quarterly*, LXV (1966), 355–370.

Russell, James Henderson. *The Free Negro in Virginia, 1619–1865* (Baltimore, Md., 1913).

Vaughan, Alden T. "Blacks in Virginia: A Note on the First Decade." *William and Mary Quarterly*, 3d Ser., XXIX (1972), 469–478.

The Arrival of the Negro in Virginia, 1619

1. A Relation from Master John Rolfe

> Edward Arber and A. G. Bradley, eds., *Travels and Works of Captain John Smith, President of Virginia, and Admiral of New England, 1580–1631* (Edinburgh, 1910), II, 541.

. . . About the last of August [1619] came in a dutch man of warre that sold us twenty Negars: and *Iapazous* King of *Patawomeck*, came to *James* towne, to desire two ships to come trade in his River, for a more plentifull yeere of Corne had not beene in a long time, yet very contagious, and by the trechery of one *Poule*, in a manner turned heathen, wee were very jealous the Salvages would surprize us.

The Free Negro

2. Anthony Johnson's Servant, 1655

> Northampton County Order Book, 1655–1668, fol. 10.

The deposition of Captain Samuel Goldsmith taken (in open court) 8th of March Sayth, That beinge at the howse of Anthony Johnson Negro (about the beginninge of November last to receive a hogshead of tobacco) a Negro called John Casar came to this Deponent, and told him that hee came into Virginia for seaven or Eight yeares (per Indenture) And that hee had demanded his freedome of his master Anthony Johnson; And further said that Johnson had kept him his servant seaven yeares longer than hee ought, And desired that this deponent would see that hee might have noe wronge, whereupon your Deponent demanded of Anthony Johnson his Indenture, hee answered, hee never sawe any; The said Negro (John Casor) replyed, hee came for a certayne tyme and had an Indenture Anthony Johnson said hee never did see any But that hee had him for his life; Further this deponent saith That mr. Robert Parker and George Parker they knew that the said Negro had an Indenture (in on Mr. Carye hundred on the other side of the Baye) And the said Anthony Johnson did not tell the negro goe free The said John Casor would recover most of his Cowes of him; Then Anthony Johnson (as this deponent did suppose) was in a feare. Upon this his Sonne in lawe, his wife and his 2 sonnes perswaded the said Anthony Johnson to sett the said John Casor free. more saith not

Samuel Goldsmith

This daye Anthony Johnson Negro made his complaint to the Court against mr. Robert Parker and declared that hee deteyneth his servant John Casor negro (under pretence that the said Negro is a free man.) The Court seriously consideringe and maturely weighinge the premisses, doe fynde that the said Mr. Robert Parker most unjustly keepeth the said Negro from Anthony Johnson his master as appeareth by the deposition of Captain Samuel Goldsmith and many probable circumstances. It is therefore the Judgment of the Court and ordered That the said John Casor Negro forthwith returne unto the service of his said master Anthony Johnson, And that mr. Robert Parker make payment of all charge in the suit. also Execution.

3. Francis Paine's Will, 1673

Northampton County Order Book, 1664–1674, 220–221.

In the Name of god Amen I Francis Payne of Northampton County in Virginia beinge sick of body but of perfect knowledge and understanding and being willinge to ease my minde of all worldly care Doe make this my last will and Testament as follows

Imprimis I bequeath my soule to my loveing Father my creator and to Jesus Christ who by his blood and passion suffered for my sinns and all the world trustinge through his meritt to injoy that heavenly portion prepared for mee and all true beleevers And as for my body I bequeth it unto the ground from whence it came there to receive a Christian buriall And as for my worldly Estate I doe give and bequeath itt unto my loveing wife Agnes Payne my whole Estate reall and personall moveables and immoveables makinge her my Indubitable Executrix of this my last will and Testament. And Doe here declare that by vertue of these presents all former wills by mee made and signed are rebuked and made void and this is to bee my last will and Testament. And desire that my debts may in the first place bee paid. In Testimony whereof I have subscribed my hand and putt my seale this 9th day of May Anno Domini *1673.*

Unto each of our god children a Cow Calfe a peece when they attaine to law-full age. but as for [Deura?] Driggins he is to have nothinge by this will

Francis X paine
his marke

Signed sealed and delivered in the presence of us
Nathaniel Wilkins
the marke of
Elizabeth X Pettitt

The 29th day of September 1673. This day the last will and Testament of Francis Paine Negro was proved in open Court by the Corporall oath of Nathaniel Wilkins and allowed of and ordered to be Recorded (Provided that Elizabeth Pettitt the other evidence appeare at the next Court and Con-firme the probate thereof if livinge and of ability to owne then or otherwise as sure as shee can)

Teste Daniel Neech Deputy Clerk

Recorded the 4th of October *1673*. Daniel Neech Deputy Clerk

4. *Philip Mongom Is Accused of Stealing Hogs, 1659/60*

Northampton County Order Book, 1657–1664, fol. 68.

Upon Sum presumptious Susspittion that phillip Mongom negro hath Stoll hoggs as by the Relation of John Braddum and William Planner doth appeare, It is ordered that hee put in Security for his good behaviour for the future and pay Costs of Suit. It is Ordered that phillip Mongom negro shall pay for his presumptious actions used to the Court in throughing [i.e., throwing] hoggs eares on the Court table one hundred pounds of tobacco and Caske with Court Charges.

5. *John Francisco Maintains a Bastard Child, 1668*

Northampton County Order Book, 1664–1674, fol. 53.

Whereas John Franciscoe Negro have moved the Court that hee might have the Negro child of Thomas Driggins Negro, slave to Lt. Col. [William] Kendall and John Eyre, with the Consent of the same Lt. Col. Kendall for himselfe and John Eyre; Itt is ordered that the said John Franciscoe in whose Custody the said Child now is, shall Keepe it in his Custody, and have the tuition and Care of it untill it attaynes the age of one and Twenty yeares and then to sett it free for Ever; from the Claime of any person to make it a slave.

6. *An Example of Intermarriage, 1671*

Lower Norfolk County Order Book, 1665–1675, fol. 73.

It is the opinion and Judgement of the Court that francis Stripes ought to pay Leavyes and tythes for his wife (shee being a negro) It being according to

Law; and therefore ordered that he pay the Same for the Last year past, as well as this present and so for the future.

7. *John Francisco's Suit in Chancery, 1673/74*

Accomack County Order Book, 1673–1676, 31.

In the difference dependinge between John Ayleworth plaintiff and John Franciscoe Negro defendant in Chancery the said plaintiff not haveing filed his Bill. Itt is ordered by the Court that the same bee dismissed the plaintiff paying costs of Court also Execution.

8. *Susannah's Case, 1677*

Charles City County Order Book, 1677–1679, 216.

Upon the petition of Susannah a free Negro-Woman that she may be Exempted from payeing Levyes, And Whereas the Worshipful Courte is informed of her strength and ability It is thereupon thought fit that she be not Exempted but pay Levyes.

9. *The Suit against Mary Williams, 1688*

Middlesex County Order Book, 1680–1694, 371.

Judgment is granted To mr. Christopher Robinson against Mary Williams a negro Wooman for Three Thousand three hundred and Sixty Six pounds of good Sweet sented Tobacco and Caske with Cost Also Execution.

Problems Created by the Use of Slave Labor

10. *Runaways*

A. THEODERICK BLAND TRIES TO RECAPTURE TWO RUNAWAYS, 1662

Charles City County Order Book, 1655–1665, 331.

It is ordered that Mr. Theoderick Bland by vertue hereof have power to require the sheriff of Charles Citty or James Citty (or any other) [county?] to raise such a Competent number of men and armes as shallbe needfull for the search and surprisall of two negroes runn away from the said Mr. Bland; And that the said Mr. Bland give such reasonable satisfaction to the men so imployed as their time and paines may deserve, and present a proposition to the next Assembly whether the said charge ought to be publick or private.

B. PUNISHMENT OF A RUNAWAY SLAVE, 1689

Charles City County Order Book, 1687–1695, 262.

Will a Negro slave belonging to Mrs. Mary Clarke being a runaway thevish Rogue, and here accused of several injuries that he hath done to the People of the County in the tyme of his late absence from his service, It is ordered that he receive thirty nine lashes well layd, on his bare backe.

11. *Slave Insurrections*

A. A RISING ON WILLIAM PIERCE'S PLANTATION, 1640

"Decisions of the General Court," 1640, *Virginia Magazine of History and Biography*, V (1897–1898), 236–237.

July 22d, 1640. Whereas complaint has been made to this Board by Capt. William Pierce, Esqr., that six of his servants and a negro of Mr. Reginald's has plotted to run away unto the Dutch plantation from their said masters, and did assay to put the same in Execution upon Saturday night, being the 8th day July, 1640, as appeared to the Board by the Examinations of Andrew Noxe, Richard Hill, Richard Cookeson and John Williams, and likewise by the confession of Christopher Miller, Peter Milcocke and Emanuel, the foresaid Negro, who had, at the foresaid time, taken the skiff of the said Capt. William Pierce, their master, and corn, powder and shot and guns to accomplish their said purposes, which said persons sailed down in the said skiff to Elizabeth river, where they were taken and brought back again, the court, taking the same into consideration as a dangerous precedent for the future time (if left unpunished), did order that Christopher Miller, a dutchman (a prime agent in the business), should receive the punishment of whipping, and to have thirty stripes and so be burnt in the cheek with the letter R and to work with a shackle on his legg for one whole year and longer if said master shall see cause, and after his full time of service is Expired with his said master to serve the colony for seven whole years, and the said Peter Milcocke to receive thirty stripes and to be Burnt in the cheek with the letter R, and after his term of service is Expired with his said master to serve the colony for three years, and the said Richard Cockson, after his full time Expired with his master, to serve the colony for two years and a half, and the said Richard Hill to remain upon his good behavior untill the next offence, and the said Andrew Noxe to receive thirty stripes, and the said John Williams, a dutchman and a chirurgeon after his full time of service is Expired with his master, to serve the colony for seven years, and Emanuel, the Negro, to receive thirty stripes and to be burnt in the cheek with the letter R and to work in shackles one year or more as his master shall see cause, and all those who are condemned to serve the colony after their time are Expired with their masters, then their said masters are required hereby to present to this board their said servants so condemned to the colony.

B. A RISING ON THE NORTHERN NECK, 1680

> H. R. McIlwaine and Wilmer L. Hall, eds., *Executive Journals of the Council of Colonial Virginia* (Richmond, Va., 1925–1945), I, 86–87.

His Excellency was pleased this day in Councell to acquaint the Councell that he had even then received from Mr. Secretary Spencer Intelligence of the Discovery of a Negro Plott, formed in the Northern Neck for the Distroying and killing his Majesties Subjects the Inhabitants thereof, with a designe of Carrying it through the whole Collony of Virginia which being by Gods Providence timely discovered before any part of the designes were put in Execution, and thereby their whole Evill purposes for the present defeated, and Mr. Secretary Spencer haveing by his Care Secured some of the Principall Actors and Contrivers, and the Evill and fatall Consequences that might have hapned, being by this Board Seriously considered Have found fit to Order that the Negro Conspirators now in Custody be either safely Secured untill the next Generall Court, to the Intent they may then be proceeded against according to Law, or if it be found more Necessary for the present Safety of the Country that they be brought to a Speedy Tryall, that then his Excellency will be pleased to direct a Commission to Mr. Secretary Spencer, Col. Richard Lee, and Col. Isaac Allerton three of his Majesties Councell Inhabitants in the Northern Neck to Sitt heare and try according to Law the Negro Conspirators, and to proceed to Sentence of Condemnation and Execution, or to Such other punishments as according to Law they shall be found Guilty off, by such examples of Justice to deterr other Negroes from plotting or Contriveing either the Death wrongs or Injuries of any of his Majesties Subjects. And this Board haveing Considered that the great freedome and Liberty that has beene by many Masters given to their Negro Slaves for Walking on broad on Saterdays and Sundays and permitting them to meete in great Numbers in makeing and holding of Funeralls for Dead Negroes gives them the Opportunityes under pretention of such publique meetings to Consult and advise for the carrying on of their Evill and Wichked purposes and Contrivances, for prevention whereof for the future, It is by this Board thought fitt that a Proclamation doe forthwith Issue, requiring a Strickt observance of the Severall Laws of this Collony relateing to Negroes, and to require and Comand all Masters of families haveing any Negro Slaves, not to permitt them to hold or make any Solemnity or Funeralls for any deceased Negroes.

12. *The Difficulty in Maintaining Racial Separation*

A. HUGH DAVIS'S CASE, 1630

> William Waller Hening, ed., *The Statutes at Large; Being a Collection of All the Laws of Virginia, from the First Session of the Legislature, in the Year 1619* (Richmond, New York, and Philadelphia, 1809–1823), I, 146.

"September 17th, 1630. Hugh Davis to be soundly whipped, before an assembly of Negroes and others for abusing himself to the dishonor of God and shame of Christians, by defiling his body in lying with a negro; which fault he is to acknowledge next Sabbath day."

B. WILLIAM WATTS'S AND MARY'S CASE, 1649

Lower Norfolk County Order Book, 1646–1650, 113a.

William Watts and Mary (Mr Cornelius Lloyds negro Woman) are ordered each of them to doe penance by standing in a white sheete with a white Rodd in theire hands in the Chappell of Elizabeth River in the face of the congregation on the next sabbath day that the minister shall make penince service and the said Watts to pay the court charges.

C. WILLIAM'S CASE, 1681

Lower Norfolk County Order Book, 1681–1686, 139.

Whereas upon the Information of mr. James Porter minister It hath appeared to this Court that Mary Williamson hath Comitted the filthy sin of fornication with William a negro belonging to William Basnett Squire It is therefore ordered that shee bee fined five hundred pounds of tobacco and Caske for the use of Linhaven parish, for which the said Basnet hath In open Court Ingaged himself etc. security.

Whereas It hath appeared to this Court that William a negro belonging to William Basnett Squire hath Comitted fornication with Mary Williams[on], and hath very arrogantly behaved himself in Linhaven Church in the face of the Congregation, It is therefore ordered that the Sheriff take the said William Into his Custody and give him thirty Lashes on his bare back.

D. KATHERINE WATKINS'S CASE, 1681

Henrico County Deed Book, 1677–1692, 192–195.

The examination of Katherine Watkins, the wife of Henry Watkins of Henrico County in Virginia had and taken this 13 of September 1681 before us William Byrd and John Farrar two of his Majesties Justices of the County aforesaid as followeth (vizt.)

The said Katherine aforesaid on her Oath and examination deposeth, That on fryday being in the Month of August aboute five weeks since, the said Katherine mett with John Long (a Mulatto belonging to Capt. Thomas Cocke) at or neare the pyney slash betweene the aforesaid Cockes and Henry Watkins house, and at the same tyme and place, the said John threw the said Katherine downe (He starting from behinde a tree) and stopped her Mouth with a handkerchief, and tooke up the said Katherines Coates [i.e., petticoats], and putt his yard into her and ravished her; Upon which she the said Katherine Cryed out (as she deposeth) and afterwards (being rescued by another Negroe of the said Cockes named Jack White) she departed home, and the said John departed to his Masters likewise, or that way; after which abuse she the said Katherine declares that her husband inclinable to the quakers, and therefore would not prosecute, and she being sicke and her Children likewise, she therefore did not make her complaint before she went to Lt. Col. Farrars (which was yesterday, Morning) and this day in the Morning she went to William Randolphs' and found him not at home, But at night met with the gentlemen Justices aforesaid at the house of the aforesaid Cocke in Henrico County in Virginia aforesaid before whom she hath made this complaint upon oath . . .

The deposition of John Aust aged 32 yeares or thereabouts Deposeth, That on fryday being the twelvth of August or thereabouts he came to the house of Mr. Thomas Cocke, and soe went into his Orchard where his servants were a cutting downe weeds, whoe asked the deponent to stay and drinke, soe the deponent stayed and dranke syder with them, and Jacke a Mulatto of the said Thomas Cocke went in to draw syder, and he stay'd something long whereupon the deponent followed him, and coming to the doore where the syder was, heard Katherine the wife of Henry Wakins say (Lord) Jacke what makes the[e] refraine our house that you come not oftner, for come when thou wilt thou shalt be as well come as any of My owne Children, and soe she tooke him about the necke and Kissed him, and Jacke went out and drawed Syder, and she said Jack wilt thou not drinke to me, who sayd yes if you will goe out where our Cupp is, and a little after she came out, where the said Thomas Cockes Negroes were a drinking and there dranke cupp for cupp with them (as others there did) and as she sett Negroe dirke passing by her she tooke up the taile of his shirt (saying) Dirke thou wilt have a good long thing, and soe did several tymes as he past [*sic*] by her; after this she went into the roome where the syder was and then came out againe, and between the two houses she mett Mulatto Jacke a going to draw more syder and putt her hand on his codpiece, at which he smil'd, and went on his way and drew syder and she came againe into the company but stay'd not long but went out to drinking with two of the said Thomas Cockes Negroes by the garden pale, And a while after she tooke Mingoe one of the said Cocke's Negroes about the Necke and fling on the bedd and Kissed him and putt her hand into his Codpeice, Awhile after Mulatto Jacke went into the Fish roome and she followed him, but what they did there this deponent knoweth not for it being near night this deponent left her and the Negroes together, (He thinking her to be much in drinke) and soe this deponent went home about one houre by sunn. . . .

The Deposition of William Harding aged about 35 yeares. Deposeth,
That he came to the house of Mr. Thomas Cocke to speake with his brother, where he see Katherine the wife of Henry Watkins, and soe spoke to one there and sayd, that the said Henry Watkins wife had been a drinking; And that this deponent see the said Katherine Watkins turne up the taile of Negroe Dirks shirt, and said that he would have a good pricke, whereupon this deponent sayd is that the trick of a quaker, who made him answer, that what hast thou to say to quakers, It being acted on fryday the 12 of August or thereabouts and further saith not. . . .

The Deposition of Mary Winter aged about 22 years.

Deposeth,

That Mr. Thomas Cocks Negroes and others being in company with them a drinking of syder, Then came in Katherine Watkins the wife of Henry Watkins and went to drinking with them, and tooke Mulatto Jack by the hand in the outward roome and ledd him into the inward roome doore and then thrust him in before her and told him she loved him for his Fathers sake for his Father was a very hansome young Man, and afterwards the said Mulattoe went out from her, and then she fetched him into the roome againe and hugged and kist him. And further saith not. . . .

The Deposition of Lambert Tye aged about 26 yeares.

Deposeth

That being at Worke at Mr. Thomas Cocks on fryday being the twelvth of August or thereabouts, and coming into the house with William Hobson and the rest of Mr. Thomas Cocks servants and others in Company with them to drinke syder, and being a drinking then comes in Katherine Watkins the wife of Henry Watkins having a very high Colour in her face whereupon this deponent asked Humphrey then servant to the said Thomas Cocke; what made his Countrywoman have such a high Colour; whereupon he made this answear; That the [said] Katherine was at Old Humphrey's a drinking and he gave her a Cupp or two that had turned her braines, and soe being a drinking with their company she went into the Chimney (as this deponent thinketh) to light her pipe, and soe made a posture with her body as if she would have gone to danceing, and then afterwards coming into their company againe, she told Mulatto Jack, that she loved him for his father's sake, And then having left the Company and she together a drinking, This deponent went home to his owne house, and afterwards coming from home towards the house of the said Thomas Cocke, he mett with the said Katherine Watkins about halfe an houre by sun in the pathway homewards neare to this deponents house. And further saith not. . . .

Humphrey Smith aged 26 yeares, deposeth,

That he heard John Aust say (about September last past) what Matter is it what I swore to and likewise the deponent saw Katherine's Mouth (the wife of Henry Watkins) torne and her lipps swell'd, And the handkerchief that she said the Mulatto Stopt her Mouth with very much bloody And the deponent heard the Mulatto confess that he had beene to aske the said Watkins wife forgiveness three tymes, and likewise the Mulatto sayd that Henry Watkins (the last tyme he went) bidd him keepe of[f] his plantation or else he would shoote him and further saith not. . . .

E. REBECCA CORNEY'S BASTARD, 1689

Charles City County Order Book, 1689–1695, 225.

John Baxter his servant wench namely Rebecca Corney being convicted in Courte of having a Mulatto bastard she is thereupon fined for her default as the law prescribes and the said Rebecca is ordered to reimburse her said Master in service upon his promise to pay this fine.

The Paths to Freedom

13. Mihill Gowen Is Set Free by His Master's Will, 1657/58

York County Order Book, 1657–1662 (transcript), 45.

Bee it knowne unto all Christian people that whereas Mihill Gowen Negro of late Servant to my Brother Christopher Stafford deceased by his last will and Testament having date the eighteenth of January *1654* had his freedome given unto him Therefore know all whom itt may concerne that I Anne Barnehouse for divers good causes mee thereunto receiving doth absolutely quitt and discharge the said Mihill Gowen from any service and forever sett him free from any claime of service either by mee or any on my behalfe as any part of parcell of my Estate that may be Claimed by mee the said Anne Barnehouse my heires Executors or Assignes as witness my hand this 25th of October *1657*

Bee it knowne unto all Christian people that I Anne Barnhouse of Martins hundred widdow for divers good causes and Considerations mee thereunto receiving hath given unto Mihill Gowen Negro hee being att this time Servant unto Robert Stafford a male child borne of the 25th of August in the yeare of Our Lord God *1655* of the body of my negro Rosa being baptised by Mr. Edward Johnson the 2nd of September 1655 and named William and I the said Anne Barnhouse doth bind myselfe my heyres Executors and Administrators and Assignes never to trouble or molest the said Mihill Gowen or his Sonne William or demand my Service of the said Mihill or his said Sonne William. . . .

14. Antonio to Gain Freedom after Ten Years' Service, 1678

Middlesex County Order Book, 1673–1680, fol. 126.

Know all men Whome this may Concerne That I John Indecott Cooper Inhabitant In Boston in New England have sold unto Richard Medlcoff, A Spanish Mulatto by name Antonio I haveing full power to Sell him for his life time But at the request of William Taylor I doe Sell him But for Tenn Yeares from the day that he shall Disimbarke In Virginia the Tenn Yeares to begin, and at the expiration of the Said Tenn Yeares the said Mulatto Anthony to be a free man to Wherever he pleaseth I doe acknowledge to have Record[ed] Full Satisfaction of the Said Medlcoff for the Said Mulatto . . . I Anthonio Doe Consent to the above premises as witness my marke in presence of Anthony Low and William Taylor the day above, March the 5th 1677/8.

15. John and Isabell Daule Purchase Their Freedom, 1670

Surry County Deeds and Wills, 1657–1672, 349.

Whereas John Daule and Isabell his wife are the Negro Sarvants of Mr. Arthur Jordan, and have this present day agreed for a vallueable Consideration to the end they might be acquitted of Such Service as they owe Me, and May Now enter upon the Makeinge of a Crop for their owne use be itt Knowne therefore to all men by these presents that I the said Arthur Jordan doe hereby release acquit and discharge the said John and Isabell from all Service dues and demands what soe ever which I the said Arthur Jordan my Executors or Administrators shall or may or ought to have or claime of them or either of them from the beginning of the world to the date here of witness my hand and seale the tenth day of March Anno Domini 1669 [1670]

Arthur Jordan Seale red wax

Sealed and delivered in presence
of George Jordan   George Procter
William S[h]erwood

Acknowledged in Courte by the
Subscriber Arthur Jordan 3d
May and recorded 13th 1670.

16. *The Courts as an Avenue to Freedom*

A. THE CASE OF ELIZABETH KEY, 1655/56

> Northumberland County Record Books, 1652–1658, fols. 66–67, 85, 1658–1660, fol. 28; Northumberland County Order Book, 1652–1665, fols. 40, 46, 49.

The Court doth order that Col. Thomas Speke one of the overseers of the Estate of Col. John Mottrom deceased shall have an Appeale to the Quarter Court next att James Citty in a Cause depending betweene the said overseers and Elizabeth a Moletto hee the said Col. Speke giving such caution as to Law doth belong.

Wee whose names are underwritten being impannelled upon a Jury to try a difference between Elizabeth pretended Slave to the Estate of Col. John Mottrom deceased and the overseers of the said Estate doe finde that the said Elizabeth ought to be free as by severall oathes might appeare which we desire might be Recorded and that the charges of Court be paid out of the said Estate. [names of the jury omitted]

Memorandum it is Conditioned and agreed by and betwixt Thomas Key on the one part and Humphrey Higginson on the other part [word missing] that the said Thomas Key hath put unto the said Humphrey one Negro Girle by name Elizabeth for and during the [term?] of nine yeares after the date hereof provided that the [said?] Humphrey doe find and allow the said Elizabeth meate drinke [and?] apparrell during the said tearme And allso the said Thomas Key that if that if [*sic*] the said Humphrey doe dye before the end of the said time abovespecified that then the said Girl be free from the said Humphrey Higginson and his assignes Allsoe if the said Humphrey Higginson doe goe for England with an Intention to live and remaine there that then hee shall carry [the?] said Girle with him and to pay for her passage and likewise that he put not of[f] the said Girle to any man but to keepe her himselfe In witness whereof I the said Humphrey Higginson. Sealed and delivered in the presence of us Robert Booth Francis Miryman. 20th January 1655 this writing was Recorded.

Mr. Nicholas Jurnew aged 53 yeares or thereabouts sworne and Examined Sayth That about 16 or 17 yeares past this deponent heard a flying report at Yorke that Elizabeth a Negro Servant to the Estate of Col. John Mottrom deceased was the Childe of Mr. Kaye but the said Mr. Kaye said that a Turke of Capt. Mathewes was Father to the Girle and further this deponent sayth not signed Nicholas Jurnew
20th January *1655* Jurat in Curia [i.e., "sworn in court"]

Anthony Lenton aged 41 yeares or thereabouts sworne and Examined Sayth that about 19 yeares past this deponent was a servant to Mr. Humphrey Higginson and at that time one Elizabeth a Molletto nowe servant to the Estate of Col. John Mottrom deceased was then a servant to the said mr. Higginson and as the Neighbours reported was bought of mr Higginson with the said servant both himself and his Wife intended a voyage for England and at the nine yeares end (as the Neighbours reported) the said Mr Higginson was bound to carry the said servant for England unto the said mr. Kaye, but before the said mr Kaye went his Voyage hee Dyed about Kecotan, and as the Neighbours reported the said mr. Higginson said that at the nine yeares end hee would carry the said Molletto for England and give her a portion and lett her shift for her selfe And it was a Common report amongst the Neighbours that the said Molletto was mr Kays Child begott by him and further this deponent sayth not the marke of Anthony Lenton   20th January *1655* Jurat in Curia

Mrs. Elizabeth Newman aged 80 yeares or thereabouts sworne and examined Sayth that it was a common Fame in Virginia that Elizabeth a Molletto nowe servant to the Estate of Col. John Mottrom deceased was the Daughter of mr. Kay; and the said Kaye was brought to Blunt-point Court and there fined for getting his Negro woman with Childe which said Negroe was the Mother of the said Molletto and the said fine was for getting the Negro with Childe which Childe was the said Elizabeth and further this deponent sayth not the marke of Elizabeth Newman   20th January *1655* Jurat in Curia

John Bayles aged 33 yeares or thereabouts sworne and Examined Sayth That at the House of Col. John Mottrom Black Besse was tearmed to be mr Kayes Bastard and John Keye calling her Black Bess mrs. Speke Checked him and said Sirra you must call her Sister for shee is your Sister and the said John Keye did call her Sister and further this deponent Sayth not the marke of John Bayles 20th January *1655* Jurat in Curia

The deposition of Alice Larrett aged 38 yeares or thereabouts Sworne and Examined Sayth that Elizabeth which is at Col. Mottroms is twenty five yeares of age or thereabouts and that I saw her mother goe to bed·to her Master many times and that I heard her mother Say that shee was mr. Keyes daughter and further Sayth not the marke of Alice Larrett Sworne before mr. Nicholas Morris   19th Jan. 1655.   20th January this deposition was Recorded

Anne Clark aged 39 or thereabouts Sworne and Examined Sayth that shee this deponent was present when a Condition was made betweene mr. Humphrey Higginson and mr. Kaye for a servant called Besse a Molletto and this deponents Husband William Reynolds nowe deceased was a witness but whether the said Besse after the Expiration of her time from mr Higginson was to be free from mr Kaye this deponent cannot tell and mr Higginson promised to use her as well as if shee were his own Child and further this deponent Sayth not Signum Ann Clark 20th January *1655*. Jurat in Curia

Elizabeth Newman aged 80 yeares or thereabouts Sworne and Examined Sayth that shee this deponent brought Elizabeth a Molletto, Servant to the Estate of Col. John Mottrom deceased to bed of two Children and shee layd them both to William Grinsted and further this Deponent Sayth not Elizabeth Newman her marke 20th January 1655 Jurat in Curia

A Report of a Comittee from an Assembly Concerning the freedome of Elizabeth Key

It appeareth to us that shee is the daughter of Thomas Key by severall Evidences and by a fine imposed upon the said Thomas for getting her mother with Child of the said Thomas That she hath bin by verdict of a Jury impannelled 20th January 1655 in the County of Northumberland found to be free by severall oathes which the Jury desired might be Recorded That by the Comon Law the Child of a Woman slave begott by a freeman ought to bee free That shee hath bin long since Christened Col. Higginson being her God father and that by report shee is able to give a very good account of her fayth That Thomas Key sould her onely for nine yeares to Col. Higginson with severall conditions to use her more Respectfully then a Comon servant or slave That in case Col. Higginson had gone for England within nine yeares hee was bound to carry her with him and pay her passage and not to dispose of her to any other For theise Reasons wee conceive the said Elizabeth ought to bee free and that her last Master should give her Corne and Cloathes and give her satisfaction for the time shee hath served longer then Shee ought to have done. But forasmuch as noe man appeared against the said Elizabeths petition wee think not fitt a determinative judgement should passe but that the County or Quarter Court where it shall be next tried to take notice of this to be the sence of the Burgesses of this present Assembly and that unless [original torn] shall appear to be executed and reasons [original torn] opposite part Judgement by the said Court be given [accordingly?]

Charles Norwood Clerk Assembly

James Gaylord hath deposed that this is a true coppy

James Gaylord

21th July 1656 Jurat in Curia
21th July 1656 This writeing was recorded

Att a Grand Assembly held at James Citty 20th of March 1655 Ordered that the whole business of Elizabeth Key [and?] the report of the Comittee thereupon be returned [to the?] County Court where the said Elizabeth Key liveth

This is a true copy from the book of Records of the Order granted the last Assembly
Teste Robert Booth
21th July 1656 This Order of Assembly was Recorded

Upon the petition of George Colclough one of the overseers of Col. Mottrom his Estate that the cause concerning a Negro wench named Black Besse should be heard before the Governor and Councell Whereof in regard of the Order of the late Assembly referring the said caise to the Governor and Councell at least upon Appeale made to them These are therefore in his Highness the Lord Protector his name to will and require the Commissioners of the County of Northumberland to Surcease from any further proceedings on the said Cause and to give notice to the parties interested therein to appear before the Governor at the next Quarter Court on the fourth day for a determination thereof. Given under my hand this 7th of June 1656. Edward Digges 21th *1656* This Writeing was Recorded.

Whereas mr. George Colclough and mr. William Presly overseers of the Estate of Colonell John Mottrom deceased were Summoned to theis Court at the suite of Elizabeth Kaye both Plaintiffe and Defendant being present and noe cause of action at present appearing The Court doth therefore order that the said Elizabeth Kaye shall be non-suited and that William Grinsted Atturney of the said Elizabeth shall by the tenth of November next pay fifty pounds of tobacco to the said overseers for an non-suite with Court charges else Execution. Whereas the whole business concerning Elizabeth Key by Order of Assembly was Referred to this County Court. According to the Report of a Comittee at an Assembly held at the same time which upon the Records of this County appears, It is the judgment of this Court that the Said Elizabeth Key ought to be free and forthwith to have Corne Clothes and Satisfaction according to the said Report of the Comittee. Mr. William Thomas dissents from this judgment.

These are to Certifie whome it may concerne that William Greensted and Elizabeth Key intends [*sic*] to be joyned in the Holy Estate of Matrimony. If any one can shew any Lawfull cause why they may not be joyned together lett them Speake or ever after hold their tongues Signum William Greensted Signum Elizabeth Key
21th July 1656 this Certificate was Published in open Court and is Recorded

I Capt. Richard Wright administrator of the Estate of Col. John Mottrom deceased doe assigne and transfer unto William Greensted a maid servant formerly belonging unto the Estate of the said Col. Mottrom commonly called Elizabeth Key being nowe Wife unto the said Greensted and doe warrant the said Elizabeth and doe bind my Selfe to save here [i.e., her] and the said Greensted from any molestation or trouble that shall or futurely arise from or by any person or persons that shall pretend or claime any title or interest

to any manor of service [original torn] from the said Elizabeth witness [my ha]nd this 21th of July 1659
Test William Th[omas] Richard Wright
    James Aust[en]

B. FERNANDO APPEALS HIS SUIT TO THE GENERAL COURT, 1667

Lower Norfolk County Order Book, 1666–1675, fol. 17.

Whereas Fernando a Negro sued Capt. [John] Warner for his freedome pretending hee was a Christian and had been severall yeares in England and therefore ought to serve noe longer than any other servant that came out of England according to the custome of the Country and alsoe Presented severall papers in Portugell or some other language which the Court could not understand which he alledged were papers From severall Governors where hee had lived a freeman and where hee was home. Wherefore the Court could find noe Cause wherefore he should be free but Judge him a slave for his life time, From which Judgement the said Negro hath appealed to the fifth day of the next Generall Court. [It is not possible to follow this case further owing to the destruction of the General Court records for this period.]

C. JACK PETITIONS GOVERNOR BERKELEY AND THE GENERAL COURT FOR HIS FREEDOM, 1665

Charles City County Order Book, 1655–1665, 604–605.

Whereas Jack a Negro Servant to Mr. Rice Hoe exhibited his petition to the Honorable Governor and Councell at the last Generall Court for freedome and release from further service claimed by vertue of a note produced to that effect under the hand of his foresaid Master Mr. Rice Hoe deceased, which note being conditionall for the said Negroes performance of true and faithfull service in the interim was opposed by Mr. Rice Hoe Junior arguing that he had not onely been refractory and disobedient, but also comitted several facts to impeach the force and Covenant of the said note. The execution whereof being referred (according to law, as a matter of fact) to examination of a Jury who returned their verdict that They find no notorious facts as was alleadged by the said Mr. Hoe, The Court doth therefore passe Judgement for the said Complainant Jack Negro (according to the said verdict) for release of the said Negro, according to his foresaid Masters engagement to him under his hand as aforesaid with Costs, also execution.

Rice Hoe appealeth from the Judgement abovesaid to the 4th Day of the next Generall Court

Itt is Ordered that the Appellant and defendant enter into bonds with security according to the Acts of Assembly in that Case provided

To the Right Honorable Sir William Berkeley Knight Governor of Virginia etc. with the Honorable Councell of State John a Negro humbly presenteth

That your petitioner being servant to Mr. Rice Hoe deceased and haveing carefully served him about 18 yeares the said mr. Hoe was pleased out of his good affection to the petitioner to give under his hand that when the petitioner should have served 11 years more he should be free, provided the said 11 years service were honestly and truly performed. And when your petitioner had served the said 11 years he presented the paper of his freedome to Westover Court, who told him the petitioner that the widow Hoe the pretended Mistress was an old diseased woman and that I should returne to her and serve her untill it should please God to take her; So the petitioner did and hath Continued in her service until she dyed, And now young Rice Hoe Claimes this your petitioner for his life time not withstanding his fathers paper under his hand to the contrary

May it please your Honors to examine the premises and grant the poore petitioner his freedome now after 29 years service and your petitioner shall pray.

14th October 1665. From the Generall Court

This cause of the Negro within named is referred to the next County Court for examination, and if it appeares there that the petitioner served eleven years service without comitting any notorious fault, then the said Negro forthwith to be sett free recorded feb. 8 1665

Teste Francis Kirkman
Clerk of Council

Memorandum that I Rice Hoe gentleman do by these presents engage my selfe my heirs and assignes to sett my Negro John free at the expiration of 11 yeares from the date hereof provided that he the said Negro doth carefully and honestly performe his labors dureing the said term of eleven years: But in case he the said Negro shall neglect what business I or my assignes shall imploy, or runn away or theife or purloine any thing from his said master or any other whatsoever and it shall be proved against him then this ingagement to be void and of none effect or else to remaine in full power and vertue:
Witness my hand this 26 Day of November 1653
Teste Thomas Tanner   Rice Hoe
Isaak Hermison

I Isaack Hermison witness this within written note, and that this on the inside is my hand, which time therin expressed the Negro hath faithfully served according to the testimony of the neighbors all which I have made under oath in Westover Court to which I can againe depose being called
                    Dec the 3 1665   John Cogan   Isaak Hermison

These may satisfie [w]home it may concerne that we [w]hose names are underwritten to the best of our knowledge do testifie that John Keratan Mr. Hoes Negro have done Mr. Hoe true and good service
                    John Cogan   Edward X Ames his Marke
                    John Stith   James Blascome
                    Robert Short

D. THE GENERAL COURT SETS ANDREW MOORE FREE, 1673

> H. R. McIlwaine, ed., *Minutes of the Council and General Court of Colonial Virginia, 1622–1632, 1670–1676, with Notes and Excerpts from Original Council and General Court Records, Now Lost* (Richmond, Va., 1924), 354.

Whereas Andrew Moore A Servant Negro to Mr. *George Light* Doth in Court make Appeare by Severall othes that he Come into this County but for five yeare, *It is Thereof ordered* that the Said *Moore* bee free from his said master, and that the Said Mr. *Light* pay him Corne and Clothes According to the custome of the Country and Four hundred Pounds tobacco and Caske for his service Done him Since he was free, and pay Costs.

E. JOHN TOWE'S CASE, 1686

> Accomack County Order Book, 1682/83–1692, fols. 92, 98.

Whereas John Towe appeared before this Court and complained against his Master John Waltham that haveing attained to twenty foure yeares of age his said Master refused him his freedom and the said Mr. Waltham not being present in Court but by Attorney Petitioned the Court that the said Towe was his slave and absented himself from his Said Masters Service and desired that he might be returned into his Service the Court thinke fitt that the Sherriffe give the Said Waltham notice to be and appeare at the next Court to make good his claime, as also the said Towe, and in the mean time the said Towe to return to his said Masters Service untill the next Court where if it appeares that he hath allready accomplished his time of service that then he the said Waltham make satisfaction to the said Towe for what the Court shall think fitt for his over plus Service.

   Whereas John Towes Mallatto Petitioned this Court for his freedome against his Master Mr. John Waltham which was referred last Court for the said John Towes to produce Mr. Richard Vahans will and this day presented the same which being read in open Court after the plea of the Plaintiff and defendant heard the Court considering upon debate thereof that it was a case of great weight and moment and that the like case never occured or was brought before them the Court thought fitt to Respit Judgment therein and order that against the next Court the case be justly and truly Stated and then to be presented to the Court in order that the same may be humbly presented to his Excellency [Francis, Lord Howard of Effingham] and Councell for their Judgment and determination therein that their excellencies opinion therein may be a Rule to proceed in this Court in resembling cases and in the mean time the said John Towes to returne to his said Masters service and if shall appeare and is adjudged that the said Towes is free then to have satisfaction for his overplus service according to Law. [No further record of the case appears.]

The Evolution of Slavery's Definition in the Law

17. Acts of the General Assembly, 1640–1680

A. AN ACT PREVENTING NEGROES FROM BEARING ARMS, 1640

"Acts of General Assembly, Jan. 6, 1639–40," *William and Mary Quarterly*, 2d Ser., IV (1924), 147.

It is likewise enacted that all masters of families shall use their best endeavours for the firnishing of themselves and all those of their families which shall be capable of arms (excepting negros) with arms both offensive and defensive (vizt) that all persons shall provide themselves as aforesaid with armes offensive the ensueing year, and with half armes both offensive and defensive the following year (vizt) in the year 1641 upon such penalty as shall be thought fitt by the Governor and council. And that for the present all persons shall cause their pieces to be fixed within three months upon such penalty as aforesaid.

B. AN ACT TAXING NEGRO WOMEN, MARCH 1642/43

Hening, ed., *Statutes at Large*, I, 242.

Be it also enacted and confirmed That there be tenn pounds of tobacco per poll and a bushell of corne per poll paid to the ministers within the severall parishes of the collony for all tithable persons, that is to say, as well for all youths of sixteen years of age as upwards, as also for all negro women at the age of sixteen years. . . .

C. AN ACT DEFINING THE STATUS OF MULATTO BASTARDS, DECEMBER 1662

Hening, ed., *Statutes at Large*, II, 170.

WHEREAS some doubts have arrisen whether children got by any Englishman upon a negro woman should be slave or Free, *Be it therefore enacted and declared by this present grand assembly*, that all children borne in this country shalbe held bond or free only according to the condition of the mother, *And* that if any christian shall committ Fornication with a negro man or woman, hee or shee soe offending shall pay double the Fines imposed by the former act.

D. AN ACT DECLARING THAT BAPTISM DOES NOT BRING FREEDOM, SEPTEMBER 1667

Hening, ed., *Statutes at Large*, II, 260.

WHEREAS some doubts have risen whether children that are slaves by birth, and by the charity and piety of their owners made pertakers of the blessed sacrament of baptisme, should by vertue of their baptisme be made Free; *It is enacted and declared by this grand assembly, and the authority thereof*, that the conferring of baptisme doth not alter the condition of the person as to his bondage or Freedome; that diverse masters, Freed from this doubt, may more carefully endeavour the propagation of christianity by permitting children, though slaves, or those of greater growth if capable to be admitted to that sacrament.

E. AN ACT DECLARING HOW NEGROES BELONGING TO INTESTATES
SHALL BE DISPOSED OF, SEPTEMBER 1671

Hening, ed., *Statutes at Large,* II, 288.

WHEREAS in the former act concerning the estates of persons dying intestate, it is provided that sheep, horses, and cattle should be delivered in kind to the orphant, when they came of age, according to the several ages the said cattle were of when the guardian tooke them into his possession, to which some have desired that negroes may be added; this assembly considering the difficulty of procureing negroes in kind as alsoe the value and hazard of their lives have doubted whither any suffitient men would be found who would engage themselves to deliver negroes of equall ages if the specificall negroes should dye, or become by age or accident unserviceable; *Be it therefore enacted and ordayned by this grand assembly and the authority thereof* that the consideration of this be referred to the county courts who are hereby authorized and impowred either to cause such negroes to be duly apprized, sold at an outcry, or preserved in kind, as they then find it most expedient for preservation, improvement or advancement of the estate and interest of such orphants.

F. AN ACT FOR PREVENTING INSURRECTIONS AMONG SLAVES,
JUNE 1680

Hening, ed., *Statutes at Large,* II, 481–482.

WHEREAS the frequent meeting of considerable numbers of negroe slaves under pretence of feasts and burialls is judged of dangerous consequence; for prevention whereof for the future, *Bee it enacted by the kings most excellent majestie by and with the consent of the generall assembly, and it is hereby enacted by the authority aforesaid,* that from and after the publication of this law, it shall not be lawfull for any negroe or other slave to carry or arme himselfe with any club, staffe, gunn, sword or any other weapon of defence or offence, nor to goe or depart from of his masters ground without a certificate from his master, mistris or overseer, and such permission not to be granted but upon perticuler and necessary occasions; and every negroe or slave soe offending not haveing a certificate as aforesaid shalbe sent to the next constable, who is hereby enjoyned and required to give the said negroe twenty lashes on his bare back well layd on, and soe sent home to his said master, mistris or overseer. *And it is further enacted by the authority aforesaid* that if any negroe or other slave shall presume to lift up his hand in opposition against any christian, shall for every such offence, upon due proofe made thereof by the oath of the party before a magistrate, have and receive thirty lashes on his bare back well laid on. *And it is hereby further enacted by the authoriy aforesaid* that if any negroe or other slave shall absent himself from his masters service and lye hid and lurking in obscure places, comitting injuries to the inhabitants, and shall resist any person or persons that shalby any lawful authority be imployed to apprehend and take the said negroe, that then in case of such resistance, it shalbe lawfull for such person or persons to kill the said negroe or slave soe lying out and resisting, and that this law be once every six months published at the respective county courts and parish churches within this colony.

Chapter Seven

Tobacco and Trade

Virginia's economic lifeblood was the production and marketing of tobacco. Tobacco made the colony's most abundant resource, the land, a valuable commodity, thereby turning Virginia into an agricultural community and luring to the Old Dominion thousands of Englishmen who dreamed of becoming prosperous tobacco planters. In a nascent economy, where money was in short supply, tobacco became the principal medium of exchange. Because Virginians never developed the capacity for producing manufactured goods during the seventeenth century, the colonists depended upon the tobacco trade for the necessities of life; the colony's need for goods and services presented widespread opportunities for business enterprise to colonist and home-bound Englishman alike. Tobacco helped to fit the Old Dominion into the English conception of the ideal colony: a place that supplied useful raw materials, but did not compete with England's own industries, and in addition generated new markets, trade, and royal revenues. The Englishmen's early experiences with Virginia and tobacco germinated ideas that matured after 1660 into England's colonial system.

John Rolfe's successful experiments with West Indian tobacco between 1612 and 1614 had saved Virginia from collapse. By demonstrating the feasibility of growing a desirable strain of the plant in the colony, Rolfe had shown that a way to Virginia's survival lay in raising a single cash crop. Rolfe pointed the way to a realization of the English dream of furthering the nation's commerce through colonial enterprise when he shipped four hogsheads of tobacco to a London merchant in 1614. Before that shipment Virginia offered few commodities that could have become the basis of a trade between English merchants and the colonists. Now, however, the colony was a potential producer of something the English wanted. This demand for tobacco made Virginia's uncultivated land the more attractive to prospective settlers already drawn to the colony by a hunger for land ownership. Once in the Old Dominion, these colonists depended upon the mother country for finished goods of all sorts, as well as for labor, financial assistance, and the means of getting their crop to market. The possibilities for trade were boundless, if only the English could exploit them.

Although the settlers had quickly abandoned other experimental crops in favor of tobacco, company officials in England did not regard the weed as an answer to the colony's economic woes. Indeed, the members of the London Company were dismayed by the rapidity with which other colonists tried to emulate Rolfe, but the colonists' fascination with tobacco alerted company officials to the possibility that salvation for their colony might lie in exploiting Virginia's agricultural potential. Accordingly the company had tried in 1618 to salvage its investment through the introduction of private land tenure, common law, and representative government. In part, then, Rolfe's successes had also contributed to the transformation of Virginia from a quasi-military outpost to an agricultural society. Following Virginia's reorganization in 1618, all efforts to discover viable alternatives to tobacco failed, and by the time the company lost its charter, Englishmen on both sides of the Atlantic had already developed an extensive long-distance trade in the staple—a trade that Arthur Pierce Middleton has called "one of the most remarkable aspects of our colonial history."

Perhaps the allure of tobacco, apart from its cash value, was its suitability to the Virginia settlers' needs. Its yield per acre was high, it kept well when cured properly, and its shipping weight was low in comparison to other staples. To men who possessed only a rudimentary knowledge of farming, tobacco appeared relatively simple to cultivate. Before 1607 Englishmen had raised the plant in England, and even as Rolfe conducted his experiments, English agriculturalists were writing treatises on its cultivation. A would-be planter had only to go to America, acquire land and seeds, and then adapt to the Virginia setting the instructions of a writer like the unidentified author of *An Advice how to plant Tobacco in England* (Document 1). In practice, however, growing and exporting a crop of tobacco proved to be a more difficult occupation than it seemed in theory.

Once in Virginia, a colonist discovered that the chance to prosper depended upon his ability to produce a cured crop that would be ready for shipment to market when the tobacco fleets came each fall. In order to meet this deadline, the planter soon realized that he had to farm according to a timetable that allowed little margin for error and that required a careful husbanding of the time between sowing and shipping. Raising tobacco, he learned, was a time-consuming process that invited financial ruin if he did not adhere to a strict regimen or failed to wring maximum efficiency from his workers.

A new Virginia planter's first task, after he had acquired his land, was to prepare the uncultivated wilderness for planting—a chore made the more arduous because of primitive farm tools. Because tobacco culture is highly destructive of a soil's nutritive qualities, the colonist, who knew little of fertilizers, found that his acreage wore out after several plantings, and this discovery necessitated the continual acquisition of more land. In order to realize a high yield, planters also learned that their tobacco needed constant, close attention throughout the growing season. During the spring there were seed beds to prepare, fields to plow, and seedlings to transplant, while over the summer the maturing plants required weeding, worming, suckering, and topping. When ready for harvest in the fall, the plants had to be cut and individually stripped of their leaves, which were then cured and packed for shipping.

Besides having a troublesome crop to raise, the planter faced other obstacles to prosperity and success. Like any farmer, he risked crop loss through drought, disease, or other natural disaster, but he also faced the prospect of losing his tobacco at sea. Lacking many labor-saving devices, the planter relied upon as much servant labor as his means allowed, but recruiting and maintaining a work force required time and energies that he could scarcely afford to spare. Moreover, he was penalized by the vagaries of a single-crop economy.

Until the navigation acts excluded them, the Dutch regularly bought Virginia tobacco, but by preference the colonists sold most of what they grew in England. Being English, they displayed a natural affinity for the products of the mother country, and at a time when one did business mainly on the basis of kinship and personal ties, they also tended to follow traditional habits of commercial intercourse. Once the English mercantile community and the government appreciated the value of the tobacco trade to the national economy, they sought to eliminate foreign competition. To that end, Parliament adopted policies that bound the Virginia planter even more tightly to his English markets. Consequently, as a result of these impulses, Virginia tobacco trade was limited to one market, and despite the obvious advantages of such an arrangement, its ultimate effect was to depress tobacco prices.

Down to the 1630s tobacco brought high prices on the English market. But as successive waves of immigrants reached Virginia's shores in the decades after the mid—1630s and as the size of the colony's annual crops rose, tobacco prices fell. By 1650 overproduction was a serious problem. A product that was generally of poor quality, growing competition from Maryland and Carolina, and the restrictions that were imposed on the tobacco trade by the English government after 1660 only aggravated the condition still further. In some years between mid-century and 1700 enormous gluts in the market drove tobacco prices so low that the planters could barely subsist on the profits of their labors. What usually spared the planters from financial ruin in these years was the willingness of their creditors to carry them until better times prevailed. The extension of credit in such circumstances was but one part of the commercial arrangements comprising the tobacco trade.

While there are many little mysteries surrounding its mechanics, the basis of the tobacco trade was the consignment system. Every year the planter arranged to have his crop shipped abroad to merchants who acted as sales agents. Any English businessman could be a consignment merchant. All he needed to become one was a source of supply and access to the market. Consequently, virtually every mercantile calling from grocer to vintner was represented in the tobacco trade. A particular merchant to whom a cargo of tobacco was consigned handled all the details of its sale, but he assumed none of the risks involved in getting it to the marketplace because the planter retained ownership of the tobacco until it was sold. After selling the tobacco for the best price he could obtain, the merchant deducted duties, shipping, storing, and hauling costs, in addition to his own commission. Next he deposited the net proceeds of the transaction in the planter's account and rendered a statement of his balance (Document 2). The planter could then use the account by drawing against it bills of exchange, which were the precursors of modern checks (Document 3).

Besides selling the planter's tobacco, the consignment merchant also bought whatever the planter required and sent those items to Virginia, after deducting their cost from the colonist's account. Because nearly everything the colonists needed had to be imported, these merchants dealt in an immense range of commodities. In a given year they might supply anything from furniture to laborers (Document 4).

Filling the planter's orders could be a trying experience for merchant and colonist alike, because even under ideal conditions conducting business at a distance of three thousand miles was anything but satisfactory. Besides selling tobacco and buying goods, the consignment merchants performed petty tasks or otherwise looked after their customers' overseas affairs (Documents 5A through 5C). At best this was a tedious responsibility; at worst it wasted much of the time needed to dispose of a tobacco crop. Frequently the tobacco that a merchant handled was difficult to vend because of its inferior quality, which was made the poorer by improper care in transit to the marketplace. Also, the planter sometimes overestimated the value of his crop and purchased more than his funds would cover. As a result, some planters were heavily indebted to English merchants.

Debt or no debt, settling a planter's accounts could involve a merchant in lengthy dealings with his Virginia customers. If court action was ultimately required, through a document known as a power of attorney the merchant deputed some friend or relative who lived in Virginia to act in his stead before the colony's courts (Document 6). The deputy then sought whatever remedies Virginia law provided, and if they were insufficient, the merchant could always seek relief in English courts. These means were time-consuming. Letters of attorney had to be attested by an English magistrate, sent to America, and then recorded in the colony's records before an attorney could act. Because debt actions clogged local court dockets, months might elapse before a case ever came to trial, while an appeal to England took even more time. In short, a debt suit could drag on for years without ever being resolved, and the costs of its prosecution could far exceed the original debt.

Apart from the risk of falling into debt, from the planter's viewpoint there were other drawbacks to dealing with consignment merchants. Usually a lag of twelve to eighteen months intervened between the time a planter ordered his purchases and their arrival at his plantation. When they arrived, they were often damaged, not what he wanted, or of poor quality. Merchants disregarded their instructions or displayed poor taste in their choice of articles, and they occasionally charged exorbitant prices for what they sold. A planter who became dissatisfied with buying from a consignment merchant, however, had other ways to acquire what he needed.

Like tobacco, merchandise could also be sold on consignment. With the profits of his business the tobacco merchant could buy goods and then sell them through his customers, whom he employed as his agents in Virginia. The planter who received the shipments of clothing, foodstuffs, or laborers might pay shipping costs, but he assumed none of the other risks in getting the cargo to Virginia (Document 7). Once it arrived, the planter exchanged the cargo for tobacco. The arrangement was not always that direct, however, as both goods and tobacco might pass through several hands before being sold. Frequently, for example, a shipper in the New England colonies might take commodities assigned to him on commission and consign them and the ship to someone in Virginia, who then disposed of what he could, loaded the ship with tobacco, and sent it elsewhere (Document 8).

In addition to these arrangements, another variation in the commodity trade was possible. Besides raising tobacco, some planters doubled as merchants. Using their contacts in England and elsewhere, they exchanged their tobacco for merchandise, set up stores on their plantations, and catered to their neighbors' requirements. Usually these storekeepers stocked only essential items, but there were some, like Jonathan Newell, who could furnish all their customers' wants (Document 9).

Merchant-planters like Jonathan Newell constituted an important segment of Virginia society. Of mercantile origins, not a few of these men had even belonged to London guilds, such as the grocers' or haberdashers' companies, before moving to America. Often they had emigrated to the Old Dominion to search for new trade outlets or to look after the already-established business interests of family and friends. Once in the colony, they took up tobacco farming and used their knowledge of business to set themselves up as intermediaries between their fellow planters and English-based merchants. Their connections with England's financial and commercial centers drew their neighbors to them for credit and easier access to the marketplace. In turn, as the merchant-planters' acquaintances and ties with the other colonists enlarged, the scope of their activities and influence widened. At his death Newell had developed his business to a point where it extended over a four-county area, as well as to London, Bristol, and several other colonies; among his customers were several justices of the peace, councillors of state, two ministers, and a governor (Document 10).

Unlike Newell, however, many of his counterparts used their economic positions to ease themselves into places of power. Employing their status as the principal merchants in their respective counties, plus whatever other influence they had gained through marriage or political alliances, these men pushed their way into the county courts, the House of Burgesses, and even the Council of State. Indeed, probably over one-half of the men who held political office between 1634 and 1689 were merchant-planters. Thus, quite apart from their economic roles, tobacco and the tobacco trade played a part in shaping Virginia's social and political institutions.

The Virginia experience with tobacco also contributed to the emergence of England's colonial system. Early in the seventeenth century the home government had given little thought to regulating the tobacco trade beyond trying to collect customs revenues. By mid-century, however, the commercial rivalry between England and the Netherlands had reached a stage where Englishmen were greatly alarmed by Dutch competition. This growing fear of the Hollanders dovetailed with English acceptance of the century's prevailing economic theory, mercantilism. Accordingly, at the behest of the merchant community, the English government began to take steps to exclude the Dutch from the American colonies and to bind those colonies more closely to the mother country's economy. A move in that direction came in 1651 when the Interregnum Parliament adopted England's first navigation act. That statute failed in its intended purpose, and the task of realizing the mercantilist ideal fell to the restored Stuart monarchs. In the years after 1660 they and their parliaments laid the foundations for England's commercial empire—an empire that rested in part upon smoke.

SUGGESTED READINGS

Bruce, Philip Alexander. *Economic History of Virginia in the Seventeenth Century: An Inquiry into the Material Condition of the People, Based upon Original and Contemporaneous Records.* 2 vols. (New York, 1895), I, 189–572, II, 258–522.

*Carrier, Lyman. *Agriculture in Virginia, 1607–1699.* Jamestown 350th Anniversary Historical Booklet 14 (Williamsburg, Va., 1957).

Gray, Lewis Cecil. *History of Agriculture in the Southern United States to 1860.* 2 vols. (Washington, D.C., 1933).

*Herndon, Melvin. *Tobacco in Colonial Virginia: "The Sovereign Remedy."* Jamestown 350th Anniversary Historical Booklet 20 (Williamsburg, Va., 1957).

* Available in paperback.

Middleton, Arthur Pierce. *Tobacco Coast: A Maritime History of Chesapeake Bay in the Colonial Era* (Newport News, Va., 1953).

————. "The Chesapeake Convoy System, 1662–1763." *William and Mary Quarterly*, 3d Ser., III (1946), 182–207.

Williams, Neville. "England's Tobacco Trade in the Reign of Charles I." *Virginia Magazine of History and Biography*, LXV (1957), 403–449.

————. "The Tribulations of John Bland, Merchant, London, Seville, Jamestown, Tangier, 1643–1680." *Virginia Magazine of History and Biography*, LXXII (1964), 19–41.

The Production of Tobacco

1. *How to Plant Tobacco, 1615*

C. T., *An Advice how to plant Tobacco in England* (London, 1615), sig. B.

Now the first thing that you are to take care for, must be the soyle: of which the ground naturally fertile, is the best, and that which hath not borne any other but grasse: for if you sow your seede in ground enriched with dung, except you stay two yeare at least, til the dung and the vapour thereof be consumed, your Tobacco will retain the savour of it.

If you sow it where Cabbage and Turnips have beene lately sowne; those rootes will also infect your Tobacco with their smell. Nay you must take care your ground be not over-fat: for the fattest grounds bring forth so thicke and so rugged a leafe, and so fild with moysture, as it will never be brought to any colour, never to any strength, nor never burne well in the pipe: A good soyle, neither too rich nor too poore, is the best, and the best helpe to better the barren, is dung of sheep.

The seedes which you are to sowe, are of two kindes, the male and female; the male is the lesser leafe, and beares a yellow flower; of which kinde is that of Brasill, which the people of the land call *Pet un.*

The female brings a very large leafe, and fatte larger and longer in England, and in France, then in the Indies; by reason of their sandy grounds, and want of raine there; and it beares a pale incarnate flower. If this latter kinde would ripen in England, in certainty it would yeeld farre more profite to the planters, it requireth less labour in the gathering, withering and making up: and being ripe, it will come to a perfect tawny colour, without any other Act then the stoving [i.e., curing with heat]; but the lesser leafe is generally the stronger, subject to lesse hazard then the greater.

In all the months betweene September and April you may cast your seed into the ground: for as that seed which falleth of it selfe in the end of September, and lyeth as it falleth uncovered, doth grow and thrive as well as that which is sowne in January, February, or March: so doth the last sowing in Aprill prosper as well, and grows as soone ripe as any of the rest. When it is sowne it must be covered but thinly with earth: for if you Cake too much over it, it will come up too late to ripen for that yeare.

If Spring bee dry, you must water it often to bring it out of the ground: your water must be river or pond water; for that of the well is too cold, except you set it all the day in the Sunne.

After your seedes are growne up to a stalke of three inches high, you must take them up and replant them, leaving two foot betweene each plant of the lesser kinde, and three foote between each of the greater. If you leave your plants so long on the ground ere you set them abroad, that the stalke have sixe inches in length, then must you either bury in the ground foure of the sixe inches, or else they will hang the head and be long ere they recover: and having set them in so deepe you bury that part of the stalke which would bring out your fairest and strongest leaves: you must therefore replant as soone as you have a stalke able to be set abrode.

You must also take care to water your plants once a day: in the morning, if the Spring bee cold; in the evening if it bee warme; otherwise they will wither or stand long ere they recover.

After they are growne a foote high, or somewhat more, they will offer a knob, and cast out little buttons for seede; which they will doe the sooner if you sowe them in the increase of the Moone, which you must avoyd. These knobbes you must every day nippe off, so must you doe all the by-branches that it casteth out, and all the stalkes but one that shoots out of the same root: you must leave but one stalke, and upon it not above 8 or 10 leaves. This pruning must be continued from the time that your Tobacco begins to yeeld shuttes and buttons for seed, even to the time that you gather it: which if you shall neglect coveting to have many stalkes, because many leaves, your Tobacco will be weake and worth nothing.

Your next and greatest care must bee, your patience to attend the ripening: for if you gather your leaves before they change colour on the stalke, they will be good for nothing. Your corne and all other fruits and grains may teach you this, that nothing hath any great vertue where nature is prevented. When your leaves be toward ripening they will be full of yellow spottes, which you shal best discerne if you hold a leafe between you and the light.

And yet you must not so love your owne as to take it greene: for when you cut it and dry it, how strong soever it prove in the taking of it, the great-nesse shewes that either it wants ripenesse or fermentation; it must look yellow at the least, or otherwise it may prove equally harmfull with that which is sophisticate. I must also advise you, not to slubber your English with *Mel rosarum*; and other trumpery, as many of our owne Artificers do, thereby to bring it to the Indian colour: it is an impious practise to play with the health of men, and to make profite by their destruction. Your English Tobacco if you give it time to ripen, and time to ferment will change colour, and cast off all her naughty and unwholsome moysture, and change her greene garment for that which is perfect yellow or tawny, without any art or addition.

When you have gathered the ripe leaves; for all will not be ripe at once, you may lay them in the Sunne for two or three houres, otherwise they will be so brickle [i.e., brittle], as they will breake in the stringing; and if the weather bee cloudy, then you may leave them in your baskets two or three dayes, and then string them upon threed, and so hang them in a close roome, where no winde entreth, or lay them on a cleane boorded floore, till they wither and become yellowish, which they will do in 10, 12, or 14 dayes, but you may not over-dry them; for then they will not sweat and change colour.

When they are thus withered, but not dried to crumble, you must stove them in heapes, in a heat somewhat stronger than a hot-house, and like unto the heate of an Oven after the bread drawne: for if your heate bee too great, it will burne, if too little, it will require a long time in their sweating, or fermentation, ere they bee brought to perfection. But if you suffer your leaves to be perfect ere you gather them, then they will ferment in a short time, and obtaine a perfect Indian colour, I meane the naural Indian colour, though not the artificiall and blacke. . . .

The Tobacco Trade

2. The Sale of Tobacco, 1651

Northampton County Deeds and Wills, Book 5, 1654–1655, fols. 88–89.

Amsterdam this 9th of July 1651

Mr. John Browne

Lloveinge friend I shalbe glad to heare of your Safe arrivall I have weighed your tobacco The one and Thirty hogsheads which are as followeth (vizt)

li tobacco		*li tobacco*	
[Hogshead] No. 30	399	[Hogshead] No. 25	395
24	366	23	370
13	372	10	336
7	425	2	374
3	330	16	390
14	352	6	306
29	374	4	352
27	384	15	392
1	380	21	380
31	364	19	372
22	342	11	380
18	360	9	416
28	390	26	370
12	416	8	394
20	406	[5?]	352
18	397		

16 hogsheads weight 6050   15 hogsheads 5569
                                  16 hogsheads 6050
                                  ———————
                                  11619

*9609
[–]576
 9033 lb at 9—4014=17=   1860
                                                                          ————
                                                                          9759

For fraight of 31 hogsheads tobacco with other charge heither att
24 per hogshead and the sume of 744* (for damaged tobacco)   150

paid mr. Browne at twice 20 [word illegible] at 63   63

Charge of your Tobacco for Laborers att [word illegible] out of
the shipp and stapling it upp   3–17–8

per house hiere at 4 s per hogshead   6–4

½ weigh money and Bookeinge   18–6

porter and [stepidge?] att the weight   4–13
                                                                  ————
         3089[guilders]–05[stivers]–8[pence]/[£]924–11–8

Mr. Browne
You are to receive of Capt. Mitchell (if he will stand to his bargaine) which
I question not 308–18–6 sterling hee beinge to paye you 12 li. for dutye 10
sterling holland money by agreement betwixt you. The 924 guilders 11
stivers 8 pence which you owe me, I have put downe to Capt. Mitchells Account, and made him debtor for it (as by his and your order) I desire to heare
from you with what speed you can, heere is a shipp goeinge from Rotterdam
towards Virginia; with the first Easterly winde I suppose The newes more
then ordinary doeings I have not else, but rest
                                                 Yours Lawrence Coughen

3. A Bill of Exchange, 1668

Isle of Wight County Deeds and Wills, 1666–1712, I, 141.

Virginia Aprill the 27th 1668
In Twenty dayes after sight of this my second Bill of Exchange[,] my First
and third not being paid, pay or Cause to be paid unto Mr. Stephen Watts
Merchant in Bristoll or his Order the full Just sume of Seaventeen pounds
Tenne Shillings good and lawfull money of England it being for the like vallue
received here in Virginia of John Scott Marriner of Bristoll make good payment and Charge it to the Accompt of him that is
                                                 Your loveing Unkle
                                                 Henry Filmer
To mr. Robert Filmer Esq.
liveing near the Talbott
att the signe of the Goat in London.

4. *Captain Yardley Buys Five Negroes, 1648*

Lower Norfolk County Order Book, 1646–1651, 116.

To all Christian people to whome these presents shall come I Daniell Peirce of the Iland of the Barbadoes, and of the shipp Swallow, now Rideing att anchor in Virginia, Merchant, send greeting in our Lord god everlasting, know ye, that I the said Daniell peirce, for and in Consideration of full and ample satisfaction by me in hand allready received have bargained and sould, and by these presents doe bargaine sell, assigne, and Confirme unto Captain Francis Yardley of Linhaven in Virginia aforesaid, five negroes, That is to say fower men and one woman namely francisco Emanuell, antonyo Lewis, and Maria, to have hould possess and peaceably Injoy the said five negroes to [serve?] the said Francis Yardley his heirs Executors, administrators, or assignes for ever without any [let?] hindrance Molestation or trouble, of mee the said daniell peirce, my heirs executors, Administrators or assignes or any other person or persons whatsoever, which warrantie and warranties of and from all and all manner of Tytles, Claimes and Interest, at present or that hereafter, may canst or shallbe layd, or pretended, to all or any of the aforesaid negroes, by mee the said Daniell peirce my heirs, executors, administrators or assignes, or any other person or persons what soever, and in witness and Consideration of the premises, I the said Daniell peirce have hereunto sett my hand and seale this 22th of February Anno Domini *1648*

Signed sealed and delivered in the   Daniell peirce
presence of Edward Windham   and his seale
        John Healey

5. *Correspondence between Merchants and Planters*

A. WILLIAM SCOPES TO THOMAS WILLOUGHBY, LEMUEL MASON, AND JOHN HOLMES, 1653

Lower Norfolk County Order Book, 1651–1656, fol. 79.

In Yarmouth the 6th December *1653*
Capt. [Thomas] Willoughby
Mr. Lemuel Mason
and Mr. John Holmes
And Loveinge Frends and kind I kindly salute you desieringe your helth in the Lord, your letter dated the 11th July I have Received per concerninge your desire of an account for the tobacco which I have Received for [the care and schooling of] Henry Sewell, as alsoe what, I am out for him, the which you shall receive heerein closed, per what you will finde there is, 64 £:3:8d due in holland cost me more, it cost me 200 guilders per Annum for his schooling done for him as if he had beene my owne, and as I did and doe by any of my famely soe I hope you will consider it, also that I have bin out of my money a longe tyme, its reason if I stand to the expenditure that I should have Tobacco, at 2d per hogshead but if otherwise then you must send soe much tobacco as will make that some [i.e., sum] out with Consideration for the

time, but I know you are Jueditious men and will doe what is reason[able],
soe I refferr my selfe to you for that part[.] I pray what Tobacco you send
lett it be good all that I have had it hath bene verry poore, if you send good it
shalbe advanced accordingly[.] I have as you ordered Taken fraught [i.e.,
freight] by Capt. Phillip Ewers, in the shipp called William of London, as
per the Coppie of an agreement sent you. Mr. Mason will appear, for the
further, dispose of the youth, you have resolved verry well for his good for it
were [a] pittey he should go to Virginia till he be able to manage his owne
businesse for if he should, he would soone lose all that he hath gayned, I
doubt not but he will gaine more in one yeere now then in two yeeres before[.] he hath beene hither to verry sickley, he brought a distemper uppon
him from Virginia which hath stucke him almost all this time, which was a
hardnesse in his boddy which is now desolved and doeth begin to threive,
he can wright and siffer [i.e., cipher] well and could have spoake French and
dutch, but I am afraid he will forgett booth, but I shall doe my best that he doe
not for his future dispose[.] seeinge I have keept him all this while I doe not
much ceare if I take him to bee my prentice[.] if you will allowe me that
[it] is fitt I could have a 100 li with a prentice if you please to give me 4
hogshead of good, tobacco per Annum for fower yeeres, and seaven yeeres service. I will take him, I doe not doubt but soe to bringe him upp that he shalbe
able to live of himselfe and soe soone as I find him capable I shall send him
on to Virginia with cargoe and then he may doe some thinge for himselfe and
I shall further him therein as well as I can for his best advantage, I pray wright
your minds with the first, I shall order my kinsman John Scopes to come to
you to know your resolution therein this being in some hast[e] I rest

> Your Loveinge Frend to use
> William Scopes

Directed to the Worshipfull Capt. Thomas Willoughby and Mr. Lemuell
Mason, and Mr. John Holmes merchants in Virginia

B. JAMES GILBERT TO WILLIAM CARVER, 1667

> Lower Norfolk County Deeds and Wills, 1666–1675, fol.
> 63.

> London december the 24th 1667

Capt. Carver—
And Loveing frend my kind Love unto you and to your wife, this is to give
you notice That I have sent you a Silver Cadle [caudle] Cup and a small
dram Cup which I have ordered Thomas Blanck to deliver you, and I desire
you to deliver my bill unto him, I was forced to send It in a box with goods
that I sent him because I had noe other way to send It that It might Come
safe to your hand, the plate Cost 50s sterling which is the full produce of 500
li. of Tobacco Beesides all Charges out of It, I should have beene veary glad if
that It had Come to a better markett soe I might have sent you a Better Return Butt this Is the utmost I have made of It, soe I hoope you will bee satisfied
with It, I have nott yett had tyme to Loock after your business concerning
Thomas alexander butt when I have I shall bee mindfull of It, and you shall
have notice of It, I doe not know your wifes name, that is the Cause It is nott
upon the plate, I hoope you have delivered my coate to Thomas Blanck. I have

sent one other letter of the same business least one should miscarry, nott Else att present butt my kind Love unto you and the Rest of my acquantance there I Remaine

Your frend
James Gillbartt

The Coate Received by mee
Thomas B Blanck   his marke

This for my Loveing frend Capt. William Carver
Liveing in Elizabeth River this letter with Care.

C. ABRAHAM WHEELOCK TO JOHN BOWERY, 1676

Lancaster County Inventories and Deeds, 1666–1682, 251–252.

London November 17th 1676

Mr. John Bowery

Yours I have received by Capt. Smith Dated July the 2nd. but I wish it [had] bin of a [later?] date that I might have heard how Conditions have bin amongst your greate troubles with the Indians, for Capt. Smyth sailed aboute 10 weekes after Your Date[.] I neede not write noe more about my not comeing in the Ship againe, but referr you to what Letters have come before[.] it was very unfortunate that none came into [i.e., in] that Ship[.] I shall Desire your care and be punctuall for I thank God it was the best of my play[.] I have sent Samuel Bryan to receive of you my tobacco, you received for mee, And have given hym a full account together with Mr. hastedd, desireing you would assist him what Debts cannot bee gotten this year, lett hym leave the Ballance with Col. William Traverse and take his receipt to bee received next year pray mr. Bowery faile not but let mee have what tobacco can possible bee had[.] I know my debts bee good I have made a very bad Voyage to my selfe as debtor I did being much out of purse. The tobacco may make mee something amend, mr. Farrington is Deceased mr. Hasted should take the Command and Shipp them home what tobacco received and bring what goods left home, what bills not received to put them into Col. Travers hands for our use, hee was please wee did not Credite his Brother with goods I hope you have noe account with hym only to pay from mee the ballance of what I promised hym though hee writt home I received nothing from him If you can dispatch your business betimes come home in some forward ship for if you please you may joyne with mee the next yere in a better concerne, I hope to bee in as early as I was before, but smallest Ship and I hope so good a Ship, and pray when you come to London take my house to your home whilst you are at London[.] your wife is well, when I was in the Countrey she sent some Side saddles to the shipps side but hearing I was not Master careyed them back supposeing as I understand by her last Letter to my wife I was Deade, as I beleeve she have given an accompt in her Letter to you[.] I shall send to her speedily and give her an accompt you are well and received a Letter from you pray bee carefull of Mr. Trotts concernes for hee serves it wholy to your selfe to give hym a returne for the goods and the sale and what Debts you make in his name leave them with Col. Travers and take his receipte, hee have charged you with 80 bushells, 60 is in your hands and about 20 I solde, charge hym for Storidge you know what Damages the salte did mee and let it bee out of what the last I solde and pay hym the rest out of my Concernes you may acquainte the neighbours I shall bee with them the next yere I thought to come my selfe this yere but servants are soe scarce cannot bee had under 3 li–05s–00d sterling per head If any of them myte have any Desire to Shipp tobacco home by the first ships and Consigne it to mee I shall Doe for them to theire Desire for the first Shipp the Best markett this yere Tobacco now at this tyme 5d½ but it is Falling by the report of Smith's Arrival with the newes of the Governors takeing James Towne and the Shipps I hope Mr. Browne have acknowledged the [parcel?] of Lande in the Court, If hee will not, lett hym pay mee for it my Cost hee shall have it. Remember mee to hym and her Kindly I could wish hee had lett Anne feerey come to mee If hee pleases to send her I shall receive her my Love to all our Neighbours and your selfe I remaine your Loveing friend.

Abraham Wheelock

To mr. John Bowery merchant liveing at Mr. Nathaniel Browns In Deepe Creeke in Rappahannock River
These Virginia [Debts?]

6. A Power of Attorney, 1657

Lower Norfolk County Order Book, 1656–1666, 82–83.

Bee it knowne unto all men by these presents that I Isaac Davis of the Citty of Bristoll Merchant, Have made constituted and ordained and in my Stead and place put my loving Friend Richard Hargrave of Elizabeth River in the County of Lower Norfolk in Virginia, my true and Lawfull attorney for mee in my name and to my use to aske[,] Levy[, and] sue for taks [i.e., taxes] recover and receive all such summes or sumes of tobacco, or any other debts or Merchandizes due and oweing unto mee within the Collony of Virginia Giving and by these presents granting unto my said atturney my full power and Lawfull authority to doe execute[,] performe[,] compound, Conclude[,] fulfill and finish in and about the premises all and whatsoever shalbee requisite and necessary as amply and effectually in every respect and to all intents and purposes by any lawfull waies or meanes Whatsoever, And upon recovery and receipt thereof or any part thereof for mee and in my name and as for my act and deed to make and give such acquitances or other discharges as shalbee thought fitting, one atturney or more under him to make Constitute and ordain Rattifieing and Confirming Whatsoever my said atturney in that behalfe shall doe or cause to bee done in or about the premises in as full and ample manner as if I my selfe were personally present, In witness whereof I have hereunto sett my hand and Seale this 21th of June *1657*

Isaack Davis and his Seale

Sealed and delivered in the presence of
Thomas Brereton   Henry Poole   Arthur Moseley

7. *A Bill of Lading and an Invoice of Goods*
Bound for Virginia, 1661

Lancaster County Inventories and Deeds, 1666–1682, 31–32.

Shipped by the grace of God in good order and well conditioned by mee John Berwick, merchant upon the good ship called the Charles of Southampton, whereof is master under God for this present voyadge James Knowles and now ridding at anchor in Carlile Bay and by Gods grace bound for Virginia to say six hogsheads of Bay salt[,] three men, and seaven women Negroes for the account of the said Barwick, and consigned to Mr. Joseph Smith now goeing in the said Ship being [included and numbered?] as in the Margent [i.e., margin], and are to be delivered in the like good order and well conditioned at the aforesaid port of Virginia, the danger of the Seas and mortality only excepted unto Mr. Joseph Smith or to his Assigns, he or they payeing fraight for the said goods already in hand with primage and overage accustomed, In witness whereof the Master, or purser of the said Ship hath affirmed to three bills of Ladeing all of this tenor and date the one of which three bills being accomplished the other two to stand voyde. And soe God send the good Ship to her desired port in safetie Amen Dated in Barbadoes October the first 1661

James Knowles

I underwritten Isaac hill Attorney of Capt. John Barwicke of the Island of Barbadoes doe hereby acknowledge to have received in full satissfaction for the negroes and goods in the within mentioned bill of ladeing from Robert Price Administrator of the estate of Joseph Smith deceased of the which I forever discharge him as witness my hand this 15th of May *1665*
Witness   Cuthbert Potter   Isaac Hill
          John Curtys

Invoyce of 6 hogsheads of bay salt, 3 dozen of Cards, 9 ivory combes, 8 pair of white cotten drawers, 8 red Jacketts, 13 pair of course stockings, 33 yards of Bayes [i.e., baize, a coarse woolen cloth], and 3 men and 7 woemen negroes, shipt aboard the Charles of Southampton, James Knowles Commander bound for Virginia being included and numbered as per Margent and is for the No. 1 to 8 account of John Barwick merchant now in Barbadoes and Consigned to Mr. Joseph Smith now goeing in the said Ship. Barbadoes October the first *1661.*

6 hogsheads of bay salt containing 56 bushels and ¼ at 12 li per bushel....675
3 dozen of cards at 30 li 090
9 ivory Combes at 20 li 180
8 pair of white Cotton drawers at 20 li 160
8 pair of red Jacketts at 20 li 160
13 pair of Course stockings at 15 li 195
33 yards of bayes at 13 li per yard 429
3 men and 7 women negroes at 3000 li per head 30000
For 6 hogsheads at 180 li per tonne Cask 270
For Cooperage and nailes at 8 li per cask 48

For Freight of 6 hogsheads of salt at 300 li per tonne 450
For freight of 10 negroes at 300 li per head 3000
Soma total is   35657

Received the 15th day of May 1665 of Mr. Robert price in full satisfaction
for the goods and above specified as Attorney to Capt. John Berwick of
Barbadoes Merchant

per Isaac Hill

Teste: Cuthbert Potter
          John Curtys.

8. *Correspondence between James Barton and Thomas Wilke, 1680*

Lancaster County Deeds and Wills, 1666–1682, 437–438.

Boston New England 14th December 1680

Mr. Thomas Wilke

These are to let you know that by the same conveyance you will receive a let-
ter subscribed by Mr. Robert Brunsden and my selfe wherein wee consigne the
Ketch Roberta Joseph Nash Comander her Cargo according to Invoice and
bills of Lading to your selfe, And therein did advise you to give the said
Vessell what speedy dispatch you could and consigne her and her Ladeing to
Mr. William [Hurst? of?] Barbados. Now this serves further to advise you that
In regard I have consigned severall goods to you to a considerable value by
severall persons which I doubt not but you have secured and disposed of for
my account and have the effects thereof in your hands I would desire you
therefore for the more speedy dispatch of the Ketch you would loade upon her
upon the joynt account (which you cannot [convert?] of her present Cargo
for ready pay to ship aboard her) as much out of the Effects of what you have
already in your hands on my proper account as will fill her up. And make good
the like value to my proper account out of the sale of the Cargo that comes to
you by this Katch, soe as that it may bee in [word illegible] for the dispatch of
the ship which I have already consigned whereof I doubt not but you have
received my former advise and if you have received the twenty hogsheads of
tobacco of Mr. Sampson Waters be sure to reserve for the ship and pray Sir
doe what you can to git in the debts you desire mee to send you a power to
receive, which I have accordingly done here enclosed. And what [ever?] you
doe give this Katch a speedy dispatch though you put aboard the more of my
proper effects consigning her to the person abovementioned and get in what
hides and tobacco you can possibly procure and keepe them till the Katch
returnes to you from Barbadoes, pray doe what you can In saveinge what Custome you can In giveing her a quick dispatch and hastening the master that
I may not be disapointed in my Voyage to Holland, besides I am [at] greate
charge in having his third parte soe that my whole returnes depend upon you
for a quick dispatch, therefore pray if possibly you can let her not stay in
Virginia above ten dayes. I have sent here enclosed a Coppy of a Bond of Col.
John Stringer to pay to Joseph Dole Forty thousand pounds of tobacco which
bond I have bought of him, therefore would desire you to send to him to get
the tobacco ready by the 20th of February by which time I hope I may bee
with you in Virginia or else shall send his obligation to you to receive it of

him, pray if you can meete with my opportunity send mee word whether the
tobacco wilbee received for I have paide Mr. Dole for it already thus hopeing
and expecting to heare from you by the first instant—hereunto subscribe my
selfe your Loveing freind

James Barton

Postscripte
The Negro that I have sent is a quiet honest fellowe and one that you may
commend to anyone that hath occasion to buy one for I have had above a
twelve moneths tryall of him.

9. *A Virginia Merchant's Stock*

York County Order Book 6 (transcript), 1675–1684, 139–
142.

An Appraisement of the estate of Mr. Jonathan Newell late of York Parish
and County Merchant Deceased taken in Obedience to an order of York
County bearing Test at Yorke February the 29th 1671/2 By Mr John Smith
Mr. Edward Moss, Mr. Hethersall and Mr. William Paddison being first
Sworne By Capt. John Scarsbrooke one of his Majesties Justices of the peace
of the said County.

No.	In the Store	lb.	s	d
1.	8 yds. ½ redd Kersey [i.e., a coarse, ribbed light woolen cloth] at 2–8 per yd.	1	2	8
2.	10 yds. almost ditto 2 remnants at 2–4	1	3	4
3.	17 yds. broad cloth at 5–6 per yd.	4	13	6
4.	15 yds. ¼ of Cotton damnified [i.e., damaged] at 12d per yd. [The frequent notation that goods were "damnified" was probably made because nearly six years had elapsed between the time when the court ordered the inventory and when it was actually taken. Thus some of the store's contents had deteriorated.]	0	15	3
5.	7 yds. ½ cotton more at 12d per yd.	0	7	6
6.	8 yds. ½ red penniston [i.e., a woolen cloth used for linings] at 1–6 per yd.	0	12	9
7.	5 yds. more at 1–6 per yd.	0	7	6
8.	1 yd. ½ cotton	0	1	6
9.	5 match Coats almost 2 yds. each at 3 and 6	0	17	6
10.	17 yds. and ½ of redd trading Cloth at 1 and 10 per yd.	1	12	1
11.	12 yds. white Kersey at 4d per yd.	0	4	0
12.	10 yds. ¼ dark colored Kersey at 3d per yd.	1	10	9
13.	7 yds. dark colored broad cloth at 7d	2	12	6
14.	7 yds. linsey woolsey at 9d per yd.	0	12	9
15.	7 yds. ½ of Saloon Cloth colored at 2–4	0	17	6
16.	14 yds. ½ of Striped stuff [i.e., a generic term for cloth and/or a woolen fabric] at 12d per yd.	0	14	6
17.	8 yds. in 2 remnants of Stuff at 1–3 per yd.	0	10	0
18.	22 yds. ¼ x ½ yds. wide Linsey Woolsey at 10d per yd.	0	18	6

No.	In the Store	lb.	s	d
19.	4 yds. ¾ of stuff at 1–3 per yd.	0	5	3
20.	7 yds. ½ stuff more at 10d per yd.	0	6	3
21.	28 yds. Tawney dark colored at 10d per yd.	1	3	4
22.	30 yds. ditto green att 2d per yd.	1	10	0
23.	24 yds. ¾ stuff all damnified	0	12	4
24.	5 yds. ½ of drugg stuff [i.e., a woolen used for heavy cloaks] at 2d	0	10	6
25.	2 yds. ½ of Stuff at 10d per yd.	0	2	1
26.	4 yds. ½ stuff at 12d per yd.	0	4	6
27.	1 end Dimitty [i.e., a corded cotton fabric] and 2 ends colored	1	11	4
28.	23 ells [i.e., an archaic unit of measure equal to 45 inches] canvas at 9½d	0	18	2
29.	14 ells ditto at 6d	0	7	0
30.	18 ells ditto at 9d per ell	0	3	6
31.	92 ells ditto at 12d per ell	4	12	0
32.	79 ells ditto damaged at 8d per ell	3	5	0
33.	47 ells Canvas at 11d per ell	2	3	1
34.	55 ells ozenburg [i.e., osnaburg, a coarse linen fabric] at 8d per ell	1	16	8
35.	16 ells ditto thin at 7d per ell	0	9	4
36.	23 ells ditto at 7d per ell	0	13	5
37.	43 ells Lockeram [i.e., a linen fabric] at 12d per ell	2	3	0
38.	24 ells ¾ of Course Lockram at 9d per ell	0	18	2¾
39.	39 ells Lockram at 10d per ell	1	8	5
40.	15 ells ¼ sayle diaper [i.e., a coarse linen] at 7d	0	8	10¼
41.	39 ells ¾ ditto in Remnants at 8d	1	6	6
42.	22 ells ¼ of ¾ dowles [i.e., a coarse linen] at 5–6	1	13	4½
43.	12 ells ¼ ditto Linnen at 15d	0	15	3
	2 dozen Callico neck Cloths at 1–6	0	15	0
44.	46 ells Lockram very course at 3d	2	2	2
45.	34 ells ¼ Hambrough Cloth at 8d per ell	1	2	10
46.	40 ells ½ Lockram at 10d per ell	1	13	9
47.	27 ells of very Course Canvas at 5d	0	10	5
48.	11 ells ¾ course Lockram at 11d per ell	0	10	8
49.	1 ell ½ more	0	0	10
50.	22 yds. Callico 2 remnants at 12d	1	2	0
51.	9 yds. ditto more	0	9	0
52.	1 booke Callico stained	0	2	0
53.	17 ells broken ozenburg at 8d per ell	0	11	4
1.	17 yds. ¼ of blew Linnen at 9d per yd.	0	12	11
2.	32 yds. ¼ more at 6d per yd.	0	16	1½
3.	32 yds ditto at 6½d per yd.	0	17	4
4.	34 yds. ¾ ditto in 2 Remnants at 8d per yd.	1	2	10
5.	8 yds. more at 9d per yd.	0	6	0
6.	19 yds. ¼ more at 9d per yd.	0	14	5
7.	26 yds. more at 7d per yd.	0	15	2

No.	In the Store	lb.	s	d
8.	22 yds. more in 2 remnants at 9d per yd.	0	16	6
9.	30 yds. more at 9d per yd.	1	2	6
10.	19 yds. ¾ of blew Linnen more at 10½d per yard	0	17	2½
1.	one suite striped curtens and val[ance]	0	17	0
2.	2 yds ½ Red Callico at 6d per yd.	0	1	3

Haberdashery Ware

No.		lb.	s	d
1.	4 peeces Colored Inckle [i.e., a linen tape] at 8d per peece	0	2	8
2.	4 yds ferret Ribbon at 2d per yd.	0	0	8
3.	13 peeces Inckle at 8d per peece	0	8	4
4.	86 yds. of mixt Colored ferret [i.e., ribbon]	0	7	2
5.	82 yds. Cotton Ribbon several Sorts	0	4	6
6.	53 yds. ½ and 1 pair Incles several sorts	0	1	6
7.	29 yds. Manchester binding	0	1	3
	3 doz. and 3 Collers 7 doz and 5 Coller peeces	0	10	8
8.	5 yd. and 9 doz. of Laces	0	12	6
	10000 pins at 6d per 1000	0	5	0
	8 packs of Cards }			
	½ Reame of White paper }	0	3	4
	5 doz. and 4 thred blew black and Colored	4	16	0
	3 doz. boyes and girles stockeins old and Motheaten	1	16	0
	1 doz. mens worsted hose motheaten	1	0	0
	1 Burnt Hammock	0	5	0
	9 porrengers 3 broken 2 bruised at 7d per porrenger	0	5	3
	4 Basons and Sawcers	0	16	0
	10 dishes of several sorts	1	10	0
	1 Bedd pan 1 porcelain Chamber pott 1 salt cellar			
	2 small tankards, bruised	0	10	0
	10 small skins	0	7	0
17.	219 yds. Ribbon at 1d per yd	0	18	3
18.	1 yd. Silke Loop Lace	0	1	6
19.	614 yds. Red, gray and green Galloone [i.e., a cotton or silk braid used for trimming]	0	10	0
20.	729 yds. of old Rotten Statute Lace	0	10	0
21.	4 doz. 1 pr. very old hat band strings	0	1	0
22.	1 old Rotten Shoulder Belt	0	0	0
23.	6 old Red Seamens Capps	0	3	0
24.	one Musty old hat	0	0	6
05.	old holland bandd rotten	0	1	6
25.	1 doz. Child gloves damnified	0	3	0
26.	7 pr. womens Gloves and 1 pr. mens	0	4	0
27.	6 small black Whisks [i.e., women's neckerchiefs]	0	9	0
	6 ditto laced with Loom Lace: 1 plaine	0	14	0
	1 Childs sattin capp	0	0	6
	1 laced prise	0	2	0
	13 Tobbacco stoppers (Bone)	0	0	6½

No.	In the Store	lb.	s	d
	A parcel of old wormseed [i.e., seeds considered to have anthelmintic properties]	0	0	1
	2 Razors Rusty	0	1	6
	3 cards of Statute Lace	0	2	0
	5 Beaver [word illegible]	0	0	2
	1 quilted night Capp	0	2	0
	2 Ink hornes	0	0	8
	1 pound sealing wax	0	3	0
	5 Rideing Kanes Small and Rotten	0	0	2
	3 doz. ½ horne Combes	0	8	0
	8 Ivory [combs?]	0	5	4
	10 Bone Combs	0	1	6
29.	2 doz. and 2 Knives Sheffield	0	3	3
	3 Joynt Rules	0	4	6
	2 Shoemakers Knives and some wooden tools	0	2	0
30.	5 doz. of sissers Several sorts	0	10	0
31.	a parcel silke and a parcel Loop Lace	0	10	0
	21 Tinn panns	0	13	2
	4 gross Leather Buttons	0	12	0
	14 doz. Thimbles and 41 Taylors Thimbles	0	8	0
	½ a gross Cloak Buttons	0	4	0
	a parcel of buttons	0	12	0
	a parcel of hookes and eyes	0	5	0
	6[?] and 17 Felts and 20 bands	1	5	6
	4 Course Castovers for men eaten with rats about the brims	0	16	0
	1 doz. womens castovers some damnified	3	0	0
	4 Leather hatt Cases old	0	4	0
	10 Looking glasses	2	0	0
	9 pr. wool cards	0	9	0
	8 Horne Bookes	0	0	8
	2 Beef Fatts [words illegible]	0	2	0
	21 pr. Childrens shooes	1	4	0
	4 pound Whale Bone	0	8	0
	1 Jack	0	7	0
	4 yds. ½ haire Cloth	0	5	0
	5 pr. Children yarne Gloves	0	1	3
	14 Canvas Jacketts and 2 pr. drawers	0	16	0
	2 Dimity Suites drawers and Jacketts	0	8	0
	9 small wast coats for children	0	7	6
	8 womens wast coats	0	13	4
	9 pr. womens Bodices	1	1	0
	4 pr. Boys Stockens	0	3	4
	1 childs petty coat and wast-coat damnified	0	1	6
	5 Childrens Capps old	0	1	0
	10 pr. Socks	0	2	6
	17 yds. ½ Buckram at 9d per yd.	0	13	1½
	one yd. of Drest Leather	0	3	6

No.	In the Store	lb.	s	d
186 gimbletts [i.e., gimlet, a small boring tool] at 1½d per gimblett		1	3	3
2 pr. garden sheares		0	5	0
11 Weeding hoes at 17d		0	15	7
16 White Latches for doores		1	4	0
12 hand sawes		0	17	4
26 Chisells		0	19	6
6 Stock Locks and Keys		0	7	0
12 Trowells		0	16	0
26 pr. hookes and hinges for doores		1	6	0
4 grubbing hoes		0	6	0
4 adzes		0	8	0
5 Hammers		0	4	2
3 Round shaves		0	3	0
2 Froes [i.e., a wedge-shaped cleaving tool]		0	4	0
1 pare large Compasses		0	1	0
13 files Rusty		0	1	6
1 Box Iron and Heatters		0	1	6
11 Bitts		0	0	11
32 Augers		0	15	0
2 bitts		0	2	0
16 falling axes one with another		1	0	0
2 reape hookes		0	1	0
2 Bedd Cords		0	2	0
1 pr. sheep sheares		0	0	4
22 Tinn Tobacco boxes		0	1	10
A parcel of old Fish hookes		0	12	0
2 fishing lines		0	4	0
A parcel of pictures of several Sorts and sizes		1	19	4
6 oyled pictures more		0	8	4
63 Bookes of severall sorts		0	12	0
6 pay Bookes some large		0	16	0
4 Large Inkhornes		0	2	0
8 parchment skins Rotten		0	2	0
1 slate frame		0	1	0
5 pad-Locks		0	6	8
3 Spring Locks		0	6	0
3 Hat Brushes		0	1	0
6 Wooden busks [i.e., a stiffening material used in corsets]		0	0	3
4 whale bone busks		0	0	2
6 Roles [i.e., rolls, either a padding worn around the top of the sleeve or a padding used in certain hair styles] for Women		0	1	6
3 old oyle cases		0	1	6
2 Chafeing dishes		0	3	0
2 balls of cotton week [i.e., wick]		0	1	4
a parcel of small boxes		0	0	8

No.	*In the Store*	lb.	s	d
	26 pr. of stirrop irons, 28 straps and 2 pr. Stirrup Leathers	0	8	8
	9 girthes	0	3	0
	23 Cow Bells	0	11	6
	8 small tin graters	0	0	8
	5 bread Graters	0	2	0
	17 Sauce panns of Tinn	0	2	10
	18 Funnels small	0	3	0
	4 bale tinn panns	0	2	0
	9 Tinn Candlesticks	0	3	0
	13 tin drinking potts	0	4	4
	28 tinn porrengers small	0	3	6
	4 doz. and 4 Ratt eaten Cabbidg netts	0	1	6
	2 pr. old bootes	0	5	0
	6 sithes of several sizes	0	12	0
	5 pr. small Bellows	0	5	0
	2 Bale pailes	0	2	6
	11 Cross Cutt Sawes	2	15	0
	3 spitts	0	6	0
	7 pr. pott Racks	0	17	6
	4 pr. pott hookes	0	5	0
	4 spades damnified	0	6	0
	1 plow Chaine	0	5	0
	1 Iron pestle	0	2	6
	2 old Saddles Old Shop keepers	0	12	0
	1 old Bridle	0	2	0
	2 old Port mantles [i.e., portmanteaux, overcoats]	0	1	6
	A parcel of earthen ware most broke	0	0	0
	2 unmoveable watches one broke	0	10	0
	3 old swords	0	4	6
	1 great pr. of scales with a beame	1	0	0
	5 pr. Scales more with 5 setts of weights	2	10	0
	1 chest of drawers	1	10	0
	1 Desk	0	10	0
	3 Chests without Locks and Keys	1	4	0
	3 old small Trunks broken	0	6	0
	1 Iron pott small	0	4	0
	1 bird cage	0	4	0
	7500 of 20d nails at 8s per M	3	0	0
	39584 of 10d nayls at 5–6 per M	10	17	0
	76334 of 6d nails at 3s	11	9	0
	40017 of 4d nails at 2–4	4	18	4
	A parcell of Rusty hobb nailes	0	2	0
	80 lb. of goos shott at 2d per lb.	0	13	4
	6 pr. of [word missing] 1 pr. small	3	10	0
	1 pr. scales and a parcel of small weights	0	15	0
	a parcell Glass about 170 foot at 5d	3	10	10
	91 lb. powder at 14d	5	7	10

No.	*In the Store*	*lb.*	*s*	*d*
1 grapnell, a parcell of old rigging and old rotten sailes one bed stead a suit of old Curtens and valens rodd, 3 Rodds and a matt		1	10	0

. . . .

10. *Jonathan Newell's Accounts, 1677*

York County Order Book 6 (transcript), 145–147.

New Kent County Debts Due to the Estate

	Tobacco
Bill and Account Charles Edmonds date April 1671 for	1140
Bill Robert Harman Oct. the 24 1671	1110
Ambrose Clare, Judgement Sept. 1671 for	32000
Ballance of William Mosshill in 1671	941
Bill 3 Negroes as Security date 4 May 1671 for	2000
Bill Richard Littlepage Oct. 1 1670 for	663
Bill Robert Jarratt 23 March 1670	2780
Bill William Wetherford 6th May 1671	1000
Account upon Mr. Thomas Balls upon Ballance	365
Bill Philip Benbridge date 1670 in worke	1664
Thomas Hollowaye and Mascall their bills Oct. 1671 account	1641
Account of Mr. William Hall for	735
Account of Benjamin Brock for	455
Bill James Forrest 22 March 1670 for	538
Nicholas Amos upon ballance per bill 17 Jan. 1671	1767
Daniel Knittons bill for 913 upon balance of a bill 1449	913
Capt. Will Jones per bill 1st May 1671	452
Richard Wethersford bill 24 June 70	451
William Woodwards bill 23 Nov. 1670 for	259
Howel Rogers 45 lbs. Porke upon ballance	
John Walch bill 16 April 1670 and Account	305
Timothy [Purton?] per Account	165
John Jackson per bill 22 March 1670	200
William Randall per bill 6 May 1671 and Account	215
William [Custis?] bill and account in 1666	594
Susanna Wilkins per bill Feb. 1670 for	80
Account Leonard Tompson for	195
Bill John Davies March 15 1670	200
Bill from Sarah Sparkes in 1664	1150
Bill John Parker for	159
Thomas London's bill and account	116
William Rolph per bill and account	1113
Bill date November 18 1665	[no amount in original]
Thomas Minns per bill 19 Jan. 1671 for	405
Edward Harrison per bill 22 March 1670 upon balance	444
	58,837

Account to be settled with Mr. Thomas Hall
Account to be settled with Mr. John Duncomb
Account to be settled with Lt. Col. Gooch
Claim of 4264 lbs. from James Perry per bill and account to be settled
Claims with Col. Abrahall to be settled
Bill and accounts with Gregory Barnett to be settled
Bill and account with Valentine Napier and Nicholas Thompson to be settled
Account to be settled with Charles Turner
Account to be settled with Capt. Blackley
Account with Mr. Austin to be settled
Account with Mr. Thomas Michell to be settled
Account with Mr. George Chapman to be settled
papers of Capt. Bassett to be settled
Account with Capt. Parkes to be settled
Account with John Winslow to be settled
Account with Capt. Mallory to be settled
Account with Mr. John Hilliard to be settled
Account with Capt. Lyddal to be settled
Account with Flanders to be settled
Papers Mr. John Mohun
Account with Thomas Hancock to be settled
Account to be settled with Capt. Claiborne in 1669
Account with Major Wyat to be settled.
Account with Thomas Hartley to be settled 1670
Account to be settled with Crump in 70 and 71
Account to be settled with Mr. John Smith
Mr. William House his account to be settled
Mrs. Frances Izard her account to be settled
Account to be settled with Doctor Philips
Engagement Major West for Beaver to be settled
Account Peter Ford to be settled
Severall accounts and bills between Lane and Newell to be settled
Account of William Tompson about 1392 to be settled
Account Stephen Petters to be settled
Account John Walker to be settled
Account Robert Wallis to be settled
papers James Coale to be settled
Account to be settled with John Vaughan
Benjamin Dowle account to be settled
Bill and account William Morgan 1670 to be settled
Papers William Horne to be settled
An account to be settled with John Twilly
Account William Parker to be settled
Account with John Pigges to be settled
Will Drakeford Account to be settled
Arnold Mann his account to be settled
Mr. John Lane his account to be settled

A List of the hogsheads of Tobacco Received in New Kent County by David Crawford Lying at the severall plantations underwritten

G.R. No. 1 att Mr. Cookes of Woodland neate [i.e., net weight]	338
2. At John Jacksons house Nicholas Amos neate	406
3. At John Jacksons house Robert Jarratt	420
4. At John Jacksons house Robert Jarratt	396
5. At John Jacksons house Robert Jarratt	468
6. At John Jacksons house Robert Jarratt	468
7. At John Jacksons house Robert Jarratt	508
8. At John Jacksons house Robert Jarratt	430
9. At John Jacksons house John Cape	400
10. At John Jacksons House Mr. Mosse neate	450
11. At John Jacksons house William Moss neate	408
	4742

James County Debts

No. 1 Major Thomas Waidsons bill 13 May 1671 and No. 2	1000
Henry Chester per bill Assigned for James Bullock for	500
Edward Walker his bill date 7 April 1678 for	630
Mr. Chisse minister his account assigned per Cooper 1670 for	225
Richard Davis his noat at William Comans 1671 for	60
Mr. Robert Colchy per noate date 2 Nov. 1670 either in Fees or Expenses at Towne for	300
Mr. John Stevenson his bill assigned per Cooper for	130
Capt. Thomas Williams per Vinegar as per Receipt under Raynolds his hand date 29 March 1671 will appear otherwise Raynolds to pay it.	40
Robert Sorrell an account to be settled but upon ballance	3000
John Hawkins bill and account to be settled	520
Will Smith bill 1669 and account to be settled	1322
	7727

No. 1 Henry Reades his account to be settled

Mr. Robert Sorrell upon ballance of his bill 3000 and an account therein to be settled

Mr. John Barber his account to be settled in 67 and 68

Mr. Richard Awbourne his bill and account to be settled 1669

Mr. Richard Lawrence his account to be settled 1670

James Alsopp his account to be settled 13 Nov. 1671

Note to Major Marriott about [Rec?] 2 Bills

Mr. Mason and Mr. Linny their account to be settled 1671

Mr. David Crawford noate per service and other Account to bee settled

No. 2 William Paulett his account to be settled

Account with the Right honorable Governor [Sir William Berkeley] to be settled

William Belvins account and papers to be settled

Mr. William Cooke his account to be settled

1670 ballance 318 lb. per note
Thomas Ballard Esq. his papers and accounts to be settled
John Hawkins his bill and account 1671 for 520 to be settled
William Smith his bill 1669 and Account for 1322 to be settled
William Roberts his accounts to be settled
John Linge his bill for plants and Tobbacco
Robert Weekes
Richard Farthing per bill date Nov. 1678
Mr. David Newell bills and account in a particular bundle
No. 2 to be settled per bill 1019, 882 and 100 gal. Rum
One Man servant named Peter Trusdell came not in the praisement David
   Newill kept him
One new saddle
One Mare and Colt praised
4 ounces old plate

York County Debts

No. 1 John Potthin Jr. per bill date 21 Dec. 1670	170
Gerrard Conner and Edward Wyndham payable 1672	494
Thomas Gardner per noate	50
Bill Edmund Ivory August 1669	3169
Francis Browne bound per Alex Ashton per bill December 1671	493
Christopher Dedmond upon ballance of a bill December 24 1670 and his estate bound over for payment therefore 437 received in ballance	2637
Thomas Townell per bill date 23 Feb. 1670 for	276
Mr. James Woody security for Robert Neale December 1671 for	1040
Mr. Edward Wade per bill date 20 May 1671	692
Mr. William Major per bill and account to symons	815
Humphrey Beale his bill 1669 for	225
No. 2 James Price Edward Miller and John Hallam their bills date 24 December 1670 for	893
Mr. John Hallam per bill date 23 August 1671 per 4,000, 1,000 payable the last october and the other 3000 in 1672	
Mr. Thomas Mann Assigne of Gawen Dunbar	520
Thomas Isles per bill 200 and 1671 per Blackstons 100	300
John Babb Assigne of Thomas Gulley	200
No. 3	
John Lawson per bill 121 lb. porke and per another in tobacco	40
Mr. George Reade Debtor one Knife 21d Francis Kniveton and Crispe upon ballance	756
William Allen Shoomaker Assigne of Cooper	20
Richard Wheeler upon ballance of the noate	20
George Johnson Assigne per Cooper	106
Mr. Nicholas Clarke per 330 gal. syder and 1/4 caske Quince pickles	270
Mr. Clement Marsh	2500
Mr. [Collier?] Lucas	390

John Macoy   460
Thomas Dunston   336
Thomas Wardley and Thomas Isles   934
Mr. Thomas Bushrod per note debtor 1000 of 6d nayls, 1000
     10d nayls, 500 of 4d nails, 1000 of 6d, more 6d nails 300
Major Robert Baldrey per 9 bushel Corne 1669
Mr. Thomas Wardley his obligation for 10 gal. and 4 inches of Cyder
                                                                              _____
                                                                              21806

No. 1
Mr. Henry Freemans papers to be settled
Richard Trotter and Walter Blake their account
Mr. John Hetherfall his account to be settled
Mr. Thomas Beale Jr. his account to be settled
John Ruston his account to be settled
Mr. John Rogers Undersherriff his bill and account to be settled
     per Christopher Deadman 334 lb. Tobbacco and Caske
Mr. William Wetherall his account to be settled
Mr. James and Edward Miller their bills and accounts to be settled
Mr. William Allen the Smith his account to be settled
John Baskerville his account to be settled
Mr. Ralph Flowers his bill and account to be settled

No. 2
Will Aylesberry his bills and accounts to be settled
Mr. Samuel Docope his papers to be settled
Mr. James Butler his account to be settled
Mr. John Roger his papers to be settled
Account to be settled Between Col. Bacon and Jonathan Newell deceased
Thomas Spelmans bill and account to be settled
Richard Groves his account to be settled
Peter Hargrave his account to be settled

No. 3
Major James Goodwins papers to be settled
Mr. Job Vergetts accounts to be settled
Account between Mr. Jonathan Newell deceased and doctor Francis Haddon
James Bullock his account to be settled
Mr. Will Pattison his papers to be settled
Jeremiah Wale his papers to be settled
Mr. John Smith his papers to be settled
Thomas Watkinson per account and bill 245 to be settled

Rapahannock
Account between Robert Beverley to be settled
Account between Col. Potter to be settled
Account with Capt. Wormely to be settled
Account with Mr. James Key and Owen Lloyd to be settled
Capt. Edmund Lester his papers to be settled
Mr. John Appleton his papers to be settled

Warwick County

John Rich per bill assigned per Mr. Robert [Weersmore?] in Anno 1668	150
Mr. Thomas Reed per 3 bills 67:69:71 besides Accounts	12383
William Moore the Miller per assignment	
Leake per account	150
Margaret Stevens alias Crews per bill 1670	400
Francis Cooke per bill 1670	951
Mr. Humphrey Harwood per ballance of the bill	11
Thomas Green and John Podgett per bills 1669	1389
Mr. Francis Rice per assignment James Millers bills to Mr. Jonathan Newell of 2 lb. o s o d sterling	
William Elmes per bill 1669	428
William Coman per bill date July 1671	2000
Richard Lloyd Fidler per bill 1671	476
John Grunsell per bill date Oct. 1669	602
Mr. Samuel Clarke deceased per bill and account	5479
Mr. Anthony Haynes and Mr. Ambrose Lloyd per bills	14836
Richard Lloyd Fidler black swampe	476

Glocester County Debts
March 18 1671/2

Mr. Robert Brian per bill and account	1428
per another bill Thomas Seawells for	154
Francis symonds per bill	6500
John Gardner per assignment of 2 bills of Richard Welch as due from the said Welch	1660
Doctor Henry Whiting	1518
Mr. Thomas Vicars	10800
James Collison per bill	808
Richard Austin per bill 100 lb. of potatoes and one peck of English flower and 40 lb. of Tobbacco per note charged per Mr. Ireland	40
Mr. John Leake	6196
One gill and one pint Juse	
John Gregory Capt. Ludwells overseer	73
Mr. Gawin Dunbar, besides 2 notes to be Cleared	
Richard Edmunds	410
	20436

Glocester County

Mr. Thomas Tilley	400
Mr. Richard Whitebread per bill	1105
	21941

Account Mr. Robert Lee to be Settled
Account Mr. John Payte Esq. to be settled

Account to be settled with Mr. Whitebread
Account made up with Mr. Richard Whitebread
Mr. Dearows accounts to be settled and his papers a note of
Dr. Whitings in them
Accounts with Capt. John Lightfoote to be settled
Some papers as to Kentiss
Account with Mr. Hugh Nevett to be settled
Accounts relating Mr. Hawling to be examined
Capt. Jennings papers to be settled
Papers Mr. Ralph Harwood to be settled
Will Dixons [desputed?] and therefore not entred

Chapter Eight

Indians and Whites
The Conflict of Cultures

At the time the English settled Jamestown, what became Virginia was populated by an aboriginal people who spoke languages belonging to three linguistic stocks, Algonquian, Iroquoian, and Siouan. Of the three groups, the Algonquian-speaking Indians were the most numerous. Consisting of some three dozen tribes who were united in a loose confederacy imposed upon them by the chieftain Powhatan, these natives lived in an area between the fall line and the Atlantic Ocean (see the map of Virginia from 1607 to 1624, in chapter 1, for locations of Indian villages). West of the falls the Siouan tribes inhabited the remainder of modern Virginia, except for a small wedge of territory along the Carolina border in the southeastern portion of the state, which was the homeland of the Iroquoian-speaking tribes. Estimates of the number of preconquest natives are conjectural. John Smith put the number of Indians living within a sixty-mile radius of Jamestown at five thousand, but modern scholars estimate that the size of the Powhatan Confederacy in 1607 may have been more than double Smith's estimate (Document 1).

Because the English pushed their line of settlement no farther west than the fall line during the seventeenth century, the tribes of Powhatan's Confederacy bore the brunt of the colonists' intrusion. The discovery of these Indians was a disappointment to the English. Having learned of highly developed native civilizations in the Spanish New World, Englishmen were eager to capitalize on an opportunity for contact and trade with similar indigenous cultures in the part of the Americas that they had selected for exploitation. What they found was not another Aztec or Inca civilization, but a people who were in the late woodland phase of cultural development.

All of what modern scholars know about the Powhatan Confederacy comes from archaeological evidence or English depictions of Virginia's original inhabitants. While the descriptions of native life left by such colonists as Ralph Hamor, William Strachey, and John Smith are classics in the literature of Europe's exploration of America, their usefulness is limited because of their authors' cultural chauvinism and because they reveal nothing about the Indians after the first decade of settlement. Once the English perceived the Indian as an obstacle to settlement in the wilderness, they became more interested in removing a menace to their security than in preserving a record of Indian ways. More unfortunate, there are no records representing the native point of view, because the Indians had no written language. Consequently there are gaps in our understanding of how the tribes of the Powhatan Confederacy withstood the onslaught against their culture. Despite the handicaps imposed by an unsophisticated technology, Powhatan's people stoutly resisted English assaults on their lands and life-style. Until overwhelmed by sheer force of numbers, they kept the English at bay for nearly half a century. Their success lay in the potency of the confederation that Powhatan had erected.

Shortly before 1607 Powhatan had forged the confederation of all the Algonquian tribes by force of arms. Each of these tribes had a recognized territory marked out for it, and every native family had its own plot upon which to raise crops. Most of the individual tribes lived in villages surrounded by palisades, which were situated on lowlands near rivers and creeks, where there was rich soil and easy access to food from the streams.

Their economy, which depended primarily upon agriculture, was fairly advanced. To supplement the foodstuffs that could be gathered in the forests or caught in the rivers, the Indians cultivated a variety of crops. Their skill as farmers saved the English more than once: the native women produced surpluses of corn that kept the colonists from starvation. Surrounded by an abundant variety of fish and wild life, Indian men were accomplished hunters and fishermen, having developed such harvesting techniques and devices as the community hunt, the net, the weir, and the fishhook. Their tools were fashioned of wood, bone, or stone, but many of them were similar in design and function to European implements. Although before 1607 the Indians had not developed an extensive system of trade outside the confederation, they understood bartering. Once they perceived the advantages to be gained by employing European technology, the Indians quickly began to barter for English tools, pots, cloth, and the like. As the seventeenth century wore on, a trade that was both lucrative and troublesome became a mainstay of relations between the two alien cultures.

Within the Powhatan Confederacy the largest unit of social organization was the tribe. In contrast to the English, the line of descent in the family was matrilineal, and some chiefs practiced polygamy. The Indian religion centered on propitiating evil spirits and maintaining a balance among the forces of nature; the priesthood was a recognized social status. Games, ceremonies, and ritual dancing often attended occasions of great social moment, such as religious festivals or making war. Potsherds, pipe fragments, and colonists' accounts also attest to the Indians having had an appreciation of artistic design for both aesthetic and functional purposes.

The Indians lacked a formal system of laws but not a sense of morality and justice. Marriage was regarded as sacred, but divorce was permissible, and infidelity was considered the most unpardonable of crimes. Chiefs held the power of life and death over their people, and they visited retribution upon those who stole, murdered, or otherwise offended against tribal morality.

Although its cohesive force was fear of Powhatan, the confederation had a clearly defined political organization. Governing each tribe was a chief, who was often a woman. A number of individual tribes might be ruled over by a chieftain known as a lesser *werowance.* The lesser werowances were subordinate to a council consisting of werowances, priests, and relatives, who assisted the great werowance, Powhatan, in administering his dominion. That the confederation was in its formative stages in 1607 may account for the relatively friendly reception Powhatan accorded the English when they first arrived in Virginia.

In the beginning the Englishmen posed no threat to the confederacy. The colony was small, the settlers had been instructed to make friends with the natives, and the wilderness killed off the colonists almost as rapidly as they came. Still, the Indians were wary and occasionally hostile. After 1609, when it became increasingly apparent that the English were determined to remain, this hostility stiffened into war. Using their traditional tactics of surprise and mobility, the Indians waged an intermittent war of attrition on the English that lasted until Samuel Argall kidnapped one of Powhatan's daughters, Pocahontas, in 1613. Following her capture, Pocahontas met John Rolfe, who became so smitten by the Indian girl that he wished to marry her. After a lengthy inquiry into his motives had been conducted, Rolfe secured Sir Thomas Dale's permission to make the marriage (Document 2). The Pocahontas-Rolfe marriage, one of the few Indian-white marriages in seventeenth-century Virginia for which there is a record, plus the English threat of a concerted attack on the confederacy, caused Powhatan to make peace with the colonists. Thereafter, as long as Powhatan lived, relations between the two peoples remained stable.

A shift in Indian attitudes began to occur following Powhatan's death and the accession of Opechancanough as chief werowance in 1618. By then it was apparent to Opechancanough that the English planned to stay in Virginia. Their settlements already extended from the mouth of the James to the falls, and some Englishmen were pushing north towards the York River. Opechancanough bided his time, waiting for the right moment to remove this menace to his people and their way of life. Feigning continued friendship with the English, he made his plans and marshaled his men for a concentrated attack on all the colonial settlements. On Good Friday morning of 1622, a day he reckoned the English would be least cautious, Opechancanough made his move. Without warning, parties of Indians simultaneously struck all the English settlements. Opechancanough's intention to extirpate the colony was clear: none of the Indians took any prisoners that day or in the subsequent attacks (Document 3).

Opechancanough's offensive claimed 347 lives—a third of the colony's population. Jamestown escaped destruction only because a friendly Indian had given the town advance warning on the morning of the attack. The entire colony might have been wiped out had the Indians pursued their advantage. For weeks the English reeled from continuing assaults; then they were struck by famine and plague. But gradually they mounted a counteroffensive. The English resorted to a policy of systematically hunting down the Indians, destroying their villages, and crippling their capacity to make war. This pattern of raids and counterattacks continued sporadically until the late 1620s, when both sides finally tired of fighting (Document 4).

The consequences of the fighting were calamitous: both sides suffered frightful losses of life and property. For the Indians the waste of life was irreplaceable. Beyond the physical scars that it left, the Indians' attack served notice that they refused to be assimilated into the white man's world, while the colonists' response indicated a change in English attitudes toward the red man. After 1622 the settlers made fewer attempts at establishing friendly relations with the natives; no longer was there as much concern for educating or converting them. More than ever the colonists now looked upon the Indians as unfit barbarians who stood in the way of the orderly settlement of their newfound homes. These were savages with whom to trade—if the trade were profitable. Otherwise they were to be avoided or exterminated, as the occasion demanded.

When a degree of peace returned in the 1630s, the English were still too few in numbers to launch an all-out campaign of extermination or removal. Nevertheless they continued to harass the Indians with periodic raids upon their settlements (Document 5). The tactic of burning villages and destroying crops kept the natives off balance, while it allowed the English time to recover from the devastation wrought by years of fighting. A more destructive method of eradicating the Indian rivals was the extension of the colony's settled area. As the colony's English population multiplied, the new immigrants put the plow to more land, leaving the natives the choice of moving west into the territories of their enemies or standing to fight once again.

By the 1640s the pressure on the Powhatan Confederacy was so great that the Indians decided to fight. Now an old man, but still the great werowance, Opechancanough had lost none of his inveterate hatred of the whites. As he had done two decades before, the aged chief laid another carefully conceived plan to attack the fringe settlements. His warriors struck in April 1644 and in the first two days of fighting killed perhaps as many as five hundred colonists. But the eventual outcome of the war that followed was never in doubt. This time the English enjoyed superiority in numbers, and they had acquired the skill to defeat the Indians decisively. The fighting lasted for two years; Opechancanough was captured and later murdered by his guards in the jail at Jamestown. Finally, in October 1646, the surviving Indians sued for peace.

By terms of a treaty with the General Assembly adopted in the fall of 1644, the Indians surrendered all of their claims to the areas of English settlement. In return for their recognition of English sovereignty over the land, the Indians received a reservation north of the York River, where whites were forbidden to enter except by special license. Additionally, the colonists forced Opechancanough's successor, Necotowance, to acknowledge Charles I as his overlord and the Indians as crown subjects. As a reminder of their subjection, the treaty required the Indians to pay an annual tribute of twenty beaver skins (Document 6).

The treaty of 1646 marks the colonists' first real effort to devise a program for governing Indian relations. In adopting the treaty the General Assembly laid the foundation of a policy that remained in effect for nearly thirty years. As adumbrated in the treaty it contained three points: erecting a defensive perimeter on the frontier, eliminating as many contacts between the two peoples as possible, and subjugating all those Indians who lived within or near English settlements. A string of forts had been constructed in 1645; after 1646 more were added, and these became the colony's main defense against future attacks. To reduce tensions, in October 1649 the assembly outlawed the casual killing of Indians, which had been permitted in the treaty, and forbade the English from keeping Indian children (Documents 7A and 7B). During the same session the assembly also sanctioned the creation of new reservations for two additional tribes of tributary Indians (Document 7C). Throughout the Interregnum and the 1660s the General Assembly continued to add to this core legislation in the hope of reducing the causes of friction still further.

By an unfortunate coincidence the formulation of Virginia's Indian policy came at the very time the colony's population began to burgeon rapidly. Based as it was, in part, upon reserving tracts of land for the natives, the policy's failure was assured by the sudden influx of large numbers of Englishmen into the Old Dominion during the 1650s. In the territory north of the York River alone, the General Assembly created three new counties out of Indian lands by 1653. Save for delaying settlement, the governor and the assembly could do little to prevent the eventual overrunning of Indian land.

The effects of this encroachment were predictable. Scattered outbreaks of violence occurred in frontier areas throughout the 1650s, but they subsided briefly as the decade drew to a close. By March 1661/62 the situation had worsened to the point that the assembly felt the necessity for acting to prevent scattered incidents from becoming widespread. For the next dozen years relations remained tense. Twice before 1675 they became so strained that a full-scale war threatened.

These known incidents of hostility were only the extreme manifestations of the continuing tensions that existed between the English and the Indians from 1646 to 1675. Given the wide cultural differences between the two and the Englishmen's aggressive land hunger, the development of such tensions was probably unavoidable. For the Indians the stolen land, dishonest dealings, and loss of their independence and identity, and for the English the pilferage, trespassing, and threat of unexpected attack by the natives stood out as constantly irritating reminders of the daily conflict of cultures. (Documents 8A through 8I). While the official policy of the colony's government was peace, those colonists who routinely came into contact with the Indians took a less tolerant view when their neighbors were set upon by the natives. A small raid upon a remote settlement was likely to be inflated in reports from the frontier into an attack of unequaled proportion. To be sure, the settler could blame his aggressiveness for much of the trouble, but the ever-present threat of attack produced an attitude of mind that, when a general Indian war again became a possibility in the summer of 1675, made the frontier settlers more than willing to remove the Indians forever.

Indian-white relations had reached a critical point by the summer of 1675. Several isolated raids initiated by the Doegs and the Susquehannocks on the outlying settlements along Virginia's northwestern frontier set the stage for another war. The Doegs and the Susquehannocks were Siouan-speaking tribes who had been driven from their traditional homelands north of Virginia by the Iroquois. In July 1675 small parties of Doegs slipped into the Old Dominion, stole some hogs, killed a few settlers, and then drifted back into Maryland. When local militia officers learned of the raids, they gathered a force of men, crossed into Maryland, and killed several Doegs and a few friendly Susquehannocks before returning to Virginia (Document 9A).

On the face of it, the episode seemed typical of other such incidents that had happened in recent years, but this one led to more serious trouble. Alarmed by the Virginians' strike into their colony, Maryland authorities protested the invasion to Governor Sir William Berkeley, but they also indicated a willingness to cooperate in any future assault on hostile natives. Late in August, Berkeley, who correctly surmised that the situation threatened to get out of hand, ordered John Washington and Isaac Allerton to raise a force of militia, investigate the causes of the recent troubles, and punish the guilty Indians (Document 9B).

Washington and Allerton seem to have interpreted their instructions rather loosely, for they displayed no apparent inclination to conduct a thorough investigation. Instead, as soon as they had mustered the militia, they contacted the Maryland government for assistance in tracking down the Indians. The Marylanders dispatched a troop of men, and the combined force set out in search of the Susquehannocks, who were now thought to be as responsible as the Doegs for the recent troubles. Late in September when the party reached the Susquehannock stronghold and arranged a parley, the Virginians accused the natives of murdering whites. The Indians vigorously disclaimed any responsibility, but Washington and Allerton were unconvinced. Five chiefs were led away and executed (Document 9C). The English then besieged the stronghold, but a few days later, under cover of darkness, the Indians slipped off.

Whether or not the Susquehannocks had been with the Doegs in July no longer mattered. Now they were bent upon avenging their murdered chiefs, and in January 1676 they hit the settlements along the Rappahannock and Potomac Rivers, killing thirty-six persons. Electrifying in its effect, the raid terrorized the English into mass panic and divided opinion about how best to prevent further attacks. Governor Berkeley sought to calm passions and to protect the friendly, tributary Indians; so he downplayed the seriousness of the natives' depredations. The frontiersmen clamored for an all-out assault on "the Indians," without distinction between friend or foe. Sir William's inability to allay fears of a general Indian uprising throughout the colony caused the agitated colonists to seek extralegal means of ending the threat to their security. In the end the disagreement over Indian policy became entangled with other issues, which led to Bacon's Rebellion.

The English never again engaged the Susquehannocks after their attack in January 1676. Instead the remnants of the Powhatan Confederacy became the targets of the colonists' frustrations and wrath. On the pretext that one tribe, the Pamunkeys, was secretly aiding the Susquehannocks, a party of colonists led by Nathaniel Bacon attacked the tribe's main encampment in the summer of 1676. The Pamunkeys offered little resistance: several were killed, a number captured, and the remainder scattered. Although the Powhatan Confederacy was later exonerated of any cooperation with the Susquehannocks, the English made the surviving Indians sign another peace treaty that again acknowledged their dependence upon the crown.

With the signing of the treaty, the destruction of the Powhatan Confederacy was complete. Eastern Virginia was cleared of any Indian "problem," and the remaining tribes of the confederation dwindled rapidly over the last years of the seventeenth century. Within the first years of the eighteenth century, their number had so diminished that the historian Robert Beverley concluded, "The *Indians* of *Virginia* are almost wasted" (Document 10).

A century of proximity to the English had been disastrous to the Indians of eastern Virginia. Disease and warfare had exacted a terrible tribute. English settlement patterns had destroyed the Indians' economy, and their desire for English tools, clothing, and weapons had reduced the natives to dependence upon the colonists. Overwhelmed by superior numbers and weakened by the gradual erosion of their cultural identity, the tribes of the Powhatan Confederacy finally lost the will to survive. Broken in spirit, their lands and way of life forever lost, these Indians passed into the pages of the tragic history of Indian-white relations.

SUGGESTED READINGS

*Beverley, Robert. *The History and Present State of Virginia,* ed. Louis B. Wright (Chapel Hill, N.C., 1947), 159–237.

Bruce, Philip Alexander. *Economic History of Virginia in the Seventeenth Century: An Inquiry into the Material Condition of the People, Based upon Original and Contemporaneous Records.* 2 vols. (New York, 1895), I, 140–189.

Craven, Wesley Frank. *White, Red, and Black: The Seventeenth-Century Virginian* (Charlottesville, Va., 1971), 39–72.

————. "Indian Policy in Early Virginia." *William and Mary Quarterly,* 3d Ser., I (1944), 65–82.

*Lurie, Nancy Oestreich. "Indian Cultural Adjustment to European Civilization." In *Seventeenth-Century America: Essays in Colonial History,* ed. James Morton Smith (Chapel Hill, N.C., 1959), 33–63.

*McCary, Ben C. *Indians in Seventeenth-Century Virginia.* Jamestown 350th Anniversary Historical Booklet 18 (Williamsburg, Va., 1957).

Nash, Gary B. "The Image of the Indian in the Southern Colonial Mind." *William and Mary Quarterly,* 3d Ser., XXIX (1972), 197–230.

Robinson, W. Stitt. "The Legal Status of the Indian in Colonial Virginia." *Virginia Magazine of History and Biography,* LXI (1953), 247–259.

————. "Tributary Indians in Colonial Virginia." *Virginia Magazine of History and Biography,* LXVII (1959), 49–64.

*Available in paperback.

The Virginia Indians on the Eve of Colonization

1. John Smith's Description of the Indian Way, 1612

John Smith, *A Map of Virginia. With a Description of the Countrey, the Commodities, People, Government and Religion* . . . (Oxford, 1612), 19–36.

The land is not populous, for the men be fewe; their far greater number is of women and children. Within 60 miles of *James* Towne there are about some 5000 people, but of able men fit for their warres scarse 1500. To nourish so many together they have yet no means, because they make so smal a benefit of their land, be it never so fertill.

6 or 700 have beene the most [that] hath beene seene together, when they gathered themselves to *have surprised Captaine Smyth* at *Pamunke*, having but 15 to withstand the worst of their furie. As small as the proportion of ground that hath beene discovered, is in comparison of that yet unknowne. The people differ very much in stature, especially in language, as before is expressed.

Some being very great as the *Sesquesahamocks* [i.e., Susquehannocks], others very little as the *Wighcocomocoes*: but generally tall and straight, of a comely proportion, and of a colour browne when they are of any age, but they are borne white. Their haire is generally black; but few have any beards. The men weare halfe their heads shaven, the other halfe long. For Barbers they use their women, who with 2 shels will grate away the haire, of any fashion they please. The women are cut in many fashions agreeable to their yeares, but ever some part remaineth long.

They are very strong, of an able body and full of agilitie, able to endure to lie in the woods under a tree by the fire, in the worst of winter, or in the weedes and grasse, in *Ambuscado* in the Sommer.

They are inconstant in everie thing, but what feare constraineth them to keepe. Craftie, timerous, quicke of apprehension and very ingenuous. Some are of disposition fearefull, some bold, most cautelous [i.e., crafty, cautious] all *Savage*. Generally covetous of copper, beads, and such like trash. They are soone moved to anger, and so malitious, that they seldome forget an injury: they seldome steale one from another, least their conjurers should reveale it, and so they be pursued and punished. That they are thus feared is certaine, but that any can reveale their offences by conjuration I am doubtfull. Their women are carefull not to bee suspected of dishonesty without the leave of their husbands.

Each household knoweth their owne lands and gardens, and most live of their owne labours.

For their apparell, they are some time covered with the skinnes of wilde beasts, which in winter are dressed with the haire, but in sommer without. The better sort use large mantels of deare skins not much differing in fashion from the Irish mantels. . . .

Their buildings and habitations are for the most part by the rivers or not farre distant from some fresh spring. Their houses are built like our Arbors of small young springs [saplings?] bowed and tyed, and so close covered with mats or the barkes of trees very handsomely, that not withstanding either winde raine or weather, they are as warme as stooves, but very smoaky; yet at the toppe of the house there is a hole made for the smoake to goe into right over the fire. . . .

Their houses are in the midst of their fields or gardens; which are smal plots of ground, some 20 [acres?], some 40, some 100. some 200. some more, some lesse. Some times from 2 to 100 of these houses [are] togither, or but a little separated by groves of trees. Neare their habitations is [a] little small wood, or old trees on the ground, by reason of their burning of them for fire. . . .

Men women and children have their severall names according to the severall humour[s] of their parents. Their women (they say) are easilie delivered of childe, yet doe they love children verie dearly. To make them hardy, in the coldest mornings they wash them in the rivers, and by painting and ointments so tanne their skins, that after [a] year or two, no weather will hurt them.

The men bestowe their times in fishing, hunting, wars, and such manlike exercises, scorning to be seene in any woman like exercise; which is the cause that the women be verie painefull and the men often idle. The women and children do the rest of the worke. They make mats, baskets, pots, morters; pound their corne, make their bread, prepare their victuals, plant their corne, gather their corne, beare al kind of burdens, and such like. . . .

Their fishing is much in Boats. These they make of one tree by bowing [i.e., burning] and scratching away the coles with ston[e]s and shels till they have made it in [the] forme of a Trough. Some of them are an elne [i.e., an ell, a unit of measure equal to 45 inches] deepe, and 40 or 50 foot in length, and some will beare 40 men; but the most ordinary are smaller, and will beare 10, 20, or 30. according to their bignes. Instead of oares, they use paddles and sticks, with which they will row faster then our Barges. . . .

Their manner of trading is for copper, beades, and such like; for which they give such commodities as they have, as skins, fowle, fish, flesh, and their country corne. But their victuall is their chiefest riches. . . .

There is yet in *Virginia* no place discovered to bee so *Savage* in which the *Savages* have not a religion, Deare, and Bow and Arrowes. All thinges that were able to do them hurt beyond their prevention, they adore with their kinde of divine worship; as the fire, water, lightening, thunder, our ordinance peeces [i.e., ordnance pieces, large guns], horses, etc.

But their chiefe God they worship is the Divell. Him they call *Oke* and serve him more of feare than love. They say they have conference with him, and fashion themselves as neare to his shape as they can imagine. In their Temples, they have his image evill favouredly carved, and then painted and adorned with chaines, copper, and beades; and covered with a skin, in such manner as the deformity may well suit with such a God. . . .

Although the countrie people be very barbarous; yet have they amongst them such government, as that their Magistrats for good commanding, and their people for du[e] subjection and obeying, excell many places that would be counted very civill.

The forme of their Common wealth is a monarchicall governement. One as Emperour ruleth over many kings or governours. Their chiefe ruler is called *Powhatan*. . . .

His kingdome descendeth not to his sonnes nor children: but first to his brethren, whereof he hath 3 . . . ; and after their decease to his sisters. First to the eldest sister, then to the rest: and after them to the heires male and female of the eldest sister; but never to the heires of the males.

He nor any of his people understand any letters wherby to write or read; the only lawes whereby he ruleth is custome. Yet when he listeth, his will is a law and must bee obeyed: not only as a king, but as halfe a God they esteeme him.

His inferiour kings whom they cal *werowances* are tyed to rule by customes, and have power of life and death as their command in that nature. But this word *Werowance* which we call and conster for a king, is a common worde whereby they call all commanders: for they have but fewe words in their language, and but few occasions to use anie officers more then one commander, which commonly they call *werowances*.

They all knowe their severall landes, and habitations, and limits to fish, fowle, or hunt in: but they hold all of their great *Werowances Powhatan*, unto whome they pay tribute of skinnes, beades, copper, pearle, deare, turkies, wild beasts, and corne. What he commandeth they dare not disobey in the least thing. It is strange to see with what great feare and adoration all these people doe obay this *Powhatan*. For at his feet, they present whatsoever he commandeth, and at the least frowne of his browe, their greatest spirits will tremble with feare: and no marvell, for he is very terrible and tyrannous in punishing such as offend him.

The Conflict of Cultures

2. *John Rolfe Requests Permission to Marry Pocahontas, 1614*

> Ra[l]ph Hamor, *A True Discourse of the Present Estate of Virginia, and the successe of the affaires there till the 18 of June. 1614* . . . (London, 1615), 61–68.

The coppie of the Gentle-mans letters to Sir Thomas Dale,
that after maried Powhatans daughter,
containing the reasons moving him thereunto.
Honourable Sir, and most worthy Governor:

WHEN your leasure shall best serve you to peruse these lines, I trust in God, the beginning will not strike you into a greater admiration, then the end will give you good content. It is a matter of no small moment, concerning my own particular, which here I impart unto you, and which toucheth mee so neerely, as the tendernesse of my salvation. Howbeit I freely subject my selfe to your grave and mature judgement, deliberation, approbation and determination; assuring my selfe of your zealous admonitions, and godly comforts, either perswading me to desist, or incouraging me to persist therein, with a religious feare and godly care, for which (from the very instant, that this began to roote it selfe within the secret bosome of my brest) my daily and earnest praiers have bin, still are, and ever shall be produced forth with as sincere a godly zeale as I possibly may to be directed, aided and governed in all my thoughts, words and deedes, to the glory of God, and for my eternal consolation. To persevere wherein I never had more neede, nor (till now) could ever imagine to have bin moved with the like occasion.

But (my case standing as it doth) what better worldly refuge can I here seeke, then to shelter my selfe under the safety of your favourable protection? And did not my ease proceede from an unspotted conscience, I should not dare to offer to your view and approved judgement, these passions of my troubled soule, so full of feare and trembling is hypocrisie and dissimulation. But knowing my owne innocency and godly fervor, in the whole prosecution hereof, I doubt not of your benigne acceptance, and clement construction. As for malicious depravers, and turbulent spirits, to whom nothing is tastful, but what pleaseth their unsavory pallat, I passe not for them being well assured in my perswasion (by the often triall and proving of my selfe, in my holiest meditations and praiers) that I am called hereunto by the spirit of God; and it shall be sufficient for me to be protected by your selfe in all vertuous and pious indevours. And for my more happie proceeding herein, my daily oblations shall ever be addressed to bring to passe so good effects, that your selfe, and all the world may truely say: This is the worke of God, and it is marvelous in our eies.

But to avoid tedious preambles, and to come neerer the matter: first suffer me with your patence, to sweepe and make cleane the way wherein I walke, from all suspicions and doubts, which may be covered therein, and faithfully to reveale unto you what should move me hereunto.

Let therefore this my well advised protestation, which here I make betweene God and my own conscience, be a sufficient witnesse, at the dreadfull day of judgement (when the secret of all mens harts shall be opened) to condemne me herein, if my chiefest intent and purpose be not, to strive with all my power of body and minde, in the undertaking of so mightie a matter, no way led (so farre forth as mans weakenesse may permit) with the unbridled desire of carnall affection: but for the good of this plantation, for the honour of our countrie, for the glory of God, for my owne salvation, and for the converting to the true knowledge of God and Jesus Christ, an unbeleeving creature, namely Pokahuntas. To whom my hartie and best thoughts are, and have a long time bin so intangled, and inthralled in so intricate a laborinth, that I was even awearied to unwinde my selfe thereout. But almighty God, who never faileth his, that truely invocate his holy name hath opened the gate, and led me by the hand that I might plainely see and discerne the safe paths wherein to treade.

To you therefore (most noble Sir) the patron and Father of us in this countrey doe I utter the effects of this my setled and long continued affection (which hath made a mightie warre in my meditations) and here I doe truely relate, to what issue this dangerous combate is come unto, wherein I have not onely examined, but throughly [i.e., thoroughly] tried and pared my thoughts even to the quicke, before I could finde any fit wholesome and apt applications to cure so daungerous an ulcer. I never failed to offer my daily and faithfull praiers to God, for his sacred and holy assistance. I forgot not to set before mine eies the frailty of mankinde, his prones [i.e., proneness] to evill, his indulgencie of wicked thoughts, with many other imperfections wherein man is daily insnared, and oftentimes overthrowne, and them compared to my present estate. Nor was I ignorant of the heavie displeasure which almightie God conceived against the sonnes of Levie and Israel for marrying strange wives, nor of the inconveniences which may thereby arise, with other the like good motions which made me looke about warily and with good circumspection, into the grounds and principall agitations, which thus should provoke me to be in love with one whose education hath bin rude, her manners barbarous, her generation accursed, and so discrepant in all nurtriture from my selfe, that oftentimes with feare and trembling, I have ended my private controversie with this: surely these are wicked instigations, hatched by him who seeketh and delighteth in mans destruction; and so with fervant praiers to be ever preserved from such diabolical assaults (as I tooke those to be) I have taken some rest.

Thus when I had thought I had obtained my peace and quietnesse, beholde another, but more gracious tentation [i.e., temptation] hath made breaches into my holiest and strongest meditations; with which I have bin put to a new triall, in a straighter manner then the former: for besides the many passions and sufferings which I have daily, hourely, yea and in my sleepe indured, even awaking mee to astonishment, taxing mee with remisnesse, and carelesnesse, refusing and neglecting to performe the duetie of a good Christian, pulling me by the eare, and crying: why dost not thou indevour to make her a Christian? And these have happened to my greater wonder, even when she hath bin furthest seperated from me, which in common reason (were it not an undoubted worke of God) might breede forgetfulnesse of a farre more worthie creature. Besides, I say the holy spirit of God hath often demaunded of me, why I was created? If not for transitory pleasures and worldly vanities, but to labour in the Lords vineyard, there to sow and plant, to nourish and increase the fruites thereof, daily adding with the good husband in the Gospell, somewhat to the tallent, that in the end the fruites may be reaped, to the comfort of the laborer in this life, and his salvation in the world to come? And if this be, as undoubtedly this is, the service Jesus Christ requireth of his best servant: wo unto him that hath these instruments of pietie put into his hands, and wilfully despiseth to worke with them. Likewise, adding hereunto her great apparance of love to me, her desire to be taught and instructed in the knowledge of God, her capablenesse of understanding, her aptnesse and willingnesse to receive anie good impression, and also the spirituall, besides her owne incitements stirring me up hereunto.

What should I doe? shall I be of so untoward a disposition, as to refuse to leade the blind into the right way? Shall I be so unnaturall, as not to give bread to the hungrie? or uncharitable, as not to cover the naked? Shall I despise to actuate these pious dueties of a Christian? Shall the base feare of displeasing the world, overpower and with holde mee from revealing unto man these spirituall workes of the Lord, which in my meditations and praiers, I have daily made knowne unto him? God forbid. I assuredly trust hee hath thus delt with me for my eternall felicitie, and for his glorie: and I hope so to be guided by his heavenly graice, that in the end by my faithfull paines, and christianlike labour, I shall attaine to that blessed promise, Pronounced by that holy Prophet Daniell unto the righteous that bring many unto the knowledge of God. Namely, that they shall shine like the starres forever and ever. A sweeter comfort cannot be to a true Christian, nor a greater incouragement for him to labour all the daies of his life, in the performance thereof, nor a greater gaine of consolation, to be desired at the hower of death, and in the day of judgement.

Againe by my reading, and conference with honest and religious persons, have I received no small encouragement, besides *serena mea conscientia* [i.e., "at peace with myself"], the cleerenesse of my conscience, clean from the filth of impurity, *quae est instar muri ahenei*, which is unto me, as a brasen wall. If I should set down at large, the perturbations and godly motions, which have striven within meé, I should but make a tedious and unnecessary volume. But I doubt not these shall be sufficient both to certifie you of my tru intents, in discharging of my dutie to God, and to your selfe, to whose gracious providence I humbly submit my selfe, for his glory, your honour, our Countreys good, the benefit of this Plantation, and for the converting of one unregenerate, to regeneration; which I beseech God to graunt, for his deere Sonne Christ Jesus his sake.

Now if the vulgar sort, who square all mens actions by the base rule of their own filthinesse, shall taxe or taunt me in this my godly labour: let them know, it is not any hungry appetite, to gorge my selfe with incontinency; sure (if I would, and were so sensually inclined) I might satisfie such desire, though not without a seared conscience, yet with Christians more pleasing to the eie, and lesse fearefull in the offence unlawfully committed. Nor am I in so desperate an estate, that I regard not what becommeth of mee; nor am I out of hope but one day to see my Country, nor so void of friends, nor mean in birth, but there to obtain a mach [i.e., match] to my great content: nor have I ignorantly passed over my hopes there, or regardlesly seek to loose the love of my friends, by taking this course: I know them all, and have not rashly overslipped any.

But shal it please God thus to dispose of me (which I earnestly desire to fulfill my ends before sette down) I will heartely accept of it as a godly taxe appointed me, and I will never cease, (God assisting me) untill I have accomplished, and brought to perfection so holy a worke, in which I will daily pray God to blesse me, to mine, and her eternall happines. And thus desiring no longer to live, to enjoy the blessings of God, then [i.e., than] this my resolution doth tend to such godly ends, as are by me before declared: not doubting of your favourable acceptance, I take my leave, beseeching Almighty God to raine downe upon you, such plenitude of his heavenly graces, as your heart can wish and desire, and so I rest,

At your commaund most willing to be disposed off

JOHN ROLFE.

3. *The Massacre of 1622*

Edward Waterhouse, "A Declaration of the state of the Colonie and Affaires in Virginia. With a Relation of the barbarous Massacre . . ." (1622), in Susan Myra Kingsbury, ed., *The Records of the Virginia Company of London* (Washington, D.C., 1906–1935), III, 549–556.

The last *May* there came Letters from *Sir Francis Wiat* [i.e., Wyatt] *Governor* in VIRGINIA, which did advertise that when in *November* last [1621] he arived in VIRGINIA, and entred upon his Government, he found the Country setled in a peace (as all men there thought) sure and unviolable, not onely because it was solemnly ratified and sworne, and at the request of the Native King stamped in Brasse, and fixed to one of his Oakes of note, but as being advantagious to both parts; to the Savages as the weaker, under which they were safely sheltred and defended; to us, as being the easiest way then thought to pursue and advance our projects of buildings, plantings, and effecting their conversion by peaceable and fayre meanes. And such was the conceit of firme peace and amitie, as that there was seldome or never a sword worne, and a Peece seldomer, except for a Deere or Fowle. By which assurance of securitie, the Plantations of particular Adventurers and Planters were placed scatteringly and straglingly as a choyce veyne of rich ground invited them, and the further from neighbors held the better. The houses generally set open to the Savages, who were alwaies friendly entertained at the tables of the English, and commonly lodged in their bed-chambers. The old planters (as they thought now come to reape the benefit of their long travels) placed with wonderfull content upon their private dividents, and the planting of particular Hundreds and Colonies pursued with an hopefull alacrity, all our projects (saith he) in a faire way, and their familarity with the Natives, seeming to open a faire gate for their conversion to Christianitie.

The Country being in this estate, an occasion was ministred of sending to *Opachankano* [i.e., Opechancanough] the King of these Savages, about the middle of *March* last, what time the Messenger returned backe with these words from him, That he held the peace concluded so firme, as the Skie should sooner fall then it dissolve: yea, such was the treacherous dissimulation of that people who then had contrived our destruction, that even two dayes before the Massacre, some of our men were guided thorow the woods by them in safety: and one *Browne*, who then to learne the language lived among the *Warrascoyacks* (a Province of that King) was in friendly manner sent backe by them to Captaine *Hamor* his Master, and many the like passages, rather increasing our former confidence, then any wise in the world ministring the least suspition of the breach of the peace, or of what instantly ensued; yea, they borrowed our owne Boates to convey themselves crosse the River (on the bankes of both sides whereof all our Plantations were) to consult of the divellish murder that ensued, and of our utter extirpation, which God of his mercy (by the meanes of some of themselves converted to Christianitie) prevented; and as well on the Friday morning (the fatal day) the 22 of *March*, as also in the evening, as in other dayes before, they came unarmed into our houses, without Bowes or arrowes, or other weapons, with Deere, Turkies,

Fish, Furres, and other provisions, to sell, and trucke with us, for glasse, beades, and other trifles: yea in some places, sate downe at Breakfast with our people at their tables, whom immediately with their owne tooles and weapons, eyther laid downe, or standing in their houses, they basely and barbarously murthered, not sparing eyther age or sexe, man, woman or childe; so sodaine in their cruell execution, that few or none discerned the weapon or blow that brought them to destruction. In which manner they also slew many of our people then at their severall workes and husbandries in the fields, and without their houses, some in planting Corne and Tobacco, some in gardening, some in making Bricke, building, sawing, and other kindes of husbandry, they well knowing in what places and quarters each of our men were, in regard of their daily familiarity, and resort to us for trading and other negotiations, which the more willingly was by us continued and cherished for the desire we had of effecting that great master-peece of workes, their conversion. And by this meanes that fatall Friday morning, there fell under the bloudy and barbarous hands of that perfidious and inhumane people, contrary to all lawes of God and men, of Nature and Nations, three hundred forty seven men, women, and children, most by their owne weapons; and not being content with taking away life alone, they fell after againe upon the dead, making as well as they could, a fresh murder, defacing, dragging, and mangling the dead carkasses into many pieces, and carrying some parts away in derision, with base and bruitish triumph.

Neither yet did these beasts spare those amongst the rest well knowne untthem, from whom they had daily received many benefits and favours, but spitefully also massacred them, without remorse or pitty, being in this more fell then Lyons and Dragons, which (as Histories record) have beene so farre from hurting, as they have both acknowledged, and gratefully requited their Benefactors; such is the force of good deeds, though done to cruell beasts, as to make them put off the very nature of beasts, and to put on humanity upon them. But these miscreants, contrariwise in this kinde, put not off onely all humanity, but put on a worse and more then unnaturall bruitishnesse. One instance of it, amongst too many, shall serve for all. That worthy religious Gentleman, Master *George Thorpe* Esquire, Deputie of the Colledge lands, sometimes one of his Majesties Pentioners, and in one of the Principall places of command in VIRGINIA, did so truly and earnestly affect their conversion, and was so tender over them, that whosoever under his authority had given them but the least displeasure or discontent, he punished them severely. He thought nothing too deare for them, and as being desirous to binde them unto him by his many courtesies, hee never denyed them any thing that they asked him, insomuch that when these *Savages* complained unto him of the fiercenesse of our Mastives [i.e., mastiffs], most implacable and terrible unto them, (knowing them by instinct it seemes, to be but treacherous and false-hearted friends to us, better then our selves) he to gratifie them in all things, for the winning of them by degrees, caused some of them to be killed in their presence, to the great displeasure of the owners, and would have had all the rest guelt (had he not beene hindered) to make them the gentler and the milder to them. Hee was not onely too kinde and beneficiall to the common sort, but also to their King, to whom hee oft resorted, and gave many presents which hee knew to be highly pleasing to him. And whereas this king before dwelt onely in a cottage, or rather a denne or hog-stye, made with a few poles and stickes, and covered with mats after their wyld manner, to civilize him, he first, built him a fayre house according to the English fashion, in which hee tooke such joy, especially in his locke and key, which hee so admired, as locking and unlocking his doore an hundred times aday, hee thought no device in all the world was comparable to it.

Thus insinuating himselfe to this King for his religious purposes, he conferred after with him oft, and intimated to him matters of our Religion; and thus far the *Pagan* confessed, moved by naturall Principles, that our God was a good God, and better much then theirs, in that he had with so many good things above them endowed us. Hee told him, if hee would serve our God, hee should bee partaker of all those good things wee had, and of farre greater then sense or reason ever could imagine. Hee wonne upon him, as hee thought in many things, so as hee gave him fayre hearing and good answer, and seemed to be much pleased with his discourse and in his company. And both hee and his people for the daily courtesies this good Gentleman did to one or other of them, did professe such outward love and respect unto him, as nothing could seeme more: but all was little regarded after by this Viperous brood, as the sequell shewed: for they not only wilfully murdered him, but cruelly and felly [i.e., foully], out of devillish malice, did so many barbarous despights and foule scornes after to his dead corpes, as are unbefitting to be heard by any civill eare. One thing I cannot omit, that when this good Gentleman upon his fatall hower, was warned by his man (who perceived some treachery intended to them by these hell-hounds) to looke to himselfe, and withall ranne away for feare of the mischiefe he strongly apprehended, and so saved his owne life; yet his Master, out of the conscience of his owne good meaning, and faire deserts ever towards them, was so void of all suspition, and so full of confidence, that they had sooner killed him, then hee could or would beleeve they meant any ill against him. Thus the sinnes of these wicked Infidels, have made them unworthy of enjoying him, and the eternall good that he most zealously alwayes intended to them.

And thus these miserable wretches, not hee, hath lost by it, who to the comfort of us all, hath gayned a Crowne of endlesse blisse, and is assuredly become a glorious Martyr, in which thrice-happy and blessed state we leave him. But these miscreants, who have thus despised Gods great mercies so freely offered to them, must needs in time therefore be corrected by his justice: So as those who by the way of mercies would not be drawne unto him, shall some of them at length (no doubt) be brought unto him by his way of judgements: to which leaving them, I will knit againe together now the thred of my Discourse, and proceed to tell you, That at the time of this Massacre there were three or foure of our ships in *James-River*, and one in the next River, and daily more to come in, as three did within fourteene dayes after; one of which they endevored to have surprised, but in vaine, as had also beene their whole attempt, had any the least fore-knowledge beene in those places where the Massacre was committed: yet were the hearts of the English ever stupid, and averted from beleeving any thing that might weaken their hopes of speedy winning the Savages to Civilitie and Religion, by kinde usage and fayre conversing amongst them. Hee, and the whole Councell write further, That Almighty God (they doubt not) hath his great worke to doe in this Tragedy, and will thereout draw honor and glory to his great Name; safety, and a more flourishing estate to themselves, and the whole Plantation there; and the more speedy conversion of the Children of those Savages to himselfe, since hee so miraculously preserved so many of the English (there being, God be praysed about eleven parts of twelve still remayning) whose desire to draw those people to Religion by the carelesse neglect of their owne safeties, seemes to have beene the greatest cause of their own ensuing destruction. Yet it pleased God to use some of them as instruments to save many of their lives, whose soules they had formerly saved, as at *James-Citie*, and other places, and the Pinnace trading in *Pamounkey* River, all whose lives were saved by a converted *Indian*, disclosing the plot in the instant (whereof though our sinnes (say they) made us unworthy to be instruments of so glorious a conversion in generall[)], yet his infinite wisedome can neverthelesse bring it to passe with some more of them, and with other Provinces there in his good time, and by such meanes as wee thinke most unlikely. For even in the delivery of us that now survive, no mans particular carefulnesse saved any one person, but the meere goodnesse of himselfe, freely and miraculously preserved whom it pleased him.

The Letters of Mr. *George Sandis* a worthy Gentleman and Treasurer there, likewise have advertised (as many others from many particular persons of note and worth) besides the Relations of many returned in the Sea-flower (the ship that brought us this unwelcome newes) have beene heard at large in the publike Courts, that whilst all their affayres were full of succcesse, and such intercourse of familiaritie, as if the *Indians* and themselves had beene of one Nation, those treacherous Natives, after five yeares peace, by a generall combination in one day plotted to subvert their whole Colony, and at one instant of time, though our severall Plantations were an hundred and forty miles up one River on both sides.

But before I goe any further, for the better understanding of all things, you shall know that these wyld naked Natives live not in great numbers together, but dispersed, and in small companies; and where most together, not above two hundred, and that very rare, in other places fifty or forty, or thereabouts, and many miles distant from one another, in such places among the Woods where they either found, or might easiliest make some cleared plots of ground, which they imploy wholly in setting of Corne, whereby to sustaine their lives. These small and scattered Companies (as I have said) had warning given from one another in all their habitations to meete at the day and houre appointed for our destruction, at all our severall Townes and places seated upon the River; some were directed to goe to one place, some to another, all to be done at the same day and time, which they did accordingly: some entring their Houses under colour of trucking, and so taking advantage, others drawing our men abroad upon faire pretences, and the rest suddenly falling upon those that were at their labours.

They certifie further, that besides Master *George Thorpe*, before mentioned, Master *John Berkeley*, Captaine *Nathanael Powel*, and his wife, (daughter of Master *William Tracy*, and great with childe) and Captaine *Maycock*, all Gentlemen of birth, vertue, and industry, and of the Councell there, suffered under this their cruelty and treason.

That the slaughter had beene universall, if God had not put it into the heart of an Indian belonging to one *Perry*, to disclose it, who living in the house of one *Pace*, was urged by another Indian his Brother (who came the night before and lay with him) to kill *Pace*, (so commanded by their King as he declared) as hee would kill *Perry*: telling further that by such an houre in the morning a number would come from divers places to finish the Execution, who failed not at the time: *Perries* Indian rose out of his bed and reveales it to *Pace*, that used him as a Sonne: And thus the rest of the Colony that had warning given them, by this meanes was saved. . . .

Pace upon this discovery, securing his house, before day rowed over the River to *James*-City (in that place neere three miles in bredth) and gave notice thereof to the Governor, by which meanes they were prevented there, and at such other Plantations as was possible for a timely intelligence to be given; for where they saw us standing upon our Guard, at the sight of a Peece they all ranne away. In other places that could have no notice, some Peeces with munition (the use whereof they know not) were there carried away, and some few Cattell also were destroyed by them. And as Fame divulgeth (not without probable grounds) their King hath since caused the most part of the Gunpowder by him surprized, to bee sowne, to draw therefrom the like increase, as of his Maize or Corne, in Harvest next. And that it is since discovered, that the last Summer *Opachankano* practised with a King of the Eastern shore (no well-willer of his) to furnish him with store of poison (naturally growing in his country) for our destruction, which he absolutely refused, though he sent him great store of Beades, and other presents to winne him thereunto: which he, with five or sixe of his great men, offered to be ready to justifie against him. That the true cause of this surprize was most by the instigation of the Devill, (enemy to their salvation) and the dayly feare that possest them, that in time we by our growing continually upon them, would dispossesse them of this Country, as they had beene formerly of the West Indies by the Spaniard: produced this bloody act. That never griefe and shame possessed any people more then themselves, to be thus butchered by so naked and cowardly a people, who dare not stand the presentment of a staffe in manner of a Peece, nor an uncharged Peece in the hands of a woman, from which they flye as so many Hares; much faster then from their tormenting Devill, whom they worship for feare, though they acknowledge they love him not.

Thus have you seene the particulars of this massacre, out of Letters from thence written, wherein treachery and cruelty have done their worst to us, or rather to themselves; for whose understanding is so shallow, as not to perceive that this must needs bee for the good of the Plantation after, and the losse of this blood to make the body more healthfull, as by these reasons may be manifest. . . .

4. *The Governor and Council Threaten Reprisals against the Indians, 1629*

> H. R. McIlwaine, ed., *Minutes of the Council and General Court of Colonial Virginia, 1622–1632, 1670–1676, with Notes and Excerpts from Original Council and General Court Records, into 1683, Now Lost* (Richmond, Va., 1924), 198.

[A Court At James Citty] . . . 1629
present
John Pott Esqr. Governor etc. Capt. *Smyth* Capt. *Mathewes*

At this Court was held a serious Consultation concerning the Massacre of Mr. *Pooly* and fower other of Our men with him by the Indians, And at lenght it was Concluded that one of the Indians now remayning with us should bee sent unto the greate King with a Messuage to this effecte *Vizt.*, that whereas by the last treaty of peace it was agreed on that none of their people should come to any of our plantations or howses nor call or parley with our men, But if any should come a[bout] any speciall businesse from the greate king they should come to the Governor and in other places to the Commaunder only and that they should st[eale] nothing from us, nor kill or hurt our Cattle [among?] dyvers other thinges conteyned in the said treaty since which tyme an Indian Came in contrary to the said agreement who not withstanding wee forbore to kill or punishe but sent him backe with a [word of] strickt warning that none of the Indians what[soever] should presume to come in without the [words missing], and those only to come to the appoynted place at *Pasbyhey* which order they have nevertheless not observed, but have come to dyvers of our plantations stollen our hoes, killed our hoggs and done us many other wronges, some of whome alsoe althoughe wee have deteyned, yett wee have not offered them any vyolence but have used them well and Courteously notwithstanding all which they ha[ve] killed five of our men which wee conceave to bee by the kinges knowledge and Consent and therefo[re] wee demaund satisfaction, which if hee refuse to give wee determined by force and armes to Revenge both deathe of our men and repaire all other wronges they have done us

[*It is*] *ordered* that Mr. *Robert* [words missing] forther [i.e., further] attende uppon the Court to interpr[et] betweene the Indians and then untill [*Christmas?*] next as occasion shall require, shall have one thousand pounds weight of tobacco paid at the next Cropp.

5. *Lower Norfolk County Sends Its Militia against the Nanticokes, 1639*

> Lower Norfolk County Order Book, 1637–1646 (transcript), 35.

Whereas, at a court holden by the Grand Council at York the first of the present July, it was ordered that there should be appointed fifteen sufficient

men out of the Lower county of Norfolk to March against the Nenticoke
Indians, according therefore to the said order, The Commander and Commissioners of this county have made choice of these men whose names are here
mentioned to go the said march.

[names omitted]

Every 20 persons being [chosen] to provide 2 lbs. of powder and 2 lbs. of
shot and 40 lbs. of biscuit and half a bushel of peas a man for them sent
for the said march.

6. *The Peace Treaty That Ended the Indian War of 1644–1646*

> William Waller Hening, ed., *The Statutes at Large; Being
> a Collection of All the Laws of Virginia, from the First
> Session of the Legislature, in the Year 1619* (Richmond,
> New York, and Philadelphia, 1809–1823), I, 323–326.

Art. 1. *BE it enacted by this Grand Assembly*, That the articles of peace following between the inhabitants of this collony, and Necotowance King of the
Indians bee duely and inviolably observed upon the penaltie within mentioned
as followeth:

Imp. That Necotowance do acknowledge to hold his kingdome from the
King's Majestie of England, and that his successors be appointed or confirmed by the King's Governours from time to time, And on the other side,
This Assembly on the behalfe of the collony, doth, undertake to protect him
or them against any rebells or other enemies whatsoever, and as an ac-
knowledgment and tribute for such protection, the said Necotowance and
his successors are to pay unto the King's Governor the number of twenty
beaver skins att the goeing away of Geese yearely.

Art. 2. That it shall be free for the said Necotowance and his people, to
inhabit and hunt on the northside of Yorke River, without any interruption
from the English. *Provided* that if hereafter, It shall be thought fitt by the
Governor and Council to permitt any English to inhabitt from Poropotanke
downewards, that first Necotowance be acquainted therewith.

Art. 3. That Necotowance and his people leave free that tract of land betweene Yorke river and James river, from the falls of both the rivers to
Kequotan, to the English to inhabitt on, and that neither he the said Necotowance nor any Indians do repaire to or make any abode upon the said
tract of land, upon paine of death, and it shall be lawfull for any person to
kill any such Indian, And in case any such Indian or Indians being seen
upon the said tract of land shall make an escape, That the said Necotowance
shall uppon demand deliver the said Indian or Indians to the Englishmen,
upon knowledge had of him or them, unles such Indian or Indians be sent
upon a message from the said Necotowance.

And to the intent to avoid all injury to such a messenger, and that no ignorance may be pretended to such as shall offer any outrage, *It is thought fitt
and hereby enacted*, That the badge worne by a messenger, or, in case there
shall be more than one, by one of the company, be a coate of striped stuffe
which is to be left by the messenger from time to time so often as he shall
returne at the places appointed for coming in.

Art. 4. *And it is further enacted*, That in case any English shall repaire contrary to the articles agreed upon, to the said north side of Yorke river, such persons soe offending, being lawfully convicted, be adjudged as felons; *Provided* that this article shall not extend to such persons who by stresse of weather are forced upon the said land, *Provided alsoe* and it is agreed by the said Necotowance, that it may be lawfull for any Englishman to goe over to the said north side haveing occasion to fall timber trees or cut sedge, soe as the said persons have warrant for theyre soe doeing under the hand of the Governor. *Provided alsoe* notwithstandinge any thing in this act to the contrary, That it shall bee free and lawfull for any English whatsoever between this present day and the first of March next to kill and bring away what cattle or hoggs that they can by any meanes kill or take upon the said north side of the said river.

Art. 5. *And it is further enacted* that neither for the said Necotowance nor any of his people, do frequent come in to hunt or make any abode nearer the English plantations then the lymits of Yapin the black water, and from the head of the black water upon a straite line to the old Monakin Towne, upon such paine and penaltie as aforesaid.

Art. 6. *And it is further ordered enacted* that if any English do entertain any Indian or Indians or doe conceale any Indian or Indians that shall come within the said limits, such persons being lawfully convicted thereof shall suffer death as in case of felony, without benefit of clergy, except such as shall be authorized thereto by vertue of this act.

Art. 7. *And it is further enacted* that the said Necotowance and his people upon all occasions of message to the Governor for trade, doe repaire unto the Fort Royall onely on the north side, at which place they are to receive the aforesaid badges, which shall shew them to be messengers, and therefore to be freed from all injury in their passage to the Governor, upon payne of death to any person or persons whatsoever that shall kill them, the badge being worn by one of the company, And in case of any other affront, the offence to be punished according to the quality thereof, and the trade admitted as aforesaid to the said Necotowance and his people with the commander of the said Fort onely on the north side.

Art. 8. *And it is further thought fitt and enacted*, that upon any occasion of message to the Governor or trade, The said Necotowance and his people the Indians doe repair to Forte Henery *alias* Appamattucke Forte, or to the house of Capt. John Floud, and to no other place or places of the south side of the river, att which places the aforesayd badges of striped stuffe are to be and remaine.

Art. 9. *And it is further thought fitt and enacted*, That Necotowance doe with all convenience bring in the English prisoners, And all such negroes and guns which are yet remaining either in the possession of himselfe or any Indians, and that he deliver upon demand such Indian servants as have been taken prisoners and shall hereafter run away, In case such Indian or Indians shall be found within the limitts of his dominions; provided that such Indian or Indians be under the age of twelve years at theire running away.

Art. 10. *And it is further enacted and consented*, That such Indian children as shall or will freely and voluntarily come in and live with the English, may remain without breach of the articles of peace provided they be not above twelve yeares old.

Art. 11. *And it is further thought fitt and enacted* That the several commanders of the Forts and places as aforesaid unto which the said Indians as aforesaid are admitted to repaire, In case of trade or Message doe forthwith provide the said coats in manner striped as aforesaid.

7. *The English Formulate an Indian Policy*

A. AN ACT OUTLAWING THE KILLING OF INDIANS, OCTOBER 1649

> Warren M. Billings, ed., "Acts Not in Hening's *Statutes:* Acts of Assembly, April 1652, November 1652, and July 1653," *Virginia Magazine of History and Biography,* LXXXIII (1975).

Whereas it was Enacted at an Assemblye in October 1646 the 5th day that it should be lawfull for any person to kill any Indian within such Limmitts as the said Act is Expressed, Exceptinge such as were Imployed uppon messages haveinge a Badge for the better Knowledge of them which Act is thought Fitt by this Assemblye to be Restrayned, the Collonye beinge Subject to manye prejuduces by Reason of the Lattitude, and gennerallitye of such allowance, and that the breach of the peace may probablye be the Consequence thereof through the Rashness, and inadvicednesse of Divers persons whoe by such Act Rather vindicate some private mallice, then provide for theire owne; or Public Indempnitye. It is now therefore Enacted that noe man shall heerafter kill any Indian within the Lymmitts aforesaid unless such Indian shall be taken in the Act of doeinge tresspasse, or other harme, in which the oath of that partie by whome the Indian shall be discovered or killed shall be Full, and sufficient Evidence.

B. AN ACT PREVENTING THE KIDNAPPING OF INDIAN CHILDREN, OCTOBER 1649

> Billings, ed., "Acts Not in Hening's *Statutes,*" *Virginia Magazine of History and Biography,* LXXXIII (1975).

Whereas Divers Informations are taken notice of by this Assemblye of severall persons whoe by theire Indirect practices have Corrupted some of the Indians to steale, and Conveigh away some other Indians Children, and others whoe pretendinge to have bought or purchased Indians of theire Parents, or some of their great men, haveinge violentlye, or fraudelentlye forced them from them to the great Scandall of christianitye, and of the English nation by such theire perfidious dealinge Renderinge Religion Comtemptible, and the name of Englishmen odious to them, and may be a very Dangerous, and Important Consequence to the Collonye if not timelye Prevented, It is therefore Enacted that noe person, or persons whatsoever dare, or presume, after the Date of this Act, to buy any Indian, or Indians vizt. from, or of the English, and in case of Complaint made that any person hath transgressed this Act, the truth thereof being proved, such persons shall Returne such Indian, or Indians within tenn dayes to the place from whence he was taken, And it is Further Enacted that whosoever shall Enforme against any person for the breach of this Act, and the Information beinge found against the partie accused, the offender shall pay unto the Enformer 500 tobacco to be Recovered in any Court of Justice within the Collonye.

C. AN ACT GRANTING LAND TO THE INDIANS, OCTOBER 1649

Billings, ed., "Acts Not in Hening's *Statutes*," *Virginia Magazine of History and Biography*, LXXXIII (1975).

Whereas Ascomowett King of the South Indians, vizt. Waianoake hath by Petition Presented to this Assemblye, and subscribed under his owne hand writinge, and Ossakican King of the north Indians, and Totepotomey Comander, and Leader over the Pymunckee Indians have by theire severall Petitions Exhibited likewise to this Assemblye, humblye acknowledged themselves tributaryes to his Sacred Majestye, and that the Soverainitye of the land where on they live doth belong to his most Excelent Majestye, our most gracious, and Royall King, and have therefore prayed that a Convenient proportion of land may be granted unto them by Pattent, whereon they, and theire people may Inhabitt, and Injoy the priviledges of Range and huntinge free from mollestation, and Incroachments of any person, whither Indians, or English which this Assemblye for manye Reasons of State have thought Fitt should be assigned, and granted unto them accordinge to theire severall Petitions wherein Consideration was had of the Readye meanes, and fayre oppertunityes afforesaid in this Course for theire Reducement to Civillitye, and a hopefull progresse there to theire Conversion to Christianitye which is the Principall and primarye Intent of this Act, And have therefore Enacted that there shall be layde out, and Surveighed for Ascomowett the South king five thousand Acres of land on the South Side James River without the Bounds [and] Limmited by the treatye, to be called, and knowne by the name Wanecke accordinge to his desyre in his Petition, with Priveledge to hunt uppon all Waste land thereunto adjacent without the bounds as afforesaid, which priveledge is to be Inserted into his Pattent.

That there shall be layde out, and Surveighed for Totopotomey five thousand Acres of land adjacent to the place where he now liveth, and that after surveigh thereof a Pattent be alsoe granted to him. That there shall be layde out, and Surveighed for Ossakican King of the north Indians 5000 Acres of land more, or lesse, the place Whereon he now liveth to be part thereof, and from thence Runninge toward land of mr. Heugh Gwinn, beinge [secured?] by a Small Creeke, and uppon Surveigh thereof, a Pattent to be alsoe granted to him, and in case any of the said land shall be found to be formerlye granted to any other by Pattent, It is Included that for Everye five hundred Acres taken from any former Pattents, there shall be a Thousand pounds of tobaccoe Allowed from the Publick to be [paid] the next Assemblye, And that the said Pattentes shall have liberty uppon the same Rights to take upp the like quantetye of land in any place not formerlye granted, and it is further Enacted that in all the said Pattents afforesaid there be a Reservation of the Accustomed

Rent to his Majestye with the usuall Limitation of seaven yeares for the payment thereof. Mr. James [Cookett?] was ordered Surveighor.

8. *Sources of Potential Trouble between the Indians and the English, 1661–1675*

A. INDIANS FINED FOR HOG STEALING, 1660/61

Northampton County Order Book, 1657–1664, fol. 93.

Whereas Complaint hath ben made to the Court by Severall of the Inhabitants of the upper part of the County against Tapatiapan and the Indians of Accomack for hoggs Stollen by the said Indians and other Cattle killed by dogs belonging to the said Indians as appeared by Severall testimoneys, The Court taken the premises into their Serious Consideration to prevent the like injuries for future Order that Tapatiapan shall within fifteene dayes make payment of three hundred arms length of Roanoke els execution.

B. INDIANS ACCUSED OF BEATING AN ENGLISHMAN, 1663/64

Accomack County Order Book, 1663–1666, fol. 54.

Whereas Complaint hath bin made in the Court by John Die and by the deposition of Henry Michel it appeareth that the King of Matomkin and his great men have beaten and abused him the said John Die. The Court taking the premises into their Consideration doe Request Col. Edmund Scarburgh to make for them enquiry into the business and doe therein according to Justice as hee shall thinke necessary and Convenient to be donne in the premises and to give Report thereof to the Court. [There is no further record of the matter.]

C. STAFFORD COURT FORBIDS INDIANS TO HUNT IN SETTLED AREAS, 1664

Stafford County Order Book, 1664–1668, 12.

Whereas many sad Accidents have happen'd by the Indians hunting in the Woods as by firing the same [i.e., setting the woods afire to drive out the game] and that Particular Persons doe harber them[,] Then the Court doth Order that noe Indian by any person whatsoever shall be Suffer'd to hunt in any parte of the English habitation such only excepted as by publique Order are Allowed to find out the residue of the Murtherers [this reference is not explained in the records] on the forfiture of 500 li. Tobacco and Cask and it is further Order'd that the Grand Jury present all such offenders to be prosecuted accordingly.

D. INDIANS LOSE SUIT TO RECOVER LAND, 1665/66

Accomack County Order Book, 1663–1666, fol. 109.

Whereas the Indians of Pokomoke this Day complained against John Williams for intruding upon their Land and upon tryall it appeared by the Evidence of Robert Houston and Roger Hobson that the Indian whome the Indian King of Pokomoke did acknowledge and owne as proprietor of the Land where the said John Williams is seated did sell to the said John Williams that tract of Land whereon the pretended intrusion is made, It is therefore ordered that the said John Williams make payment to the Indian proprietor for the Land according to his agreement: and for this yeare noe Cattle or hoggs to be transported and Remaine upon the said Land this Yeare, nor the said John Williams to plant or prejudice the Indians in planting or useing their Fields

E. GOVERNOR BERKELEY'S FORMULA FOR QUIETING THE NORTHERN INDIANS, 1666

Rappahannock County Deeds and Wills, 1665–1668, 57.

Sir—

I wrote my first Letter to you in hast the minute after I read Yours but since I have collected my Selfe I thinke it is necessary to Distroy all these Northerne Indians for they must Needs be Conscious of the Coming of these other Indians, twill be a great Terror and Exemple of Instruction to all other Indians, If the Councell nere you and the Councell of Warr bee of this opinion it may be done without Charge, for the Women and Children will Defray it, lett me heare from you what you thinke of it and if the first impulse of our first resentments doe not Deceive me and lead to much I thinke this Resolution to be of absolute necessity if your young men will not Undertake it alone there will be enow [i.e., enough] from hence [who] will undertake it for their Share of the Booty

June 22th *1666*   Your Most Affectionate Humble Servant

Signed

William Berkeley

To My Most Honr'd Friend Maj. Gen. [Robert] Smyth   These
Hast post Hast for the Service of his Majestie and the Country

F. INDIANS SUSPECTED OF KIDNAPPING A SERVANT GIRL, 1668

Northumberland County Order Book, 1666–1678, fol. 21.

Whereas Andrew Pettegrew did exhibit a Complaynt against the great men the Indians of Wiccocomako, for that the said Indians vizt. Owasawas, [Appeneman?] and Chicatomen did oblige them selves to bring one Norwas an Indian who hath entertained a run away mayd servant of the said Pettegrews, to this Court who having failed to produce the said Indian or the said Servant the Court fearing that the said mayd may be made away by the Indians, doe order that the Sheriff keep the said Indians in safe Custody without Bayle or Main prize untill that they produce the said Mayd.

G. INDIANS BREAK INTO ROBERT JONES'S HOUSE, 1669

Northumberland County Order Book, 1666–1678, fol. 31.

Whereas Mr. Robert Jones Complayned to this Court that the Indians of Wecocomaco did in the night break open his house, and did him further outrage, the Court doe order that Mr. Peter Knight, and Capt. Edmund Lyster summon the Indians before them, and punish the delinquents according to the nature of their Crime.

H. ACCOMACK COURT ORDERS INDIANS WHIPPED, 1671

Accomack County Order Book, 1671–1673, 41.

Whereas itt appeares by the complaint of William Marshall Constable and the Deposition of Henry Williams That a certain Indyan called John the Bowlemaker and one Indyan called Jack of Morocco did contimptuosly disobey a Warrant brought to them by the said Constable, and that the said John did perticulerly take the said Constable by the hayre of the head and drew blood from him: whereto the said Jack of Morocco was assisting It is therefore Ordered that the Sherriff doe take the said Indyans into his Custody and to see that the said John the Bowlemaker have Thirty Lashes well layd on his naked Back for contempt of the said Warrant and Thirty lashes more for his abuse of the Constable: and that Jack of Morocco have Thirty Lashes well layd on for ayding and abetting the said John the Bowlemaker in abusing the Constable and the said Indyans to remain in the Sheriffs Custody till they have paid Costs and fees accruing.

I. WHITES CONVICTED OF STEALING FROM THE INDIANS, 1675

Accomack County Order Book, 1673–1676, 285.

Upon the Complaint of the Qiquotanck Indians for being robbed of Corne: and John Stockley Junior, John Field, John Jackson Confessing the same by petition Craveing the Courts mercy, It is the Judgment of the Court and Accordingly ordered, That the said deliquants pay unto the Indians Six Yards of new Trading Cloth and pay all Costs of Suit also Execution, and it is further ordered that the Constable forthwith returne the Corne by him found and now in his possession unto the said Indians.

9. *The Indian War of 1675–1677*

A. THE INCIDENT THAT LED TO WAR, 1675

Thomas Mathew, "The Beginning, Progress, and Conclusion of Bacon's Rebellion, 1675–1676," in Charles M. Andrews, ed., *Narratives of the Insurrections, 1675–1690*, Original Narratives of Early American History (New York, 1915), 17.

Of this horrid Action [the Doeg attack] Col. [George] Mason who commanded the Militia Regiment of Foot and Capt. [George] Brent the Troop of Horse in that County [Stafford], (both dwelling Six or Eight Miles Downwards) having speedy notice raised 30 or more men, and pursu'd those Indians 20 Miles up and 4 Miles over that River [the Potomac] into Maryland, where landing at Dawn of Day, they found two small Paths. Each Leader with his Party took a Separate Path and in less than a furlong, either found a Cabin, which they Silently Surrounded. Capt. Brent went to the Doegs Cabin (as it proved to be) Who Speaking the Indian Tongue Called to have a *Matchacomicha Weewhip* i.e. a Councill, called presently Such being the usuall manner with Indians. The King came Trembling forth, and wou'd have fled, when Capt. Brent, Catching hold of his twisted Lock (which was all the Hair he wore) told him he was come for the Murderer of Robert Hen, the King pleaded Ignorance and Slipt loos, whom Brent shot Dead with his Pistoll. Th' Indians Shot Two or Three Guns out of the Cabin, th' English shot into it, th' Indians throng'd out at the Door and fled, The English Shot as many as they cou'd, so that they Kill'd Ten, as Capt. Brent told me, and brought away the Kings Son of about 8 Years old, . . . the Noise of this Shooting awaken'd th' Indians in the Cabin which Col. Mason had Encompassed, who likewise Rush'd out and fled, of whom his Company (supposing from that Noise of Shooting Brent's party to be Engaged) shott (as the Col. Inform'd me) Fourteen before an Indian Came, who with both hands Shook him (friendly) by one Arm Saying *Susquehanougs Netoughs i.e.* Susquehanaugh friends, and fled, Whereupon he ran amongst his Men, Crying out "For the Lords sake Shoot no more, these are our friends the Susquehanoughs."

B. THE GOVERNOR AND COUNCIL ACT TO PREVENT WAR, 1675

Westmoreland County Deeds and Wills, 1665–1677, fol. 232.

At a meeting at Green Spring the 31th August, *1675*

Sir William Berkeley, Knight Governor etc.

Col. Nathaniel Bacon	Col. Joseph Bridger
Col. Thomas Swann	Col. Phillip Ludwell, Deputy Secretary
Thomas Ballard esq.	James Bray Esq.

Lt. Col. William Cole

Whereas information was lately given to the Right Honorable Governor that the Doeg Indians of Maryland Killed one of his Majesties Subjects in the upper parts of Stafford County within this Government wherupon his Honor was pleased by Letter to acquaint the Honorable [Lieutenant?] of Maryland with the said Murther who by his answer to the said Letter hath expressed a willingness that necessary forces be sent from Virginia into that province for the assaulting and distroying of the Barbarous Ennimies And whereas since the former Murther the Doegs and Sucahanno [i.e., Susquehannock] Indians as confederates with them have murthered two more Englishmen cutt up severall feilds of corne and Tobacco and distroyed severall stocks of cattle in the said upper parts of Stafford County and make Daly incursions uppon them appearing Armed in considerable numbers to the terrifing the inhabitants of those parts and to the apparant indainger of the whole County and Whereas also the Honorable Governor immediately uppon notice of the Murthers above mentioned was pleased to send Orders to the Malittia Officers of Stafford County to raise such force uppon all Emmergencies as might be sufficient to expell the Enimy if they made further Attempts uppon them Requiring thereby the severall Counties of Rappahannock and patomeck River to give them all necessary assistance of men and Armes The Governor and Councell takeing the premises into serious Consideration thought fitt to Order as well for the prevention of future Mischiefes from the Indians and security of the County as Sattisfaction may be had for the Murthers already perpetrated and Spoyles Comitted within this his Majesties Colony of Virginia That Col. John Washington and Maj. Isaac Allerton and together the Several Malittia Officers of the

Severall regiments on the North side of Rappahannock and South side [of] patomeck Rivers and that a full And thorough inquisittion be made of the true causes of the severall Murthers and spoyles by which Nation or Nations of Indians donne And that theruppon the said Col. Washington and Major Allerton demand sattisfaction And take such further course in this Emergency as shall be thought requisite and necessary And that if they find cause they raise a fitt number of men within the Lymitts aforesaid sufficiently furnished with such Armes and ammunition And with them doe Attacque and doe such Executions uppon the said Indians as shall be found necessary and Just And that from time to time they give speedy notice to the Honorable Governor of theire severall proceedings therein Who [will?] please to give such further Orders as shall be requisite And that they Transmitt the whole business to the next Generall Court And it is further Ordered that in case there be necessity of pursuing the Ennimy into Maryland that an Account thereof be given to the Honorable Governor of that province Who is pleased by his Letter to promise if occasion be[,] all necessary assistance therein

Vera Copia Teste Henry Hartwell Clerk of Council

C. AN ACCOUNT OF THE ATTACK ON THE SUSQUEHANNOCK STRONGHOLD, 1675

Westmoreland County Deeds and Wills, 1665–1677, fol. 288.

A narative of the transactions of the Susquehannock Fort. Soe fare as I know concerning the Killing of the five Indians   Assoone as our Virginia forces were landed in Maryland wee found five susquehannock Indians, under a guard and inquireing the reason of theire restraint, where [i.e., were] answered they endeavoured an escape and thereof were secured till our comeing in order to a treaty wee informing the Marylanders our businesse was first to treat and require satisfaction for the murder perpetrated before wee declared ourselves open enimies and proceeded to hostile actions Lt. Col. John Washington and Major Isaac Allerton upon this information thought it convenient to have them stronger guarded and themselves alsoe dureing the treaty which being donne and Col. Washington and Major Alerton accordingly treating there first demand was Satisfaction for the murder and spoyles committed on Virginia Shore Major Tilghman in the interim remaining silent: after long debate [word illegible] therein made by Col. Washington and Major Alerton the Indians disowned all that was Aledged to them and imputed it all to [the] senacas[.] Col. Washington and Major Alerton urged that severall Cannoes loaded with beefe and pork had bin carried into theire fort alleadging that theire enimyes would not be soe kinde as to supply them with provisions and farther that some of their men had a little before been taken on Virginia side who had the Cloathes of such as had bin a little before murdered, upon there backes which made it appeare that they had bin the murderers: for these reasons Major Alerton and Col. Washington demanded Satisfaction or else they must proceed against them as enimyes and storme there fort and accordingly commanded the interpreter to bid them defiance[.] dureing the time of their Treaty Major [Thomas] Trewman came and asked the Gentlemen wheather they had finished[,] saying when you have donne I will Say something to them:

And when Col. Washington and Major Alerton had ended there treatie he sent and comanded his interpreter John Shanks to ask them how theire Indians came to be buried at [Hutsons?] and after a little further discourse caused them to be bound and told them he would Carry them to the place and show them theire owne Indians where they lay dead: Major Alerton asked him what he did intend to doe with them afterwards[.] Major Trewman answered he thought they deserved the like to which Major Alerton replyed I doe not thinke soe[.] noe sooner was this discourse ended between Major Allerton and Major Trewman than the Marylanders carried away those five Indians and before they had got five hundred yards distance from the place of this discourse and treaty spoken of[,] the Marylanders killed them and further saith not

John Gerrard

Sworne before us by virtue of an order to us from the right Honorable the Governor

Nicholas Spencer   June the 13th 1677 recorded
Richard Lee

The Virginia Indians a Century after Colonization

10. Robert Beverley's Estimate of the Indian Population, ca. 1705

Robert Beverley, The History and Present State of Virginia,
ed. Louis B. Wright (Chapel Hill, N.C., 1947), 232–233.

The *Indians* of *Virginia* are almost wasted, but such Towns, or People as retain their Names, and live in Bodies, . . . All which together can't raise five hundred fighting men. They live poorly, and much in fear of the Neighbouring *Indians*. Each Town, by the Articles of Peace in 1677. pays 3 *Indian* Arrows for their Land, and 20 Beaver Skins for protection every year. . . .

Thus I have given a succinct account of the *Indians*; happy, I think, in their simple State of Nature, and in their enjoyment of Plenty, without the Curse of Labour. They have on several accounts reason to lament the arrival of the *Europeans*, by whose means they seem to have lost their Felicity, as well as their Innocence. The *English* have taken away great part of their Country, and consequently made every thing less plenty amongst them. They have introduc'd Drunkenness and Luxury amongst them, which have multiply'd their Wants, and put them upon desiring a thousand things, they never dreamt of before. . . .

Chapter Nine

Upheaval and Rebellion

Throughout the seventeenth century Virginia was periodically beset by assaults on the colony's duly constituted authorities. In 1634 the Council of State drove from the Old Dominion an unpopular royal governor, Sir John Harvey. Less than a decade after Harvey's expulsion, civil war broke out in England. That and the subsequent overthrow of the Stuart monarchy plunged Virginia into a period of turmoil and uncertainty that lasted for nearly two decades. Some years later, in the midst of the Third Anglo-Dutch War, a group of dissident colonists from Lawne's Creek Parish in Surry County challenged the power of local magistrates by refusing to pay taxes. Hardly had the Lawne's Creek rising abated when Bacon's Rebellion burst upon the colony. In the aftermath of the rebellion a band of planters, called "plant cutters" by their contemporaries, rioted and went about the countryside destroying tobacco in the fields in the hope of bolstering sagging tobacco prices.

These upheavals, which were sometimes quite violent, were not merely isolated incidents or mindless acts of rebellion. Although each one originated from the peculiar circumstances surrounding its occurrence, they shared a common characteristic: each reflected the turbulence of a swiftly developing colonial society in the throes of adjusting Old World values to an American setting where European conceptions of a stable social order operated badly or not at all. Englishmen came to the New World expecting to duplicate familiar social and political relationships, but these expectations were never to be realized fully. Throughout the seventeenth century the disparity between expectation and actuality was ever widening.

In the relatively short space of time between "the thrusting out" of Sir John Harvey in 1635 and the plant-cutter riots of 1682, Virginia experienced profound social change. As the population increased prodigiously, the entire face of the colony was altered in dramatic fashion. The presence of great numbers of unruly servants and a smaller collection of graspingly ambitious, competitive men, insured continuing social unrest. A whole new system of government and justice began to replace the almost formless structure that had served as the colony's governing authority between the fall of the London Company and the mid–1630s. New counties sprang up almost as quickly as men could be found to fill the offices occasioned by their creation. So numerous were the problems of law and order generated by the high rate of immigration that the General Assembly could not quickly enough enact the legislation needed to cope with the rapid expansion. Moreover, the assembly itself was in the midst of a significant modification of its role in relation to the colony's overall political structure. There were also economic adjustments brought on by chronic overproduction of tobacco and the commercial policies adopted by the home government after 1660.

Because the colony's institutions were still evolving during most of these years, there was little in them to give the colonists a sense that change was taking place within a stable, recognizable framework. Until they became rooted in tradition and won the settlers' acceptance, those institutions contained no effective means of dissipating tensions generated by fundamental social change. Their extreme fragility always carried the potential for violence. In such circumstances the recurring upheavals can be seen as purifying agents that alleviated pent-up pressures, clarified the lines of authority, and brought Virginians, however grudgingly, to accept that their world demanded its own rules for an orderly society.

Sir John Harvey's troubles with his council came at a moment of uncertainty in the colony. Virginia was still recovering from the massacre of 1622. Apart from the damage wrought by protracted fighting, the Indian wars had also contributed to the dissolution of the London Company. Charles I and his advisers, however, had still not come to a decision as to the final disposition of Virginia's government. In the meanwhile necessity had forced the Virginians to conduct their affairs in accordance with the provisions in the company's 1618 charter, but there were no assurances that those provisions would be sanctioned in the future. As long as the crown remained indecisive, grave doubt surrounded such important concerns as the validity of the colonists' land titles and the legitimacy of the General Assembly or the newly established county courts. The colony's leadership was also in transition. Before 1624 company officials had recruited leaders from the traditional English ruling classes, but after the company lost its charter, these men either returned home or died in Virginia. They were replaced by men whose claim to power lay only in their success at wresting a living from the wilderness. Lacking the usual attributes of the English ruling class, the new leaders were ever sensitive to any interference in their exercise of local power. A final contributor to the uncertainty that gripped Virginia in the mid–1630s was Lord Baltimore's founding of Maryland. Besides raising the specter of Virginia's being overrun with papists, the new colony lay within the territorial limits of the London Company's original land grant. It also conflicted with trading and settlement rights to the northern reaches of Chesapeake Bay, which the crown had previously given to one of Virginia's most important permanent residents, William Claiborne.

Governing Virginia under such circumstances would have been a trial for any governor. Harvey, however, proceeded to make matters worse by so antagonizing Claiborne and other members of the Council of State that they drove him from Virginia. Characterized by a friend as "a proper man, though perhaps somewhat choleric and impatient," Harvey had received his commission as governor from Charles in 1628. After he arrived in 1630, Sir John's prickly personality quickly abraded the councillors' sensibilities. Soon Harvey and the council were embroiled in a dispute over the extent to which the governor could act independently of the will of a majority of the council. Relations between the antagonists worsened when Harvey, against the advice of Dr. John Pott and several other council members, made peace with the Indians. Harvey's position became untenable when he backed Lord Baltimore's claims to the northern Chesapeake region against those of William Claiborne. By supporting Baltimore, Harvey not only jeopardized Claiborne's interests but also opened himself to charges of being friendly to the hated papists. Such allegations received widespread credence because Sir John, acting on the king's orders, sent the Marylanders supplies and did whatever else he could to ease Baltimore's colonists through the difficult days of their initial settlement.

The events leading to Harvey's deposition had their beginning in a meeting of some discontented colonists in April 1635. At this gathering several dissidents complained of the governor's arbitrariness and expressed the fear that his handling of Indian affairs would lead to another massacre. Learning of the meeting, Harvey ordered the participants arrested and summoned the council to dispose of the suspected mutineers according to martial law. Demurring, several councillors defended the validity of the malcontents' complaints, whereupon Harvey demanded from each councilman a written opinion of what should be done with the dissidents. They refused, and after a vigorous argument that failed to resolve anything, the meeting broke up. At the next sitting of the council the debate continued. This time, however, it focused on the councillors' dissatisfaction with Harvey's government and in particular his refusal to transmit certain letters from the General Assembly to the king. Enraged at this harangue, which was delivered by George Menefie, Harvey rose from his chair and arrested Menefie for treasonable utterances. No sooner had the governor acted than he was seized by John Utie and Samuel Mathews. They released him only on the condition that he would go to England to answer their charges. As if to reinforce the demand, Dr. Pott signaled for the appearance of an armed guard. Having gained the upper hand, the council replaced Sir John with one of their number, John West, and convened the General Assembly to hear charges against the governor. After some tense days of negotiation, Harvey at last agreed to return to England (Documents 1 and 2).

Once in England, Harvey obtained a hearing before the Privy Council. Proving that the charges against him were groundless and that the Virginians had personal reasons for wanting him removed, Sir John won the king's renewed support. Armed with a new commission and orders to arrest the rebellious councillors for trial in England, he returned to Virginia in 1637. The apprehension of Mathews, Utie, West, and William Peirce soon followed, but sending them to England finally undid Harvey. Instead of being tried, the four were able to lobby against the governor through their connections at court. Three thousand miles away in Virginia, Harvey could not defend himself against their machinations. In January 1639 the Privy Council replaced him with Sir Francis Wyatt.

Although the council had made it appear that the colonists generally opposed his government, Harvey's downfall in no way represented a triumph of the popular will. He had clashed with ambitious men who were intent upon establishing a share of political control over Virginia's affairs, and Harvey had lost. His loss helped to pave the way for the emergence of Virginia's ruling elite during the next four decades.

Having made their point with Harvey, the councillors cooperated with his successors. Indeed, the crown's appointment of Sir William

Berkeley in 1641 ushered in an era of harmony between governor and council that remained virtually uninterrupted until Berkeley's removal in 1677. A more artful politician than Harvey, Berkeley won over the councillors by deferring to their sensibilities and by recognizing their right to a share of power that comported with the dignity of their office. Thus they retained what they had wrested from Harvey, though the prize was diminished somewhat by the growing delegation of authority to local government.

Scarcely had the dust of the Harvey affair settled when new troubles befell Virginia. The wrangling between Charles I and the Parliament men gave way to civil war in August 1642, and the outbreak of armed conflict in England put the Virginians in a tenuous position. As Englishmen they were not unmindful of the issues that separated their kinsmen. Indeed, some shared the Puritans' distaste for Archbishop William Laud and Charles's recent attempt to rule England without Parliament, while others remained dedicated churchmen and fiercely steadfast in their loyalty to the Stuarts. At bottom, though, most distressing to the colonists was the certain knowledge that whatever happened in England would deeply affect their most vital interests, at a time when their own world in Virginia still lacked permanence and stability.

Civil war disrupted the normal commercial intercourse between colony and mother country. Because the trade in tobacco was essential to Virginia's economic survival, prolonged disruption could seriously impair not only the planters' ability to survive in the wilderness but also the welfare of the entire colony. Of equal concern was the apprehension that a triumph of the parliamentary forces would lead to a revival of the Virginia Company, since the old Virginia adventurers had sided with the king's opponents. Resurrecting the company would threaten those privileges and rights that the crown had allowed the colonists since 1624. Such fears had been momentarily allayed in 1641, however, when Governor Berkeley brought the king's promise that the status quo would be maintained, but in light of more recent events no one could be certain of the future.

In these circumstances, the Virginians understandably continued their loyalty to their sovereign. Not wishing to offend Parliament unnecessarily, they also attempted to remain as aloof from the contest as their condition would allow. So long as the issue between royalist and roundhead hung in the balance, the colonists succeeded in maintaining their neutrality. But when the monarchy was overthrown, the situation changed; Virginia was too important a colony to remain long outside the control of Oliver Cromwell's government.

News of Charles I's execution brought forth a hostile reaction to Cromwell from Governor Berkeley and the General Assembly. In reply to this hostility Parliament enacted in October 1650 a statute forbidding foreign ships from trading with Virginia. Again the Virginians responded with defiance.

The Commonwealth government now resolved to bring the colony under its dominion, and to that end it dispatched to Virginia a four-man commission in charge of a military force. Under orders to reduce Virginia by peaceful means if possible, the commissioners set sail in the fall of 1651. Arriving at the mouth of the James early in 1652, the two who survived the crossing sought to negotiate the colony's surrender with Berkeley, but the governor refused to meet them. Their patience at an end, at length the commissioners sailed their fleet upriver to Jamestown. Berkeley hastily raised a force of men, and for a brief time it appeared that blood might be shed. Realizing that his Virginians were no match for the parliamentary force, Berkeley apparently sought only to make a show of the colony's loyalty to the late king. Having made his point, he promptly surrendered to the parliamentary forces on March 12, 1651/52.

The terms of Virginia's submission were generous. Berkeley and other staunch royalists in the provincial government retired to private life. Political control of the colony was vested in the House of Burgesses. The entire legal code was revised to bring it into conformity with the new situation, but the basic fabric of the law remained untouched. All colonists would "enjoy such freedomes and priviledges as belong to the free borne people of England." Use of the *Book of Common Prayer* could continue for a time. And those colonists not wishing to submit to the authority of Parliament were given a year to remove themselves and their property from Virginia.

Surrendering to Oliver Cromwell did not throw the colony into a conflict between cavalier and roundhead. Indeed, the transition was quite smooth: there was a marked continuity of leadership in both provincial and local government. With few exceptions, the councillors, burgesses, and justices of the peace who held office under the king continued to do so under Cromwell.

Royalist sentiment ran high throughout the eight years Parliament ruled Virginia, and because of their feelings, the Virginians regarded their new masters with suspicion. Those suspicions were in no way diminished by Cromwell's commercial policies, which attempted to exclude the Dutch from the colonial trade and eventually led to the First Anglo-Dutch War in 1654. Moreover, while the men Parliament chose as the colony's governors were all residents of Virginia, each managed to embroil himself in controversies with the burgesses. Unfortunately, these skirmishes did little to endear London's authority to the colonists. Yet in the end, it cannot be said that the Interregnum had many lasting effects upon Virginia.

It did have one important consequence, however. The subordination of the governor to the House of Burgesses established a precedent of lessened gubernatorial control in local affairs. This change came at the very time when immigration and the expansion of the number of counties were at their highest levels in the century. Their position weakened by the terms of Virginia's surrender to Parliament, the Interregnum governors were unable to forestall the assembly's vesting of additional powers in the county courts. And by the time royal authority was restored in 1660, the almost complete control of local affairs by the justices of the peace had been assured.

Rumors of a change in governments at home began to filter into Virginia in the early months of 1660. The death of the colony's last Interregnum governor, Samuel Mathews, dictated the need for a change in the Old Dominion as well, and in March, Sir William Berkeley agreed to assume the office temporarily until the situation in England had clarified itself. In July 1660 Charles II formally commissioned Sir William as the colony's governor. Unloved and unmourned, parliamentary rule had crumbled in Virginia almost as quickly as it had in England.

The return of Virginia to its old allegiance freed the colonists from some of the disturbing uncertainties of the preceding two decades, but others were still unresolved. One of the more vexing problems that confronted the colonists in this period was the maintenance of an adequate defense against the Indians and foreign invasion. A remedy lay in arming the colonists and developing a system of local militias. To that end the General Assembly repeatedly adopted legislation to provide a store of arms and to train settlers in the art of warfare. When the Indian War of 1644–1646 broke out, the colony was so ill-prepared that Governor Berkeley made a hasty trip to England to buy much-needed ammunition and weapons. Virginia's loyalty to the House of Stuart in the 1640s had raised the added possibility of an invasion by a parliamentary army. Such an attack could scarcely be prevented because, as the deputy-governor, Richard Kemp, observed in 1645, Virginia was "destitute both of Fortification and ammunition, and neither fitted for offence or defence." The truth of Kemp's observation had been borne out in the spring of 1652 when without a struggle the colony submitted to Parliament.

By the 1660s the matter of defense had become even more acute. Smoldering relations with the Indians threatened to engulf the frontier anew, and as the home government again sought to eliminate its commercial rival, the Dutch, the prospect of invasion was once more a distinct probability. Alarmed by the inadequate store of military hardware, Berkeley, the Council of State, and others charged with defending Virginia deluged London with letters hammering out the same theme: the colony lacked the resources to defend itself, and help from the crown was needed. No help was forthcoming. Instead, in the mid–1660s, the crown forced Berkeley to abandon his own expensive scheme for protecting the colony and compelled him to build a costly, but useless, fort on the mouth of the James River. Berkeley argued that the fort was a folly because no ordnance could traverse the river's width. Events soon demonstrated the wisdom of Berkeley's argument: during the Second Anglo-Dutch War a fleet of Dutch warships sailed up the James out of range of the fort's guns and burned a tobacco convoy as it lay at anchor. Six years later, in the midst of the Third Anglo-Dutch War, the same thing happened (Document 3A).

The burning of the tobacco fleet in July 1673 pointed up the provincial government's long-standing inability to protect the Old Dominion. All of the taxes that the General Assembly had raised for forts and arms had brought no results. In the months following the latest Dutch raid, the disaffection with Berkeley's handling of the defense issue seems to have mounted, especially after the assembly, meeting in October, required local militias to rearm and authorized the county courts to defray the expenses by raising new taxes. It was against this background that fourteen residents of Lawne's Creek Parish in Surry County refused to pay their taxes.

Sometime before December 12, 1673, four of the men, John Barnes, Mathew Swan, John Sheppard, and William Hancock, hatched their protest during a meeting at Barnes's house. Their scheme was simple enough: they would recruit a group of other like-minded men and persuade the authorities not to raise the year's levies. Failing that, they would try to prevent the sheriff from collecting taxes within Lawne's Creek Parish. The protest began on December 12 when several of the justices and the sheriff came to the parish church to announce and to collect the parishioners' levies. As the day progressed, Barnes, Swan, Sheppard, and Hancock, together with ten other men, arrived at the church and attempted to make their feelings known. They were ordered to disperse, but instead of disbanding, Barnes and the other ringleaders called for a second, and hopefully larger, meeting of disgruntled taxpayers. Ignoring a warning by the sheriff against such an unlawful gathering, the dissidents proceeded to assemble at a place called Devil's Field, whereupon the magistrates arrested all fourteen protestors for trial (Document 4A).

Charged with illegal assembly, contempt, and obstructing the sheriff, the fourteen were tried before the Surry County Court in January 1673/74. Nine of the men whom the court regarded as lesser actors merely posted peace bonds, paid court costs, and were released. A tenth protestor, Roger Delke, was fined one thousand pounds of tobacco for seditious utterances. Three of the ringleaders, Barnes, Sheppard, and Hancock, were fined a thousand pounds of tobacco apiece. Mathew Swan, the reputed architect of the whole affair, was bound over to the General Court (Documents 4B and 4C) and the following April was convicted and fined two thousand pounds of tobacco (Document 4D). Then in an apparent gesture of conciliation, in September 1674 Governor Berkeley remitted all of the fines on the condition that the convicts confess their error in open court (Document 4E).

Neither conciliation nor the end of the Third Anglo-Dutch War laid to rest the issue of the adequacy of the colony's defenses. Within a year of Berkeley's remission of the Lawne's Creek malcontents' fines, the Indians began raiding the northern and western frontier settlements, and the defense question came to life once more. By the spring of 1676 the settlers in these areas were so alarmed by the seeming ineffectiveness of the governor's latest defensive measures, plus his apparent unwillingness to honor their requests to settle things themselves (Document 5A), that many of them were determined to resist the Indians by acting outside the law. That determination resulted in Bacon's Rebellion.

The revolt began in earnest in April 1676 when a recently arrived young colonist named Nathaniel Bacon took command of an illegally assembled group of volunteer Indian fighters. Of Bacon little is known except that he was a ne'er-do-well whose father had sent him to Virginia in 1674 in hopes of getting him a fresh start under the watchful eye of his cousin, Councillor Nathaniel Bacon, Sr. Once he was in the colony, the younger Bacon's fortunes improved; he soon bought a plantation on the frontier of Henrico County, where he apparently developed a distaste for Indians. Within a year of his arrival Berkeley elevated him to a seat on the Council of State, but Bacon seldom attended council meetings. His position and his known antipathy towards the natives are the probable reasons for his neighbors' prevailing upon him to lead them.

Possibly angered by the governor's refusal to allow him to raise volunteers as he had requested, Bacon paid no heed to Sir William's warning that the acceptance of the unauthorized command was tantamount to mutiny. Instead Bacon and his men set out into the wilderness southwest of Henrico to find some Indians. Soon they fell in company with some friendly Indians who informed them that a band of marauding Susquehannocks was close at hand. Bacon talked his newfound friends into attacking the Susquehannocks, but in the aftermath of their victory the Indians and the English quarreled over the spoils. Bacon and his men fell upon their erstwhile allies and destroyed their village. Now he had killed some Indians—a fact that enhanced Bacon's popularity when he returned to Henrico (Document 5B).

In the meantime the governor had not been idle. Infuriated by Bacon's disobedience, Berkeley had taken three hundred men to head off Bacon before he slipped into the wilderness. But when he reached Henrico, Bacon was gone. Realizing that the situation was more precarious than he had first imagined and that his control had slipped badly, Berkeley took steps to reassert his authority. He proclaimed Bacon a rebel and removed him from the council. Then "to satisfye the Importunity of the People in their soe earnest desires for a new Assembly," the governor issued a proclamation dissolving the General Assembly and calling the first general election in fourteen years (Document 6A). In a move to erode Bacon's popular support, Berkeley drafted a remonstrance, which he ordered read in every county court, setting forth his reasons for outlawing Bacon, reminding people of their duty to the king, and promising to look into the popular complaints in the upcoming meeting of the assembly (Document 6B). Yet in the end the governor may have wavered in his conviction that these measures would have the desired effect; just two days before the new assembly opened, Sir William wrote to London asking to be replaced (Document 7).

On June 5 the General Assembly convened in an atmosphere of tension. Rumors of an imminent Indian attack were rife, and because of them the colony verged on mutiny. Of more immediate concern to the assemblymen was what would happen between the governor and Bacon. Flush with his "victory" over the natives, Bacon had been elected burgess for Henrico upon his return from the wilderness (Document 8). Since he was still an outlaw, the question arose as to whether Berkeley would allow him to take his seat with the other burgesses, some of whom were his adherents and sympathizers. Seeking an answer, Bacon arrived off Jamestown in his sloop but was driven away when the governor ordered the vessel fired upon. Bacon then stole into town, and following a secret meeting with some friends, he and his sloop were captured. He was subsequently brought before Berkeley and the council, where he confessed his errors and begged Sir William's forgiveness (Document 9). The governor restored him to his place on the council and apparently promised to put him in charge of the forces being raised against the Indians. A few days later Bacon returned upriver to his plantation while the assembly proceeded to its business.

The June General Assembly met for twenty days and adopted a series of twenty acts (Document 10A). Contrary to the opinion of some scholars, these laws did not radically alter existing political arrangements, nor were they the handiwork of a reform-minded Nathaniel Bacon, since he was absent from most of the session. Several statutes established procedures for prosecuting the war against the Indians. Other acts were designed to strengthen local government by closing loopholes in existing legislation. Still others were attempts to quell popular complaints by prohibiting certain abuses of power that had crept into the county courts over recent years. As the assembly was completing its work on these laws, Bacon suddenly reappeared in Jamestown at the head of five hundred armed men and terrorized the members into giving him command of the Indian campaign. Having won that office, plus restitution of his sloop, Bacon marched off to fight Indians (Document 10B).

Throughout the summer and early fall of 1676 the rebellion took a more serious turn. As Bacon scouted for Indians near the falls of the James, he learned that Berkeley had again declared him a rebel and was trying to capture him. Armed with this intelligence, Bacon returned to the vicinity of Jamestown, only to discover that Berkeley had fled to Accomack on the Eastern Shore. At that point the rebel moved to wrest control of Virginia entirely from the governor. He published several emotionally charged documents attacking the governor's credibility (Document 11) and sent men across the Chesapeake Bay to carry the fight to Sir William. To prove his prowess as the people's guardian, Bacon again went off to hunt Indians, but the only ones he could find were the tattered remnants of the Powhatan

Confederacy. These he attacked and scattered. Bacon then returned to Jamestown and discovered that Berkeley, who by now had gained control over parts of the Western Shore, was in possession of the capital. Laying seige to it, he forced the governor to quit the town and repair to his stronghold in Accomack. Then Bacon burned Jamestown to the ground. From that point, however, the rebellion began to fall apart. A month after he had destroyed the capital, Bacon died of the "Bloody Flux" and "Lousey Disease," and by February 1676/77 Berkeley had stamped out the last vestiges of the revolt.

The rebellion's repercussions were wide ranging. There had not been a heavy loss of life, but property damage was extensive. Inflamed by the revolt, passions were slow to cool; the possibility of renewed violence continued for some years. Despite the efforts of a royal commission of investigation, many of the underlying problems that had turned a dispute over Indian affairs into the most serious colonial challenge to royal authority before 1776 remained unresolved (Document 12). Bacon's Rebellion also forced the crown to pay closer heed to Virginia than it had done since the 1620s. When the home government learned how serious the situation in the Old Dominion was, it dispatched over a thousand troops to the colony. In a departure from past practice, the king issued a proclamation annulling the legislation adopted by the June assembly, thus opening the door to more careful scrutiny of colonial law by the crown. Berkeley was recalled, and he returned to England in disgrace to die before he could defend his handling of the revolt in the presence of Charles II. The experiences with the rebellion led royal officials to seek a more centralized and efficient system of colonial administration. That intention would be reflected in the political contests between Berkeley's successors and the General Assembly throughout the last decades of the seventeenth century.

Virginia recovered slowly from the effects of Bacon's Rebellion. Impeding recovery was the continued low price of tobacco—the cause of the plant-cutter riots in 1682. In the late 1670s the colonists grew several large crops of tobacco, thereby glutting the English market and keeping prices down. Faced with this situation, the planters began to clamor for the General Assembly to enact a stay law that would prohibit the growing of tobacco for a whole year. But in the aftermath of Bacon's Rebellion the governors had abandoned the custom of annual assembly sessions because of disputes between themselves and the burgesses over the assembly's powers. Thus, when the governor, Thomas, Lord Culpeper, went to England in the summer of

1680 after having just prorogued a particularly troublesome assembly, he commanded his deputy, Sir Henry Chicheley, not to call it back into session until his return.

As Culpeper's stay in England lengthened and the economic situation worsened, pressure for reconvening the General Assembly mounted. By December 1681 some colonists were petitioning Chicheley for an assembly, while several local politicians used what influence they had with the deputy-governor to effect the same end. A tobacco planter and a long-time resident of Virginia himself, Sir Henry's sympathies probably lay with the distressed planters. In any case, Chicheley yielded to the planters' wishes, and in April 1682 he ordered the assembly back into session. However, before the members assembled, the deputy-governor received instructions from Lord Culpeper not to convene the assembly before November, when his lordship expected to return to the colony.

Gathering in Jamestown on April 23, the assembly received Chicheley's news. Bitterly disappointed by it, the burgesses begged Chicheley to let them attend to the colony's urgent business. After four days of wrangling, Chicheley and the council prorogued the assembly until November. A week later the plant-cutter rioting began.

Frustrated by the dismissal of the General Assembly before it could adopt a stay law, groups of planters from Gloucester County started destroying their own and their neighbors' tobacco plants as they grew in their beds. The spontaneous rioting spread quickly to nearby Middlesex and New Kent counties. When Chicheley learned about the riots, he forbade all meetings and called out the militias in the affected areas. Before local officials quelled them, the plant-cutters destroyed tobacco on about two hundred plantations (Documents 13A and 13B). The ringleaders were arrested, and Chicheley pardoned all but Robert Beverley, the burgesses' clerk, who was suspected of being the perpetrator of the riots. When Culpeper finally returned to the colony, he came with orders to try those responsible for the plant-cutting. Beverley was released for lack of evidence, but four other men were convicted of treason, and two of these were eventually executed (Document 14).

Remarkably, the plant-cutter riots had not reached the proportions of earlier disturbances. That they did not is attributable to the dispatch with which Chicheley moved to quell the rioting and to Culpeper's treatment of Beverley and the other putative ringleaders. But there is perhaps a further explanation of why plant-cutting did not turn into a more generalized rebellion. Unlike earlier disruptions, these riots were purely economic in their origin. Harvey's troubles with the council, the uncertainties bred by the English civil wars and the Interregnum, the inadequacies of the colony's defenses, and the Indian troubles that led Nathaniel Bacon to revolt were manifestations of much deeper causes of social unrest that gripped Virginia from the mid–1630s to the mid–1670s.

Harvey was tossed out of the colony because he would not share power with men who wanted a role in governing that was commensurate with their newly acquired place at the head of Virginia society. Having won their point with Sir John and the crown, Claiborne, Utie, Mathews, and the others had to establish their societal and political control with the rest of the planters. That they and their successors to the council, the House of Burgesses, and the county courts could not do so before 1676 helps to explain Bacon's Rebellion.

In part the rebellion has to be viewed as an attempt by the planters outside the governing elite to seize by force what they had lost in less violent competition with the great planters. If Bacon's Rebellion accomplished nothing else, its failure to unseat the great planters demonstrated that they could hold onto their places despite the gravest of challenges. Defeated, Bacon's adherents had only one choice: to submit to the rule of their betters.

For their part the great planters also learned from Bacon's Rebellion. Governing others demanded a sensitivity to those beneath them. It also required a willingness to check unnecessary taxation, corruption, waste, or the outright abuse of enormous power over the lives of so many people. Magnanimity was a further requisite to the exercise of power, and after 1676 the great planters could afford to be magnanimous because their position was assured. Outstripping all comers, they had achieved social and political distinction, and they had succeeded in reproducing the traditional nexus between the two.

A final reason why plant-cutting did not give way to more disruption lay in the increasing vitality of local government and the growing permanence of life in Virginia by the 1680s. From its inception in 1634 the county court system held the promise of providing order and stability in many of the planters' affairs. But the system had grown with such rapidity, and had been so strained by the pressures of phenomenal population growth, that the county courts could barely keep pace with their expanded jurisdictions. Although the swift rate of change began to abate by the 1660s, the colonists did not sufficiently comprehend the process in time to forestall Bacon's Rebellion.

Again it was the upheaval of 1676 that brought an awareness of the courts' durability. All during the rebellion, courts met, probated wills, settled debts, and collected taxes; in short, they did their job, and life went on. To judge from the court records of all but a few counties, Bacon's Rebellion was a non-event. That fact is significant, for it indicates that local institutions now had the vitality to withstand social violence without sustaining serious injury.

This stability in the face of the rebellion also indicates a similar permanence in the life-styles of the colonists themselves. In the course of the century the tidewater area had been transformed from a collection of frontier outposts into a region of settled communities. There was a rhythm to life that rebellion and plant-cutting could disrupt only momentarily. And with the maturing of the second and third generations of Virginians, there was less concern with how things ought to have been and more regard for how they were in Virginia. Robert Beverley stated the change in attitude in a forceful metaphor some years after the plant-cutter riots when he observed in his *History and Present State of Virginia*, "I am an Indian, and don't pretend to be exact in my language." He meant that he had become, above all, a native of Virginia.

The plant-cutter riots marked the end of an era of violent upheaval in colonial Virginia. Thereafter a high degree of social stability was possible because the colonists finally saw that life in the Old Dominion demanded a departure from Old World norms. That realization ushered in an era of domestic tranquility that remained unbroken until the Revolution.

SUGGESTED READINGS

Billings, Warren M. "The Causes of Bacon's Rebellion: Some Suggestions." *Virginia Magazine of History and Biography*, LXXVIII (1970), 409–435.

Boddie, John Bennett. *Colonial Surry* (Richmond, Va., 1948).

Morton, Richard L. *Colonial Virginia*. 2 vols. (Chapel Hill, N.C., 1960), I, 297–309.

Thornton, J. Mills, III. "The Thrusting Out of Governor Harvey: A Seventeenth-Century Rebellion." *Virginia Magazine of History and Biography*, LXXVI (1968), 11–26.

*Washburn, Wilcomb E. *The Governor and the Rebel: A History of Bacon's Rebellion* (Chapel Hill, N.C., 1957).

*Available in paperback.

Wertenbaker, Thomas J. *Torchbearer of the Revolution: The Story of Bacon's Rebellion and Its Leader* (Princeton, N.J., 1940).

The Thrusting Out of Sir John Harvey, 1635

1. The Mutineers' Complaints against Harvey:
Samuel Mathews to Sir John Wolstenholme

Virginia Magazine of History and Biography, I (1894), 416–424.

HONORED SIR:

I have made bold to present you with divers passages concerning our late governor by the hands of my worthy friend Sir John Zouch. But such was the miserable condition wee lived in that it dayly gives just occasion of new complaints which I doe hereby presume to acquaint you withall, which I beseech you to creditt as they are true in every particular. Sir, you may please to take notice that since Sir John Harvie his deteyning of the Letters to his Majestie the Lords and others concerning a contract, of which Sir John Zouch had onely bare copies, such as the Secretary would give without either his or the clarkes hand. Notwithstanding he promised me to certefie them under his hand, whereupon Sir John Zouch declared before his departure that it was not safe for him to deale as agent in the countreyes affaires as they had desired him to do, having no warrant for his proceedings. And therefore desired that if the colony would then deale therein for them, they should give him further authority under their hands. To that purpose when a letter was drawn and carried to the Burgesses to subscribe; the consideration of the wrong done by the Governor to the whole colony in detayning the foresaid Letters to his Majesty did exceedingly perplex them, whereby they were made sensible of the miserable condition of the present Govenor, wherein the Govenor usurped the whole power, in all causes without any respect to the votes of the councell, whereby justice was now done but soe farr as suited with his will to the great losse of Many Mens estates and a generall feare in all. They had heard him in open court revile all the councell and tell them they were to give their attendance as assistants onely to advise with him, which if liked of should pass, otherwise the power lay in himselfe to dispose of all matters as his Majesties substitute. Next that he had reduced the colony to a great straight by complying with the Marylanders soe farr that betweene them and himselfe all places of trade fore corne were shutt up from them, and no meanes left to relieve their wants without transgressing his commands which was very dangerous for any to attempt. This want came upon us the increase of above 2000 persons this yeare to the colony as alsoe by an unusuall kind of wevell that last yeare eate our corne, againe they saw a dangerous peace made by him with the Indians against the councells and countreyes advice, that although the Indians had offered many insolent injuries yet he withheld us from revenging ourselves and had taken of them satisfaction for many Hoggs, of which in one place a Lyst was brought in of above 500; which satisfaction the Interpreter instefies he had received for the Governors owne use. The inhabitants also understood with indignation that the Marylanders had taken Captaine Clayborne's Pinnasses and men with the goods in them, whereof they had made prize and shared the goods amongst them, which action of theirs Sir John Harvey upheld contrary to his Majestie's express comands in his Royall Letters, and the Letters of the Lords which Letter from his Majestie he did not communicate to the rest of the councell though Captaine Clayborne in his Petition had directed them to the whole Board. But said they were surreptitiously gotten. Sir, these and infinite number of perticular mens injuries, were the grounds of their greife and the occasion of the Petition and Letter that they exhibited to the councell for some speedy redress of these evills which would otherwise ruine the Colony.

These general grievances made some of the people meete in some numbers and in an unlawfull manner, yet without any manifestation of bad intents, only desires to exhibit their complaints, as did appeare upon strict examination, though Captain [Thomas] Purfrey [Purifoy] had in a Letter accused them in a neare sense to rebellion which since he denyed under his owne hand, being usuall with him to affirme and deny often the same things. The governor having intelligence of this Petition grew inraged, and sent out his warrants to apprehend the complaynants, which some of the councell accordingly executed; upon these appearances he himself onely, constituted a new sheriff at James Citty, a defamed fellow to whom he committed the Keeping of the Prisoners in Irons. Some of them desiring the cause of their comittment, to whom he answered that they should at the gallowes, presently the councell being called together he declared it necessary that Marshall law should be executed upon the Prisoners, but it was desired they might have legall tryall; soe growing into extreame coller and passion, after many passings and repassings to and fro, at length sate downe in the chayre and with a frowning countenance bid all the councell sit. After a long pause he drew a paper out of his pockett and reading it to himself said to the councell; I am to propound a question unto you; I require every man, in his Majestie's name, to deliver his opinion in writing under his hand, and no man to advise or councell with the other, but to make a direct answer unto this proposition (which is this): What do you think they deserve that have gone about to persuade the people from their obedience to his Majestie's substitute; And to this I doe require you to make your present answer and no man to advise or interrupt with other. And I begin with you Mr. [George] Menefie; who answered, I am but a young Lawyer and dare not upon the suddain deliver my opinion. The governor required that should be his answer under his hand; Mr. [William] Farrar begann to complaine of that strong comand, the governor cutt of[f] his speech saying in his Majestie's name I comand you not to speake till your turne. Then myselfe replyed, I conceive this a strange kind of proceeding; instantly in his Majesties name he comanded me silence; I said further there was no Presedent for such a comand, whereupon he gave me leave to speake further. But it was by a Tyrant meaning that passage of Richard the third against the Lord Hastings; after which relation the rest of the councell begann to speake and refused that course. Then followed many bitter languages from him, till the sitting ended. The next meeting in a most sterne manner he demanded the reason that wee conceived of the countreye's Petition against him. Mr. Menefee made answer, the chiefest cause was the detayning of the Letters to his Majestie and the Lords. Then he rising in a great rage sayd to Mr. Menefee; and do you say soe? He replied, yes: presently the governor in a fury went and striking him on the shoulder as hard as I can imagine he could said, I arrest you of suspicion of Treason to his Majestie. Then Captain [John] Utie being neare said, and wee the like to you sir. Whereupon I seeing him in a rage, tooke him in my armes and said: Sir, there is no harm intended against you save only to acquaint you with the grievances of the Inhabitants and to that end I desire you to sitt downe in youre chayre. And soe I related to him the aforesaid grievances of the colony desiring him that their just complaint might receive some satisfaction which he altogether denied, soe that sitting ended. After wee were parted the Secretary Shewed a letter sent up by Captain Purfrey to the Governor which spake of dangerous times, that to his knowledge the wayes were layd, which when wee had considered with the things before specified, wee much doubted least the Inhabitants would not be kept in due obedience if the Governor continued as formerly and soe acquainted him therewith. The which opinion of ours he desired under our hands the which being granted him he was requested the sight of his Majestie's Comission, and the same being publiquely read (notwithstanding any former passages) wee of the Councell tendred the continuance of our assistance provided that he would be pleased to conforme himselfe to his Majesties pleasure expressed by his Comission and Instructions, the which request was in no part satisfied, whereupon being doubtfull of some Tyrannicall proceeding wee requested the Secretary to take charge of the Comission and Instructions untill we had some time to consider of a safe course for the satisfying the Inhabitants Petition and the safety of the Governours Person which by reason of Captain Purfreys letter wee conceived to be in some danger; whereupon wee appointed an Assembly of all the late Burgesses whereby they might acquaint us with their grievances as may appeare by theire Petition; wee broke up for that meeting with a resolution to return againe within six dayes, having, according to Sir John Harvey's desire appointed a sufficient gard for the safety of his Person, within three dayes after he departed from James Citty and went into the Mills to the house of one William Brockas, whose wife was generally suspected to have more familiarity with him than befitted a modest woman where he thought himselfe soe secure that he dismissed his guard. Soone after the Councell and Burgesses according to the time prefixed mett at James Citty. But before wee entered upon any business the Secretary shewed us a Letter which he had received that morning from Sir John Harvey (the true coppie whereof I have here inclosed) And notwithstanding his threats therein the Assembly proceeded according to their former Intentions. The next morning the Secretary shewed us another letter from Sir John Harvey wherein he had required him to redeliver him his Majesties Comission and Instructions charging him upon his alleageance to keepe Secresie therein. But the Councell had before thought of his late practises with the Secretary concerning the detayning of the former proceedings, had comitted the charge of the Comission and Instructions to Mr. George Menefie until all differences were setled. And for the effecting of the same wee proceeded to give a hearing unto the grievances of the Inhabitants which were innumerable, and theretofore it thought fit that their generall grievances only should be presented to the Right Honorable Lords Comissions for Plantations omitting particular complaints which should have beene over tedious untill a fitter opportunity. Sir, wee were once resolved not to proceed to the election of a New Governor but finding his Majesties comands to the contrary that upon the death or absence of any governor to make a new election. Therefore untill we heare of his Majesties further pleasure wee have made choice of Captaine John West an anntient Inhabitant who is a very honest gentlemen of a noble family being brother to the Lord Laward [i.e., Lord Delaware] sometimes governor of Virginia. I beseech God to direct his Majestie in appointing of some worthy religious gentleman, for to take charge of this his colony, and I doubt not by God's assistance and the industry of the people, but Virginia in few yeares will flourish. You may please to take notice that Captaine Clayborne two dayes since repayred unto us for redress against the oppressions of the Marylanders who have slaine three and hurt others of the Inhabitants of the Isle of Kent. Notwithstanding their Knowledge of his Majesties late express Letter to comand freedome of trade, the true coppie whereof I have here inclosed, I doe believe that they would not have comitted such outrages without Sir John Harvey's instigation, however in conformity to his Majesties comand wee have entreated Captaine Utie and Captain Pierce to sayle for Maryland with Instructions and Letters from the Governor and councell desiring them to desist their violent proceedings promising them all fayre correspondence on the behalfe of the Inhabitants of the Isle of Kent untill wee understood his Majesties further pleasure.

In the meane time we rest in expectation of their answere according to which wee intend to proceed. In the which I beseech God to direct us for the best. I conclude with an assured hope that Sir John Harvey's returne will be acceptable to God not displeasing to his Majestie, and an assured happiness unto this Colony, wherein whilst I live, I shall be ready to doe you all the true offices of a faythfull friend and servant.

Signed SAMUEL MATHEWS.

From Newport Newes this 25th May, 1635.

2. *Harvey's Account of His Troubles*

Virginia Magazine of History and Biography, I (1894), 425–430.

To the Right Honorable the Lords Commissions for forraigne Plantations:
The humble Declaration of Sir John Harvey his Majesties Lieutenant
    Governor of Virginia touching the Mutinous proceedings of the
    councell there and their confederates with the causes thereof.

Sheweth:

That about seaven yeares since I was by his Majestie imployed to serve him as Governor of Virginia, during which time I have faithfully and diligently served his Majestie to the uttermost of my power: And that Mr. John West, Samuell Mathews, John Utye, William Clayborne, William Farrer, William Perry, William Pearse, and George Minefie with some others are all of the councell of Virginia, and thereby joyned with mee in the said Government.

And by the Comission all things are to be ordered by the Governor and councell, only the Governor is of the Quorum.

That about December last and many times since secret and unlawfull meetings were had by the said Mathewes with the rest of the foresaid councellors, and divers of the inhabitants drawn to the said meetings and assemblies. That coming to the Knowledge of the said unlawfull and factious meetings, I caused William English Captain [Nicholas] Martu and Francis Pott, who were chiefe actors therein, to be apprehended and comitted, and sent for the said councellors to give their assistance to the suppressing and punishing the mutinous meetings. And that upon the 28 day of Aprill last which was the time when they were to meet for his Majesties said service, the said Mathewes, Utye, Farrer, Pearce, Minefie and John Pott came all armed and brought with them about 50 Musketeers, and besett mee in my owne house, which was the place which I appointed for our meeting. That I and Mr. [Richard] Kemp (his Majesties Secretary there) were then sitting together expecting the councell, when the said mutinous company entered the place, and John Utye in the presence of the rest gave me a very greate and violent stroake upon the shoulder and sayd with a loud voyce, I arrest you for treason; and thereupon Mathewes and the rest of the said company, came all about mee, and layd hould on me, and there held me so as I was not able to stirr from the place, and all of them sayd to me; you must prepare yourself to goe for England, for you must and shall goe, to answer the complainte that are against you.

That upon this Uproare John Pott, (who by the said company was pleased [i.e., placed] at the doore of said house) with his hand gave a signe and immediately the Musketeers which before that time lay hid, came presently running with their pieces presented towards my house; and when one of my servants saw them coming so hastily towards my house, he asked the said Pott what the said Shott meant; he said unto him; Stirr not for your life; and when they were come neare to him, he sayd to the Musketeers: Stay there untill there be use of you; and there upon they retired again.

That to prepare their way to the meeting they caused guards to be sett in all wayes and passages, so that no man could travel or come from place to place, nor had I meanes or power to raise any force to suppress this meeting they having restrayned me, and sett a guard upon me.

That the said councellors did then sett at liberty the said William English, Martu and Francis Pott, having before contrived a petition made in the name of the countrey to themselves wherein they pretended to lay many aspersions upon mee, which they sent by Francis Pott upp and downe the Colonie, whom they caused to meet in severall places for that purpose to gett their hands to it, who by feare and persuasion being told by him that it was for the generall good of the countrey and that the councell and the best in the Land did approve of it, were brought to subscribe thereto, only they of Accomack refused to subscribe with them.

That upon pretence of this petition thus by themselves contrived, they caused an Assembly of the Countrey to be called, who mett at James Towne, upon the seaventh day of May last, and there and in severall other places they made Proclamation that if any man could say ought against Sir John Harvey he should be heard. And the said councellors then chose Mr. John West for Governor, who thereupon tooke the place and title of Governor upon him, and gave orders and directions as Governor.

That when I saw things come to this height that they had sent mee a proscription under their hands, and that they had sumoned the Countrey together under pretence of calling an Assembly (which is their Parliament) and chosen another Governor; seeing them runn into such dangerous and desperate courses, I wrote unto the councell and Assembly of Burgesses and comanded them, in his Majesties name, all to depart from that mutinous Assembly: but this the councell, (after they had heard it read unto them by Mr. Kemp) supprest and concealed it from the people, the better to worke their mutinous intentions. And still persisting in their malice towards mee, they contrived amongst themselves to share my house and estate amongst them.

1. All which did proceed from these motives following: Sir John Wolstenholme hath long kept the countrey in expectation of a change of the Governor and the renewing of a corporation, which hath much distracted the minds of the people there.

2. These mutinous Councellors Mathewes, Utye, Pearce, and Clayborne, who are the heads and contrivers of this outrage, are the same men that both myself and Mr. Kemp have complayned of to your Lordships for their opposition to his Majesties service in severall occasions. And they have contrived to raise this storme uppon mee, hoping thereby to shelter themselves.

3. The maine occasion, which they pretend to proceed upon, is that which is mentioned in the councellors letter or petition to themselves, but made in the name of the countrey, and that is, for my not sending a letter, which was by them written in answere to his Majesties letter touching the Tobacco contract; a true copy whereof Mr. Kemp sent to Mr. Secretary Windebank, but the originall I thought fitt to keepe, both for their owne good and his Majesties service; doubting that as his Majestie would therein finde cause to mislike the matter it being in effect a deniall of his Majesties proposition; so he would not take well the manner thereof, that they should make it a popular business, by subscribing a multitude of hands thereto, as thinking thereby to give it countenance.

4. Mathewes hath particular quarrells to mee, for that I have endeavoured to obey his Majesties command in assisting Captaine Yonge, whom Mathewes opposed for no other cause then for that he came not to present his service to him and sought not his favour: And thereupon he tould mee, before divers persons that such condissions as Captaine Yonges would breed bad blood in Virginia. And for that I laboured to performe your Lordshipps comands in restrayning Constable a Dutchman from trading for Tobacco, which your

Lordshipps expresly comaunded mee; but Constable was a favorite of his, and by him patronized, and this gave him no small offence. And of both these I formerly complayned to your Lordshipps.

5. Utye hath a quarrell to me, for that I have called often upon him to give an account of a great stock of Cattell which belong to his Majestie since the dissolution of the Company; which Cattell he hath kept ever since, without giving any account of them; except it be to Sir John Wolstenholme, who hath written unto him touching the same, and expects to have them when he getts the Virginia Company renewed.

6. Clayborne hath his quarrells to mee for that I endeavoured to discover his practice with the Indians against the Lord Baltemore's plantation in Maryland. And for that I sent a warrant to take the papers which belonged to the Secretaries place out of his hand; when his Majestie sent Mr. Kemp over to be Secretary, which he refused to deliver; and putting the warrant in his pockett, went out of the Colony of Virginia, and hath absented himself thence ever since.

7. Pearce is discontented for that I comitted one Walker (the Master of a shipp wherein he is a partner) for his saucy behaviour before mee and the Councell of Virginia.

8. John Pott retaines an old grudge, for that at my first coming to be governor of Virginia, I was the meanes of displacing him from the government; who, therein had behaved himself so ill, as that he came very shortly after to be arraigned and condemned for felonie comitted when he supplyed the place of governor and in truth I must confesse I deserve some blame, for that I was a sutor to his Majestie for his pardon, which therupon was given him.

9. Francis Pott brother of John Pott, was by mee made Captaine of the Fort at Point Comfort and after, for his misbehaviour, displaycd [i.e., displaced]; whereof he still retaynes the memory.

10. Sir John Wolstenholme appeared to be angry with mee when he wrote about foure yeares since to one Tucker (then one of the councell in Virginia) that Sir John Harvey stunke in court and citty; which letter was there published to my no little disgrace. And all the cause of offence that I know was ever by mee given him was, for that I gave to the late Lord Treasurer a larger amount of the affaires of Virginia, then I did to him.

These things being thus as I am ready to prove, I humbly leave the consideration thereof to your Lordshipps judgments, who are best able to judge of these insolencies, and of the dangerous consequences thereof. And do humbly beseech your Lordshipps that you will be pleased by your wisdomes to give some timely remedy, that his Majesties subjects there, may be reduced to their obedience, the offenders receive condigne punishment, and I who have suffered so much in the execution of his Majesties comandments may be repayred in my reputation and otherwise, as to his Majestie and your Lordshipps wisdomes shall seem best.

And he shall daily pray, etc.

The Lawne's Creek Rising, December 1673

3. The Causes of Discontent

A. THE DUTCH BURN THE TOBACCO FLEET, JULY 1673: THE PROBLEM
OF DEFENDING VIRGINIA AGAINST ATTACK

C.O. 1/30, 114–115, Public Record Office.

To the Kings Most Excellent Majestie and the Lords of Your
Majesties most Honorable Privy Councell
The Governor and Councell of his Majesties Collony of Virginia
In all Humility Present
That on Fryday the 11th of this Instant July (which was foure Dayes before
the Fleet was ordered to Saile from hence) To our very great Griefe and
Damage, arrived on our Coast Foure Saile of Holland Men of Warr from
above thirty to Fourty foure Gunns Under the Command of Jacob Bincke
and as many Flushingers one of Six Gunns and three from thirty to Fourty
Six Gunns With one Fire Ship, under the Command of Cornelius Everson
Junior, and on Saturday the 12th anchor'd in Lynhaven Bay within our Capes;
That upon their first Arrivall on Fryday they were discovered by our Centinalls
on the Coasts, and [Sundry?] advice Given to Capt. Gardner and Capt. Cotterell, who Commanded your Majesties Shipps here, Who presently Commanded Severall Masters of the abler Merchants Shipps in James River on
Board, and order'd them to Cleare their Shipps for fight, and Press'd as many
men as they thought fitt out of the Weaker Shipps, But may it Please Your
Majestie and your Most Honorable Councell, before that could be Done
Capt. Gardner Saw Eight Shipps of Maryland under Saile in the Bay who he
judged wo[u]ld fall A Prey to the Enemy for Want of Advice, and [there-
upon?] with Capt. Cotterell weighed Ancher, and with them Six Merchant
Shipps to Engage the Enemy thereby to Save the Marylanders, Butt before they
came within Reach of Gunn Shott foure of the Merchant Shipps came on
Ground One Stood backe and one Commanded by Capt. Grove in Fighting
came on Ground Soe the Two men of Warr were left to encounter Six of
their biggest Ships[.] The two Smaller with the Fire Shipps being not yett
come upp to them, The Fight Continued with Great resolution about three
houres, After which Capt. Gardner Supposeing Capt. Grove (who fought well
Whilest on float) to be [Gotten?] of[f] the Ground resolved not to lose him,
and Judging that the Enemy (if hee Checkt them not) would be in with our
Merchant shipps Rideing in James River before they could Gett from them,
Hee tacked alone upon them with Exterordinary Courage, and for at least
one houre fought them all, But findeing himselfe mistaken in the Condition
of Groves his Shipp, and the night in hand, it being A Quarter past Eight
before the fight ended, Hee with as much Courage and Conduct (and beyond
the hopes or expectation of those who saw that brave Action) disingaged
himselfe from them, as he had before ingaged them, and brought off all the
Marylanders but one and foure of ours which were on Ground, and Gave the

rest, which Were nere fourty Saile almost A Tides Way before the Enemy, Which Undoubtedly Saved Many who otherwise Would have bin lost, Butt haveing all his Great Masts and his Fore topmast desperately wounded, and most of his Rigging Shott, he was forced with Capt. Cotterell to goe into Elizabeth River to Refitt with Roapes and Sailes Which brought the Enemy to Anchor, not Dareing to Persue the James River Fleet in a Strange Channell, and Leave your Majesties Friggetts behind them [word missing?] Two and twenty of our Shipps Stood upp James River and the Rest went under the Fort at Nansemond, Where the Enemy looked on them five Dayes but Attempted them not; Five of those which stood upp James River Comeing on Ground, They Sent upp three of their Smallest Shipps to them And Gott of[f] one, and burnt the other foure, the rest Getting above the Fort at James Towne were Safe; And here wee expect it will be Objected that had not Soe long A Time bene given for the Departure of our Fleet this Misfortune had bin Avoided; To Which wee humbly Offer this answer That Capt. Cotterell arriveing here neere the 20th of June and representing to us Some Dayes after (in presence of all the Masters) that for want of Wood and water and other necessaries, he could not be ready before the 15th of July, was the Reason for the appointing that Day; Next the Masters of the Yorke Shipps were not ready till then, and the Enemy was within our Capes before the most Considerable Shipps of Maryland came to us besides Five Saile in Rappahannocke not Ready and two upp the Bay which in all two and twenty Saile, A Number Too Considerable to be left behind by your Majesties Convoy; This May it please your Majestie and your most Honorable Councell being the true State of our Misfortune in the present losse of Eleaven Shipps and Goods (wherein the Inhabitants of James River bore A very Great Share) Wee thought it our Duty, for the Better Vindication of our Selves from Such Injuries as the Mallice of Some may indeavor to fix on us, by Misrepresenting us and our indeavors to your Majestie and most Honorable Councell, to Sett forth in this our Declaration, the true State and Condition of this Country in Generall and our particular disadvantages and disabilities to entertaine A Warr at the time of this Invasion, And therefore doe most humbly beseech your Majesty and your most Honorable Councell to Consider that though all that Land which now bares the name of Virginia be Reduced to little more than sixty Miles in breadth towards the Sea, Yet that Small Tract is intersected by Soe many Vast Rivers as makes more Miles to Defend, then wee have men of trust to Defend them, For by our neerest computation Wee leave at our backs as Many Servants (besides Negroes as their are freemen to defend the Shoars and all our Frontiers, [against] the Indians) Both which gives men fearfull apprehentions of the dainger they Leave their Estates and Families in, Whilest they are drawne from their houses to defend the Borders, Of which number alsoe at least one third are Single freemen (whose labour Will hardly maintaine them) or men much in debt, both which Wee may reasonably expect upon any Small advantage the Enemy may gaine upon us, wo[u]ld revolt to them in hopes of bettering their Condition by Shareing the Plunder of the Countrey With them, Nor can wee Keepe any number of Soldiers long together in A Place for Want of Provissions, For the aire being hott and Moist wee could never yett find the way of keeping any Sort of Corne A Yeare from Being eaten out by Vermine Which hinders our haveing Publique Magazines of Provisions necessary for Such occations, and our men (though their has bin Great Care taken in Exercizing them) haveing for Many yeares bene unacquainted with dainger. wee cannot with much Confidence rely on their Courage against an Enemy better practiced in the Hazards of Warr; But may it please your most Sacred Majestie and your most Honorable Councell, Their were many more difficulties from this last attempt, for diseases this Winter before haveing destroyed at least fifty thousand Cattell and their Owners to preserve them haveing given them almost all their Corne Brought Soe great A Scarcety of Provision amongst us as men Could not have bene keept long together, and the Enemies Arrivall being in A time when all mens Cropps both of tobacco and corne lay hardest upon their hands (being much in the weeds by reason of the great Raine which fell Sometime before) It Troubled them much to be drawne away from their Worke (though for their Common defense) Yett notwithstanding these and many more disadvantages they appeared Soe ready in Every place that the Enemy desended not on the Land though they wanted water to great Extremety, The losse then being wholy on the Shipps and Loading (Except some fugative Servants who escapeing our dilligence gott to them and were Carryed away) Our industry for their defense wee humbly hope will appeare in this that their was not A Shipp lost which run not on Ground before She gott within the protection of one or other of our Forts, Nor did Your Majesties Shipps or any of the Merchant men want any Assistance wee could possibly helpe them too, Though in this alsoe their lay very great difficulty, For In these times of warr, the Merchant gives our Inhabitants Soe very little for their Labour as will not Cloath them and their Famelies, which Soe disasorts them as they rather rejoyce at their loss, then Shew any desire to defend them nor would they have bene brought to appeare for them by any other Motive then the affection they have to the Gentleness and Justice of the Government they have Soe long lived under, Yet though wee have Certainly done our utmost for them to our very great expense and hazard of our Cropps Wee expect A Complaint against us for not haveing A Fort at Point Comfort, which Some Suppose wo[u]ld have prevented all this losse, though the Considerable part of it happened farr off in the Bay beyond the reach of any Gunn; To which Objection for our Justification Wee doe humbly Offer our Reasons to your most Excellent Majestie and most Honorable Councell against A Fort there, because it being A direct Chanell and A great Tide, A Shipp may ride in Safety in the Bay till it hath A Good Wind and upon A Tide may runn by A better Fort then all the Wealth and Skill of this Countrey can build, Especially Considering the distance they may goe from it, which were it but halfe A Mile wo[u]ld be to [i.e., too] farr for us to depend Certainly on its defense; Then, the time of Loading being five or Six Monthes in every River, wee thought it best to build Forts in the most Convenient places for their defense, during their stay, Rather then one at Point Comfort, which at best Could but Secure James River, Butt by these two losses Receaved the last Warr [i.e., the Second Anglo-Dutch War] and now they doe conceade it necessary that Point Comfort were fortified Soe as to Secure

their Comeing together, and wee doe truely wish Soe too, But Since wee be-
leive the doeing or not doeing of it will Something depend upon our advice
to Your Majestie Wee dare not propose A battery of lesse then fourty or fifty
dimmy [i.e., demi] cannon and Culvarine of A Good length, And that will
Cost Considering the inconveniency of the place (which affoards not Soe much
as A Foundation to build on, much less any Materialls[,] at least Fifteene
thousand pounds sterling, which being A Some [i.e., sum] wee have not in
our Power The Publique revenue not exceeding two and twenty hundred
pounds A yeare of which the Governor has twelve hundred, The Councell
two hundred and the rest expended in necessary workes, and the labour of
our Inhabitants Scarcely Cloathing them, Wee humbly hope Your Majestie
will not expect it From us, Nor Dare wee propose lesse Strength, least A Weaker defense Should leave the Shipps (by depending to [i.e., too] much upon it)
more open to the Attempts of the Enemy then hither to they bin; And if
your Majestie Shall be graciously pleased to build such A Fort as wee propose,
Wee are not able to maintaine A Garrison in it unlesse their [be] Such duties
laid on Shipps through the whole Countrey as may Support the Charge For
Soldiers will not Serve for tobacco, because the Merchants (working on their
necessities) give them Soe little for it as A Yeares Sallery will hardly Cloth[e]
them, And the present Fort duties are Soe Small as not to Pay the Gunners
finde Powder and repaire them but Most of that Charge lies upon the Countrey But Wee Doe most Humbly Offer it to your Majestie and your most
Honorable Councells Consideration, Wether it may not be better to Send a
Convoy proportioned to Such Strength as the Enemy may bring against us,
Which may in Some Measure be knowne, by advice of their first setting out,
And that the Charge of Such Convoy be upon the Fraight of the Merchant
men, And to ease them of part of the Charge every hired man of Warr may
be permitted to take two teire [i.e., tier] of tobacco in the hoald which would
Serve to ballast them and not hinder their workeing Such A Convoy would
Secure the Shipps and us who dare not be Soe confident in Our defense (the
dainger of our Servants and the Indians Considered) as not to give your
Majestie This State of our present condition and to implead Your Assistance;
And haveing thus in all humillity laid our cause before your Majestie and your
Most Honorable Councell Wee appeale to your Goodness and Justice to Determine of it Most Heartily Praiseing God for his favour to us in giveing
your Majestie Soe discerning A Judgment and Soe tender A heart towards
all Your Subjects And for Assisting you with Soe wise A Councell As wee
doubt not Will direct all your great and Royall Undertakings to A Glorious
end Which is the earnest Desire of
Your Majesties Most Loyall and Obedient Subject and Servants

William Berkeley	Augustine Warner
Henry Chicheley	Henry Corbin
Edward Digges	Daniel Parke
Thomas Ludwell	Thomas Ballard
Nathaniel Bacon	Nicholas Spencer

B. DISSATISFACTION WITH SIR WILLIAM BERKELEY'S LEADERSHIP:
THE COUNCIL OF STATE DEFENDS THE GOVERNOR AGAINST
COMPLAINTS OF MISMANAGEMENT, OCTOBER 1673

C.O. 1/30, fol. 179, Public Record Office.

To the Kings Most Excellent Majestie and the Lords of Your
Majesties most Honorable Privy Councell
The Governor and Councell of his Majesties Collony of Virginia
In all Humility Present

That haveing the Honor to Serve your Majestie as your Councell for this
Place under the Right Honorable Sir William Berkeley your Majesties Governor here and Doubting Some ill affected Persons Who are vexed with their
losse in this late Unhappy Accident may unjustly asperse his Fame and give
your Majestie ill Impressions of him Wee have thought it our Duty to your
Majestie and Justice to your Governor for here, To give your Majestie and
your most Honorable Councell This true Character and Accompt of him and his
Actions, That he hath for nere Thirty yeares Governed this Collony with that
Prudence and Justice which hath gained him both Love and reverence from all
the Inhabitants here, which wee looke on as our greatest Strength, for in this
Very Conjuncture had the People Distaste of All Governors they Would have
hazarded the losse of this Countrey, and then rather because they doe believe
their Condition would not be Soe bad Under the Dutch in Point of Traffique as
it is under the Merchants who now use them hardly (even to extremity) But
this Governor Oppresseth them not, but on the Contrary Spends all his revenue
amongst them in Setting up Manufactures to their advantage who will follow
his Example; nor ought wee in gratitude to pretermitt the advantage this
whole Countrey hath received from the Conquest of the Indians and the peace
Wee have Soe long enjoyed; which Wee owe to his indefatigable Indevour
and Vigerous Prosecution of that Warr for Severall yeares in most of the
greatest expedition whereof he was himselfe in person, to the very great
hazard of his health and life, Then for his behaviour in this last Conjuncture
Wee doe assure your Majestie and your most Honorable Councell that it was
wonderfully beyond what could be expected from A man of his age for he
exposed his person to the greatest Dainger of the Enemy by night and Day on
the water and on the land, Visiting the remoter parts, and with his presence
encouraging every one to doe well in their places, and at the Same time
takeing Care for the heart of the Countrey in Soe much as he Scarce eat or
Sleept to the hazard of his health nor did he Leave any part of A Prudent
Governor or Valliant Generall unperformed but shewed very great Vigour
and Conduct on all occations where he Saw it necessary nor could he be
blamed unlesse it were for exposing his person to much, and some of us who
living neere him are most Conversant with him, Doe assure your Majestie
and most Honorable Councell That he Spends most of his time and Thoughts
in the Contemplation of your Majesties Interests and in Contriveing which
way (on all Occasions offered) he may be most Serviceable to your Majestie,
This being the truth (though farre Short of his Merritts) Wee doe pray to

God to give him A much longer life and Continue long in Your Majesties favour, which is the very harty Prayer of
Your Majesties Most Loyall and Obedient Subjects and Servants

Henry Chicheley	Henry Corbin
Edward Digges	Daniel Parke
Thomas Ludwell	Thomas Ballard
Nathaniel Bacon	Nicholas Spencer
Augustine Warner	

4. *The Prosecution of the Lawne's Creek Dissidents, January 1673/74*

A. THE WARRANTS FOR THE ARREST OF THE DISSIDENTS, JANUARY 3, 1673/74

Surry County Deed Book, 1671–1684, fols. 41, 42.

Surry

Whereas a Company of rude and disorderly persons to the Number of Fourteene did unlawfully Assemble on or about the 12th day of December last at the parish Church of Lawnes Creeke in this County with Intent to alter the Late Levy, or not to pay the Same: and that they Expected divers others of theire Confederates to meete with them and for that it appears by the Confession of Mathew Swan, John Barnes, William Hancock, Robert Lacy, John Grigory, Thomas Cley, Michael Upchurch, John Sheppard, William Tooke, George Peters, William Little, John Greene, and James Chessett that they did meete att the Time and place aforesaid, and for that the greatest part of the persons aforesaid did this day alsoe Riottously meete togeather in the feild, commonly called the Divells feild, not withstanding some of them were advertised to the Contrary: Which we Conceive to be against the peace of our said Sovereign Lord the King, and the quiett of this County: these are Therefore in the Kings Majesties name to will and require you to take into your Custody the bodyes of the Severall persons before named, and them in Safe Custody to Keepe, untell they Enter into Bond with Sufficient Security for there appearance att the Ware Neck on Tuesday the 6th Instant at the Court there; there to be proceeded against according to Law and alsoe that they be of the good behavior and Keepe the peace of our Sovereign Lord the King, and for soe doeing this shall be your warrant. Given under our hands this 3rd January 1673.

Lawrence Baker
Robert Spencer

To the Sheriff of the Said County or his deputy
Vera Recordat
Teste William Edwards Clerk of Court

Surry County

Whereas by the Examination and Confession of Roger Delke and by the Testimony of William Sherwood Sub Sheriff of this County, it is Apparent that the said Delk (being one of the unlawfull Assembly on the 12th [of] December last) did this day discourseing of that meeteing, Jusifye the same and said we will burne all, before one shall Suffer, which words being Spoaken in A Terrifieing manner and tending to the breach of his Majesties peace, being alsoe spoaken by the said Delke before us, These are Therefore in the Kings Majesties Name to will and require you to take into your Custody the Body of the said Roger Delk, and him in Safe Custody to Keepe untill the next Court to be held for this County on Tuesday the Sixth of this Instant, and that you have Delke at the said Court there to be Dealt with according to Law, unless he find good Security for his personall appearance att the Court and that he be of the good behavior and keep the peace of our Sovereigne Lord the King, and for your soe doing this shall be your Sufficient Warrant. Given under our hands this 3d January *1673*

Lawrence Baker
Robert Spencer

To the Sheriff of the said County or his deputy these
Vera Recordat. Teste William Edwards Clerk of Court

B. FRANCIS TAYLOR'S EVIDENCE, JANUARY 1673/74

Surry County Deed Book, 1671–1684, fol. 43.

The deposition of Francis Taylor being Called before Captain Lawrence Baker Mr. Robert Caufield and Captain Robert Spencer, to sweare his true Knowledge concerning a meeteing of some of the parish on fryday the 12th [of] December 1673 att Lawnes Creek parish Church is as followeth That being at home at my lodgeing lookeing out I Espyed John Grigory goeing through the feild, and called him to desire him to make me Wastcoate, which he told me he would, but he asked me If I would not be at the Church for there was to be a great part of the parish mett there this morneing concerneing the Levys; I told him I knew nothing of it Neither was I Concerned in it as being noe housekeeper, but I did not much care if I went with him to see what was done, he told me he was going to Mr Caufeilds to take measure of one of his men, to make his freedome Cloathes, and he would hallow for me as he Came back, which Accordingly he did and wee went togeather, and when wee Came there we found about halfe A Score of men Sitting there, and askeing them how they did, and what they met for, they said they did Expect some more to come Intendinge Civilly to Treate Concerneing the Levy, for that they did understand, that there was Severall Officers to be paid tobacco out of the Leavy, which they Knew noe Reason for, by Reason they were put to as much Trouble and Expense as they were, and that Colonel [Thomas] Swan was to have five Thousand pounds of tobacco for his trouble and Charge, that which tobacco for the Officers and the Colonel was to be Leavied on this parish onely, theire Company not meeteing they stayed about an hower, and soe resolved to Speake about it on the next Sabbath being Sermon day, In the Interim on the Saturday, I being att Mr. Sherwoods, requested him to see the list of the Leavy, which he did show me, and there I saw that the Charge was

Leavied on the whole County, which I spoak of at the Church, they heareing that said noe more and further Saith not

Francis Taylor

[names of the dissidents omitted]

Jurat Coram Nobis
January 3d *1673*
Lawrence Baker
Robert Caufield
Robert Spencer

Vera Recordat   Teste William Edwards Clerk of Court

C. THE SURRY COUNTY COURT'S VERDICT, JANUARY 6, 1673/74

Surry County Order Book, 1671–1691, 41–42.

Whereas a Certaine Company of Giddy Headed and Turbulent persons Inhabiting in Lawnes Creeke Parish to the number of 14, Tis to say Mathew Swan, John Barnes, William Hancock, Robert Lacy, John Grigory, Thomas Cley, Michael Upchurch, John Sheppard, William Tooke, George Peters, William Little, John Greene, James Chessett and Roger Delke, upon the 12 of December last, factiously and in contempt of Governor and contrary to the peace of our soverigne Lord the King and to the Disturbance of this county, and the bad example of [others?], did unlawfully assemble themselves at the parish church of Lawnes Creeke with intent and designe to oppose not only the just and lawfull order of this court but alsoe the sheriff in the due execution of his office, but a greater number being by now invited and expected, which by reason of the weather did not come, they perswaded John Grigory one of the above named to list and give number of men and appoynted a second meeteing or unlawful assembly, but being by the Sheriff, by order from Capt. Lawrence Baker and Capt. Robert Spenser commanded to appeare before them and ordered by the Sheriff not to goe above two or three togeather, did not stand planing to meete the most part of them in the Divells field, and goe before the magistrates with great clubbe, where being come they demeaned themselves of great stubborness and contempt, and were bound out by the magestrates to answer theire Offenses at this court, and according to persons being of this day brought before the said court and after a longe serious admonition of the dangerous and mischevious effecte of such unlawfull and factious proceedings, and being also desired by the court to show the cause of theire agrevance and the intent of their meeteing, they answered the levy was unjustly laid upon them, and they met with intent to remedy that oppression, but the court having publickly repeated the order according to Record, every particular of the levy which they pretended unjust, and Showed by them as justness and reasonabless there of and theire bond, and [how] carefull they [i.e., the justices] had been not to impose one pound of tobacco upon the county but [what] Justice and nessessity required. And that all which they complained of did not exceed three pounds of tobacco, some of them answered that they were exceeding well satisfied in the case, and were heartily sorry for what they had done and the rest were stuborne and silent and went out in the sheriff's custody.

And being called again one by one and strictly examined how and by whom and to the unlawful assembly was projected, and set on foote, it appeared, that the said Mathew Swan, John Sheppard, and William Hancock at the house of the said John Barnes, did first resolve and conclude upon the meeteing, and that the rest (of a great many more whome they Intended to perswade were only drawne in from the beginning) the said John Grigory, Robert Lacy, James Chessett, Thomas Cley, Michael Upchurch, William Tooke, William Little and John Greene, it is therefore ordered and resolved by this court that the said John Gregory, Robert Lacy, James Chissett, Thomas Cley, Michael Upchurch, William Tooke, William Little and John Greene, for which they are sorry for theire offence and were not [the] projection of the same, be comitted untill they give bond for their future good behavior and pay court [costs] and be dismissed and that the said John Barnes, John Sheppard, and William Hancock be committed untill they give the like bond and pay each of them one thousand pounds of tobacco fine to the use of his Majesty and for the said Roger Delke although he were noe ring leader in the faction, yet for saying after much faire admonition that if one of them suffered they would burne all, he shall stand comitted untill he give the like bond and pay the like fine of one thousand pounds of tobacco and for the said Mathew Swan[, who] was the cheife projector of the designe and being asked if he were convinced of his offence, he answered that he was not convinced and said that the court had unjustly proceeded in the levy and charged the court therewith at the [word illegible], it is therefore ordered that he stand comitted untill for his good [Behavior?] he give bond with security for his appearance on the 3rd day of the next General Court before the Right Honorable the Governor and Councell for his Dangerous Contempt and unlawful project and his wicked persisting in the same and that the order be enforced for every single person herein named according to this general order.

D. THE GENERAL COURT CONFIRMS THE SURRY COURT'S VERDICT,
APRIL 1674

> H. R. McIlwaine, ed., *Minutes of the Council and General Court of Colonial Virginia, 1622–1632, 1670–1676, with Notes and Excerpts from Original Council and General Court Records, into 1683, Now Lost* (Richmond, Va., 1924), 367.

It is ordered that the order of *Surry Court* Against the mutinuss persons be Confirmed and that *Mathew Swann* the ringleader of them, who was bound over to this Court be Fined Two Thousand pound of tobacco and Caske and that all fines of the persons goe towards the Fort at *James Citty* And that they pay all Just Costs and Charges.

E. GOVERNOR BERKELEY CANCELS THE DISSIDENTS' FINES,
SEPTEMBER 1674

> Surry County Deed Book, 1671–1684, fol. 69.

By the Governor and Captain Generall of Virginia I doe hereby remitt the fines of Mathew Swann, and alsoe the fines of the other poore men, that were fined in Surry County Court, provided they acknowledge there fault in the said County Court, and pay the Court Charges, Dated this 23rd September 1674.

William Berkeley

vera recordat. Teste William Edwards Clerk of Court

Bacon's Rebellion, 1676

5. The Causes of Discontent

A. FRONTIER PLANTERS PETITION GOVERNOR BERKELEY TO COMMISSION VOLUNTEERS AGAINST THE INDIANS, CA. SPRING 1676

C.O. 1/36, fol. 139, Public Record Office.

To the Right Honorable Sir William Barkly Knight governour and Capt. Generall of verginia: The Humble petition of the poore distressed subjects in the upper parts of James River in verginia Humbly Complain that the Indians hath allready most barberously and Inhumanly taken and Murdered severall of our bretheren and put them to most cruell torture by burning of them alive and by cruell torturing of them which makes our harts Ready to bleed to heare and wee the poore subjects are in dayly dandger of loosing our lives by the Heathen in soe much that wee are all afraid of goeing about our demesticall affaires. Wherefore we Most Humbly request that your gratious Honor would be pleased to grant us a Committion and to make choice of Committioned Officers to lead this party now redy to take armes in defence of our lives and estates which without speedy prevention lie liable to the Injury of such insulting enimmies not that your petitioners desires to make any disturbance or put the Country to any charge wherefore we Humbly implead your Honnours speedy answer for we are informed that the Indians dayly approach our habitations and we your petitioners as in duty bound shall ever pray.

B. NATHANIEL BACON'S VICTORY OVER THE INDIANS, APRIL 1676

C.O. 1/36, 77, Public Record Office.

Wee found the Indians in all places unwilling to assist us against the Common Enemy, they having received orders to the contrary from the Right Honourable the Governer, soe that wee were forced to goe quite out of our way Southward to gett of the Nottowaies and Mayherings what assistance wee could, who at last amounted but to 24 men, during which time our provisions were soe much wasted That when wee came to Action wee had not to half the company one dayes provision, and very many none at all, soe that upon equall sharing which was prepared wee found ourselves not able to subsist 3 daies[.] yett being promised some Releife from the Hockinnechy [i.e., Occaneechee] King Posseclay by name wee entrd the iland hoping to find some small releif to the weary and faint; wee had made our Agreement That the Manakins and Annalectins, who joyned with the Susquahanocks and lived with their King in the fort should at a signe given cutt of[f] the Susquahanocks being in number but 30 men besides woeman and children, this accordingly was effected, and the Prisoners by the King brought in with triumph, and severall of the Susquahanocks, by them put to death soe that wee refused to take that Office which they first offered to us. After these were destroid wee againe complained to the King for want of provision and demanded the expected supply. But He having viewed the posture of our men (who were many of them leaving the Island at the very instant and returning home) began to alter his story, and desired us to stay six daies, and went from us gathering togither all his Indians, as also the Hayhelocks, and Manakins and Annalectons, mand all his Forts and lined the other side of the River thick with men so that wee could neither well attack them, nor depart the Island, without some danger, wee neither saw nor heard from him but having some jealousie of his proceedings, wee sent for him, and by further discourses being yet more and more dissatisfied, wee ordered our men to surround the fort with all expedition, and if they could to enter it, but tho the Indians had allready possest 3 Forts, and were in a condition to fight, soe that what wee could doe was to hinder the rest from entering the Fort which were very many still crowding in and to demand satisfaction of their King, But he cunningly threw all the blame upon the Manakins and Annalecktons, whom he said were so many he could not Rule them but pretended to persuade them, which he presuming to doe, making faire pretences of lying in guard with us all night or what else would be thought convenient provide wee would withdraw[.]

Which was onely to secure his magazine his wife and children who were in his fort which wee destroid, But wee absolutely denied to remoove untill he gave us better satisfaction of his intentions, Hee perceiving That no Artifices would prevaile [in?] way of treaty (as wee guessed) entered the middle Fort, and pretended that his men would not let him come out any more but seeing wee had in our custodies in our Cabins severall men, woemen and children he pretended wee might take them for Hostages, who before were our Prisoners. In this Posture things stood[,] when by a watchword from the other side of the River they began and killed one of our men which wee quickly repaid them[,] firing at all their owne forts, holes and other places soe thick That the groans of men, woemen and children were soe loud that all their howling and singing could not hinder them from being heard, Immediately wee fell upon the men woemen and children without, disarmed and destroid them all, and the King's Forts where all his Treasure his wife children and ammunition were with a strong guard of men, woemen and children, wee stuck close to the Port holes fired and destroid them[.] a great number of men, woemen and children whose groans were heard but they all burnt except 3 or 4 men who happening to escape brok out and had a Welcome by a liberall volley of shott from our men who lay close upon them, This was night work [and] wee lost 4 men, they lost as wee know off [i.e., of] about 40 besides what wee know not off [i.e., of] and besides woemen and children[.] Next day our Fight continued till towards night during which time they made severall sculking attempts but our men were soe conveniently placed everywhere and ambuscadoed soe that they presently received and had such welcomes that few or none of them escaped but were shott behind Trees as they stood which the King perceiving was resolved to make one brave sally and came very boldly out running and shouting into the Field, with about 20 men and continued firing about 2 or 3 Rounds running all the while in a Ring a course about half a quarter of a mile, but he was soe entertained on all hands that he was shott dead in the Feild and many that from the banck of the River fell in there, soe that of this partie wee could not perceive that 7 escaped, After which the Remander made all post haste to escape not firing one gun from the Forts. During all this time the people having no refreshment of meat or drink or sleep began to grow very faint, seeing the Enemy had caried away all their provisions woemen and children excepting about ten that remaned in the middle Fort being jealous of Raine[,] the weather being very hott, and a small rain[e] would have made it impossible to have brought our Horses over, soe that wee unanimously agreed rather to acquitt the Iland than hazard being starved there, so that in short what wee did in that short time and poor condition wee were in was to destroy the King of the Susquahannocks and the King of Oconogee [i.e., Occaneechee] and the Manakin King with a 100 men, besides what [was?] unknown to us. The King's daughter wee took Prisonner with some others and could have brought more, But in the heat of the Fight wee regarded not the advantage of the Prisoners nor any plunder, but burn't and destroid all. And what we reckon most materiall is That wee have left all nations of Indians [where wee have bin] ingaged in a civill warre amongst themselves, soe that with great ease wee hope to manadge this advantage to their utter Ruine and destruction.

6. *Berkeley Attempts to Regain His Popularity*

A. BERKELEY'S ELECTION PROCLAMATION, MAY 10, 1676

Tracy W. McGregor Manuscripts, Alderman Library, University of Virginia, Charlottesville.

By the Governor and Captain Generall of Virginia
When I considder that the more experienced men are in any Act Profession or Practice the more exact and perfect they are in that Profession or Practice it cannot but seeme somewhat strange to mee that the Inhabitants of this Country should bee dissatisfied with those Gentlemen as their Burgesses of the Grand Assembly who were by themselves freely elected and chosen to that great Task for no other reason but because they have soe often mett and consulted the great affaires of the Country in that quallity: However findeing by the too great complaints I have heard that soe long continuance of the present great Assembly is looked upon as a Greviance by many of the Inhabitants of this Country And being most willing and desirous as I have beene ever to endeavor the Redresse of all just Greviances, although I cannot but with respect and honor take notice of the deliberate consultations and Judicious proceedings of the present Burgesses yet to satisfye the Importunity of the People in theire soe earnest desires for a new Assembly I have thought fitt and doe hereby with the consent of the Councell of State dissolve the present

Assembly And for the redress of all such Greviances of the Country may justly complaine of and for the better security of the Country from our Barbarous Enemies the Indians and better settling and quieting our domestick discords and discontents Doe order and Appoint that a grand Assembly bee held at James Citty in June next and I doe heartily wish and hope that the persons elected Burgesses in this conjuncture will discharge that duty of their owne personall charge for the ease of the Country as the Councell shall: These are therefore in his Majesties name to Will and require you at the usuall place or places within your County to cause two of the most Sage best experienced and most understanding persons to bee elected Burgesses for the said County to meet mee and the Councell of State at James citty on the 5th day of June next then and there to consult and advise of such matters as may be for the Glory of God the honor of his Majestie and the publique Weale of this Country And because the Country may perhaps perceive some Defects to be in the present Government I doe will and Require that at the Election of the said Burgesses all and every person or persons there present have liberty to present freely to their said Burgesses all just Complaints as they or any of them have against mee as Governor for any Act of Injustice by mee done or any receeved Bribe or Present by mee accepted or taken from any person whatsoever and the same bee by the said Burgesses presented to the Assembly and duly examined and supposeing I who am head of the Assembly may bee their greatest Greviance I will most gladly joine with them in a Petition to his Sacred Majestie to appoint a new Governor of Virginia and thereby to ease and discharge mee from the great care and trouble thereof in my old age: Given under my hand this 10th day of May 1676 in Henrico County as alsoe to make true returne hereof

William Berk[e]ley

Vera Copia

The time and place of Election is at York Courte house the 25th of this Instant May when all persons whom this may or doth concerne are hereby required to make their Appearance then and there to make a Legall Election of their Burgesses

Gideon Macon
Subsheriff of York County

B. BERKELEY'S "DECLARATION AND REMONSTRANCE," MAY 29, 1676

Henry Coventry Papers, LXXVII, fols. 157–158, Estate of the Marquis of Bath, Longleat, Warminster, Wiltshire, Eng.

Sheweth that about the Yeare 1660 Col. [Samuel] Mathewes the then Governor Died and then in Consideration of the service I had donne the Country in defending them from and destroying greate numbers of the Indians without the losse of theire men in al the time that warr lasted and in contemplation of the Equal and uncorrupt Justice I had distributed to al men not only the Assembly but the unanimous Votes of al the Country Concurred to make me Governor in a time when if the Rebels in England had prevailed I had certainly died for accepting of it and was there an unfortunate love shewed to me for to shew my selfe grateful for this I was willing to accept of this Goverment againe when by my Gracious Kings favour I might have had other places much more profitable and lesse toylesome then this has beene since that time I returned into the Country I cal the Great God Judge of al things in heaven and Earth to Witnesse that I doe not know of any thing Relative to this country wherein I have acted unjustly corruptly or neglegently in distributing Equal Justice to al men and taking al possible care to preserve their properties and to defend them from their Barbarous Enimies

But for al this perhaps I have Erred in things I know not of if I have I am so conscious of humane fraylty and my owne defects that I wil not only acknowledge them but repent of them and amend them and not like that Rebel Bacon persist in an Error only because I have Committed it and tells me in Divers of his letters that tis not for his honor to Acknowledge a fault But I am of opinion it is only for Divels to be incorrigeable and men of Principles like the worst of Divels and these if truth be reported to me of divers of his Expressions of Atheisme, tending to take away al Religion and lawes

And NOW loving frends I wil State the Question betweene me as Governor and Mr. Bacon and Say that if any Ennimies should envade England any councelor Justice of the peace or other superior Officer might rayse what forces they could to protect his majesties subjects But I say againe if after the Kings knowledge of this invasion any the greatest Peare of England should rayse forces against the Kings prohibition this would be now and was ever in al Ages and nations accounted Treason Nay I wil goe farther (and it shal be printed) that though this Peere were truly sealous [i.e., zealous] for the preservation of his King and subjects to doe his King and Country service Yet if the King though by false information should suspect the contrary it were treason in this Noble Peere to proceed after the Kings prohibition and for the Truth of this I appeale to al the lawes of England and the lawes and constitutions of al other nations in the World and yet further it is declared by this Parliament that the taking up Armes for the King and Parliament is declared Treason for the Event shewed that what ever the Pretence was to seduce Ignorant and wel affected people yet the end was such as told to King and People as this wil be if not prevented I doe therefore againe declare that Bacon proceeding against al lawes of al nations modern and ancient is a Rebel to his Sacred majestie and the country nor will I insist uppon his swearing of men to live and dye together which is Treason by the very words of the law

Now my friends I have liv'd amongst you fower and thirty years as uncorrupt and diligent as ever governor was: Bacon is a man of two years amongst you his person and qualities unknown to most of you and to al men Its by any vertuous action that ever I heard of, and this very action wherein he so much boasted was fully foolishly and as I am informed Treacherously carried to the dishonor of the English nation. Yet in it he lost more men then I did in three wars and by the Grace of god wil put myselfe to the same dangers and troubles again when I have brought Bacon to acknowledge the lawes are above him and I doubt not by the assistance of god to have better successe than Mr. Bacon has had the reason of my hopes are that I wil take councel of wiser men then my selfe But Mr. Bacon has none aboute him but the lowest of the people.

Yet I must farther enlarge that I can not without your helpe doe anything in this but Dye in the defence of my King his lawes and subjects which I wil cherfully doe though alone I doe it: and considering my poore fortunes I cannot leave my poore wife and frends a better legacy then by diyng for the King and you for his sacred majestie wil easily distinguish betweene Mr. Bacons actions and mine and Kings long hands either to reward or punish.

Now after al this if Mr. Bacon can shew me presedent or example where such actings in any nation what soever was approved of I wil mediate with the King and you for a pardon and excuse for him, But I can shew him an hundred examples where brave and greate men have ben put to death for gaining victories against the command of their superiors.

Lastly my most assured frends I would have preserved those Indians that I knew were hourely at our mercy to have beene our spies and intelligence that they also were also treacherous Ennimies I have given out commissions to destroy them al as the commissions wil speake it to conclude I have donne what was possible both to frend and Ennimies have granted Mr. Bacon Pardons which he has scornfully rejected supposing himselfe stronger to [subvert?] then I and you to maintaine the lawes by which only and [good?] assisting grace and mercy al men must hope for Peace and safety I wil add no more thoughe much more is yet remaining to justifye me and condemne Mr. Bacon but to desire that this Declaration may be made in every county court in the country and that a court be presently cald to doe it before the Assembly meet that your approbation or dissatisfaction of this Declaration may be knowne to al the country and to the Kings Councel to whose most revered judgements it is submitted. Given this 29 of May a happy day in the 28 yeare of his most sacred majesties Raigne Charles the Second whome god grant long and prosperously to reing [*sic*] and let al his good subjects say amen Amen

Your incessant Servant
William Berkeley

7. *Berkeley Asks to Be Replaced*

Coventry Papers, LXXVII, fol. 103, Longleat.

Right Honorable [Henry Coventry]
in my last letter I thinke I told you that the Blood of King Charles the first was the cause of the Indian warre in New England and I fear'd would be the cause of more Calamities to the Universal English Nation then they had ever yet felt But Indeed Sir I then thought this country would have beene the last that would have Expected Gods Anger for that wicked act for the whole Country was in a most serene calme none suspecting the least suspicion of any troubles When a young fellow one Bacon Massinello like [i.e., a reference to Tommaso Aniello, a Neopolitan fishseller who revolted against the rule of Spain in the 1640s] infused into the People the great Charge and uselessnesse of the forts which our Assembly had most wisely provided to resist the Ennimie and tis wonderful what a monstrous number of the basest of the People declared for him in lesse then ten dayes in al parts of the country tis impossible for me to tel you the Particulars but al the Papers that concern it are sent home to our Agents who wil give your honor an Exact account of it. This Rebellion

is the more formidible because it has no ground and is not against any particular Person but the whole Assembly Sir I am so over weaned with riding into al parts of the Country to stop this violent Rebellion that *I am not able to support my selfe at this Age six months longer and therefore on my Knees I beg his sacred majesty would send a more Vigorous Governor.* Sir if I out live this I shal ever be
June the 3d 1676

Your most obedient servant
Will Berkeley

8. *Bacon Is Elected Burgess for Henrico*

Coventry Papers, LXXVII, fol. 102, Longleat.

2 June 1676

Honored Sir [Nathaniel Bacon, Sr.]
This morning the Sherife of Henrico County brought back the Proclamation of the Governors with that of [the] Counsells: they having in that County Chosen Bacon and [James] Crewes Burgesses[.] Bacon was there with a garde of Thirty or forty men and tould the Sherife if he durst reade a line of that Proclamation he would make him repent it. Soe the Comissioners thought fitt that the Sherife did desist and return the Proclamation with the other papers[.] he [Bacon] intends to be in town with a guarde, so I know not what to doe with out yours and some of the other Councells advise[.] Pray be pleased to come over hither with al speed possibly you can and send this or another letter forward to Colonel [William] Cole.

Sir Your affectionate frend and humble servant
Henry Chicheley

9. *Bacon's Submission*

Coventry Papers, LXXVII, fol. 116, Longleat.

I Nathaniel Bacon, Jr. of Henrico County in Virginia doe hereby most Readily freely and most Willingly Acknowledge that I have been Guilty of diverse late unlawfull mutinous and Rebellious Practices Contrary to my duty to his most Sacred Majesties Governor and this Country by beating up of drums raiseing of men in Armes marching with them into Severall parts of this his most Sacred Majesties Colony not only without Order and Comission but Contrary to the Expresse Orders and Comands of the Right Honorable Sir William Berkeley Knight his Majesties Most Worthy Governor and Captain General of Virginia. And I doe further Acknowledge that the said Honourable Governor hath been very favorable to me by his severall Reiterated Gracious offers of Pardon thereby to Reclaime me from the prosecution of those my unjust proceedings (who[se] noble and Generous mercy and Clemency I Can never Sufficiently Acknowledge) and for the Resetlement of this whole Country in peace and Quietness. And I doe hereby upon my Knees most humbly begg of Almighty god and of his Majesties said Governor that upon this my most Harty and unfeigned Acknowledgement of my said Miscarriages and unwarrantable practices he will please to grant me his Gracious Pardon and Indempnity humbly desireing alsoe the Honourable Councell of State by whose Goodness I am alsoe much obleiged and the Honorable Burgesses of the present Grand Assembly to Interseed and mediate with his Honor to grant me Such Pardon and I doe hereby promise upon the word and faith of a Christian and of a Gentleman that upon such Pardon Granted me as I shall ever Acknowledge soe great a favor soe I will alwaies beare true faith and allegiance to his most Sacred Majestie and demeane my self dutifully faithfully and peaceably to the Government and the Laws of this Country and am most Ready and willing to Enter into bond of Two Thousand pound sterling for Security thereof [and] bind my whole Estate in Virginia to the Country for my Good and Quiett behavior for one whole yeare from this date And I doe promise and Obleige my selfe to Continue my Said duty and Allegiance at all times afterwards[.] In Testimony of this my free and Harty Recognition I have hereunto Subscribed my Name this 9th [of] June *1676.*

Nathaniel Bacon

10. *The June Assembly*

A. A PRÉCIS OF THE JUNE LAWS

> William Waller Hening, ed., *The Statutes at Large; Being a Collection of All the Laws of Virginia from the First Session of the Legislature, in the Year 1619* (Richmond, New York, and Philadelphia, 1809–1823), II, 341–365.

ACT I. *An act for carrying on a warre against the barbarous Indians.*
Declared war against enemy Indians and ordered the raising of a thousand troops. Bacon was named "generall and commander in cheife of the force raised."

ACT II. *An act concerning Indian trade and traders.*
Prohibited all trade with the Indians, except for "friendly Indians."

ACT III. *An act concerning Indian lands deserted.*
Lands deserted by the Indians reverted to the colony; these lands were to "dispose to the use of the publique towards defraying the charge of this warr."

ACT IV. *An act for suppressing of tumults, routs, etc.*
Every officer and magistrate was authorized to suppress unlawfull "routs, riotts and tumults."

ACT V. *An act for the regulateing of officers and offices.*
Prohibited sheriffs from holding office "more than one year successively," abolished plural officeholding, regulated fees, and denied office to anyone not a resident of the colony for at least three years.

ACT VI. *An act for chooseing of Vestries.*
Gave freemen as well as freeholders the right to elect parish vestries.

ACT VII. *An act enabling freemen to vote for burgesses and preventing false returnes of burgesses.*

Repealed an act of 1670 that had restricted the franchise to freeholders and imposed a stiff fine on any sheriff who made a false election return.

ACT VIII. *An act for representatives to vote with the justices at Levie Courts, and makeing bye lawes.*

Authorized county voters to elect a number of representatives equal to the numbers of justices of the peace, "to have equal votes with them . . . in laying the countie assessments, and of making wholesome by lawes. . . ."

ACT IX. *An act for countie courts to appoint their collectors and disabling counsellours to vote in countie courts.*

Forbade members of the Council of State from "vot[ing] or determin[ing] any matter or cause" in county courts.

ACT X. *An act for limitting Sherriffs, etc. a time to demand the levies and for tenders to be made them.*

Limited collection of taxes to certain times of the year; made tobacco legal tender.

ACT XI. *Two Justices of the Quorum to signe probates, etc.*

Authorized two senior justices of the peace to sign probates instead of the governor.

ACT XII. *Councellors and Ministers families to pay levies, and money allowed them.*

Removed tax exempt status of conciliar and ministerial families, gave councillors a fixed salary.

ACT XIII. *An act altering the encouragement for killing wolves.*

Allowed county courts to fix size of bounties on wolves.

ACT XIV. *An act for the further prevention of mischief from unrulie horses.*

ACT XV. *An act against exportation of corne.*

ACT XVI. *An act for the suppressing of ordinaries.*

Closed all ordinaries except in "James Citty, and at each side of York River. . . ."

ACT XVII. *An act for limmitting the bounds of James Cittie.*

ACT XVIII. *An act repealing lawes concerning Accomack and Northampton.*

Permitted appeals from the courts in these counties to the General Court.

ACT XIX. *An act of general pardon and oblivion.*

Pardoned all "treasons, misprison of treasons, murders, fellonies, offences, crimes, contempts and misdemeanors" committed between March 1 and June 25, 1676.

ACT XX. *An act disabling Edward Hill and John Stith to beare office.*

Debarred two justices of the peace in Charles City County from office.

B. WILLIAM SHERWOOD'S ACCOUNT OF THE ASSEMBLY'S PROCEEDINGS

[William Sherwood], "Virginias Deploured Condition . . . ," Massachusetts Historical Society, *Collections,* 4th Ser., IX (1871), 170–172.

Mr. Bacon resolved to force his admittance amongst the Burgesses and thereupon came in his sloope, with fifty armed men, and in the night with his guards, privately getts into Towne, where he associated with [William] Drummond (that perfidious scott) and [Richard] Lawrence (that Athisticall and scandalous person) who informed him of what had passed att Towne, by breake of day he returneing on board his sloope was discovered, and an Allarum in the towne, and imediately severall small Boates were well manned to take him, who persued him to Sandy point, where the Shipps ridd, by whome he was fyred att, and perticulerly by Capt. Gardner in the ship Adam and Eve, who had the Governors order to that purpose, and soe Mr. Bacon was forced to come to Anchor, and he and his men were taken, brought to Towne by Capt. Gardner and Capt. Hubert Farrell. Now great hopes was, that those intestine troubles would be ended, and noe obstruction in carrying on the Indian Warr, the Burgesses the next Morning mett, and that all private animosities and grudges might be laid aside, upon Mr. Bacons submission, on his knees in open Court, and faithfull promises of future good behaviour, he was pardoned, and he and his souldiers discharged.

The Assembly proceeded in forming an Army of 1000 Men, to be imediately raised, and sent out against the Indians, But Mr. Bacon goes home, harbouring private discontent, and studying revenge for his late confinement, sends to the factious, discontented people of New Kent, and those parts, that severall affronts were offered to him in his confinement, for his vindicateing them, that the Assembly were bringing a great charg by raiseing more forces, and that instead of reduceing the 500 men now in pay, they had ordered a thousand souldiers to be raised, suggesting to them that the only way for carrying on the Warr would be by Volunteeres, of which he would be Generall soe that (as bad actions are useually attended with worse) he getts the discontented rabble togeather, and with them resolved to putt himselfe, once more on the stage, and on the xxith day of June he entred James Towne, with 400 foot, and 120 horse, sett guards att the state howse, kept the Governor, Councell and Burgesses prisoners, and would suffer none to pass in or out of Towne, and haveing drawne up all his forces to the very doore and windows of the state howse, he demanded a Commission to be Generall of all the forces that should be raised dureing the Indian Warr, he and all his souldiers crying out Noe Levies, Noe Levies. The Assembly acquainted him they had taken all possible care for carrying on the Indian Warr at the easiest charge that could be, that they had redressed all theire Complaints, and desiered that for sattisfaction of the people, what they had don might be publickly read, Mr. Bacon answered there should be noe Laws read there, that he would not admitt of any delays, that he came for a Comission, and would imediately have itt, thereupon sending his souldiers into the State howse, where the Governor Councell and Burgesses were sitting and thretning them with fyer and sword iff itt was not granted, his souldiers mounting their Guns ready to fyer, Soe that for feer all would be in a flame, the Councell and Burgesses Joyned in a request to the Governor to grant Mr. Bacon such a Comission as he would have, the Governor declaired he would rather loose his life then consent to the granting such unreasonable things as he demanded, but for prevention of that ruin, which was then threatened upon their second request, Order was given for such a Comission as Mr. Bacon would have himselfe, and according to his own dictates. The next morning the (forced) Comission was delivered to him, and the Assembly judged he was fully answered, and soe were in hopes they should without restraint proceed in dispatch of the publick affaires, but now Mr. Bacon haveing a Comission, shews himselfe in his cullers [i.e., colors], and hangs out his flagg of defiance (that is) Imprisoning severall loyall Gentlemen and his rabble used reproachfull words of the Governor (not calling to mind the eminent services he hath don, not onely in takeing prisoner the great Indian Emperour Opechauckenough [i.e., Opechancanough] makeing tributary all the Neighbouring Indians, without the loss of any English blood, and maineteyning peace for many yeares amongst them) Mr. Bacon alsoe with his guard forceably entred amongst the Burgesses, and demanded that severall persons who had beene active in obeying the Governors comands, should be made uncapable of beareing any publick office, and for that he was informed the Governor had lately supplicated his Majesty for aid to suppress the tumulto's, itt should be contradicted by the grand Assembly and Letters writt to the Kings Majesty in favour of his proceedeings: he also required order against Capt. Gardner (who then was his prisoner) for seventy pounds sterling for his sloope, when in truth she was not worth thirty pounds. The Burgesses answered they were not Court of Judicature, and that the Courts were open from whome he might expect Justice. Att this he swore his useuall Oath (God dam his blood) he would have their order for the £70. These thretnings and compulsions being upon them, the Assembly granted what ever he demanded, soe that itt was imagined he and his souldiers would martch out of Towne, yett they continued drinking and domineereing, the fronteere Countys being left with very little force, and the next day came the sad news that the Indians had that morning killed Eight people within thirty Myles of towne, in the familys of some of them that were with Mr. Bacon, yett they hastned not away, but the next day haveing forced an Act of Indemnity, and the Assembly being att the Burgesses request disolved, Mr. Bacon after fower days stay, marched out of Towne. . . .

11. Bacon's "Manifesto"

Virginia Magazine of History and Biography, I (1893), 55–58.

If vertue be a sin, if Piety be giult, all the Principles of morality goodness and Justice be perverted, Wee must confesse That those who are now called Rebells may be in danger of those high imputations, Those loud and severall Bulls would affright Innocents and render the defence of our Brethren and the enquiry into our sad and heavy oppressions, Treason. But if there bee as sure there is, a just God to appeal too, if Religion and Justice be a sanctuary here, If to plead the cause of the oppressed, If sincerely to aime at his Majesties Honour and the Publick good without any reservation or by Interest, If to stand in the Gap after soe much blood of our dear Brethren bought and sold, If after the losse of a great part of his Majesties Colony deserted and dispeopled, freely with our lives and estates to indeavor to save the remaynders bee Treason God Almighty Judge and lett guilty dye, But since wee cannot in our hearts find one single spott of Rebellion or Treason or that wee have in any manner aimed at subverting the setled Government or attempting of the Person of any either magistrate or private man not with standing the severall Reproaches and Threats of some who for sinister ends were disaffected to us and censured our ino[cent] and honest designes, and since all people in all places where wee have yet bin can attest our civill quiet peaseable behaviour farre different from that of Rebellion and tumultuous persons let Trueth be bold and all the world know the real Foundations of pretended giult, Wee appeale to the Country itselfe what and of what nature their Oppressions have bin or by what Caball and mistery the designes of many of those whom wee call great men have bin transacted and caryed on, but let us trace these men in Authority and Favour to whose hands the dispensation of the Countries wealth has been commited; let us observe the sudden Rise of their Estates composed with the Quality in which they first entered this Country Or the Reputation they have held here amongst wise and discerning men, And lett us see wither their extractions and Education have not bin vile, And by what pretence of learning and vertue they could soe soon into Imployments of so great Trust and consequence, let us consider their sudden advancement and let us also consider wither any Publick work for our safety and defence or for the Advancement and propogation of Trade, liberall Arts or sciences is here Extant in any [way] adaquate to our vast chardg, now let us compare these things togit[her] and see what spounges have suckt up the Publique Treasure and wither it hath not bin privately contrived away by unworthy Favourites and juggling Parasites whose tottering Fortunes have bin repaired and supported at the Publique chardg, now if it be so Judg what greater giult can bee then to offer to pry into these and to unriddle the misterious wiles of a powerfull Cabal let all people Judge what can be of more dangerous Import then to suspect the soe long Safe proceedings of Some of our Grandees and wither People may with safety open their Eyes in soe nice a Concerne.

Another main article of our Giult is our open and manifest aversion of all, not onely the Foreign but the protected and Darling Indians, this wee are informed is Rebellion of a deep dye For that both the Governour and Councell are by Colonell Coales Assertion bound to defend the Queen and Appamatocks with their blood Now whereas we doe declare and can prove that they have bin for these Many years enemies to the King and Country, Robbers and Theeves and Invaders of his Majesties' Right and our Interest and Estates, but yet have by persons in Authority bin defended and protected even against His Majesties loyall Subjects and that in soe high a Nature that even the Complaints and oaths of his Majesties Most loyall Subjects in a lawfull Manner proffered by them against those barborous Outlawes have bin by the right honourable Governour rejected and the Delinquents from his presence dismissed not only with pardon and indemnitye but with all incouragement and favour, Their Fire Arms soe destructfull to us and by our lawes prohibited, Commanded to be restored them, and open Declaration before Witness made That they must have Ammunition although directly contrary to our law, Now what greater giult can be then to oppose and indeavour the destruction of these Honest quiet neighbours of ours.

Another main article of our Giult is our Design not only to ruine and extirpate all Indians in Generall but all Manner of Trade and Commerce with them, Judge who can be innocent that strike at this tender Eye of Interest; Since the Right honourable the Governour hath bin pleased by his Commission to warrant this trade who dare oppose it, or opposing it can be innocent, Although Plantations be deserted, the blood of our dear Brethren Spilt, on all Sides our complaints, continually Murder upon Murder renewed upon us, who may or dare think of the generall Subversion of all Mannor of Trade and Commerce with our enemies who can or dare impeach any of [word missing] Traders at the Heades of the Rivers if contrary to the wholesome provision made by lawes for the countries safety, they dare continue their illegall practises and dare asperse the right honourable Governours wisdome and Justice soe highly to pretend to have his warrant to break that law which himself made, who dare say That these Men at the Heads of the Rivers buy and sell our blood, and doe still notwithstanding the late Act made to the contrary, admit Indians painted and continue to Commerce, although these things can be proved yet who dare bee soe guilty as to doe it.

Another Article of our Guilt is To Assert all those neighbour Indians as well as others to be outlawed, wholly unqualifyed for the benefitt and Protection of the law, For that the law does reciprocally protect and punish, and that all people offending must either in person or Estate make equivalent satisfaction or Restitution according to the manner and merit of the Offences Debts or Trespasses; Now since the Indians cannot according to the tenure and forme of any law to us known be prosecuted, Seised or Complained against, Their Persons being difficulty distinguished or known, Their many nations languages, and their subterfuges such as makes them incapeable to make us Restitution or satisfaction would it not be very giulty to say They have bin unjustly defended and protected these many years.

If it should be said that the very foundation of all these disasters the Grant of the Beaver trade to the Right Honourable Governour was illegall and not granteable by any power here present as being a monopoly, were not this to deserve the name of Rebell and Traytor.

Judge therefore all wise and unprejudiced men who may or can faithfully or truely with an honest heart attempt the country's good, their vindication and libertie without the aspersion of Traitor and Rebell, since as soe doing they must of necessity gall such tender and dear concernes, But to manifest Sincerity and loyalty to the World, and how much wee abhorre those bitter names, may all the world know that we doe unanimously desire to represent our sad and heavy grievances to his most sacred Majesty as our Refuge and Sanctuary, where wee doe well know that all our Causes will be impartially heard and Equall Justice administred to all men.

12. *Postrebellion Grievances*

C.O. 1/39, 244, Public Record Office.

Whereas His Majesties Comissioners Herbert Jeffreys Esq. Sir John Berry, Knight and Francis Morryson Esq., by their Declaration, have commanded us the Subscribers, in the behalfe of Gloster County to give in our Grievances: In Obedience thereunto, we have drawne up our Grievances, and they are as followeth.

AGGRIEVANCES

1. WHEREAS about 17 yeares since there was a Tax layd upon Tobacco shipt in this Country of 2*s* per hogshead by Act of Assembly; under pretence of defraying the publick charge of the Country therewith; in order to the preventing of other publick Taxes, which hath not taken its effects: For that the Country Levies, hath notwithstanding this Tax, beene ever since as great, or more then before: Therefore they Humbly conceave, the said Tax of 2*s* per hogshead to be a Grievance; Unless it may be imployed, (as pretended) when first raysed.

2. That whereas, about 3. or 4. yeares since, by the pretence of some Persons, insensing the Assembly, That the Lord Arlington, Culpeper and others had obteined a Pattent from his Sacred Majesty, which tended to the enslaving of the Inhabitants of this Country; for prevention whereof, they did persuade the said Assembly, to consent to the raysing of 60 lbs. of Tobacco per pole [i.e., poll, or head], for two yeares together; which, in the whole Country amounts to a considerable sume: Which said Tobacco was to be imployed as pretended, to beare the charge of Agents, imployed to prevent or remove the abovesaid Pattentees. Now, if his Majesty gave no such Grant, to the said Persons; Then wee Humbly conceive the said 120 lb. Tobacco Tax per pole, was a cheate, and Oppressive; and doe Humbly beg Restitution from the Authors. This Tax occasioned the first Discontents among the People.

3. That within this 14. or 15. months, it is conceaved, there hath beene near 300 Christian persons, barbarously murthered by the Indians; and after the murther of severall Numbers of the said Persons, the Assembly (called for that purpose) Order'd 500 men to be raysed against the said Murtherers; by whom Forts were erected: Wee were informed That, the Commanders of the said Souldiers, had order, not to molest an Indian; unless they knew them to be the Murtherers; or, began to act in an hostile way first: which Lenity, we humbly conceive gave the Indians incouragement to persist in their bloody Practice; and was Occasion in part, of the Peoples arming themselves without command from their Superiors in a Rebellious manner; with whom the Rebell Bacon, having before by extravagancy lost his fortunes, takes the Opportunity and Joynes: and being amongst them reputed a Witt, was adhered to by the rest: and after he had Illegally obtained a Commission, which was published, as Legally obtained, in the severall County's, by Consent of the Grand Assembly: By which, many people were ignorantly deluded and drawn into his Party, that thought of no other designe then the Indian War; Most of which persons though never so Innocent, are persecuted with Rigour; The which, with the Ill-Management of this Warr at first, wee complaine of, as Grievances.

4. That whereas There were severall Grievances presented to the Assembly

in June last, in order to prevent many exorbitant fees, and other Disorders in Government; upon which many good lawes were consented to, and agreed upon by that grand Assembly; before the Rebell Bacon came to interrupt the said Assembly: Wee beg that those good and wholsome Lawes, may be confirmed by this Assembly.

5. Wee complaine, That since the Late Rebellion, the Rebells have taken and plundered divers good Subjects estates: Wee beg that this Assembly will take some course that right Owners may be impowered to be revested, in all that was so taken from them (and not imbezzell'd) of what quality soever.

6. Wee complaine, That some particular Persons neare about the Governor have obtained Commission to plunder and destroy the Rebells, which they have made use of to the Imprisonment of the Persons and rifling their estates, and converting them to their owne uses; of some of his Majesties good subjects, as well as of the Rebells: And Wee do pray that such may have Redress, according to Law and Justice.

7. Wee Complain, That whereas there was an Order from a Councell of Warr, lately held at Green Spring, directed to the Militia Officers of our County, to raise 60 men to be an Out-guard for the Governor and be under the Command of Lt. Col. [Edward] Ramsey; which men, were accordingly raised and sent: but not finding the Governor nor their Commander there were commanded by Maj. Robert Beverley to go to work, fall trees, mawl [i.e., split] and toat railes: which many of them refusing to do, he presently disarmed them and sent them home: Which we take to be a great affront, done by the said Beverly to the whole County; and the rather seeing by disaster we had, a small time before, lost most of our Armes, and were then infested by the Indians, who cutt off 6. persons in one family, and attempted others Wee therefore humbly begg of this grand Assembly, reporation against the said Beverly, as an Affront done to this whole County, though it is well known that this County with stood the Rebell Bacon and his Adherents, the most of any in Virginia; insomuch that he never could place a guard in it: though we must needs acknowledge, that many of us were forced, to preserve our lives, to take his execrable Oath: for which wee heartily repent, and beg his Majesties and Our Governors Pardon.

8. That whereas His Majesty hath been graciously pleased, to send in Armes and Ammunition for the use of the Country; That this Grand Assembly would be pleased to take Order, that they be distributed in each County, according to the proportion of the titheables: And, That in each County they be put into the hands of some Person of Trust where most safety is, for a Magazine for that County: That, when there shall be occasion to raise men for his Majesties service, they may be there armed, as late experience hath manifested: Which way we complaine of as a Grievance

9. Whereas by the too frequent Assemblyes and the high Charges of the Burgesses, the Country is exposed to a great charge which we doe complaine [of] as a grievance.

10. We doe complaine that there are Severall Considerable Summs of money Collected from the Ships, for Fort Duties, and great Summs of money is now Lying dead in some particular mens hands, we doe humbly desire that the said money may be laid out for a Magazine for the good of the Country.

11. Whereas There is a proclamation prohibiting all Masters of Ships and Marchants from selling to any inhabitant in the Country Gunns or Ammunition the Heathen makeing dayly incursions upon us which we doe complaine of as Grievance unless it be removed

Philip Lightfoot	James Taylor
John Buckner	John Rogers
Llewis Burwell	Thomas Kemp

The Plant-Cutter Riots, 1681–1683

13. Two Accounts of the Riots

A. SIR HENRY CHICHELEY TO SECRETARY LEOLINE JENKINS, MAY 1682

C.O. 5/1356, 66–69, Public Record Office.

Right Honorable

I am heartily sorry I have occasion to give you soe speedy an account of this Countrys estate, the people of our County of Glocester having last week in a tumultous manner, cut up half the Tobacco plants among them some whereof voluntarily destroyed their owne and then joyned forces and, in several parties to the number of twenty or more, meagre opposition by the planters that owned them, cut up all plants wherever they came. They had begun three or four days before I had notice of it being then at a General Court at James Citty, immediately I issued out my Proclamation to that County and soon after to all others to stop their proceedings, seconded with a Commission to Col. [Mathew] Kemp one of the Council here, to suppress them by force which, with all possible hast, hee effectually put in execution taking two and twenty of them in the fact, all which except two more violent and incorrigible than the rest immediately submitted, begged pardon and promised amendment and were dismissed home. The two beforementioned were remitted to mee and the Council at James Citty and are now in safe custody. I hope my endeavors, which shall not bee wanting, may quench this growing flame. Of the further progress and total quelling of it I shall give your Honor speedy notice by a ship that I expect will sail ten days hence. The probable occasion as farr as I can yet see, of this commotion is briefly thus. The Lord Culpeper adjourning the Assembly, which he called when here, to the 15th of February after which was prorogued till Januarie last, and the next month Mr. [Nathaniel] Bacon [i.e., a cousin to the late rebel] by letter to mee reciting part of his Lordships letter (the purport whereof was that an Assembly should bee called some time last month, by which time it was hoped his Lordship would arive here) and my selfe having not received a sillable from any Publick Minister nor indeed till neer the middle of April, about which time Capt. Jeffries arrived with pay for the Soldiers [i.e., a reference to troops sent to Virginia at the time of Bacon's Rebellion]; the beginning of March I issued out Writs for the convening the Assembly, I fear unhappily because when I receiv'd His Majestie's commands not to call them to sit some of them were then on their way to James Citty and by consequence too late to prorogue them untill they met and they big with expectation to enact a Cessation, by the most, but not the wisest, thought the only expedient to advance the price of Tobacco and being advised by the Council to propose to the House of Burgesses whether they would continue His Majestie's Soldiers on the Countrys pay before their Prorogation according to the tenor of his Majestie's letter, by strange pretence they delayed for fewer [four?] days their answer as will appear by their Journal and ours to bee remitted you by the Secretary here to whom I further referr you at present. They were prorogued with unanimous advice of the Council till the 10th of November next in obedience to his Majesties' command. But before their prorogation, as I since understand, they voted their Journal should bee publickly read by their Burgesses when they got home to their respective Counties, upon the perusal of which it will bee easy for your Honor to observe how the people came inflamed and the Soldiers, by abridgement of their pay and some delay occasioned by my necessary presence at the General Court being apter to mutiny than to serve His Majesty here, must of necessity, in this juncture of time, bee with all expedition, disbanded cannot as yet see the bottom nor discover who are cheifly concerned in this tumult, nor indeed what will bee the issue. It hath an ill face in many respects. I can only say for my selfe your Honor may bee assured I shall manifest my allegiance, upon all occasions, submit the whole matter to your prudent consideration and depend upon your generosity for all the just favor can be shown to Right Honorable Your Honor's most faithful and obedient servant Henry Chicheley. Middle Plantation May the 8th 1682.

B. NICHOLAS SPENCER TO SECRETARY LEOLINE JENKINS, MAY 1682

C.O. 1/1356, 74–79, Public Record Office.

Right Honorable   James-Citty   May 8th 1682
I have not of late presumed to trouble your Honor with my letters and doe most heartily wish had other matter to signify to your Honor than the substance of this letter, for know the contents will bee as unwelcome to your Honor as they are grevious to mee to write, being now to tell your Honor the quiet and peace of this His Majesty's Colony is not only hazarded by unruly and tumultous persons, but is at present under such sufferings, by a combination of many inhabitants in Glocester-County entering into a resoluion to force a Law, by their Wills, That noe Tobaccos should bee this year planted, the which readily to effect on the first of this month began their evil underakings, first with cutting up their own plants and soe proceeded, from Plantation to Plantation, using a forcible way of perswasion by telling the Masters of Plantations where they came, if not willing to have their plants cut up, they would create a willingness in them by force and, in an hours time, destroy as many plants as would well have imployed twenty men a Summers tendance to have perfected. These outrages were in progress near three days before the Lt. Gov-

ernor had any intimation thereof himselfe and the Council being then at James Citty holding the General Court as soon as received advice thereof issued forth Proclamations whereby to restrain such riots, tumults, outrages and violences the which to make effectual dispatched one Col. [Mathew] Kemp a worthy gentleman of the Council and Commander of Glocester Militia, with orders to raise such numbers of the Militia Horse and Foot as might bee effectual to suppress and reduce the Mutineers whom, with his horse, he surrounded and took every man of them in the very act of destroying of Plants. Two of the principal and incorrigible rogues are committed, the rest submitting and giving assurances of their quiet and peaceable demeanor and behavior were remitted[. I] hope by this time other parties of the Mutineers may bee reduced, tho it's to bee feared the contagion will spread. This day have received intelligence that the next adjacent County being new kent was lately broke forth committing the like spoyls on plants as in Glocester County, the which to suppress is the like care taken, by way of the Militia Horse and Foot or soe many of them as may, in this juncture, bee admitted to arms, and least [i.e., lest] the infection should grow, general orders are gone forth to the Commanders of the Militia of each County to provide a party of horse to bee in continual motion, by which vigilancy are in some hopes the growth of these Insurrections and outrages may bee prevented and in it should not write doubtfully did I not know the necessities of the inhabitants to bee such, by their only commodity Tobacco, soe now sunk to nothing that their low estate makes them desperate and resolve a Law of Cessation of their own making, if goe forward the only destroying Tobacco-plants will not satiate their (it's to be feared) rebellious appetites who, if encrease and find the strength of their own arms, will not hound themselves. Too add to this unexpected evil His Majesty's Soldiers, being two Companies and just upon the point of disbanding and sensible His Majesty hath been pleased to comand their disbanding on the first of April and noe pay appointed after that day, are soe farr from being serviceable in this only time of assistance from them since their arrival, that their mutinous tempers double our apprehensions of evil events. Had not the Ship on which was loaded the Soldiers mony been long wind-bound and on her passage beyond usual time, His Majestie's Soldiers had been paid off before these present commotions hapned, the Soldiers quarters are now accounting for and the Soldiers and Landlords will day after day bee paid off and the Soldiers disbanded and the Country freed of their mischeifs which may bee from their mutinous demeanors, His Majesty was pleased to command the disbanding of the two Companies if the Country would not continue them on publick charge. The Assembly met in five days after the arival of those His Majesty's commands being by writ from the Lt. Governor Sir Henry Chicheley soe appointed near forty days before the arrival of the Ship Concord; by which ship His Majesty was likewise pleas'd to signify His Royall Will and pleasure that no Assembly should bee held or permitted to sit until the tenth of November next, by which time his Excellencie the Lord Culpeper would be remanded to this his Government, by whom his Majesty would be pleased to signify his Royal Will and pleasure to the last addresses of the General Assembly; and that his Lordship's arrival will bee in time for an Assembly the said tenth of November. The Assembly convened by the Lt. Governor being met hee communicated to the Council his Majestie's commands, both as to the disbanding the soldiers (unless continued at the Countrys Charge) and likewise His Majesties commands that noe Assembly should sit until the tenth of November to both of which that the Council according to their duty might pay and yeild all due obedience were of the opinion the Assembly being met then convened without the consent or advice of any one member of the Council, yet should bee permitted to sit only to advise whether to continue the Guards at the Countries charge or not, in which proposition the House of Burgesses seemed to spend some days without any other answer then desiring, from day to day, time to resolve being a point on which to gain time, to carry on other imaginations, the principle part of which was a Cessation for which as the Assembly was called peculiarly by the importunate motions of the over-active Clerk of the House of Burgesses Major Robert Beverley, soe his influence was noe less in the House when convened. The continuance of the Assembly not being agreeable to his Majestie's commands they were prorogued on the twenty seaventh of April to the tenth of November, by which prorogation the selfish purposes of some persons were frustrated, most particularly the Clerk of the House of Burgesses who to accomplish his designes of noe Tobacco this year to bee planted, to advance those great quantities of Tobaccos now on his hands, hath instilled into the multitude (as it is vehemently suspected) to justify the right of making a Cessation by cutting up of plants; soe that the ground and rise of our present troubles and disorders is from the ill timed Assembly.

Sir About ten days hence will sayl other Ships, by them shall bee able to speak more positively to our commotions than at present, therefore will now beg leave to close with subscribing Right Honorable Your Honor's most faithful and obedient Servant.

Nicholas Spencer.

14. *Governor Culpeper's Handling of the Plant Cutters, January 1681/82*

> Further representation of Lord Culpeper (to the Committee for Plantations), September 20, 1683, C.O. 5/1356, 155–160, Public Record Office.

On the 10th of January [1682/83] I called a full Council and strictly examined the Business of plant-cutting and all the Evidences relating thereunto, by which it most plainly appeared that the Vigorous advice given by Mr. Secretary [Nicholas] Spencer for the securing the person of the said Mr. [Robert] Beverley, and the faithful and courageous execution thereof by Major General [Robert] Smith (though to his own great loss of 2, or 300 li. by the Rabbles cutting up his Tobacco-plants within two days after out of spight) was the Cheif cause of the peace and quiet of the Country, as well as lucky to the said Mr. Beverley himself, who had hee been at liberty, had in all probability been ingaged therein, whereas, upon the utmost scrutiny, I could find no proofs of any thing against him but only rudeness and sauciness and an endeavor to compass his ends by prevailing on the easiness of an inclining Governor; and causing Sir Henry Chicheley to stop Shipps, to countenance petitions for an Assembly, and afterwards to call an Assembly contrary to positive Instructions and the express advice of the Council who, at their very last meeting had agreed on a Proclamation to adjourn the Assembly till November; but Sir Henry had noe sooner got to his own House then hee was perswaded not only not to signe it but, ex mero motu [i.e., "of his own mere motion"], to issue out Proclamations for its meeting in April, *1682* following, without mentioning the Council therein. And yet persuant to the above mentioned Order of the 17th June, *1682* I put him the said Beverley out of all Officers and Imployments whatsoever until His Majesty's Pleasure should be further known. In the next place notwithstanding the several disencouragements I lay under by Sir Henry's General Pardon to all then present in the feild without naming who, which in effect included alsoe that day, and by his particular pardon to one John Suckler (the cheif contriver and promoter of the said Plant destroying) on condition hee should build a Bridge near adjacent and convenient to the Plantation Sir Henry liv'd in, for his performance whereof his [i.e., Sir Henry's] Son in law Mr. Ralph Wormley one of his Majesty's Council (with one Mr. Christopher Robinson) was security; And by his taking Bayl for the appearance of all the rest, whereby hee did not only declare the same to bee but a Ryot and noe more, since bayleable [i.e., bailable], but did make that appear alsoe as slight as possible to the people. And though I was little used to the practical part of Criminal matters, yet according to Bradshaw's and Burton's case, 39 Elizabeth [i.e., a reference to a case argued before the Court of Queen's Bench in the thirty-ninth year of Elizabeth's reign] making the intent only of a Universal flinging up of all Inclosures to bee Treason though it did not succeed, I found, a fortiore, the universal cutting up and actual destroying of the Tobacco-plants by force and Arms, though none killed, to bee Treason also (not only by the Thirteenth of this King [i.e., Charles II], but even within the 25th of Edward the third [i.e., references to cases involving treason]) and the Council being unanimously of the same judgement and th' Evidence most plain, I some time after committed the persons of Somerset Davies, Bartholomew al[ia]s Black Austin, Richard Baily and [blank in original] Cocklin to prison for Treason. And having in the interim on the 13th of March, issued out the two Proclamations about John Haley, and the Impannelling Grand Juries etc. I caused them to bee indicted and tryed the next General Court, according to the usual forms and methods where, notwithstanding the noe small endeavors of some to imitate Ignoramus-Jurys [i.e., juries that do not find true bills of indictment], and the high words and threats of others both Grand and Petty Jury (as great in every respect, if not the greatest that was impannelled in that Colony) found the three first Guilty. But the Evidence not coming up so full against the last, hee was acquitted. Of the three condemned, I ordered the cheif Somerset Davies to bee executed during the sitting of the Court at James Citty, and Black Austin before the Court house in Glocester-County, where the Insurrection first broke out, and where the Justices had too much inclined that way. But for Richard Baily, hee was extremely young not past 19, meerly drawn in and very penitent. And therefore, having soe fully asserted the Dignity of the Government in the exemplory punishment of the other two to deterr others, I thought fitt to mingle mercy with Justice and Repreeved him; promising to intercede with His Majesty not only to pardon his life, but to restore the little estate hee had alsoe, to the end the whole Country might bee convinced, that there was noe other motive in the thing but purely to maintain Government and their own peace and quiet. And I the rather enclined thereunto and thought myselfe obliged, in some part to grant the General Pardon alsoe, because before my arrival the crime was reputed, even by many good men, to bee but a great Riot only and not Treason. And if that had been the case and a Ryot only found, the Country could never have been safe; for then there could have been noe punishment beyond Fine and Imprisonment. Both which would bee greater to the Government than to the offenders, for scarce one of them was worth a farthing and soe must bee maintained, and there are in effect noe prisons but what are soe easily broken that I count it almost a miracle the four I committed did not escape, I am sure I was in pain all the while and could scarsly sleep for fear thereof. In a word I concluded, soe the thing were prevented for the future, as I am confident it is for ever and that the humour will never break out that way again, that all other particulars were inconsiderable to the main business. If your Lordships think there is not enough done, I have on purpose excepted Mr. Beverley and others out of the Proclamation that you may proceed against him if you can, and the others if you will.

Chapter Ten

Life in Seventeenth-Century Virginia

What was life like for the colonist who lived in Virginia during the seventeenth century? The preceding documentation offers much incidental information that the ingenious historian can cull. But at best, an answer to that question must be tentative because of the sparsity of the surviving evidence. Unlike the New England Puritans, the Englishmen who settled the Old Dominion were quite circumspect in recording their experiences, and in Virginia's first one hundred years, the colony produced no counterparts to William Bradford, Anne Bradstreet, or Samuel Sewell. Few Virginia colonists ever described their life-style, and fewer still are the number of such descriptions that have withstood the hazards of time. In the absence of a sufficiency of letters, diaries, or sermons, legal records and archaeological remains become vital for recreating certain aspects of colonial life. For example, they provide the foundation for a reasonably accurate reconstruction of the colonists' material culture—what their houses were like, what they owned, what they wore, and how they amused themselves. Wills, inventories of estates, and artifacts are of less value, however, in determining dietary patterns, the nature of family life, social habits, or the settler's perceptions of his environment. Occasionally an extant letter provides a clue, but because of the dearth of information, the nonmaterial side of the colonial Virginian's mode of living is generally the least understood facet of his culture.

Anyone who went to America confronted the wrenching prospects of a rigorous sea voyage and the substitution of the uncertainties of a new land for the familiar surroundings of home. Going to sea was likely to be a terrifying experience for men and women who were unaccustomed to ocean travel, and the conditions they had to endure in transit were far from ideal (Document 1). Under favorable circumstances an Atlantic crossing took between six and eight weeks. Storms, contrary winds, or navigational errors often lengthened the passage, which only added to the miseries of seasickness and cramped quarters. Seldom exceeding a waterline length of one hundred feet, deep-water sailing vessels were not planned with an eye towards easing the passenger's journey to Virginia. Shipbuilders had not yet learned to design and rig vessels to make maximum use of the power from air currents. Consequently seventeenth-century merchantmen were slow and inefficient sailers. Every inch of cargo space was precious; so a skipper jammed colonists, belongings, livestock, and cargo together in his ship's small hold. Disease was common since sanitary facilities were minimal, fresh water was scarce, and even hot meals invited the risk of setting the ship afire. Forced to bear such trials, one colonist not surprisingly described his arrival in Virginia as "no smale joy."

For many settlers that joy was surely short-lived, because when they finally got to the colony, they traded one ordeal for another. Until they took up settlements there, the New World was a fascinating mystery to the English, and their lack of accurate information about Virginia proved to be a severe handicap during the initial phase of settlement. In their efforts to attract settlers, promoters—who themselves had never seen the place—often made extravagant claims about what Virginia had to offer the adventurous colonist (Document 2). Fed by sometimes fabulous stories of instant riches and easy living, the English came to Virginia with high hopes for early success in their colonial endeavors. Some of these expectations were soon realized (Document 3A), but others were just as quickly and cruelly dashed (Document 3B). Once the colonists were in Virginia, much of the mystery and inaccurate knowledge soon faded, but their fascination with the country's natural attributes remained unchecked.

In its pristine state Virginia presented the English with a formidable challenge. A land of great beauty and abundance, it was just different enough from England to render unusable much of what the colonists knew about the world they had left. Staying alive in the Virginia wilderness was risky business. Only those men and women survived who could adapt their experiences to the new situations, and such adaptations were neither quick nor painless. In the Old Dominion's earlier years some colonists died from starvation simply because they lacked hunting skills or the ability to discern edible plants among Virginia's bountiful flora. Others succumbed to the unfavorable climate, sickness, or sheer loneliness. In time the English made those adjustments that were necessary for survival and gradually accommodated their traditional modes of living to the new environment.

Housing was of immediate concern to every immigrant, no matter at what point in the century he arrived. But contrary to popular myth, Englishmen did not spend their first days in America building log cabins. Not only were log cabins then unknown to the English, but their traditional types of houses were adequate to their needs, and an abundance and variety of building materials were readily available. The settler first sought to erect a temporary shelter against the elements, so his initial home was likely to be a one-room, thatched-roof house that Englishmen called a cottage (figure 1). Constructed of wattle and daub, the cottages often lacked windows and wooden flooring, although they sometimes included a small attic. They were heated and lit by fireplaces made of logs chinked and plastered with clay. At best the wattle-and-daub cottage was a mean abode, which sufficed until a colonist could find time to build a better structure; when he did, the cottage probably became a barn or a storage facility.

A more permanent kind of dwelling was the frame house. Customarily frame houses were of single bay, story-and-a-half construction (figure 2). To save space, outside chimneys, either catted or brick, were located at either end of the building, and instead of thatching, builders roofed these homes with wooden shingles. The bay and the attic each could be partitioned into two rooms, and depending upon the planter's means, their walls might be plastered. Access to the upper rooms, which could be used for sleeping or storage, was by a ladder (Document 4A). These dwellings were somewhat more commodious and livable than wattle-and-daub cottages because they contained greater floor space and such amenities as windows and wooden flooring. Despite these embellishments, the typical frame house was cramped, poorly lit, and underheated. There was little privacy; few families enjoyed the luxury of having individual rooms for each member of the household.

Although the colonists manufactured brick at an early point in Virginia's history, there were relatively few brick houses built in the

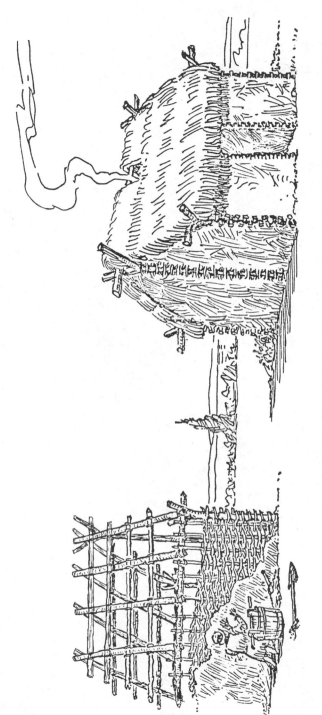

Figure 1. *Wattle-and-daub cabins at Jamestown.*
(Conjectural drawing, courtesy of H. Warren Billings, Richmond, Va.)

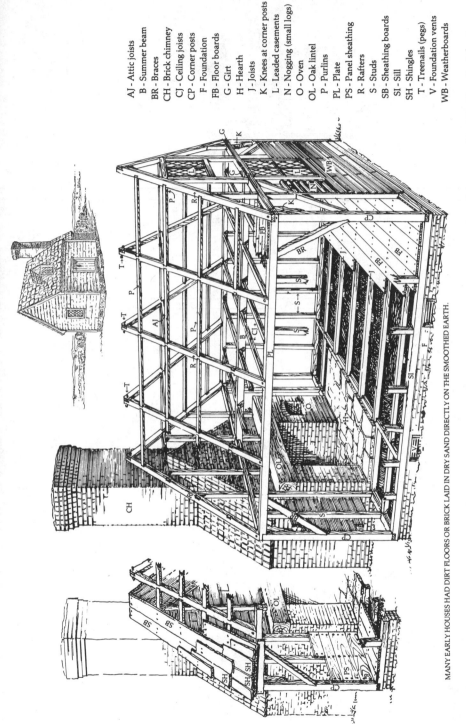

AJ - Attic joists
B - Summer beam
BR - Braces
CH - Brick chimney
CJ - Ceiling joists
CP - Corner posts
F - Foundation
FB - Floor boards
G - Girt
H - Hearth
J - Joists
K - Knees at corner posts
L - Leaded casements
N - Nogging (small logs)
O - Oven
OL - Oak lintel
P - Purlins
PL - Plate
PS - Panel sheathing
R - Rafters
S - Studs
SB - Sheathing boards
SI - Sill
SH - Shingles
T - Treenails (pegs)
V - Foundation vents
WB - Weatherboards

MANY EARLY HOUSES HAD DIRT FLOORS OR BRICK LAID IN DRY SAND DIRECTLY ON THE SMOOTHED EARTH.

Figure 2. The framing of an early seventeenth-century story-and-a-half single bay house and a similar finished dwelling (inset).

(Conjectural drawing, courtesy of H. Warren Billings, Richmond, Va.)

colony until the later years of the seventeenth century. Archaeological evidence, court records, and several extant structures hint that much of the brick that the colonists produced went into churches or public buildings rather than private residences. Some examples of the century's brick homes remain today, notably the Adam Thoroughgood House, Foster's Castle, Criss-Cross, and Bacon's Castle, but none of these is particularly noteworthy either for its scale or its architectural distinction. Instead these surviving homes, as well as archaeological evidence, suggest that bricks were used to create no more than elaborate variations on the basic plan of the common frame dwelling, made possible by their original owners' rising affluence.

An exception to this observation was Sir William Berkeley's plantation, Green Spring. Begun in the 1640s, it had by the 1660s been transformed into a manor house that the architectural historian Thomas T. Waterman has called "the greatest Virginia house of the century." As such, Green Spring set a style that the emerging planter elite sought to copy and thus contributed to the foundation of an architectural ideal that achieved full flowering in the next century. Demolished in 1806, the house became a memory until its site was subjected to intensive archaeological investigations that have produced valuable data about seventeenth-century life. (See the map of Virginia in 1668, in chapter 3, for locations of Green Spring and the other brick homes mentioned above.)

While few colonists could emulate the governor's mansion, it is evident that the quality of the colonists' housing improved as the century wore on. Robert Beverley, for example, declared in his *History and Present State of Virginia*, first printed in 1705, that "the Private Buildings are of late much improved." He went on to write that brick construction was in greater use than formerly, a fact that had also been recorded by a French Huguenot some two decades before Beverley published his *History*. The Frenchman also commented on the comfortableness of some homes, while noting that the Virginians had not lost their propensity for building the basic story-and-a-half dwellings (Document 4B).

The Virginia settlers furnished their homes with a wide range of personal belongings. What we know about this household property comes to us from thousands of inventories of personal estates that are preserved in county record books. These inventories enumerate a great variety of furnishings—so great in fact that it is difficult to deduce sound generalizations about the distribution of material goods among colonial families. Some families subsisted on the barest essentials (Document 5A), while others were of more substantial means (Document 5B). Still other families crammed an unbelievable quantity of possessions into their cramped living quarters (Document 5C). A minimally furnished home might contain only a few pieces of furniture, cooking utensils, and some tools, while the better-equipped ones contained several beds, chests, chairs, and a larger number of linens, dishes, pots, and pans.

Certain household items were highly prized for their usefulness and were therefore passed from one generation of a family to another. Usually these items either were not readily available in Virginia or were beyond the ability of the colonists to make for themselves. Weapons, cast-iron pots, tools, and flocked mattresses were commonly willed to a favorite child or relative.

Some colonists seem never to have discarded anything—no matter how useless it may seem to the inquiring eye of the scholar. The estates of those who perhaps ranked among the colony's poorest inhabitants frequently contained such items as a "peice of old melted pewter" and the "leafe of a table." Other inventories listed rotten cloth, damaged pottery, or a worn-out harness. In brief, a family's household possessions were limited only by the imagination and the means of its members.

Besides containing information about furnishings, inventories are useful for determining what sort of clothing the seventeenth-century Virginian wore. Colonial clothing was surprisingly varied in its material and construction and in the wide range of items worn by the colonists. Aside from its practical use, clothing was a mark of one's social status. Predictably, therefore, the inventories of well-to-do settlers list large wardrobes of diverse quality, from coarse linen to fine or expensive fabric. The quality, as well as the quantity, of wearing apparel diminished along the lower rungs of the social ladder. Producing clothes was a time-consuming process, and although a family might possess several changes of clothes, one did not often have the luxury of a daily fresh shirt or blouse. Because of their value, the usable dress, shoes, or stockings, like the iron pot or the flocked mattress, were willed to the next generation.

As for the family unit itself, present knowledge is limited. Until recently the seventeenth-century Virginia family has not captured the imaginations of demographic historians with the intensity of its New England counterpart. While it is not yet possible, then, to write authoritatively on the matter, certain general characteristics of the family in the Old Dominion may be noted. The first of these has to do with the number of families who settled in Virginia throughout the century. That young, mostly male, servants comprised the bulk of the colony's immigrants suggests a small number of family units in comparison to the colony's total population. If this observation is borne out by systematic research, one might postulate an absence of the family's stabilizing force as an explanation for the frailty of the Old Dominion's social institutions in the years before 1700.

In all likelihood careful investigation will also reveal that, like the New England family, Virginia families were nuclear. Instead of having several generations living together under the same roof, the model Virginia household probably consisted of father, mother, children, and servants. Although some prominent Virginia families are noteworthy for their numerous progeny, a house filled to the bursting point with offspring was not the desire of every married couple. Indeed, what scholars will perhaps discover is that colonial Virginians produced offspring in proportion to their means to care for them. Birth and death rates and ages of couples at marriage will be a bit more difficult to calculate because of the lack of evidence. But here too a methodical inquiry will quite possibly show that children survived infancy in greater numbers, that adults lived longer, and that men and women married later in life than has often been supposed. In short, many time-honored assumptions about these aspects of the family will probably lack validity when all of the available data are subjected to rigorous analysis.

With modifications, John Demos's depiction of the Plymouth family as a business, a school, a vocational institute, a church, a house of correction, and a welfare institution is perhaps equally appropriate for the colonial family in its Virginia setting.* The business of Virginia families was raising tobacco: its production demanded specialized skills, the possession of which may have made Virginians somewhat less self-sufficient than colonists in Plymouth. Since the Virginia government never adopted compulsory education laws, the opportunities for formal schooling in the colony were practically nonexistent before 1693. Consequently the little that young Virginians learned of reading and writing came from their parents, from whom they also received, either by observation or instruction, the practical knowledge that was necessary for living in the colonial world. One is likely to uncover only small amounts of information about the Virginia family's function as a "church," but still it may be safely concluded

* John Demos, *A Little Commonwealth: Family Life in Plymouth Colony* (New York, 1970).

that parents tried to impart their understanding of Anglicanism to their children by teaching them the creed or the articles of religion. Like the authorities in Plymouth, Virginia magistrates depended upon the family to provide welfare services for a local community, although they do not appear to have relied upon it as an agency for reforming petty criminals. In sum, the family was the focal point of the colonists' daily existence, and it performed a variety of roles that in modern times have been assumed by other institutions.

Outside the home, the church provided the colonists with spiritual sustenance, as well as a source of public involvement and recreation. Anglicanism came to Virginia in 1607, and except for the hiatus of the Commonwealth, it remained the Old Dominion's established religion until the General Assembly adopted Thomas Jefferson's statute for religious freedom in 1786. However, because religion was not a primary impetus for founding the colony, it is a historical commonplace to assume an absence of piety and religious commitment in the Old Dominion's colonists. In their way, the English who populated Virginia throughout the seventeenth century were probably as attached to Anglicanism as the Massachusetts colonists were to Puritanism. But the point is largely speculative, since the Virginia colonists have not favored scholars with volumes of sermons or other religious writings. Although the Anglican way may not have inspired in its practitioners the same zeal and sense of vision as the Puritan way did in its adherents, Anglicanism furnished the Virginians with that comfort of spirit and assurance that all believers require of their religion. (See the two maps in chapter 3 for locations of seventeenth-century churches.)

From the colony's earliest days, however, the institutional church experienced difficulties in meeting the colonists' spiritual needs. The most serious of these was an insufficiency of clergymen—a problem that was never solved throughout the century. Another was the failure of the church hierarchy to transfer to the colony. In the absence of bishops and ecclesiastical courts, the responsibility for governing the church devolved almost exclusively upon secular authorities. To the governor fell the power of inducting ministers, while the General Assembly assumed the authority for establishing parishes and enacting laws relating to church affairs. The county courts were empowered to punish offenses against morals and the church. As the process of adjusting the church to the needs of the colonists continued, the parish vestry came to hold a key position in church government and to serve as an important agency for introducing some men to public service.

Originally a body whose primary responsibility in an English parish was administering poor relief, the vestry in Virginia was transformed by time and circumstance into the governing authority for individual parishes. Its duties included fixing parochial boundaries, raising taxes to support the parish's operations, investigating moral offenses, building churches, and recruiting ministers (Documents 6A through 6C). Vestries were chosen at irregular intervals by the parishioners. They usually consisted of at least twelve men, each of whom took an oath in which he averred his allegiance to the Church of England and promised to perform the duties of his office (Document 6D). Since the office entailed important responsibilities, vestrymen were drawn from the upper ranks of colonial society. Not infrequently, therefore, members of the county courts, the House of Burgesses, and the Council of State served on their local parish vestries. But the position was also used to recruit men of promise into the political system: service on the vestry provided training for higher office. Indeed, where it is possible to trace the patterns of officeholding for specific individuals, it is not uncommon to discover that these men had begun their careers in public life as vestrymen.

Apart from ministering to the colony's spiritual needs and providing a stepping-stone to higher office, the church afforded the colonists a recreational outlet of sorts. A respite from the mundane chores of daily life, going to church was also an opportunity for parishioners to catch up on the latest gossip or simply to enjoy contact with people outside the family. Consequently the habit developed of tarrying a while in the churchyard after services to talk with friends—a custom that endures to this day in those seventeenth-century parishes that still serve their communities' spiritual needs.

The ordinary Virginian probably savored such occasions, for his life offered few opportunities for leisure. Community attitudes militated against idleness, and the business of staying alive was inordinately time-consuming. So when a moment came, the colonist took his pleasures wherever he found them. Often these divertissements took the form of drinking, horse racing, hunting, fishing, and gambling at ninepins, cards, and dice. An insight into colonial recreation habits can be found in local records, because by law the county courts regulated public houses and settled disputes arising from gambling debts or hunters who trespassed upon their neighbors' property in pursuit of their quarry (Documents 7A through 7E). A court might also act to preserve wild life or to suppress a company of players that it deemed offensive to community mores (Documents 7F and 7G).

The records are less revealing of forms of recreation that were unlikely to require court action. As with other areas of day-to-day living
in seventeenth-century Virginia, the whole matter of the colonists'
pursuit of leisure awaits intensive investigation. Despite the limited
chances for amusement, the severity of the wilderness, and the sheer,
unrelieved tedium of living in seventeenth-century Virginia, life in
the Old Dominion was better in some ways than what the colonists
had known in England. In Virginia they enjoyed a higher living
standard, and this, after all, is what they had come to find.

SUGGESTED READINGS

*Ames, Susie M. *Reading, Writing and Arithmetic in Virginia,
    1607–1699; Other Cultural Topics.* Jamestown 350th Anniver-
    sary Historical Booklet 15 (Williamsburg, Va., 1957).
*Beverley, Robert. *The History and Present State of Virginia*, ed.
    Louis B. Wright (Chapel Hill, N.C., 1947).
Bruce, Philip Alexander. *Institutional History of Virginia in the Sev-
    enteenth Century: An Inquiry into the Religious, Moral, Educa-
    tional, Legal, Military, and Political Condition of the People. . . .*
    2 vols. (New York, 1910), I, 3–463.
———. *Social Life of Virginia in the Seventeenth Century. An In-
    quiry into the Origin of the Higher Planting Class, Together with
    an Account of the Habits, Customs, and Diversions of the People*
    (Richmond, Va., 1907).
Brydon, George MacLaren. *Virginia's Mother Church and the Political
    Conditions Under Which It Grew.* 2 vols. (Richmond, Va., 1947–
    1952).
*Hughes, Thomas P. *Medicine in Virginia, 1607–1699.* Jamestown
    350th Anniversary Historical Booklet 21 (Williamsburg, Va.,
    1957).
*Jester, Annie Lash. *Domestic Life in Virginia in the Seventeenth
    Century.* Jamestown 350th Anniversary Historical Booklet 17
    (Williamsburg, Va., 1957).
*Seiler, William H. "The Anglican Parish in Virginia." In *Seven-
    teenth-Century America: Essays in Colonial History*, ed. James
    Morton Smith (Chapel Hill, N.C., 1959), 119–142.
Waterman, Thomas Tileston. *The Mansions of Virginia, 1706–
    1776* (Chapel Hill, N.C., 1945), 3–29.

*Available in paperback.

The Voyage to Virginia

1. Henry Norwood's Passage to Virginia, 1649

> *A Voyage to Virginia. By Colonel Norwood.* (n.p., n.d.),
> in Peter Force, ed., *Tracts and Other Papers, Relating Prin-
> cipally to the Origin, Settlement, and Progress of the Colonies
> in North America, from the Discovery of the Country to the
> Year 1776* (Washington, D.C., 1836–1844), III, no. X.

. . . It fell out to be about the first day of *September, Anno* 1649, that we grew acquainted on the *Royal-Exchange with* Capt. *John Locker,* whose bills upon the posts made us know he was master of a good ship, (untruly so call'd) *The Virginia Merchant,* burden three hundred tons, of force thirty guns, or more: We were not long in treaty with the captain, but agreed with him for ourselves and servants at six pounds a head, to be transported into *James River;* our goods to be paid for at the current price. . . .

[When the voyage was about twenty days underway, the ship stopped at the Azores port of Fayal to take on water. There the passengers enjoyed the local hospitality for about nine days while the sailors thoroughly debauched themselves. The travelers then progressed satisfactorily for two weeks, passing Bermuda. But as the ship neared Cape Hatteras, terribly rough seas surrounded it, and it was blown back out to sea.]

The seas thus enraged, and all in foam, the gale still increasing upon us, the officers on the watch made frequent visits to the round-house, to prepare the captain for some evil encounter which this mighty tempest must bring forth: and their fears proved reasonable; for, about the hours of ten or eleven, our new disasters did begin with a crash from aloft. All hands were summon'd up with loud cries, that the fore-topmast was come by the board, not alone, but in conjunction with the fore-mast head broken short off, just under the cap.

This was a sore business, and put all to their wits end to recover to any competent condition; what could be done was done to prevent further mischiefs; but the whole trim and rigging of a ship depending much upon stays and tackle fixed to that mast, we had reason to expect greater ruins to follow, than what had already befallen us. Mate *Putt* was then on the watch, and did not want his apprehension of what did soon ensue, which in all likelihood was to end in our utter perdition; for about the hours of twelve or one at night, we heard and felt a mighty sea break on our fore-ship, which made such an inundation on the deck where the mate was walking, that he retired back with all diligence up to his knees in water, with short ejaculations of prayers in his mouth, supposing the ship was foundering, and at the last gasp. This looked like a stroke of death in every seaman's opinion: the ship stood stock still, with her head under water, seeming to bore her way into the sea. My two comrades and myself lay on our platform, sharing liberally in the general consternation. We took a short leave of each other, men, women, and children. All assaulted with the fresh terror of death, made a most dolorous outcry throughout the ship, whilst mate *Putts* perceiving the deck almost freed of water, called out aloud for hands to pump. This we thought a lightning before death, but gave me occasion (as having the best sea legs) to look and learn the subject of this astonishing alarm, which proved to arise from no less cause than the loss of our forecastle, with six guns, and our anchors (all but one that was fastened to a cable) together with our two cooks, whereof one was recovered by a strange providence.

This great gap, made by want of our forecastle, did open a passage into the hold for other seas that should break there before a remedy was found out to carry them off, and this made our danger almost insuperable; but it fell out propitiously, that there were divers land-carpenter passengers, who were very helpful in this distress; and, in a little time, a slight platform of deal was tack'd to the timbers, to carry off any ordinary sea in the present straight we were in; every moment of this growing tempest cutting out new work to employ all hands to labour.

The bowsprit, too top-heavy in itself, having lost all stays and rigging that should keep it steady, sway'd to and fro with such bangs on the bows, that at no less rate than the cutting it close off, could the ship subsist.

All things were in miserable disorder, and it was evident our danger increas'd upon us: the stays of all the masts were gone, the shrouds that remained were loose and useless, and it was easy to foretel, our main-topmast would soon come by the board. *Tom Reasin* (who was always ready to expose himself) with an ax in his hand, ran up with speed to prevent that evil, hoping thereby to ease the main-mast, and preserve it; but the danger of his person in the enterprize, was so manifest, that he was called down amain; and no sooner was his foot upon the deck, but what was feared came to pass with a witness, both main and topmast all came down together, and, in one shock, fell all to the windward clear into the sea, without hurt to any man's person.

Our main-mast thus fallen to the broadside, was like to incommode us more in the sea, than in her proper station; for the shrouds and rigging not losing the hold they had of the ship, every surge did so check the mast (whose but-end lay charg'd to fall perpendicular on the ship's side) that it became a ram to batter and force the plank, and was doing the last execution upon us, if not prevented in time by edge-tools, which freed the ship from that unexpected assault and battery.

Abandon'd in this manner to the fury of the raging sea, tossed up and down without any rigging to keep the ship steady, our seamen frequently fell overboard, without any one regarding the loss of another, every man expecting the same fate, tho' in a different manner. The ceilings of this hulk (for it was no better) were for the same cause so uneasy, that, in many tumbles, the deck would touch the sea, and there stand still as if she would never make another. Our mizzen mast only remained, by which we hoped to bring the ship about in proper season, which now lay stemming to the east.

In this posture did we pass the tenth and eleventh days of *November*; the twelfth in the morning we saw an *English* merchant, who shewed his ensign, but would not speak with us, tho' the storm was abated, and the season more fit for communication. We imagined the reason was, because he would not be compelled to be civil to us: he thought our condition desperate, and we had more guns than he could resist, which might enable us to take what he would not sell or give. He shot a gun to leeward, stood his course, and turn'd his poop upon us.

Before we attempted to bring the ship about, it was necessary to refresh the seamen, who were almost worn out with toil and want of rest, having had no leisure of eating set meals for many days. The passengers overcharged with excessive fears, had no appetite to eat; and (which was worst of all) both seamen and passengers were in a deplorable state as to the remaining victuals, all like to fall under extreme want; for the storm, by taking away the forecastle, having thrown much water into the hold, our stock of bread (the staff of life) was greatly damnified; and there remained no way to dress our meat, now that the cook-room was gone; the incessant tumbling of the ship (as has been observ'd) made all such cookery wholly impracticable. The only expedient to make fire betwixt decks, was, by sawing a cask in the middle, and filling it with ballast, which made a hearth to parch pease, and broil salt beef; nor could this be done but with great attendance, which was many times frustrated by being thrown topsy-turvy in spite of all circumspection, to the great defeat of empty stomachs. . . .

[A respite of good weather made repair of the ship possible. The travelers thought they were approaching the Virginia Capes, only to be mistaken.]

Defeated thus of lively hopes we had the night before entertain'd to sleep in warm beds with our friends in *Virginia*, it was a heavy spectacle to see our selves running at a round rate from it, notwithstanding all that could be done to the contrary. Nothing was now to be heard but sighs and groans thro' all that wretched family, which must be soon reduced to so short allowance, as would just keep life and soul together. Half a bisket cake a day to each (of which five whole ones made a pound) was all we had to trust to. Of liquors there remained none to quench thirst: *Malaga* sack was given plentifully to every one, which served rather to inflame and increase thirst, than to extinguish it. . . .

[Still another storm blew them out to sea—perhaps as much as three to four hundred miles.]

It would be too great a trial of the reader's patience to be entertain'd with every circumstance of our sufferings in the remaining part of this voyage, which continued in great extremity for at least forty days from the time we left the land, our miseries increasing every hour: I shall therefore omit the greatest number of our ill encounters, which were frequently repeated on us, and remember only what has in my thoughts been most remarkable, and have made the deepest impression in my memory.

To give us a little breathing, about the nineteenth day [of November] the wind shifted to the east, but so little to our avail (the gale so gentle, and the seas made against us like a strong current) that, with the sail we were able to make, we could hardly reckon the ship shortened the way, but that she rather lost ground. In less than two watches the gale faced about; and if we saved our own by the change, it was all we could pretend unto.

Our mortal enemy, the north-west gale, began afresh to send us out to sea, and to raise our terrors to a higher pitch. One of our pumps grew so unfix'd, that it could not be repair'd; the other was kept in perpetual motion; no man was excus'd to take his turn that had strength to perform it. Amongst the manifold perils that threatened every hour to be our last, we were in mortal apprehension, that the guns which were all aloft, would shew us a slippery trick, and some of them break loose, the tackle that held them being grown very rotten: and it was another providence they held so long, considering how immoderately the ship rolled, especially when the sails were mending that should keep them steady, which was very near a third part of our time, whilst we plyed to the windward with a contrary gale.

To prevent this danger which must befal when any one gun should get loose, mate *Putts* found an expedient by a more than ordinary smooth water; and by placing timber on the hatchway, to supply the place of shrouds, he got them safe in hold; which tended much to our good, not only in removing the present danger, but by making the ship (as seamen say) more wholesome, by haveing so great weight removed from her upper works into her centre, where ballast was much wanted.

But the intolerable want of all provisions, both of meat and drink, jostled the sense of this happiness soon out of our minds. And to aggravate our misery yet the more, it was now our interest to pray, that the contrary gale might stand; for whilst the westerly wind held, we had rain water to drink, whereas at east the wind blew dry.

In this miserable posture of ship and provision, we reckoned our selves driven to the east, in less than a week's time, at least two hundred leagues, which we despaired ever to recover without a miracle of divine mercy. The storm continued so fresh against us, that it confounded the most knowing of our ship's company in advising what course to take. Some reckoned the ship had made her way most southerly, and therefore counselled we should put our selves in quest of the *Bermudas* islands, as to the nearest land we could hope to make: but that motion had great opposition in regard of the winter season, which would daily produce insuperable difficulties, and give greater puzzle in the discovery of it, than our circumstances would admit. Others would say, The furthest way about, in our case, would prove the nearest way home and judged it best to take advantage of the westerly winds, and impetuous seas made to our hands, to attempt returning back to the western islands, as a thing more likely to succeed (tho' at a great distance) than thus to strive against the stream without any hopeful prospect of gaining the capes. But that motion met with a more general aversion, because the run was so long, that, tho' the gale had been in our own power to continue it, we could not have subsisted. Backwards we could not go, nor forwards in the course we desired: it followed then of consequence, that we must take the middle way; and it was resolved, that, without further persisting in endeavouring to gain our port by a close hale, we should raise our tackle, and sail tardy for the first *American* land we could fetch, tho' we ran to the leeward as far as the coast of *New England*.

Whilst this determination was agreed and put in practice, the famine grew sharp upon us. Women and children made dismal cries and grievous complaints. The infinite number of rats that all the voyage had been our plague, we now were glad to make our prey to feed on; and as they were insnared and taken, a well grown rat was sold for sixteen shillings as a market rate. Nay, before the voyage did end (as I was credibly inform'd) a woman great with child offered twenty shillings for a rat, which the proprietor refusing, the woman died.

Many sorrowful days and nights we spun out in this manner, till the blessed feast of *Christmas* came upon us, which we began with a very melancholy solemnity; and yet, to make some distinction of times, the scrapings of the meal-tubs were all amassed together to compose a pudding. *Malaga* sack, sea water, with fruit and spice, all well fryed in oyl, were the ingredients of this regale, which raised some envy in the spectators; but allowing some privilege to the captain's mess, we met no obstruction, but did peaceably enjoy our *Christmas* pudding. . . .

[On January 4 the 104-day journey came to an end, but the travelers were still a considerable distance from the Virginia settlements. The party that disembarked to investigate the country was deserted by the ship and left without supplies. After experiencing considerable hardships, they made their way, with the aid of friendly Indians, to their destination in Virginia.]

This New Land, Virginia

2. *Samuel Purchas's Description of Virginia, 1613*

Samuel Purchas, *Purchas His Pilgrimage; or, Relations of the World and the Religions observed in all ages . . . in foure parts . . .* (London, 1613), 631–632.

Leaving New France, let us draw nearer the Sunne to New Britaine, whose Virgin soile not yet polluted with Spaniards lust, by our late *Virgin-Mother* [i.e., Elizabeth], was justly called *Virginia*. Whether shall I here beginne with Elogies or Elegies? Whether shall I warble sweet Carolls in praise of thy lovely Face, thou fairest of *Virgins*, which from our other Britaine-World, hath wonne thee Wooers and Suters, not such as *Leander*, whose loves the Poets have blazed for swimming over the Straits betwixt Sestos and Abydus, to his Lovely *Hero*; but, which for thy sake have for-saken their Mother-earth, encountered the most tempestuous forces of the Aire, and so often ploughed up *Neptunes* Plaines, furrowing the angrie Ocean, and that to make thee of a ruder Virgin, not a wanton Minion; but, an honest and Christian Wife? Or shall I change my accent, and plaine me (for I know not of whom, to whom, to complaine) of those disadventures, which these thy lovely Lovers have sustayned in seeking thy love? What envie, I know not, whether of Nature, willing to reserve this Nymph for the treasurie of her owne love, testified by the many and continuall presents of a temperate Clymate, fruitfull Soile, fresh and faire Streames, sweet and holsome Aire, except neare the shore (as if her jealous policie had prohibited forraine Suters:) or of the savage Inhabitants, unworthie to embrace with their rustike armes so sweet a bosome, and to appropriate with greatest disparagement so faire a Virgin to Savage Loves: or haply some conceived indignitie, that some Parents should send thither their most unruly Sonnes, and that our Britannia should make her Virginian lap to bee the voider, for her lewder and more disordered Inhabitants, whose ill parts have made distastfull those kinder Offices of other our Britan Worthies, which else had beene long since with greatest gladnesse, and the recompense of her selfe entertayned: Or whether it bee Virginian modestie, and after the use of Virgins, shee would say nay at first, holding that love surest in continuance, which is hardest in obtayning: Whether any, or all of these, or what else hath hindered; hindered wee have beene, and have not yet obtayned the full fruition of her Love, and possession of her gainefull Dowrie, which yet now (more than ever before) shee seemeth to promise, and doubtlesse will quickly performe, if niggardise at home doe not hinder. And should men bee niggardly in this adventure, where *Nabal* must needs verifie his name, where keeping looseth, adventuring promiseth so faire a purchase? Miserie of our times, that miserable men should here want what they alreadie have, and refuse to have there, at no rate, abundant supply to their too miserable feares of want. Lift up your eyes and see that brightnesse of Virginia's beautie: which the Mountaines lift up themselves alwayes with wilde smiles to behold, sending downe silver streames to salute her, which powre themselves greedily into her lovely lap, and after many winding embracements, loth to depart, are at last swallowed of a more mightie corrivall, the Ocean: Hee also sends Armies of Fishes to her coasts, to winne her Love, even of his best store, and that in store and abundance: the Mountaines out-bid the Ocean, in offering the secret store-houses of undoubted mines: hee againe offereth pearles: and thus while they seeke to out-face each other with their puffed and bigge-swollen cheekes, who shall get the Bride, the one laies hold on the Continent and detaines the same, maugre [i.e., in spite of] the Oceans furie, and hee againe hath gotten the Ilands all along the coast, which he guardeth and keepeth with his waterie Garrisons. Virginia betwixt these two fower-faced Suters, is almost distracted, and easily would give entertainement to English love, and accept a *Nova Britan* appellation, if her Husband be but furnished out at first in forts and sutes, befitting her marriage solemnitie: all which her rich Dowrie would maintayne for ever after with advantage.

3. *Two Views of Virginia's Promise*

A. JOHN PORY DESCRIBES THE POSSIBILITIES FOR ADVANCEMENT, 1619

> John Pory to Sir Dudley Carleton, September 30, 1619, in Lyon Gardiner Tyler, ed., *Narratives of Early Virginia, 1606–1625*, Original Narratives of Early American History (New York, 1907), 284–285.

. . . All our riches for the present doe consiste in Tobacco, wherein one man by his owne labour hath in one yeare raised to himselfe to the value of 200£ sterling; and another by the meanes of six servants hath cleared at one crop a thousand pound English [i.e., £1,000]. These be true, yet indeed rare examples, yet possible to be done by others. Our principall wealth (I should have said) consisteth in servants: But they are chardgeable to be furnished with armes, apparell, and bedding and for their transportation and casual [expenses], both at sea, and for their first yeare commonly at lande also: But if they escape [death], they prove very hardy, and sound able men.

Nowe that your lordship may knowe, that we are not the veriest beggers in the worlde, our cowekeeper here of James citty on Sundays goes accowtered all in freshe flaming silke; and a wife of one that in England had professed the black arte, not of a scholler, but of a collier of Croydon, weares her rough bever hatt with a faire perle hatband, and a silken suite thereto correspondent. But to leave the Populace, and to come higher; the Governour here, who at his first coming, besides a great deale of worth in his person, brought onely his sword with him, was at his late being in London, together with his lady, out of his meer gettings here, able to disburse very near three thousand pounde to furnishe himselfe for his voiage. And once within seven yeares, I am per-suaded (*absit invidia verbo* [i.e., "without invidious comparison"]) that the Governors place here may be as profittable as the lord Deputies of Ireland. . . .

B. RICHARD FRETHORNE'S ACCOUNT OF HIS PLIGHT IN VIRGINIA, 1623

> Richard Frethorne to his parents, March 20, April 2, 3, 1623, in Susan Myra Kingsbury, ed., *The Records of the Virginia Company of London* (Washington, D.C., 1906–1935), IV, 58–59, 62.

Loveing and kind father and mother my most humble duty remembered to you hopeing in God of your good health, as I my selfe am at the makeing hereof, this is to let you understand that I your Child am in a most heavie Case by reason of the nature of the Country is such that it Causeth much sicknes . . . and when wee are sicke there is nothing to Comfort us; for since I came out of the ship, I never at[e] anie thing but pease, and loblollie (that is water gruell) [.]as for deare or venison I never saw anie since I came into this land[.] there is indeed some foule, but Wee are not allowed to goe, and get yt, but must Worke hard both earelie, and late for a messe of water gruell, and a mouthfull of bread, and beife[.] a mouthfull of bread for a pennie loafe must serve for 4 men which is most pitifull if you did knowe as much as I, when people crie out day, and night, Oh that they were in England without their lymbes and would not care to loose anie lymbe to bee in England againe, yea though they beg from doore to doore. . . . I have nothing at all, no not a shirt to my backe, but two Ragges nor no Clothes, but one poore suite, nor but one paire of shooes, but one paire of stockins, but one Capp, but two bands, my Cloke is stollen by one of my owne fellowes, and to his dying hower would not tell mee what he did with it. . . . but I am not halfe a quarter so strong as I was in England, and all is for want of victualls, for I doe protest unto you, that I have eaten more in a day at home then I have al-lowed me here for a Weeke. . . .

O that you did see may [i.e., my] daylie and hourelie sighes, grones, and teares, and thumpes that I afford mine owne brest, and rue and Curse the time of my birth with holy Job. I thought no head had beene able to hold so much water as hath and doth dailie flow from mine eyes.

Houses and Household Property

4. Types of Houses

A. A CONTRACT FOR A FRAME HOUSE

Henrico County Deed Book, 1677–1692, 88.

An agreement made between Mr. Thomas Chamberlaine and James Gates about February last. Imprimis the said gates was to gett the frame of a forty foote dwellinge house and frame the same. And to Cover and weather board the said house and to add to the said house two outside chimneys and finish them and to ground fill the said house and to make two partitions one below and the other above farre [i.e., fair] all the joize [i.e., joists] and posts to be squared by a line and plained and all the rest of the ground worke to be squared by a line and the said Gates was allsoe to dubb the board for the said house in consideration for the above worke the above Chamberlaine is to pay the above Gates twelve hundred pounds of tobacco and casq and the said gates is to finish the above worke by the next ensueing fall of the leafe. ... The Deposition of John Bough ... That Mr. Chamberlaine made a bargaine with James Gates to build an house of 40 foote long and 20 foote .wide and a partition through the middle and the Joize all to be lin'd and plain'd and 2 outside Chimneys . . .

B. A FRENCHMAN'S DESCRIPTION OF HOUSING IN VIRGINIA, 1687

Gilbert Chinard, ed., *A Huguenot Exile in Virginia, or Voyages of a Frenchman Exiled for His Religion, with a Description of Virginia and Maryland* (New York, 1934), 119–120.

Some people in this country are comfortably housed; the farmers' houses are built entirely of wood, the roofs being made of small boards of chestnut, as are also the walls. Those who have some means, cover them inside with a coating of mortar in which they use oyster-shells for lime; it is as white as snow, so that although they look ugly from the outside, where only the wood can be seen, they are very pleasant inside, with convenient windows and openings. They have started making bricks in quantities, and I have seen several houses where the walls were entirely made of them. Whatever their rank, and I know not why, they build only two rooms with some closets on the ground floor, and two rooms in the attic above; but they build several like this, according to their means. They build also a separate kitchen, a separate house for the Christian slaves, one for the negro slaves, and several to dry the tobacco, so that when you come to the home of a person of some means, you think you are entering a fairly large village. There are no stables because they never lock up their cattle. Indeed few of the houses have a lock, for nothing is ever stolen. . . .

5. Household Property

A. WILLIAM HARRIS'S ESTATE, 1679

Henrico County Deed Book, 1677–1692, 107.

An Inventory of Major William Harris's Estate taken and appraised by us
the subscribers according to order of Court the 7th of February 1678.

	li. Tobacco
two Fether bedds with Canvas ticking	700
two old unfixt gunns	170
to 1 brasse Mortar and pestell	040
two Formes and 1 leafe of a table	060
to 1 peice of old melted pewter wt. 25 li.	125
	1095

to 1 Mare unpraised of 3 yeares old

B. JOHN WAROE'S ESTATE, 1650

Northumberland County Order Book, 1650–1652, 16.

An Inventory of the estate of John Waroe deceased taken and appraised the
15th of July Anno Domini 1650 by James Mackgregoer and Jeremiah Allen
and sworne before Mr. William Presly

	li. Tobacco
Imprimis a parcell of pewter at	048
a brass skillet at	012
three old hats at	050
two pound and an halfe of soape at	015
a parcell of Child bed Linnen at	045
a parcell of linnen more and old parcell of gloves and a parcell of thread at	060
fower smocks and a shirt at	100
a parcell of [working?] apparrell for a woman	100
a sute of mans apparrell with other old cloaths and Stockings at	250
one Gun at	080
two iron potts two wooden trayes and a pot lid	090
an old frying pan a barr of iron and hooks	050
one old whipsaw with an old fyle and Compasses	060
a parcell of wooden [wales?]	030
one halfe Ancher at	010
eight pound of Shott at	012
a Jugg and a brush at	006
one Rugg one old bed filled with Cattailes one old flock bolster one feather pillow at	120
one Childes coate three paire of old shooes and one looking glass	040
one something iron with other old things	010
two sifters one old hoe one old matt and some drinking Tobacco	015

This is a true Inventory and appraisment of the above said estate in particular
As witness our hands the day and yeare above written
Coram me   Jeremy Allan
William Presly   James Magrigger his marke
    More two Sowes and two shoates at 080
                                                1231

C. JANE HARTEY'S ESTATE, 1667

> Northampton County Deed and Will Book, 1666–1668, fols. 13–14.

An exact Inventory of the Goods and other the Estate of Mrs. Jane Hartey deceased

In the Buttery
1 greate Chest conteynige
13¾ yards greene collerd Kersey
12½ yards of Frize [i.e., frieze, a heavy woolen cloth with uncut nap]
4¾ yards of red Broad cloath
4 yards blew Cotten
6 yards blew trading cloath
3 yards gray Broadcloath
18 yards greene Cotten
15½ ells [i.e., an archaic unit of measure equal to 45 inches] Canvis
15¼ ells ditto
20½ ells ditto
32¼ ells ditto
39 ells ditto
36 ells ditto
17½ ells 3 quarters broad Doulas
30 ells corse Flemmish linnige
6 ells flaxon cloath
17½ yards blew linnige
3 ells Lockerum [i.e., a linen fabric] in 3 remnants
2 white blanketts
25 paire plaine shooes
6 paire Yrish stockins
1 paire boots
1 paire stirrupps and Irons
2 gerths
1 curb [i.e., a chain used to check an unruly animal] 1 snaffle [i.e., a simple jointed horse bit]
1 paire black raynes
8 li cotten weake [i.e., wick]
2 costnige Coates
1 paire briches [i.e., breeches]
1 parcell thred buttons
6¾ li. Hopps
1 Fishinge line

½ dozen tapps and fossets
1 parcell of Brimstone
1 li. browne thred
1 Montier Capp
1 parcell of Linne
1 parcell Leather Buttons
1 saddle with furniture
2 Tyles 1 wispe
12 Deare Skinns
5 Indian Stockins
2 new Socks
1 parcell ginger

More in the said Buttery
12 pewter dishes
9 pewter plates
7 porringers
2 salts
1 quart tankerd
1　3 pint pott
1 Candlestick
1 beker [i.e., beaker]
2 basins
1 quart pott
2 Fryinge panns
2 new Chamber potts
12 spoones
1 greater

More in the said Buttery
1 Bedstead
1 Flock bed and boulster
1 red shagd rugg
1 coverlate
1 sett old Curtins greene say

In the Hall
1 Iron bound trunk quantity
1 shag petticoate with 2 silver laces
1 satinseo petticoate
2 red sashes
1 dozen napkins not made
1 gray serge patticoate with silver lace
1 cloath wascoate with silver lace
1 watertamy petticoate with silver lace
1 red cloath petticoate with silver lace
1 Moyhaire petticoate with silver lace
1 yellow tammy petticoate

1 serge Fumpe
1 red rideinge suite
1 serge wascoate with silver lace
3 white petticoates
1 red broadcloath wascoate [with] silver lace
2 paire new [boots?] mans red wascoate
1 broad cloath suite
1 red broad cloath wascoate with silver lace
1 corse broad cloath sute and coate
1 serge suite with plate buttons
2 yards greene say
1 paire home made stockins
1 paire worsted stockins
1 paire old Drawers
1 parcell cotten weeke [i.e., wick]

In a small trunk in the said trunk
1 white sas nett Hood
1 sasnett Gorgett
1 black curld hood
1 paire thred gloves
1 satten pinpillow
1 lace neekcloath
1 lacd scarfe
1 Bible with silver claspes
1 paire Leather gloves Imbroydred
1 parcell woemens linnige

In the Cabinett in the Hall
about ½ li. whited browne thred
2 yvery combes
1 parcell black bobbin
1 parcell Cotten Ribben
1 paire blew silke stockins
3500 pinns
1 small broken silver bodkin
1 dozen tinn plates
1 grose wascoate buttons

In this Wanscott Chest in the Hall
1 Kersy [i.e., coarse, ribbed, light woolen cloth] old suite
1 old kersey coate
2 paire linnige stockins
1 Lambkin wascoate
1 broad cloath coate
1 paire red drawers
1 paire worsted hose
7 paire Irish stockins

17 ells Huswifes cloath
1 Canvis shirt
3 alcomy spoones
1 paire Lockerum drawers
11½ yards serge in 2 parcells
5 yards red Cotten
7 yards white Cotten
6 yards red Kersey

More in the Hall vizt.
1 Bedsted
1 Featherbed and Boulster
2 pillowes 2 pillow heeres
1 paire of sheetes
2 blanketts
1 red worsted Rugg
1 sett curtaines and vallance red serge with silke fringes
1 wormeinge pann
1 poplar table
1 carpett of Domicks
6 Leather Chayres, 3 Matted Chaires
1 Couch
1 round table
1 cupberd and Cloath
2 pewter scallopp porrengers
3 gilded cushions
1 cokernutt cupp
2 earthen plates
1 Lookeinge [glass?]
1 brasse charger
1 wicker baskett
1 small Daske [desk?]
3 earthen dishes
2 earthen juggs
1 pewter Caudle cupp
1 earthen sack cupp 1 pewter ditto
1 sleeke stone
1 glasse Case with 6 glasses
1 paire bellowes
1 box Iron
5 gunns 2 holster pistolls
1 brasse Lampe 1 tinn ditto
1 paire hand Irons, 1 Fendor
1 paire of tongs, 1 fire forke
1 fyer shovell
1 halfe horne glasse
2 cushions
2 sermon bookes, 1 old Bible

1 paire brasse snuffers
1 Hamocker
1 black castor
2 wodden Chaires

In the Hall Chamber

1 Empty chest
1 bed stead
1 Featherbed and bolster
1 pillowheere
1 paire holeaned sheetes
1 greene shagd rugg
1 sett curtens and vallence blew with fringes
2 chaires, 1 cushion
2 Lanthornes
1 Lookenige glasse
1 chamber pott
1 case with trumpery
1 powder Flaskett
1 powder horne

In the Kitchen

5 gunns
3 large trayes
4 speets [i.e., spits]
2 Iron drippinge panns
1 Large copperkittle
2 small brasse Kettles
1 barbors basin
1 brasse fish skinner
1 brasse stuepann
1 old brasse fryinge pann without handle
2 small brasse skilletts
2 small brasse ladle
1 small brasse skimmer
3 pewter plates
7 pewter dishes greate and small
1 pewter poringer
1 pewter gut pott
1 pewter flagon
1 tinn drippinge pann
4 tinn pudding pans
1 apple roster
1 tin cullender
1 basting ladle
2 chopping knifes
2 Yron tosters
1 gridyron

2 chaffing dishes
6 yron Kettles greate and small
3 yron potts with pott hookes
1 paire handyrons, 1 Fendor
2 paire pott racks
1 Fyre forke, 1 paire tongs
2 small pewter beakers
4 pewter, 4 alcomy spoones
2 yron bound bucketts
1 [skrewed?] Candlestick
3 little Joynt stooles
1 yron ladle
2 pewter Basins
1 paire pott racks in the quarter
1 Handmill ditto

In the Kitchen Chamber on the Southside
1 chest conteynige
3 Holland smokes [i.e., smocks]
2 Holland shirts
11 fine Diaper Napkins
4 Corse Diaper Napkins
1 large Diaper Table cloath
1 paire corse sheetes
11 Doulas Napkins
2 corse Diaper Table Claoths, 3 Doulas shirts
1 paire canvis sheetes
4 straits Napkins
6 pillow heeres
2 paire Canvis sheetes
2 paire corse ditto
2 paire corse holland sheetes
1 small Diaper table cloath
2 Corse towells

1 bedstead
1 Featherbed, 1 bolster, 2 pillowes
1 cattaile bolster
2 blanketts
1 blew sett rugg
1 sett curtaines, vallence red serge
1 trundle bed
1 flockbed, 1 cattayle bolster
1 blankett
2 plaine red ruggs
1 gunn, 2 pistolls
1 lookeing glasse
1 paire small brasse stillyard [i.e., a scale]
3 paire stillyards more

1 pewter [word illegible]
4 pewter sasers
1 pewter plate
1 white earthen porrenger
1 paire old boots
1 seale skin trunke quantity
3 paire woemens shooes
3 paire slippers
1 paire plaine shooes
1 paire white Mild stockins
1 paire yrish stockins

In the other Kitchen Chamber
2 old saddles, 2 bridles
1 bedstead
1 small featherbed, 1 bolster
1 pillow, 1 pillow heere
1 blew shagd rugg
1 plaine red rugg
2 old blanketts
1 suite old Dornicks Curtens
1 wodden Chaire
1 new sack
1 chest with Lumber
1 small trunke inked J H
1 yard black taffety
1 black hood
1 changinge taffety Neckcloath
1 parcell silke and buttons
1 glister pipe
1 small silver dram cupp

In the Kitchen Loft
1 chest quantity 108 li. shott in severall parcells
23 li. powder in severall parcells
5 [racks?]
4 empty Cask
2 empty cases of bottles
2 Funnells
1 yron pearcer

In the Porch Loft
600 20d nailes
10100 10d nailes
8400 6d nailes
33 ft. Roope
3 new stocklocks
11 new narrow axes
7 new hillinge hoes

13 new weedinge hoes
1 broad ax new
1 carpenters adz new
4 paires hookes and hinges
1 hammer
1 hatchett
24 harrow teeth

Old tooles in the said loft
1 broad Axe
1 adz
1 Hammer
1 Auger
5 playnes
2 wimble bitts
3 grubbing hoes
6 bed cords
1 paire canhookes
1 pearcer
3 Grand yrons
1 old snaffle, 1 old curb
6 reape hookes
1 handsawe
1 hatchett with other trumpery

In the Buttery Loft
25 Cakes sope quantity 34 li.
1 small cake soft sope
4 milke trayes
2 wodden platters
1 wodden funnell
2 wodden dishes
2 cheese fatts
12 cakes sope quantity 16 li.
3 wodden boules
1 barrell neare full white salt
2 cases with empty bottles

In the House Loft
2 great sawes
1 Hoggshead 2 barrells salt
1 paire small hand yrons
1 paire hand yrons wit[h] brass knops
1 shovell and tongs conforme
7 trayes
1 larke [*sic*] Haskett [i.e., hassock]
2 large trayes
1 great chest

In the little porch loft
3 matted chaires
3 earthen butter dishes
4 earthen plates
3 earthen cupps
2 earthen salts
1 earthen saser
3 earthen chamber potts
2 Joynt stooles

In the Milke house
1 pack saddle
1 coller and trayes [i.e., traces]
1 sith [i.e., scythe]
1 riddle
2 shovells
1 old spade
4 haire sifters
1 fryinge pann
1 large tubb
6 wodden dishes
11 earthern Milke pans
1 parcell of glasse in Casemates
1 churne
4 milke pales
3 barrells white salt
1 halfe bushell

In the Cart house
1 paire new Cart Wheeles
1 cart with wheeles
1 Cart saddle
1 coller and harnes
1 Coller and trases
1 paire harnes and trases
2 paire Harnes more
1 Cart horse bridle
1 wheele barrow

In the Syder house
1 Boates grapling
several empty Caske

Account of the Cattle and Horses
31 Cowes and Heifers
20 steeres aged between 3 and 8 yeares
2 Bulls
11 yearelings
1 white mare named Jany

1 old mare named Tibb
1 young mare aged 3 yeares
1 black mare aged 2 yeares
1 Horse named Tom
1 Horse named gray Jack
1 Horse named Frigott
1 Horse colt aged 1 yeare

William Spencer
George Mortimmer

Religious Life

6. *The Church*

A. THE CREATION OF CHRIST CHURCH PARISH, 1666

> Churchill G. Chamberlayne, ed., *The Vestry Book of Christ Church Parish, Middlesex County, Virginia, 1663–1767* (Richmond, Va., 1927), 5–7.

At a Generall Vestry for the South Side of [Lancaster] [C]oun[t]y held at the house of Sir Henry Chichley January 29th 1666 for Christ Church Parish

Imprimis We doe accord and Agree that the Two parishes Formerly called Lancaster and Peanckatanck from henceforth be united as one, and called Christ Church parish

Item That a Mother Church be built in the Small Indian Field next the head of Capt. [William] Brocas his ground. It being Adjudged by us to be about the Middle of the parish.

Item That the Mother Church be called by the Name of Christ Church

Item That the late reputed parish of Pyancketancke doe this yeare Levey to the late Reputed Bounds, Includeing the Thickett Plantation and Harwoods Pattent and noe more, for the repaire of theire Church and other Contingencies.

Item That the late parish of Lancaster Doe Levey to the late reputed bound [word missing] for the building of Theire Chappell of Ease, and Theire other contingenses The Thickett onely Excepted

Item That the Mother Church be forthwith built by the Undertakers Capt. Cuthbert Potter and Mr. John Appleton and that They be equally joyn[ed] in the Trouble of receiveing the whole Levey with the Foure Church-Wardens, and they be hereby Impowered to receive Thirty Thousand weight of Tobacco and Caske this present yeare within the aforesaid parish and that present and Due payment be made Thereof to the Undertakers, alsoe that Sixteene Thousand weight of Tobacco and Caske be also Levied and due payment be made Thereof to Mr. Richard Morris Parson of the Said Parish.

Item That the whole Levey be laid at Eighty Five pounds of Tobacco per pole, and the overplus when the aforesaid Sumes are paid, if any, The Collectors to be accomptable for the same

Item That Thirty Seven pounds of Tobacco and Caske per pole be Levyed and Collected by the Churchwardens of the late Reputed parish of Lancast[er] for building of theire Chappell of Ease

Item It is Unanimously Agreed That Mr. Morris, if he please, Continue Minister of our parish, and have the Same Maintenance as las[t] yeare allowed, but is opinions that he be not Inducted, and that Sir Gray Skipwith, Mr Dudley Mr. Leach Mr. Potter Mr. Perott Mr. Curt[is] Mr. Weekes or any Five of them, are appointed to Treat with Mr. Morri[s] In that affaire

Item That Mr. Corbin be appointed and Requested to take Bond of the Undertakers for building the Mother Church, In every respect to be done and Finished according to the Middle plantation Church, To be finished in Six Months, Glass and Iron worke convenient Time to be given for its Transportation out of England

Item It is Agreed That Major Gen. Robert Smith and Henry Corbin Esq. be requested to move to the Assembly for Continueing the Union of the Two late Parishes of Pyancktanke and Lancaster.

Sir Gray Shipwith

	Mr. Robert Smith	Richard Perrott
	Patrick Miller	Cuthbert Potter
	Edward Boswell	John Curtis
Vestrymen	William Butcher	John Appleton
	Richard Thacker	William Dudley
	Anthony Elliott	George Wadding
	Henry Thacker	William Leach
	Henry Corbin	John Needles

B. PETSWORTH PARISH BUILDS A CHURCH, 1677

Churchill G. Chamberlayne, ed., *The Vestry Book of Petsworth Parish, Gloucester County, Virginia, 1677–1793* (Richmond, Va., 1933), 3–4.

It is ordered, by this present vestry, that the inside worke of the Church now in Buildinge at poplare Springe, bee done in manner as followeth vizt.: the walls and ceilinge overhead to be substantially Lathed, daubed and plastered; the Chancell to be 15 foote and a Scrime [i.e., a cloth curtain] to be runn a Crosse the Church with ballisters; a Communione table 6 foote and [a] ½ to be inclosed on three sides at 3 foote distance, to be done with ballisters, 2 wainscoate double pews one of each side of the Chancell, Joyninge to the Scrime with ballisters suitable to the said Scrime. 1: double pew above the pulpitt and deske Joyninge to the Scrime, all the rest of the pews of both sides of the said church to be double, and all to be done with wainscoate Backs, the pulpit to be of wainscoate 4 foote diameter, and made with 6 sides, 6 foot allowed for the reading desks and passag[e] into the pulpitt: the ministers pew to be under the pulpitt, and raised 18 Inches and the readers deske under it, the two uppermost pews in the Body of the Church and the two pews in the Chancell to have doores. And it is further order'd that the Church wardens doe in behalfe of the parish bargaine and agree with good sufficient workmen for the doeinge and finishinge of the said worke.

C. RECRUITING A MINISTER, 1656

> Lower Norfolk County Deeds and Wills, Book D, 1656–1666, 29.

Copie of A letter sent to Mr. Moore a minister in New England
Mr. Moore—
Sir, after Saluts please to take Notice, that wee are informed by Capt. francis Emperor at his beeing at Mannadus hee treated with you Concerning your Coming over hither amongst us and that you weare unwilling to Come at such Uncertainties or without the Knowledge or good liking of those that you weare to Come amongst, and further that you were pleased to promise him, not otherwise not to dispose of your selfe, till you heard from him therefore wee underwritten in the behalfe of the Whole, gladly Imbrasing such an opportunity do Engage our selves that upon your arrival heere for the maintenance of your selfe and family to allow unto you the yearely quantity of [word illegible] tobacco and Corne and also to provide for your present entertainement. Upon arrivall and convenient habitation and Continuance amongst us to the Content of your selfe and Credit of us upon whome at our Invitation you have [threw us?] your selfe and for the transportation of your selfe and familly We have taken full and sufficient Course which Capt. Richard Whiteing and to all the premisses We underwritten have Subscribed. [no names attached to original]

D. THE VESTRYMAN'S OATH, 1664

> Chamberlayne, ed., *Vestry Book of Christ Church Parish*, 2.

I A B As I doe Acknowledge my Selfe a True Sonne of the Church of England, Soe I doe believe The Articles of Faith there profess[ed] and doe oblidge myselfe to be conformable to the Doctrine and Disipline There Taught and Established, and That as Vestry Man for this Parish of Christ Church I will well and Truely performe m[y] Duty Therein, being Directed by the Laws and Customes of This Cuntrey, and the Cannons of the Church of England, Soe Far as They will Suite with our present Capacity, And This I Shall Senseerely do According to the best of my Knowledge Skill an[d] Cuning, Without feare favour or partiallity, and Soe helpe me God.

Leisure Pursuits

7. Amusements, Games, and Sports

A. HORSE RACING, 1674

> York County Order Book, 1672–1694, 85.

James Bullocke a Tayler having made a race for his Mare with a horse belonging to mr. Mathew Slader for two thousand pounds of tobacco and Caske it being contrary to Law for a Labourer to make a race being a Sport only for Gentlemen is fined for the same one hundred pounds of tobacco and caske.

Whereas mr. Mathew Slader and James Bullocke by condition under hand and seale made a race for two thousand pounds of tobacco and caske, it appearing under the hand and seale of the said Slader that his horse should runn out of the way that Bullocks mare might winn which is an apparent cheate is ordered to be putt in the Stocks, and there sitt the Space of one houre.

B. NINEPINS, 1681

Henrico County Deed Book, 1677–1692, 191.

Richard Rabone having the last Courte (holden for this County the first of this instant October) Commenced his suite against Robert Sharpe for four hundred pounds of Tobacco and Casq (wonne at nine pins as the said Rabone affirmed;) whereupon a Jury being sent forth, who not agreeing on there verdict, were adjourned to his day to enter into new debate of the matter. . . .

Mr. Thomas Cocke Jr. aged about 17 yeares

Deposeth

That your deponent being in Company with Robert Sharpe and Richard Rabone heard a wager laid betwixt them to play at nine pinns at the ordinary the first foure games (thirty one up) for foure hundred pounds of tobacco; upon which the said Rabone desired your deponent to reckon his game, which he the said Rabone being in drinke your deponent refused to doe; And after some tyme went about other businesse, and some tyme after he came againe to the Alley; they fell at difference and at length it was agreed betweene them that Robert Sharpe had wonn three games and Richard Rabone two, and then they went to play againe and the other two games Richard Rabone wonne running. . . .

C. DICING, 1685

Henrico County Deed Book, 1677–1692, 313.

Robert Bullington aged 53 years or thereabouts

Deposeth that being at the house of Samuel Bridgewater Sometime in February or March he saw Charles Steward and Giles Webb playing at Dice a considerable time but the Deponent takeing no Notice of their play at last they left off Gameing, and upon their leaving off there was a discourse amongst Some of the Company then present That Giles Webb had wonn of Charles Steward Five hundred pounds of tobacco but whether it arose from the said Webb or the Company your deponent Knoweth nott. And further saith not. . . .

D. PUTT, 1685

Henrico County Deed Book, 1677–1692, 300.

John Iremonger aged 30 yeares

Deposeth that lately your deponent came to Mr. Davis' and Capt. Soane and Richard Dearlove were at play at Putt [i.e., a card game], and play'd about two

Games (but for what is unknown to your deponent) and then left off, Capt. Soane Saying to the said Dearlove I must go to the Falls to Night, and think we have done very well, Richard Dearlove Replyes we will light our pipes and play the first ten putts for five hundred and soe will Give over; then Setting down again Capt. Soane desired your deponent to take notice of the play which ten putts they played and Capt. Soane wonn, then Capt. Soane demanded his bill, for fifteen hundred pounds of tobacco which he had wonn and two hundred which he the said Dearlove ow'd Richard Bland, And the said Dearlove went away and said I owe you Nothing. And further saith not. . . .

E. HUNTING, 1680

York County Order Book Number 6, 1677–1684, 180.

Mr. John Rogers Entrusted with the Guardianship of the Grandchildren of John Adisson deceased, Sueing Edward Coilew to this Court, For hunting upon his Land with his Gunn and Doggs to his very greate prejudice and Contrary to the 71 Act in that Case made and provided: The said Rogers (upon failure Declining to Committ the said breach) Doth Remitt the penalty of the said Act, the said Edward Coilew paying the Costs of Suite.

F. MIDDLESEX COURT ACTS TO CONSERVE THE COUNTY'S FISH POPULATION, 1678

Middlesex County Order Book, 1673–1680, fol. 98.

Whereas, By the 15th Act of Assembly made in the yeare 1662; Lyberty is Given to each respective County to make By Lawes for themselves which Lawes by Vertue of the Said Act are to be as Bindeing upon them as any other Generall Law, And Whereas Severall of the Inhabitants of this County have Complayned against the excessive and Imoderate Strikeing and Destroying of Fish by Some fue [i.e., few] of the Inhabitants of this County By Strikeing them, by a light in the Night time with Fis[h] giggs, Whereby they not onely affright the Fish from Comeing into the Rivers and Creeks But also Wound Farre [more] times the quantity that they take, Soe that if a timely remedy be not applyed by that Meanes the fishing with hookes and Lines wilbe utterly Spoyled to the Great hurte and Greivance of most of the Inhabitants of this County,

It is therefore by this Courte Ordered that from and after the 20th day of March next ensueing: It shall not be Lawfull for any of the Inhabitants of this County to take Strike or Destroy any sorte of Fish in the Night time with Fis[h] gigg Harpin [i.e., harpoon] Iron or any other Instrument of that Nature Sorte or Kinde, Within any River Creeke or Bay, which are accounted belonging to or are within the Bounds [and?] precinques of this County, And it is further Ordered that if any person or persons being a Freeman Shall Offend against this Order, he or they Soe offending Shall for the first offense Bee fined Five hundred pounds of good tobacco to be paid to the Informer, And for every other offense Committed against this Order after the first by any person the said Fine to be Doubled, and if any Servant or Servants be permitted or Incouraged by there Masters, to keepe or have in there Possession any

Fis[h] gigg Harpin Iron or any other Instrument of that Kinde or Nature and shall therewith offend against this Order that in Such Case the Master of Such Servant or Servants Shalbe lyable to pay the Severall Fines abovementioned, And if any Servant or Servants Shall Contrary to and against there Masters Will and Knowledge offend against this Order That for every offence they receive such Corporall punishment as by this Court Shalbe thought meete.

G. ACCOMACK COURT FORBIDS A COMPANY OF PLAYERS FROM PERFORMING "THE BEAR AND THE CUB," 1663

Accomack County Order Book, 1663–1666, fol. 102.

Whereas Cornelius Watkinsons phillip Howard and William Darby were this Day accused by Mr. John Fawcett his Majesties Attorney for Accomack County for acting a play by them called the Bare and the Cubb on the 27th of August last past, Upon examination of the Same The Court have thought fitt to Suspend the Cause till the next Court and doe Order that the Said Cornelius Watkinson phillip Howard and William Darby appeare the next Court in those habilements that they then acted in, and give a draught of such verses or other Speeches and passages, which were then acted by them, and that the sherrif detaine Cornelius Watkinson and phillip Howard in his Custody untill they put in Security to performe this order.

Epilogue

Had he chosen to look backward, a colonist in 1689 might have marveled at what he and his fellow settlers had achieved in the eight decades since the first Englishmen disembarked on Virginia soil. Although he still considered himself English and part of a larger Atlantic world, Virginia was his country and his home, whereas it had been an exquisite hell for the earlier adventurers who had come seeking fortune and glory. The Virginian of 1689 had his own way of doing things; this is what set him apart from the first settlers.

The comparison between the colony at the beginning and the end of the seventeenth century was indeed stark. Virginia had changed from a tiny frontier outpost that clung to life by the merest of threads into a provincial society that verged on maturity. Almost every facet of life in 1689 reflected the truth of this observation.

Communities stood on what once had been virgin land. Immigrants who saw land, labor, and farming as the means of advancement had replaced adventurers who viewed their stay in Virginia as temporary. A relatively sound and defined social order, roughly patterned on tradition, had evolved, albeit violently at times. Since 1618 direct representative government, the dispersal of power through several levels of government, a vibrant local government, and a recognizable political structure had all sprung up. Such was the rate of transition in all of these areas that the colonists had begun to perceive rapid and profound change as a condition of living in America. Therein lay the seeds of a later American trait—a temperamental willingness to accept change as a manifestation of good.

Virginia had taught the English much about the New World. The early experiences had helped to allay the fears and uncertainties of a people easily frightened by the unknown. They had also given later immigrants to other parts of America an idea of what lay before them and what pitfalls to avoid. And settling the Old Dominion had generally contributed to the advancement of knowledge by sharpening appetites already whetted by the curiosity that had given rise to the Age of Discovery and the Scientific Revolution.

Virginia had even forced the English who stayed home to revise their conceptions of colonies. In 1607 no one spoke of an English empire. Colonies were conceived as private undertakings that had the sovereign's permission and blessing, but nothing else. The failure of the London Company as a colonizing agency had necessitated direct royal intervention in Virginia affairs, and thereafter a shift in attitudes began to occur. That change was greatly accelerated by a growing awareness of the value of the Virginia tobacco trade and rising commercial competition from the Dutch. Those two facts had occasioned the development of the navigation system after 1660, and by the 1680s Virginia was very much a part of an English empire.

The growth Virginia had sustained by 1689 had not been without cost. In the early days the hand of death had exacted a heavy toll as the price for English entry into the New World. While the threat of death by starvation or by ignorance receded, the grosser features of life in an expanding and evolving society remained. Servants were shamefully abused by masters who all too frequently cared more for profits than for human life. Nor did landowners show an appreciable concern or reverence for the land itself; there was too much of it to worry about conservation. Ambitious men asked and gave no quarter in their relentless quest for prestige and power. Their initial lack of sensitivity to others made their rough and tumble world needlessly harsh and excessively violent on occasion. And of course the destruction of the Indians and the enslavement of the Africans stand as two of seventeenth-century Virginia's most tragic monuments to aggressive acquisitiveness.

Despite the high social costs inherent in the development of the Old Dominion, seventeenth-century Virginians left succeeding generations of colonists an enduring patrimony. They passed on habits and experiences that their fellow countrymen would one day translate into fundamental rights upon which to lay the foundation for a nation. And in the creation of that inheritance hangs the significance of Virginia's first century.